March 2011

To Barbara & Michael:

In friendship and with

Best wishes

Peter B. Foller

BE YOUR BEST

A COMPREHENSIVE GUIDE TO AESTHETIC PLASTIC SURGERY

MEDICAL EDITOR: PETER BELA FODOR, M.D., F.A.C.S.

ISBN-13: 978-0-9791335-0-3 ~ ISBN-10: 0-9791335-0-5 Library of Congress Control Number: 2006939887

First Edition

Contributing plastic surgery experts for this book were selected on the basis of their American Board of Plastic Surgery certification and membership in the American Society for Aesthetic Plastic Surgery. In addition, they have paid a fee for development of Special Edition copies featuring their own Introduction and biographical information.

Note: This book is not intended to provide medical guidance, advice, or recommendations. Its purpose is to provide general information to help readers educate themselves about aesthetic plastic surgery and related treatments. Every precaution has been taken to ensure its accuracy; however, publisher, writers, contributing experts, and editors assume no responsibility for any liability, loss, risk, or damages, personal or otherwise, resulting as a consequence, direct or indirect, of the use or application of the information in this book. Publisher assumes no responsibility for errors or omissions; nor are the opinions stated in this book guaranteed or warranted to produce a particular outcome. Readers are advised to consult qualified professionals for assistance and advice and to consult their doctors to determine the treatment appropriate for them. The publisher, writers, contributing experts, and editors assume no medical or legal responsibility for any reader who uses the contents of this book as medical advice or prescription.

CONTENTS

INTRODUCTION TO AESTHETIC PLASTIC SURGERY

Starting with the essentials, from an explanation of what plastic surgery is and how to choose the surgeon who is best for you, to how you can help ensure your safety through any procedure.

FACIAL AESTHETIC SURGERY

Thinking of the face and neck as being divided into "aesthetic units" and the procedures designed to either rejuvenate or reshape specific facial features.

continued....

BREAST SURGERY

Considering the role of breast size and shape in self-image and personal satisfaction, and exploring the options for change.

BODY CONTOURING

Addressing problems such as bulging fat deposits, a protruding or wrinkled abdomen, sagging thighs or buttocks, and loose upper arms caused by heredity, aging, pregnancy, or massive weight loss.

NONSURGICAL AND ANCILLARY COSMETIC PROCEDURES

Exploring nonsurgical procedures; their benefits and effectiveness when performed alone or in combination with aesthetic surgical procedures.

SPECIAL TOPICS
Discussing special considerations for men's aesthetic surgery and making the right choices for teens.

RESOURCES

ABOUT THIS BOOK

Be *Your Best* is a totally different kind of book about aesthetic plastic surgery. It's written for the intelligent consumer who is interested in gaining a true understanding of aesthetic surgery. Throughout this book, you'll find commentary and insights from our group of highly qualified experts — board-certified plastic surgeons who share with you exactly what they do, how they do it, and why. You'll learn that for most aesthetic procedures there are a variety of effective techniques. And, because this book will expose you to a wide range of viewpoints, you'll feel better prepared to make well-informed choices about plastic surgery for yourself and your family.

Our contributing plastic surgery experts all are American Board of Plastic Surgery (ABPS) certified surgeons. ABPS certified surgeons generally perform a full range of plastic surgery procedures. Even though their clinical practice may be devoted to aesthetic surgery, they are trained in both aesthetic and reconstructive plastic surgery. This is important, because the comprehensive training that enables plastic surgeons to perform complex reconstructive procedures is invaluable to the development of highly refined skills in aesthetic surgery.

Be Your Best is organized in a way that allows you to easily find the specific information you're looking for — whether it's details of a specific cosmetic procedure or important points about surgical safety. The full-color drawings illustrating some of the more common techniques should help you to better visualize the process from "before" to "after" surgery. Whether you read only certain chapters or cover-to-cover, you'll find answers to many of your questions about aesthetic surgery.

Of course, neither this book nor any other can substitute for a personal consultation. As our experts emphasize repeatedly, good aesthetic surgery requires a highly individualized surgical plan. After reading this book, if you are interested in aesthetic surgery for yourself or a member of your family, talk with a board-certified plastic surgeon. Selecting a qualified surgeon is, after all, the best way to help ensure that the journey between your "before" and "after" is a safe and pleasant one.

FOREWORD
by Peter Bela Fodor, MD, FACS

$\mathcal{A}$s a plastic surgeon, I have always been inspired by my profession but never more than I am today, after more than 25 years in practice. That's because plastic surgery, and especially aesthetic plastic surgery, is more gratifying and challenging than ever before. What we are now able to accomplish for our patients is truly remarkable — and the speed at which new and or refined techniques and technologies are being introduced into mainstream plastic surgery practice is enough to keep every plastic surgeon on his or her toes! It is easy for us to remain very enthusiastic about what we can offer today to our patients.

Since you already have an interest in cosmetic surgery, much of what you will read in this book, *Be Your Best*, should encourage you to investigate further how plastic surgery can enhance your appearance and quality of life. I hope you will do so by seeking consultation with a board-certified plastic surgeon in your community — perhaps even one of the experts who have contributed comments to this book.

Along with all the positives about how aesthetic surgery can improve our lives, it's not surprising that there is also confusion. The *unreality* of plastic surgery "reality" television shows, excessive media hype of any procedure with a catchy name ("weekend," "lunch hour" or even "instant" face lifts, for example) and self-promotion by physicians without appropriate formal training to perform plastic surgery — all of this has contributed to the current "misinformation" about cosmetic enhancements. It is because of such misinformation, in part, that we have undertaken to develop *Be Your Best*.

In my mind, the most important thing that you, the reader, can take away from the experience of reading this book is the importance of selecting a qualified plastic surgeon for your cosmetic surgery. Physicians who obtain bona fide credentials in plastic surgery have devoted at least five and sometimes up to 10 years after medical school to specialized training in this field. This lengthy training period does not imply that we are "slow learners"; rather, it reflects the complexity of training, the magnitude of our commitment, and the love we have for our specialty. Among the fruits of this labor are the pleasure of surgical artistry and the ability to help people lead happier lives as a result of our work.

The popular media is a powerful source of information for the public. While there are excellent writers who do a responsible job of reporting on aesthetic surgery, unfortunately there are some in the media who succumb to pure commercialism, even with regard to a serious health topic such as plastic surgery. Then there are those journalists whom I believe have a keen interest in educating the public about the significance of plastic surgery training and board certification, but due to their own misunderstanding often make poor choices when it comes to selecting physicians for their interviews. I have read many magazine articles in which an interviewed physician is given the title of "plastic surgeon" when, in fact, he or she has no recognized board certification in plastic surgery.

I believe that media coverage of cosmetic surgery has had a positive impact in the sense that people are generally more aware of the possibilities for enhancing their appearance, and they are no longer shy or embarrassed about having cosmetic surgery. In fact, people today are proud of what they have done to improve their appearance. The downside of all this media coverage, however, is this: In speaking with my surgeon colleagues around the country, it is clear that many more potential cosmetic surgery patients now approach us with unrealistic requests, often encouraged by stories in the electronic and print media. I've had it happen in my practice on quite a few occasions: A patient comes in asking to "throw in a tummy tuck, and also liposuction and a breast lift," with their scheduled face lift and upper eyelid surgery, because they saw this on one of the reality television shows. The fact is that too many procedures or the wrong combinations of procedures in a single surgical session increase the risks of surgery. I'm not willing to take those kinds of risks with my patients — and neither are other responsible plastic surgeons who must balance risks and benefits in each individual case.

I suppose all of us have the desire, at times, to believe in "magic" — and plastic surgery can sometimes seem as close to magic as anything we know. As a plastic surgeon, I am often amazed at the wonderful transformations that are achieved through various cosmetic enhancements. However, I know what it takes to get from Point A to Point B, and it is often a long process with many steps. I also understand how easily one could be misled by the dramatic changes in appearance portrayed on television. These total transformations often are the result not only of multiple cosmetic surgeries but also extensive cosmetic dentistry, professionally applied makeup, hair coloring and restyling, and a new, more flattering wardrobe. Such extreme makeovers may be fine for some people, but don't think that having plastic surgery means changing who you are! Although some patients are looking for a dramatic difference, the majority say, "I don't want to look different, I just want to look my best."

Fortunately, most people realize that television usually represents anything but "reality," although they may still view it for the sole purpose of entertainment. For that matter, I happen to occasionally watch the totally fictionalized "Nip/Tuck" program, amused at how remote the storyline is from anything that really takes place in an aesthetic surgery practice!

One of the truly legitimate plastic surgery "stories" in the news is that of minimally invasive cosmetic surgery. Interest in this subject is certainly understandable — every patient and surgeon would like to reduce operating time, shorten recovery, and minimize complications. When new procedures have been adequately tested for safety and effectiveness, when patients are properly selected, and when the physician is thoroughly trained and qualified, there can be many benefits to minimally invasive techniques.

Liposuction (also called lipoplasty), the most commonly performed cosmetic operation worldwide, fits beautifully into the category of minimally invasive procedures. It produces only very tiny, well-concealed scars, has a relatively quick recovery, and achieves dramatic results. It's also a very safe procedure in well-trained hands.

Like everything in life, what suits one person may not be ideal for another. Minimally invasive facial procedures, from thread lifts to the more complex endoscopic approaches (such as endoscopic face lifts and brow lifts that leave no visible scars), work well for the right candidates but do not provide satisfactory results for everybody. While injectables, which have made great advances in recent years, are a near-perfect solution for some patients, others will need a full facial rejuvenation including a face lift and neck lift, brow lift, and upper and lower eyelid surgery to achieve the look they want. There is, of course, a wide variety of approaches between these two extremes. Custom-tailoring procedures, rather than the "one size fits all" approach, is the key and also is what separates the highly trained and experienced plastic surgeon from physicians without these qualifications and skills.

Throughout the pages of this book, you will learn about tried-and-true cosmetic procedures and those that are "on the cutting edge" — and you will gain insight into these procedures through concise comments from highly skilled plastic surgeons. In addition to chapters devoted to the full range of aesthetic procedures, other topics of importance such as how to select a qualified surgeon, what ensures a safe surgical facility, and even a little bit about the history of aesthetic surgery are also covered. You can choose to read individual chapters on specific procedures or the book in its entirety.

The text is compiled through contributions from more than 100 board-certified plastic surgeons, all members of the American Society for Aesthetic Plastic Surgery (ASAPS). ASAPS is the world's foremost organization for cosmetic plastic surgery. Its membership is comprised of plastic surgeons who are certified by the American Board of Plastic Surgery (or the Royal College of Physicians and Surgeons of Canada) and who are required not only to show evidence of significant experience in cosmetic surgery but also to demonstrate the highest ethical standards in their profession. The primary mission of ASAPS is the ongoing clinical education of plastic surgeons and education of the public about all aspects of cosmetic plastic surgery. It is notable that approximately half of the past presidents of ASAPS who are currently in active private practice are among the contributors to this book.

The book's publisher, Insight International Press, assembled a talented editorial team whose job was to synthesize information provided by the contributors into an easy-to-read text. We are fortunate, also, to have illustrations provided by William Winn, one of today's most well known medical artists.

My personal role has been to edit the product of this collaborative effort for accuracy of the information presented. It has been a painstaking process, but one that I have thoroughly enjoyed. I want to thank my wife, Barbara, for her patience and support during the many months in which I spent a great deal of our personal time working on this project.

Throughout the book, a balanced view was sought, especially because in cosmetic surgery there are often multiple surgical approaches to the same problem. Even though I provide personal comments at the end of some of the chapters under Editor's Viewpoint, I have tried to put aside any biases I may have regarding preferred surgical techniques. At times, however, it is inevitable that one must express personal preferences. Those instances in which my opinion may differ from some of our contributing surgeons only demonstrates that a satisfactory outcome and even excellent results can be obtained through different surgical approaches.

The "insider" information about aesthetic surgery presented by our experts is truly fascinating. Yet those who have contributed to this book understand that you, the reader, are a sophisticated health care consumer who is not in search of entertainment but, rather, seeks assistance in a highly individual decision-making process. I hope that you will find the book useful in gaining a better understanding of how aesthetic plastic surgery can, indeed, help you to *Be Your Best.*

INTRODUCTION
TO AESTHETIC PLASTIC SURGERY

A GLIMPSE AT THE HISTORY
of plastic surgery

The current interest in plastic surgery has focused largely on aesthetic procedures. There have been many advances in techniques and technology, as well as a broadening acceptance of aesthetic surgery as an option for all kinds of people, not just the rich and famous. Considering this, it may seem as though plastic surgery is a fairly young specialty.

It may be surprising to learn that although the term "plastic surgery" wasn't coined until 1818 by German surgeon Von Graefe in his book, *Rhinoplastik*, the origins of the specialty go back more than 5,000 years. The root of the word "plastic" is "plastikos," a Greek word meaning "to mold" or "give form."

Today, the specialty of plastic surgery is comprised of both reconstructive surgery and aesthetic, or cosmetic, surgery. Reconstructive surgery attempts to restore function and form to parts of the body that are damaged or abnormal — either from injury, disease or congenital defects. The goal of aesthetic surgery, on the other hand, is to improve and enhance essentially normal features to improve patients' overall sense of well-being.

As you might imagine, plastic surgery initially focused on reconstructive rather than aesthetic operations. In his brief but comprehensive 5,000-year review of the history of plastic surgery, *History of Rhinoplasty — An Epitome of Plastic Surgery*, plastic surgeon **Lewis Obi, MD**, of Jacksonville, Florida, states, "Egyptian reconstructive efforts are well documented in the *Edwin Smith Papyrus*, the origins of which are dated approximately 3000 BC. These documents describe surgical management of facial wounds including jaw and nasal fractures. The next significant text was that of Sushruta of India in

approximately 600 BC when his encyclopedic *Samhita* detailed many complex procedures, including operations to restore amputated noses. Sir Zachary Cope, in his *Short History of Plastic Surgery*, 1964, observed, 'The new nose was formed from flaps of skin taken either from the adjacent cheeks or from the forehead.' This became known as the 'Hindu' or 'Indian' method of nasal reconstruction."

Although early surgical interventions were reconstructive in nature, aesthetic enhancements were undertaken by various nonsurgical means. The ancient Egyptians were said to use fenugreek to try to increase breast size, and mummies of ancient Egyptian courtesans show that their breasts were tattooed.

Little information has been found relating to plastic surgery during the Greco-Roman period, and although Hippocrates and Aristole discuss the treatment of nasal fractures, they do not mention skin-shifting or molding techniques. Roman Aulus Cornelius Celsus in the 1st century AD does mention the Indian technique of nasal reconstruction in his book, *De Re Medica*.

Medical science in general experienced a period of dormancy during the Middle Ages, when a decree by Pope Innocent III in 1215 AD stated that no priest, deacon, or sub deacon should perform any surgical procedures which involved bloodshed, as it was incompatible with the divine mission. However, with the Islamic conversion of India in the 10th century, ancient Indian techniques made their way through the Middle East into Europe.

The Brancas, father and son, secretly developed the arm-flap technique of nasal reconstruction, which was finally perfected and published by Renaissance surgeon Gaspar Tagliacozzi in Bologna. "What makes Tagliacozzi's book so pivotal," says the historian, Dr. Obi, "is that his treatise of 298 pages including 47 pages of illustrations is the first book dedicated entirely to plastic surgery. Another Renaissance surgeon, Parisian Ambroise Pare, briefly mentions Tagliacozzi's rhinoplasty in his writings."

While various procedures and publications relating to plastic surgery continued to appear sporadically during the ensuing generations, it was not until the development of asepsis by Pasteur and Lister and anesthesia by Crawford Long and Horace Wells that significant advances in plastic surgery occurred. Despite reconstructive surgery's dominance of the specialty, there were also continuous attempts at various means of aesthetic enhancement. German surgeon Robert Gersuny tried to enlarge breasts in 1889 by injecting them with paraffin. The results were disastrous. The first recorded surgical attempt at breast augmentation occurred in 1895 when a doctor attempted to transplant a lipoma from the back of an actress to her breasts.

Yet, it was the advent of modern warfare, with weaponry far more destructive than the world had previously seen, that placed a tremendous demand on the evolving specialty of plastic surgery and helped hone the creative mindset of the modern plastic surgeon.

According to Dr. Obi, "At the onset of World War I in 1914, only a handful of surgeons were performing any significant amount of reconstructive surgery. Among these, Vilray Blair and John Staige Davis pioneered work in this country, whereas Sir Harold Gillies and Archibald McIndoe were the English pioneers of plastic surgery. With better anesthesia and improved management of infection, significant advances in plastic surgery occurred during and after World War I." The American Society of Plastic and Reconstructive Surgeons (now the American Society of Plastic Surgeons) was established in 1931, and the American Board of Plastic Surgery in 1941; yet, as Obi

states, "at the start of World War II there were only four dedicated plastic surgeons in Britain and approximately 60 in the United States."

Not only was there a relatively small number of plastic surgeons, the advance in weaponry produced injuries so numerous and devastating that traditional doctors were at a loss to treat them. Plastic surgeons, combining traditional medical and surgical techniques with creative problem solving, set about repairing massive injuries that had seemed hopeless. Although their methods were often unorthodox, they achieved positive, often amazing results. When most people hear the word creativity associated with plastic surgery, they think of the artistry involved in fashioning an aesthetically pleasing result. While this form of creativity is essential to the specialty, equally as important, and perhaps an even more unique element of the specialty, is the creative thought process involved. It is plastic surgery's focus on and methods of problem solving that are arguably its most defining feature.

The challenges created by modern weaponry's mutilations certainly accelerated this creative process. Traditional medicine has tried and true methods. When an appendix must be removed, the surgeon follows a rather standard "blueprint" in carrying out the procedure. Many of the injuries encountered during World War I and World War II called for new methods, and techniques had to be developed very quickly. Of course, medical science had evolved far beyond what it was during previous wars. Plastic surgeons weren't necessarily inventing new science, but they certainly were innovating new methods of problem solving. Calling upon their knowledge of medicine and the full spectrum of surgical techniques, they found new and creative solutions to the most difficult problems in restoring function, and secondarily form, to severely damaged bodies and faces.

Since World War II, plastic surgery has been on a continual ascendancy. Dr. Obi recounts in his history, "The first organ transplant was performed in 1954 by plastic surgeon Joseph Murray who later received the Nobel Prize for his great contribution. The introduction of silicone breast implants by Cronin and Gerow in 1962 propelled the field of cosmetic surgery during a decade of increasing social and aesthetic demands. The introduction of microsurgery by Harry Buncke in the 1960s led to many new organ and tissue transplantation techniques sensationalized by the John Travolta-Nicholas Cage movie *Face/Off*, and already a face transplant has been performed successfully by French plastic surgeons."

While the skills of plastic surgeons historically were honed through the performance of complex reconstructive procedures, some surgeons were drawn to the growing field of aesthetic surgery. At first, aesthetic surgery was not considered a "worthy" undertaking for a trained and reputable surgeon, and it was performed largely behind closed doors. Training in aesthetic surgery was obtained primarily through private arrangements to view operations performed by leading surgeons of the day. It wasn't until 1967 that a small group of board-certified plastic surgeons openly professing an interest and dedication to the advancement of aesthetic surgery established their own professional organization, later renamed the American Society for Aesthetic Plastic Surgery (ASAPS). Although at first regarded as a "renegade" society by the rest of organized plastic surgery, ASAPS eventually gained a strong following and has emerged today as the leading organization for the continuing education of plastic surgeons in all aspects of aesthetic surgery.

Parallel to the history of aesthetic surgery's rise to prominence within the specialty of plastic surgery is the evolution of society's changing attitudes toward aesthetic surgery. As advancements in technique have improved surgical results, and as more plastic surgeons have become highly trained in cosmetic procedures, so has society's recognition of the potential benefits of cosmetic plastic surgery deepened and broadened.

"Cosmetic surgery is no longer reserved for the rich and famous," says **Fanny dela Cruz, MD**, of West Bloomfield, Michigan. "It is not just for the Park Avenue crowd. It's for everybody in the mainstream. More and more people are going under the scalpel to enhance their looks, be it reshaping the nose, enlarging the breasts, removing fat bulges under the eyes, or tightening the skin. What was once considered 'vanity surgery' for the privileged has become common and accepted among the middle class of America."

Plastic surgeons today continue to receive extensive training in reconstructive procedures as part of their accredited plastic surgery residency programs, and this training provides an excellent foundation for their work in cosmetic surgery. By the time they have completed the minimum of five years of surgical training (which they begin following four years of medical school), they generally have had clinical experience in the full range of plastic surgery operations. This in-depth training and experience prepares them to provide patients with safe, competent, and high-quality plastic surgical care — whether for reconstructive or cosmetic purposes. Some plastic surgeons choose to specialize in cosmetic surgery and become members of the American Society for Aesthetic Plastic Surgery. The primary mission of ASAPS is ongoing education in the latest procedures and techniques in this rapidly developing field.

How the subspecialty of aesthetic plastic surgery will evolve in the future remains to be seen. Technology will certainly continue to play an increasingly important role, giving plastic surgeons new and less invasive methods for correcting many kinds of appearance problems. Further discoveries related to aging processes at the cellular level are likely to yield improved therapies for skin rejuvenation. Advances in genetics, stem cell research, and other scientific fields may ultimately teach us how to retard the aging process and stimulate physical regeneration, making many types of surgery obsolete.

Such predictions, for now, remain purely speculative. In the meantime, state-of-the-art aesthetic surgery, performed by qualified, board-certified plastic surgeons, is improving the lives of millions of Americans every year. Looking at how far we've come since the early days of plastic surgery, the results achieved by these modern-day procedures truly can be considered miraculous. ∀

CHOOSING A QUALIFIED SURGEON

Information on aesthetic (cosmetic) plastic surgery is readily available from many sources — but not all of these sources are credible, nor is all the available information accurate. Likewise, prospective cosmetic surgery patients have many choices when it comes to selecting a surgeon. Not all physicians who perform cosmetic surgery today have equivalent training and certification. In fact, the differences are significant and can have potentially devastating consequences for patient safety.

"The most important thing for any prospective cosmetic surgery patient to remember is that these operations have an excellent record of safety when performed by a qualified surgeon; but in the wrong hands, there is no question that the risks of cosmetic surgery increase," comments **R. Laurence Berkowitz, MD,** of Campbell, California.

"Many people approach aesthetic surgery as if they are having a salon or spa treatment," says **Zachary E. Gerut, MD,** Hewlett, New York. "Patients must be aware that in addition to the wonderful benefits of aesthetic surgery, there are risks involved."

Selecting a qualified surgeon does not constitute a guarantee of risk-free surgery or a perfect result. Complications or less-than-optimal outcomes can occur even when a procedure is performed by a well-trained surgeon exercising impeccable surgical judgment. That's because an individual patient's response to surgery and anesthesia is not totally predictable. Nevertheless, a board-certified plastic surgeon is trained to minimize risks and competently handle potential complications.

"When it comes to consumers of cosmetic surgery, it truly is a situation of 'buyer beware,'" says **Guy Stofman, MD,** of Pittsburgh, Pennsylvania. "People need to understand that all these techniques — from simple, light chemical peels to the most complex surgical procedures — have the potential for complications. Untrained, inexperienced practitioners can cause serious harm to patients. That's why people need to do their 'homework' and find out about the training, certification and experience of any doctor they may choose to perform their cosmetic surgery."

Wearing your seat belt when you ride in a car can reduce your risk of injury; so can obeying the speed limit, driving defensively, and keeping your vehicle well maintained. As obvious as these precautions are, it is surprising how many people do not follow them. Of course, they are not the only ones to have accidents. There are always uncontrollable variables.

While there are factors in aesthetic plastic surgery that you cannot control, there are measures you can take that will decidedly increase your chances for a successful and satisfying outcome. Perhaps the most important of these is choosing the right surgeon.

THE SHOCKING TRUTH

It is surprising that with the seemingly constant media blitz about the astounding increase in the number of people having cosmetic surgery, one disturbing fact is seldom discussed: unqualified doctors are legally allowed to perform these procedures, and they often do so in inadequate, unaccredited facilities.

These are life-threatening realities that too few people understand. The law in most states allows virtually any licensed medical doctor, including those whose training in plastic surgery may consist solely of a weekend seminar or less, to adopt the title "cosmetic surgeon" or "plastic surgeon" and to perform difficult surgical procedures without certification or peer-review of credentials. These doctors are often unprepared to handle emergencies that may arise in the course of a surgical procedure, or complications that can occur in the postsurgical period. They do not have hospital privileges to perform plastic surgery, so they may carry out their operations in unaccredited facilities lacking the necessary equipment and personnel to help ensure safety.

Why have so many doctors assumed the title of "cosmetic surgeon" or "plastic surgeon" and undertaken to build practices in cosmetic surgery? The reasons are primarily economic. Changes in our health care system in recent years have drastically reduced insurance reimbursements for physicians providing a wide range of medical and surgical services. Some of these physicians are attracted to cosmetic surgery because they can set their own fees for cosmetic procedures and are paid directly by the patient.

So, even though their formal residency training, certification (if any), and experience are unrelated to plastic or cosmetic surgery, they have decided to become "self-designated" plastic or cosmetic surgeons. They may advertise themselves by these self-designated titles, and potential patients often don't realize that the "plastic surgeon" they have selected is not board certified and has no accredited training in the procedures advertised.

"I like to draw an analogy to archery," says **Rafael C. Cabrera, MD**, of Boca Raton, Florida. "One can spend so much time researching all the arrows, how many feathers they have, how straight they are, and how long they are, but the most important part of hitting the bull's eye is who is holding the bow. Probably nothing is more important than choosing the right surgeon. I mean not only a qualified, board-certified plastic surgeon, but also somebody you have confidence in and who will address your needs and concerns."

People often assume that the government regulates the medical profession far more than it actually does. Federal laws do not regulate medical specialties or differentiate between physicians' qualifications. Hence, there are no federal regulations restricting which doctors can perform plastic surgery. Most states have laws governing hospitals but not doctors' private offices. It's a stunning revelation that thousands of so-called cosmetic or plastic surgeons are doctors from various medical specialties whose formal training is unrelated to plastic or cosmetic surgery — in fact, they may or may not have undergone any type of accredited surgical training. Many have nothing approaching the in-depth training and experience obtained through accredited residency training in plastic surgery, a requirement for every plastic surgeon certified by the American Board of Plastic Surgery (ABPS).

"Unfortunately, many patients are not armed with all the information they need to protect themselves," says **James A. Matas, MD**, of Orlando, Florida. "They need to know the right questions to ask and where to get the answers. It's usually not enough to select a doctor on the basis of a recommendation alone. You also need to really know what kind of residency training he or she has, what board certification, what hospital privileges, whether the facility in which he or she operates is accredited, and so on. I can count on one hand the number of times I've been asked those important questions."

"Referrals to a surgeon can come from a person's personal or primary care doctor, and from friends, family, and other patients," says **Barbara K. Siwy, MD**, of Carmel, Indiana, "but patient referrals are most useful when they come from someone who has had the same type of surgery you are considering. And, of course, you must still be diligent in making further inquiries about the doctor's training, certification and experience."

Well-meaning friends, relatives, and even other doctors who recommend a particular surgeon may actually be unaware of the details of the surgeon's education and credentials to perform cosmetic surgery. Likewise, finding a plastic surgeon through advertisements or Internet directories alone is not the best approach. While these resources may provide you with names of physicians in your area, some of whom may be qualified to perform plastic surgery, you always need to take the next step in researching the training, certification and experience of your doctor — and you should do so, as much as possible, prior to making an appointment for a consultation. Such research may be time consuming, but it is effort well spent.

No one should ever "shop" for a surgeon only on the basis of the lowest price. Taking a purely economic approach to selecting a surgeon ignores the seriousness of this important decision.

"Many times people spend more time and energy getting quotes, recommendations, or opinions about an appliance they want to buy than they do when choosing a plastic surgeon with whom they will have, in many cases, a life-changing surgical procedure," says Dr. Siwy.

While in recent years, more details about plastic surgery credentials have surfaced in the media, there still is a general lack of information as well as a great deal of inaccurate material in the popular press. Reporters will often conduct interviews with physicians, portraying them as plastic surgeons and even naming them as such, without checking to be certain of their training and certification. In addition, unqualified physicians seeking to build cosmetic practices may advertise in the media, sometimes providing consumers with misleading or erroneous information. One of the most blatant is the claim of "board certification."

Savvy consumers know that board certification is an important indicator of a physician's accredited training in a specific medical or surgical specialty. What they may not know, however, is that in addition to the 24 certifying boards recognized by the American Board of Medical Specialties (ABMS), there is also a host of other unrecognized, or "self-designated," boards. While a few self-designated boards are recognized in some states as equivalent to boards affiliated with the American Board of Medical Specialties, certification by many others may signify little and guarantee nothing.

All of this subterfuge can lead the prospective patient into some very dangerous territory. There are, however, factual guideposts for finding a qualified surgeon that can point you in the right direction from the start.

AMERICAN BOARD OF PLASTIC SURGERY CERTIFICATION

In contrast to the aforementioned self-designated boards, the American Board of Plastic Surgery (ABPS) is recognized by the American Board of Medical Specialties, which serves the public interest by overseeing physician certification in the United States.

Plastic surgeons certified by the ABPS have graduated from an accredited medical school and have completed at least five additional years of surgical training including an accredited plastic surgery residency program. They must satisfy certain requirements for clinical practice prior to applying for, and ultimately completing, their written and oral Board examinations.

ABPS-certified surgeons must also adhere to the Board's ethical and professional standards, including an absence of disciplinary actions by hospitals, licensing agencies, or financing programs. The Board also requires participation in peer review; participation in clinical self-assessment; operation of a safe, patient-centered practice that meets criteria for quality; and participation in measurement of clinical performance and patient care results, including patient satisfaction.

The ABPS is the only board recognized by the American Board of Medical Specialties to certify physicians in the specialty of plastic surgery. There are, however, other recognized boards that certify doctors in dermatology, ophthalmology and otolaryngology, and these specific specialty certifications may indicate qualifications to perform aesthetic procedures related to specific areas or structures of the face and body.

Some otolaryngologists (ENTs) pursue certification by the American Board of Facial Plastic and Reconstructive Surgery, which although not among the 24 ABMS boards, is recognized in some states as equivalent. In addition, the ABMS recognizes the subspecialty certification of Plastic Surgery Within the Head and Neck for diplomates of both the American Board of Plastic Surgery and the American Board of Otolaryngology.

Surgeons who are certified by the American Board of Plastic Surgery are physicians whose formal training and certification is applicable to plastic surgery procedures of the face and the entire body. Although not a guarantee of safety or results, this comprehensive training provides a significant indicator of competence.

HOSPITAL PRIVILEGES

Beyond board certification, doctors must be granted privileges if they wish to operate in a hospital. These privileges are granted only to qualified doctors who have passed muster with the hospital's credentialing committee, which is composed of other doctors who conduct extensive background checks of physicians applying for privileges. Once admitted to the staff of an accredited hospital, physicians continue to undergo peer review, and if they are ever deemed to be delivering substandard care, they can lose their privileges.

"Make sure that the surgeon you select for your plastic surgery has privileges to perform the procedure you want in a hospital, even if you're going to have it done in an office-based facility," says **Leo R. McCafferty, MD**, of Pittsburgh, Pennsylvania. "If the physician does not have such privileges, this should send up an immediate red flag."

FACILITY ACCREDITATION

Most cosmetic surgical procedures can be safely performed outside the hospital in an accredited ambulatory surgery facility that may be a freestanding surgicenter or an office-based facility. The keyword when it comes to outpatient plastic surgery is "accreditation."

Most people don't realize, however, that the majority of office-based surgical facilities are not accredited. Neither do they meet other acceptable safety standards such as state licensure or Medicare certification. As mentioned earlier, office-based facilities are often the only place where an untrained and unqualified doctor can perform cosmetic surgery without peer review.

"If you are going to have a procedure done in a surgi-center or a doctor's surgical suite," says Dr. McCafferty, "make sure that it's licensed by the state, certified by Medicare and/or accredited by one of the recognized national organizations. This is the best quality assurance that you can have."

Qualified plastic surgeons perform major surgery in a facility meeting at least one of these important safety criteria — whether it's a hospital, a freestanding surgicenter

or an office-based surgical suite. For more information on how you can be sure the facility in which you plan to have your surgery has met these high standards, read our chapter on The Surgical Facility.

ASAPS AND ASPS MEMBERSHIP

Board certification can be confusing, and patients often may find it daunting to investigate a doctor's hospital credentials or facility accreditation. Fortunately, there is yet another perhaps more direct way to determine whether your surgeon is a board-certified plastic surgeon operating in an accredited facility: find out if the surgeon is a member of the American Society for Aesthetic Plastic Surgery (ASAPS) and/or the American Society of Plastic Surgeons (ASPS).

"Just because someone is a good marketer and has good ads, doesn't mean he or she is a good surgeon, or even a qualified surgeon," says **Christopher Morea, MD**, of Raleigh, North Carolina. "Patients need to be made aware of the stark difference that can exist between those calling themselves 'cosmetic surgeons,' which can be virtually any M.D., and those who are board-certified plastic surgeons and members of the American Society for Aesthetic Plastic Surgery and the American Society of Plastic Surgeons — and therefore among the most highly qualified of all medical professionals."

ASAPS and ASPS are both membership organizations — they are not certifying boards. However, they do have requirements ensuring that all of their members are certified by the American Board of Plastic Surgery (or certified in plastic surgery by the Royal College of Physicians and Surgeons of Canada) and perform all but minor procedures in an accredited, state-licensed or Medicare-certified surgical facility. Also, members of the American Society for Aesthetic Plastic Surgery have met additional requirements for clinical experience in cosmetic surgery.

It is easy to find out if a particular doctor is a member of either one of these organizations by visiting their websites: www.surgery.org (ASAPS) and www.plasticsurgery.org (ASPS).

ASK QUESTIONS

Deciding to have aesthetic plastic surgery is a big step and one that requires your utmost attention and serious consideration. Once you choose a qualified plastic surgeon with whom you feel comfortable, your safety will be in his or her hands. Before then, the potential for a successful and satisfying surgical outcome rests squarely on your shoulders.

Do not accept claims of expertise or be impressed by important-sounding credentials without finding out the facts. Don't be embarrassed or afraid to ask about the surgeon's training, board certification, hospital privileges, and experience. Verify membership in the American Society for Aesthetic Plastic Surgery and the American Society of Plastic Surgeons. Find out where your procedure will be performed and ask about accreditation, state-licensure or Medicare certification. Your surgeon should always be willing to discuss with you what type of anesthesia will be used and the qualifications of whoever will administer it — either a board-certified/ board-eligible anesthesiologist or a certified registered nurse anesthetist (CRNA).

"You should feel comfortable with the surgeon you select," says **Linda Leffel, MD**, of Bend, Oregon. "Openly discuss any concerns you have at the consultation. Research your surgeon's training, credentials, and experience. When you select an ABPS-certified surgeon who is a member of ASAPS and ASPS, you'll feel assured that your surgeon is well trained and up to date with the advances in cosmetic surgery."

Throughout this book, you will be reminded that every person's sense of aesthetics is different. When selecting a surgeon, you need to be as certain as possible that he or she understands your aesthetic goals and is willing to try and meet your realistic expectations. You may achieve this level of comfort with your surgeon through simply discussing what bothers you about your appearance and his or her suggested solutions. Or you may have the opportunity to further evaluate your surgeon's aesthetic judgment by looking at patient photographs that are typical examples of his or her work, or through other means such as computer imaging used by some surgeons to help patients visualize the possible results of surgery.

People from all racial and ethnic backgrounds elect to undergo plastic surgery. In most cases, their goal is to improve specific features while preserving their ethnic identity. These special considerations require selecting a surgeon who has the appropriate skill, experience, and aesthetic judgment as well as knowledge and sensitivity regarding differences in cultural ideals of attractiveness.

Many potential patients arrange consultations with more than one surgeon to compare surgical approaches, comfort of communication, and fees. Don't be surprised to find that various plastic surgeons may recommend different approaches to what bothers you about your appearance. Often there are multiple techniques that can be applied to the same problem, and surgeons may have a preferred method based on what works best in their hands. In such cases, there may be no single "right" approach. Although being presented with too many options can sometimes be confusing, ultimately you must sort through the information that has been presented to you and choose a surgeon based an evaluation of training, experience and results, as well as your feeling of confidence in his or her judgment.

"Patients need to take responsibility — one of the most important choices they make is choosing a doctor. You may consult with a surgeon who likes to do a procedure only one way, and you may decide his or her approach is not appropriate for you at that time," says Dr. Siwy. "Personal feelings are extremely important. A patient and doctor must be able to 'connect' and communicate. Look for a surgeon who has the three 'A's' — ability, affability, and availability. You want someone who listens to you and addresses your goals and concerns."

There are many factors for you to consider as a potential cosmetic surgery patient. You wouldn't get in your car without educating yourself about the rules of the road and driving safety. You buckle your seat belt. Don't let someone operate on you without doing your homework. Learn the rules of the road as they apply to choosing the right surgeon, and the odds are that you'll have a safe and pleasant journey. ⫶

THE CONSULTATION

Once you've identified those surgeons who are certified by the American Board of Plastic Surgery and are members of the American Society for Aesthetic Plastic Surgery and/or American Society of Plastic Surgeons, you'll want to begin the next phase of your selection process, which is finding the surgeon you feel can best help achieve your personal goals for surgery.

Two plastic surgeons can have roughly the same training and experience, even use the same techniques, yet achieve very different results. That's because each surgeon's clinical judgment and unique personal aesthetics greatly influence the outcomes they achieve for their patients. These personal qualities that each surgeon brings to his or her work aren't credentialed and can't be evaluated on paper.

"In my view, a plastic surgeon should approach each case by trying to do the simplest thing in the best way," says **Archibald S. Miller, MD**, of Tulsa, Oklahoma. "Whatever I want to achieve for the patient, I prefer to use tried-and-true techniques, modifying them a little to provide the best result in any individual situation."

Mutaz Habal, MD, of Tampa, Florida, adds, "I use techniques that are reliable and have the least possible downsides. I do not correct one problem by producing another."

Once you have well in mind your goals and expectations for surgery, you are ready to make an appointment with one or more qualified plastic surgeons.

Prospective patients frequently have done a significant amount of research on their own about a particular procedure, often using resources on the Internet, and come to their consultation armed with a fairly comprehensive set of facts, figures and questions. Gathering such information can be very helpful to the patient education process. But even if you feel certain about the type of procedure, or technique, you want, it's best to approach your consultation with an open mind. After all, you are consulting with a plastic surgeon in order to benefit from his or her years of training and experience. Only by letting the surgeon analyze your situation and give you his or her opinion, can you evaluate how much confidence you have in that individual and whether he or she understands your objectives.

It also may be that the procedure you think you want is not the best one to solve your particular problem. For example, patients often assume that they need upper eyelid surgery to treat a "heavy" looking upper lid. In fact, many such patients may benefit more from a brow lift. Likewise, some patients may assume that a non-surgical procedure such as Botox or Restylane will give them the rejuvenated appearance they desire, when what they really need is a surgical procedure such as a face lift.

A qualified plastic surgeon can help you sort through the various options available to address the particular appearance problems that bother you. In many cases, there may be more than one alternative. It's important for you to give your surgeon an opportunity to explain these options to you and for the two of you to have a dialog that clearly establishes both what you would like to achieve and what is, or is not, possible in your particular case.

As much as your surgeon would like to fulfill every desire that you have for your improved appearance, there are always limitations; these may be a result of your particular anatomy, medical conditions you have that make certain techniques unadvisable, or expectations you have that cosmetic surgery simply cannot address. An important part of your plastic surgery consultation is the discussion that you and your surgeon will have about what you can reasonably expect as a result of plastic surgery. Your surgeon should be open and honest about the benefits, risks, and limitations of any procedures he or she recommends for you.

"In general, plastic surgeons should always remain humble," comments **R. Laurence Berkowitz, MD**, of Campbell, California. "Plastic surgery can accomplish a lot, but there are many things it cannot accomplish. Sometimes the technology is just not there yet. As plastic surgeons, we are public servants and are here to help and take care of people. We need to be sympathetic with their needs and very straightforward about their expected outcomes from any particular procedure."

Robert Brink, MD, of San Mateo, California, adds, "A surgeon's imagination should never exceed his or her ability — or the compliance of the patient's tissues. We must evaluate both factors realistically when determining what can and cannot be achieved through surgery."

Plastic surgeons generally charge a fee for consultation. This is appropriate, since the surgeon will be spending valuable time and utilizing his or her many years of training and experience to evaluate your situation and advise you on the type of procedure that would best serve your particular needs.

Some patients consult with a surgeon based on a recommendation from a friend, family member, or personal physician and, after verifying credentials and talking with the surgeon about what he or she would recommend, feel comfortable enough to schedule surgery. Other patients feel it is essential to consult with more than one surgeon — either because they do not have complete confidence in the first surgeon with whom they met or they simply want to compare opinions and personal approaches of several doctors. After seeing two or three plastic surgeons

in consultation, you most likely will feel that there is one you trust more than the others, you feel to be more experienced, knowledgeable, and skillful, and importantly, with whom you feel more "in sync." It is essential that you feel rapport with your surgeon and have good two-way communication before making your commitment to surgery.

"The more a patient understands before the operation," says **Steven K. White, Sr., MD**, of Myrtle Beach, South Carolina, "the smoother the postoperative course. If the plastic surgeon is annoyed or does not want to answer questions during the consultation, then the patient needs to find another plastic surgeon."

Gathering all the information you will need in order to make an informed decision about cosmetic surgery usually means asking a lot of questions. It also means being completely open and honest. Throughout this book, we will remind you of the importance of providing your surgeon with an accurate medical history, including an account of surgeries you have had and medications you have taken or currently take. In addition, you must be straightforward regarding what bothers you about your appearance, your motivation for having surgery, and what results you would be happy with. It is crucial to your ultimate satisfaction with surgery that you and your surgeon are on the same page — that you share an understanding of the perceived problem and the proposed solution.

Patients who are unfocused about what bothers them or what changes they would like to make are not good candidates for plastic surgery. Many of the results of cosmetic surgery are relatively permanent. That's why it is very important for you to think carefully about your goals and expectations before scheduling your first plastic surgery consultation. Some prospective patients find that bringing in photographs illustrating what they find attractive — for example, a particular type of nose or a model with breasts that are of a proportion they feel would be appropriate for them — can be helpful.

When using photographs as examples, however, keep in mind that what looks good on someone else may not be the right look, or even be achievable, for you. Your plastic surgeon may use computer imaging to help you visualize what the results of surgery might look like in your particular case. If your surgeon uses computer imaging, he or she will most likely remind you that the computer image is merely a representation of possible surgical results — it is not a guarantee. It is exactly for this reason that many plastic surgeons prefer not to offer computer imaging, believing that patients are better served by other methods of communication about surgical results.

Some plastic surgeons are happy to let patients look at before and after photographs of patients on whom they have operated. This can certainly give a prospective patient some idea of a surgeon's aesthetic judgment and taste. Patients may make their decision about which qualified surgeon to select based, in large part, upon whether they feel a particular surgeon's aesthetic sense is in sync with their own goals and expectations. Photographs can also help patients define and articulate the type of result they prefer. If you have an opportunity to view such photos, be sure to inquire as to whether the results are typical of most patients. While it is human nature to want to show one's best results, it is more appropriate for a surgeon to provide patients with examples of a range of results — from the best results to typical results and even less-than-optimal results that demonstrate the limitations of surgery.

Remember, also, that plastic surgeons have an obligation to protect patient confidentiality. Many surgeons are reluctant to ask former patients for permission to show their photos to prospective patients who are likely to be individuals in the same community and perhaps even acquaintances. If your surgeon has a limited number of patient photos to show you, do not assume that he or she is inexperienced or has only a small number of good results. The reason may simply be that the doctor has not sought permission to show a wide range of patient photographs. Some excellent surgeons elect not to demonstrate their work in this manner. They assume that patients who come to see them already know of their reputation and probably have friends who are former patients.

"Verbal communication has severe limitations," says **Edward O. Terino, MD**, of Thousand Oaks, California, "so visual communication becomes the most precise exchange between a plastic surgeon and a patient. I have found that facial contouring in particular cannot be discussed adequately without the use of visuals — computer imaging in particular. An interactive computer consultation allows patients to express to the doctor their own thoughts and feelings about the contours and shapes and overall appearance that they wish to achieve, and it allows the surgeon to decipher whether or not these aspirations are realistic."

All of these communication methods — discussion, viewing of photographs, computer imaging — are means to an end. That "end" is a well-informed patient who understands his or her surgeon's recommendations, abilities and "style." Most important, patients should leave the consultation with an accurate picture of both the potential benefits and the risks of surgery — and whether their expected results are likely to be met. The information gleaned during your consultation, and perhaps in written or video materials provided by your surgeon, will form the basis for your informed consent for surgery.

Guy Stofman, MD, of Pittsburgh, Pennsylvania, adds, "Patients must have realistic expectations. A woman will not look like Angelina Jolie after a simple pulsed light treatment, and if someone is trying to sell you that, be careful. If you've lost 100 pounds and your skin is hanging down, you don't need pulsed light. You need a major surgical procedure. The ethical physician will diagnose and give you the best treatment for your specific problem."

Ethical plastic surgeons do not operate on everyone who walks through their door. They are selective, evaluating patients' chances for success and considering both physical and psychological factors as much as possible.

"I see every patient at least twice before surgery," reports **Leo R. McCafferty, MD**, of Pittsburgh, Pennsylvania. "We talk about what they want and take pictures of areas that concern them. Then I encourage them to bring someone else with them for the second visit, a friend, relative, or significant other — another pair of ears. We look at the pictures, go over the procedure, and talk about the risks, the possibilities, and both realistic and unrealistic expectations. It helps me get to know the patient and for the patient to know me. What we really want is for the patient to be happy when they leave the office, whether they have surgery or not. Sometimes the best option is no surgery."

"I believe in spending time to help patients arrive at realistic expectations," says **Bruce I. White, MD**, of St. Louis,

Missouri. "I had one man come to see me who had been to five surgeons for opinions. He had a deeply wrinkled face but didn't want to have a surgical procedure, such as a face lift, or one that required extensive recovery such as dermabrasion. So, I advised him to look in the mirror and say, 'That guy looks like Clint Eastwood — isn't he handsome!' He said, 'Thanks, doc, now I don't have to bother seeing anyone else.'"

It is not uncommon for people to feel intimidated when talking to a surgeon. They may be afraid or embarrassed to ask their doctor questions, even when encouraged to do so, and quite often leave an appointment not really understanding all that the physician has said. The importance of communication with your plastic surgeon cannot be overstated. Going to see an aesthetic plastic surgeon is not like consulting with many other kinds of specialists, where the doctor tells the patient what's wrong and how he or she is going to fix it. In aesthetic plastic surgery, patients have to express what they perceive as wrong before any discussion of the procedures that are available and how the identified problems can be addressed. If you are bothered by more than one feature of your face or body, you need to be prepared to prioritize your goals. While it may be possible to perform multiple cosmetic procedures at the same time to address more than one concern, this will depend on the specific procedures, the condition of your health, and other factors. In all cases, your plastic surgeon will put your health and safety first.

"When considering facial plastic surgery, remember that when you look at someone you first look at the eyes, then the nose, and then track to the rest of the face," says **Gary R. Culbertson, MD**, of Sumter, South Carolina. "Write down for your plastic surgeon the top three things you do not like about your face, such as wrinkles or droopy eyes, before your consultation. Prioritize your concerns."

"The keys to successful plastic surgery," adds **Paul J. LoVerme, MD**, of Verona, New Jersey, "include investigating the procedure, educating yourself, and communicating with your plastic surgeon. Discuss the 'ations': your hesitations, aspirations, and expectations, and ask about recuperation and complications."

Although serious complications from aesthetic surgery are uncommon, they can occur. Never is it more important that you have a relationship of trust and mutual support with your plastic surgeon than during the recuperative process following an unforeseen complication, which can occur either in the surgical or postsurgical period.

Michael A. Marschall, MD, of Wheaton, Illinois, says, "The goals of aesthetic surgery are to refresh, rejuvenate, enhance and enliven. The maintenance of youth in a physical sense is understood to be an expected outcome. But patient satisfaction requires more than a plastic surgeon's technical skill. It also requires that the surgeon provide appropriate emotional support throughout the entire surgical experience. Only with this synergy can the ideal result be achieved."

Part of your consultation will likely be a discussion of fees. This discussion may take place between you and the surgeon, or you may be advised of fees by a patient coordinator or other member of the surgeon's staff. Your total fee for a surgical procedure may be broken down into several categories of expenses: the surgeon, the surgical facility, and the anesthesiology provider. You should also figure into the cost of surgery any medical tests that may be required, prescriptions, surgical garments, or other miscellaneous costs such as transportation to and from surgery or fees charged by an overnight caregiver if you do not have family or friends to provide these services.

You should also discuss with your surgeon his or her policy regarding revisionary surgery, if such surgery should be needed. In some cases, plastic surgeons will not charge patients for revisions that are necessary to achieve what the doctor considers to be a satisfactory result. However, patients may be asked to pay facility and anesthesia fees for revisionary surgery and, depending on the circumstances, a reduced surgeon's fee for reoperation may also be necessary.

The consultation process is, above all, an educational process. By preparing for your consultation, keeping an open mind, discussing your concerns and goals openly and honestly, paying close attention to the information your surgeon provides, asking questions, and satisfying yourself that you and your surgeon have established good communication and rapport, your plastic surgery consultation can provide the basis for a safe and successful surgical experience.

Body Dysmorphic Disorder

Body dysmorphic disorder (BDD) is an obsessive-compulsive disorder in which individuals are extremely preoccupied with one or more imagined, or at most slight, defects in their appearance, to the point of significant distress or inability to function normally in their personal or professional lives. While BDD can manifest in relatively minor behaviors, such as excessive grooming or mirror checking, it can also cause individuals with the disorder to seek more extreme remedies to compensate for an abnormal concern about their appearance. Some people suffering from BDD may seek numerous aesthetic surgical procedures in an attempt to see themselves differently. Due to their compulsion, however, they rarely are satisfied with the surgical outcome, regardless of how good it might appear to others.

Board-certified plastic surgeons are dedicated to maintaining the highest ethical standards, which includes the responsibility to provide services that have the purpose of improving patients' health and well-being. When it comes to BDD, one of the problems plastic surgeons face is that it can be difficult, if not impossible, to accurately diagnose the condition on the basis of the patient consultation. Plastic surgeons are not trained as psychiatrists or psychologists, and they must usually rely upon a combination of information provided by the patient and their own observations to determine appropriate candidates for cosmetic surgery. When in doubt, they may choose to refer a patient for psychological evaluation or simply decline to perform surgery. In some cases, even though a patient suffers from BDD, the consensus of medical professionals caring for the patient may be that a particular cosmetic surgical procedure is warranted and could produce some measure of psychological benefit.

A survey conducted by David Sarwer, PhD, Assistant Professor of Psychology in Psychiatry and Surgery at the University of Pennsylvania Medical Center, showed that an overwhelming majority of plastic surgeons would not knowingly perform surgery on someone they suspect may suffer from BDD. The 265 ASAPS members responding to the survey reported that only a very small number — approximately two percent — of their prospective patients exhibit behaviors associated with BDD. This is consistent with the estimated incidence of BDD in the general population.

THE SURGICAL FACILITY

Most people may think of surgical procedures being done in a hospital, but today a great number of cosmetic procedures can be performed in ambulatory surgery facilities — either freestanding surgicenters or office-based facilities. Where your surgery will be performed depends on a number of variables including the extensiveness of your operation, the condition of your health, and other unique risk factors. Additional considerations include your surgeon's preference and your comfort.

"There are many doctors, myself included, who perform a significant portion of surgeries in an office surgical suite rather than a hospital," says **Jay B. Fine, MD**, of Pembroke Pines, Florida. "In the office-based setting, as in any environment where surgery is performed, the patient's safety is paramount. Plastic surgeons must use good judgment when deciding which types of procedures to do in the office, which patients are good candidates, how lengthy the surgeries can be, and how to be prepared for handling complications that could arise. These are responsibilities of the surgeon, but it's also important that patients be aware of the factors involved in the safety of office-based cosmetic surgery and choose a surgeon who adequately addresses these important considerations."

"My office-based surgical facility has a defibrillator, a generator, all of the equipment necessary to handle emergency situations," says **James A. Matas, MD**, of Orlando, Florida. "I work with the same medical and surgical team, day in and day out. I feel this allows me to give my patients better and more personalized care."

As mentioned in the chapter of this book on choosing a plastic surgeon, it is important that your surgeon has

hospital privileges for the procedure you are undergoing — whether your procedure will be performed in the hospital or an ambulatory surgery setting. Hospital privileges are your assurance that the surgeon's qualifications have been reviewed by a credentialing committee composed of other doctors on staff at the hospital. But who checks on the qualifications of doctors who do not apply for hospital privileges to perform cosmetic surgery and who operate in a non-hospital setting such as a freestanding surgicenter or office-based surgery facility? Unfortunately, too often the answer to this question is: nobody.

As discussed in an earlier chapter, the vast majority of ambulatory surgery facilities remain uninspected, unlicensed and unaccredited. The personnel, including physicians, who operate these facilities may not have the qualifications required to perform cosmetic procedures in a hospital or in an accredited facility. Likewise, the facility's layout, equipment, and other safety features may be substandard, putting patients' welfare at risk.

Board-certified plastic surgeons were among the very first specialists to embrace the concept of accreditation for ambulatory surgery facilities. While still in the minority, today there are a growing number of freestanding and office-based surgical facilities that are accredited and meet the highest safety standards. It is important for prospective patients to make sure that any facility in which they will undergo a surgical procedure (other than a procedure requiring only minor local anesthesia, or minimal oral or intramuscular tranquilization) meets at least one of the following criteria:

- Accredited by a nationally or state-recognized accrediting organization
- State-licensed
- Medicare-certified under Title XVIII

Accreditation means that the facility has passed stringent safety requirements for the layout, emergency and monitoring equipment, staff, and physicians. In addition, only physicians who have hospital privileges for the procedure they wish to perform at the accredited facility are allowed to do so. Anesthesia is provided only by a board-certified (or board-eligible) anesthesiologist or by a certified registered nurse anesthetist (CRNA). Accredited facilities have met all local, state and national regulations applicable to sanitation and safety of the facility and its daily operations.

"Patients should ask a number of questions regarding where their surgery is going to be performed," says **Otis Allen, MD**, of Bloomington, Illinois. "For example, who owns and operates the facility? Is it accredited, and by whom? Are the doctors who work in the facility appropriately trained and certified? Who will provide my anesthesia, and what is their training? Have all of the facility and anesthesia fees been explained? How many bills will I receive, and from whom?"

"Our facility is uniquely focused on the mission of creating a center of excellence in aesthetic plastic surgery," says **Amado Ruiz-Razura, MD**, of Houston, Texas. "It is fully accredited, delivering the highest standards of patient care with an active educational and training program for medical staff and plastic surgeons. Importantly, it supports a clinical research center with a designated area and personnel to conduct clinical studies on the latest products and technologies available in aesthetic surgery."

Some of the groups that accredit facilities, and whose accreditation certificate should be prominently displayed in the facility, are the following:

- The American Association for Accreditation of Ambulatory Surgery Facilities, Inc. (AAAASF); www.aaaasf.org
- The Joint Commission on Accreditation of Healthcare Organizations (JCAHO); www.jcaho.org
- The Accreditation Association for Ambulatory Health Care, Inc. (AAAHC); www.aaahc.org

These organizations grant accreditation to qualifying facilities, maintain updated safety data and criteria, and conduct regular inspections to ensure compliance.

As mentioned earlier, in lieu of accreditation by one of the above agencies, state licensure or Medicare certification (Title XVIII) is also evidence that a facility has met satisfactory safety requirements. Not all states require licensing, but in some cases state licensing may be necessary even if a facility is accredited by another agency.

Is it better to undergo surgery as an outpatient rather than in the hospital? There is no single answer to this question, since each patient's circumstances are different. Besides the factors discussed earlier that might make hospital surgery a better choice for some patients, some individuals simply feel more comfortable in a hospital setting. And some hospitals have even developed special areas dedicated to plastic and aesthetic surgery. On the other hand, many patients appreciate the privacy, convenience, personal attention, and sometimes lower cost of surgery performed in an accredited outpatient setting. Accredited ambulatory facilities are well equipped for patient safety and in the unlikely event that emergency hospitalization is necessary, procedures are in place for rapid transport of patients to a hospital facility. So, for many patients, an ambulatory surgery facility can be the right choice.

"I do most of my surgeries as outpatient procedures in a surgery center right across the street from the hospital," says **David V. Poole, MD**, of Altamonte Springs, Florida. "I feel that the environment provided by the surgery center is preferable, and the care I can provide is enhanced. I check on my patients by phone the night following their surgery and every morning until we see them back in the office, usually about three to five days after the surgery."

The organizations that provide accreditation of ambulatory surgery facilities are dedicated to monitoring and maintaining high standards of competence and safety upon which patients can rely. It is up to you, the prospective patient, however, to do the research necessary to find surgeons and facilities that meet these approved criteria.

One thing to keep in mind is that all members of the American Society for Aesthetic Plastic Surgery (ASAPS) and the American Society of Plastic Surgeons (ASPS) are required to operate only in accredited, state-licensed or Medicare-certified facilities (except for procedures requiring only minor local anesthesia, or minimal oral or intramuscular tranquilization). This means that when you select a surgeon who is a member of either or both of these organizations, you should have assurance that the facility in which your surgery is performed will meet high standards for safety. ⚕

ANESTHESIA

Many patients have questions about anesthesia, and it is important to understand the facts. Your plastic surgeon will explain his or her recommendation, or that of the anesthesiologist, for the type of anesthesia to be used in conjunction with your procedure. In some cases, your preference may be considered, while in other instances there may be little choice due to the type of procedure you are undergoing or other factors including the condition of your health and your reaction to certain medications. However, it is important for you to take an active role in the discussion about anesthesia, particularly with regard to who will administer anesthesia during your procedure.

For all types of anesthesia (other than minor local anesthesia, or minimal oral or intramuscular tranquilization), your anesthesia provider should be either a board-certified or board eligible anesthesiologist or a certified registered nurse anesthetist (CRNA). This individual will be responsible for administering the correct type and amount of anesthetic and for monitoring every important body function throughout the operation and in the immediate postoperative period.

"Not only do I use an anesthesiologist for all procedures," says **John Burnett, MD,** of Fresno, California, "but for more complex procedures, I always select an anesthesiologist who has particular experience with those specific types of operations and understands the special considerations involved."

It is not unusual for patients to have some feelings of apprehension regarding anesthesia. The best remedy for these anxieties is to discuss any concerns you may have with your plastic surgeon who will explain the particular technique recommended for you and can provide you with specific information on risks.

Anesthesia administered by a qualified professional is safe, and it allows you to undergo even lengthy surgical procedures without experiencing pain or discomfort. However, serious complications from anesthesia are possible, so it is important for you to be thoroughly informed of the risks.

BEFORE ANESTHESIA

As mentioned in our chapter on Safety in Aesthetic Surgery, it is extremely important that you provide your surgeon with a complete and accurate medical history, including any allergies to drugs and a list of medications and or vitamin and herbal supplements you currently take, so these factors can be considered when planning your surgery and anesthesia. Interactions of even common medications, foods, and beverages with anesthesia are possible, so your surgeon may advise you to discontinue certain drugs and abstain from certain types of food and drinks (especially alcohol) for a period before and after surgery. He or she may want to consult with your personal physician, or other specialists, however, before removing you from any drug therapy that is under medical supervision.

Even if your procedure does not require an overnight stay, you will need to arrange in advance for someone to drive you home from your procedure and to stay with you until you are back to feeling like yourself.

TYPES OF ANESTHESIA

The types of anesthesia most commonly used for each of the various aesthetic procedures discussed in this book are indicated in the sections pertaining to those procedures. Oral or topical medications may be used for certain minor aesthetic procedures, but the types of anesthesia that generally are used in aesthetic surgery are general anesthesia, sedation anesthesia (often called twilight anesthesia), and regional or local anesthesia.

GENERAL ANESTHESIA

General anesthesia, administered intravenously or inhaled through a mask, causes a deep sleep with loss of consciousness. To help you breathe while under general anesthesia, the anesthesiologist may insert a tube into your trachea. You will be unaware of your surroundings and unable to feel any pain or discomfort. As the anesthesia wears off, the tube will be removed, and you will awaken after the surgery.

Upon awakening, you will generally have no memory of the procedure having taken place. Some patients may experience postsurgical nausea following general anesthesia, but this usually can be controlled with medication. If you have experienced nausea or any other side effects from anesthesia in the past, be sure to tell your surgeon and anesthesia provider. It is normal for you to feel somewhat dazed or tired for the rest of the day.

General anesthesia is usually required for, but not limited to, the more involved and complicated surgeries, such as lower body lifts, abdominoplasties and large-volume liposuction. General anesthesia is also the choice of many plastic surgeons for other operations, such as face lifts and rhinoplasties, particularly when performed in conjunction with other procedures.

SEDATION ANESTHESIA

Sedation anesthesia, which is also commonly known as twilight sleep, combines the use of an intravenous medication that sedates the patient, inducing drowsiness and relaxation, with a local anesthetic that prevents the patient from feeling any pain in the area to be operated on. Sometimes the same drugs that are used for general anesthesia can be used in lower doses to produce sedation anesthesia.

Once the patient is sedated, the surgeon injects the treatment area with a local anesthetic, such as lidocaine. Patients rarely even feel the injections.

Depending upon the dosage, or the depth of the sedation, patients may have periods of wakefulness, or they may sleep through the entire procedure. If patients do awaken, they will not feel any pain and will remain extremely relaxed and oblivious to what is taking place around them, even if they should have the faint realization that they are in an operating room.

With sedation anesthesia, patients continue to breathe on their own; breathing tubes and mechanical assistance are unnecessary.

Eyelid surgery, face lifts, rhinoplasty and many other procedures are often performed using this type of anesthesia. The recovery period for sedation anesthesia is usually shorter, with fewer potential side effects, than with general anesthesia.

REGIONAL AND LOCAL ANESTHESIA

Regional anesthesia has an effect on a targeted group of nerves to anesthetize a specific region of the body, such as an epidural that causes a loss of sensation in the legs and lower abdomen.

Local anesthesia is similar to the local anesthetics you may have when your dentist works on your teeth. A local anesthetic is injected under the skin at appropriate points and numbs the treatment area so that the patient doesn't feel any pain. It is generally used for a variety of minor procedures.

Local anesthetics take effect rather quickly and also wear off more quickly than other types of anesthesia. Side effects are minimal and relatively rare.

AFTER ANESTHESIA

Most patients find their recovery from anesthesia to be uneventful, but it is important to follow your surgeon's instructions carefully. These instructions will likely include such restrictions as not driving, operating complicated machinery, making important decisions, or signing legal documents for at least 24 hours after your procedure. As mentioned earlier, you also may be instructed to avoid certain medications, supplements, foods, and beverages. You may be advised to drink fluids for a while before progressing to light food.

With open and thorough communication between you, your surgeon, and your anesthesia provider, you should find your experience with anesthesia to be much easier and more comfortable than you may have imagined. ⍉

Editor's Viewpoint

Selection of an anesthesia provider — which should be either a board-certified anesthesiologist (MD) or a certified registered nurse anesthetist (CRNA) — as well as selection of the type of anesthesia to be administered for your procedure is usually decided with input from your plastic surgeon. It is essential, however, for you to make sure that this very important topic has been discussed to your satisfaction in advance of your procedure and that you are comfortable with the anesthesia plans for your surgery.

Plastic surgeons performing cosmetic surgery prefer working with anesthesiologists or CRNAs who have a keen interest and significant experience in providing services for cosmetic surgical patients. These anesthesia providers go out of their way to ensure that patients have a complete understanding of what their anesthesia care will entail, often going so far as to call the patient the night before surgery to make sure that preoperative instructions are followed and to answer any questions. In addition to their primary role of providing and monitoring anesthesia in the operating room, these highly trained medical professionals contribute to the safety of every aspect of your surgical experience. After your surgery, the anesthesia provider is right by your side as you are transported to the recovery room, ensuring seamless transfer of care to the recovery room staff.

Close communication and teamwork between the well-trained anesthesia provider and surgeon is an essential component of safety and quality care for the aesthetic surgery patient.

— Peter B. Fodor, MD

SAFETY
in aesthetic plastic surgery

Aesthetic plastic surgery is elective, and patients choose to undergo procedures to better their lives. In the overwhelming majority of cases in which patients select a qualified surgeon, cosmetic surgery produces the expected benefits, and patients are happy. The complications that sometimes occur are generally temporary and relatively minor. This should not lead one to be complacent, however, about the many issues involved in cosmetic surgery patient safety.

The risks of cosmetic surgery have much in common with other types of surgery. And while there is no such thing as "risk-free" surgery, many risks can be controlled.

It all begins with education. The well-informed patient has a much better chance of not only having a safe surgery, but also enjoying a more successful surgical outcome.

Before you choose to undergo any cosmetic surgical procedure, your surgeon will explain the risks to you. General risks associated with many types of surgery include bleeding, infection, and complications from anesthesia. Another significant complication, though infrequent, is blood clots that can lead to venous thromboembolism (VTE), including deep vein thrombosis (DVT) and pulmonary embolism (PE), both of which are serious or even fatal events.

Your board-certified plastic surgeon is trained in techniques to decrease and manage the risks associated with surgery and specific cosmetic procedures. Your surgeon will evaluate you carefully regarding your risk for DVT or PE, including your personal medical history, family health history and lifestyle factors. Compression devices will be used as a precaution to help prevent blood clots, especially if your surgery will be lengthy. For some patients at higher risk, drugs such as heparin or other anticoagulants can be administered.

Once you have selected a qualified surgeon you trust, you can certainly begin to rest easier about all aspects of your cosmetic surgery. But it is important to understand that throughout the surgical process, you also have responsibilities that significantly impact your safety.

MEDICAL HISTORY AND MEDICATIONS

One of the most important parts of your consultation with a plastic surgeon involves your disclosure of any medical conditions (past or current) and any previous surgeries that you have had. Your doctor also needs to know about drugs, of any kind, that you are taking or have taken recently.

Certain drugs — including aspirin, ibuprofen and other nonprescription medications such as certain cold, flu or allergy medicines — increase the risk of excessive bleeding. It is always best to check with your plastic surgeon about which drugs are safe to use in the few weeks leading up to surgery and during your recovery period. Other factors may also affect bleeding; your surgeon will want to be certain that your blood pressure is normal or under control, and your blood clotting abilities are not impaired.

In addition to prescription and nonprescription drugs, some vitamins and other over-the-counter substances can also have a damaging effect in combination with surgical procedures and anesthesia. For example, vitamin E supplements taken in certain dosages can contribute to bleeding during and after surgery. Your surgeon will advise you as to when and for how long you should discontinue vitamin supplements.

Herbal medications and supplements may seem harmless and in fact may be taken for their assumed benefits of boosting the immune system, providing more energy and improving general health, yet they could prove deleterious to surgery. Doctors have for some time suspected that these medications, such as St. John's Wort, may increase bleeding and cause other complications. Your surgeon may ask you to discontinue all herbal medications and supplements prior to surgery.

A February 2006 study published in *Plastic and Reconstructive Surgery*, the journal of the American Society of Plastic Surgeons, found that approximately 55 percent of plastic surgery patients take herbal supplements but, perhaps thinking it unimportant since the supplements are "harmless," often do not tell their surgeons. It is extremely important to your own safety that you tell your plastic surgeon about all medications, prescription and nonprescription, and any vitamins or herbal medications or supplements you are taking.

Use of illegal drugs is a serious matter, both in terms of your general health and possible effects on your surgery. While this may be a difficult subject to discuss with your doctor, not doing so could jeopardize your safety.

"Patients should be very truthful as to what medications they are taking, or medical conditions that they may have, for these can not only interfere with the anesthesia and recovery but also can jeopardize the final results of surgery," says **Edward J. Domanskis, MD**, of Newport Beach, California. "I recently had a patient who was scheduled for surgery and was truthful enough to admit to having used cocaine. Her surgery was rescheduled and she did very well. If we had not known about her recent drug use, she could have suffered grave consequences due to the drug's interaction with anesthetics."

LIFESTYLE FACTORS

Various lifestyle factors can also influence your readiness for surgery as well as the safety and outcome of your procedure. These include weight, nutrition, sleep, smoking, alcohol consumption, and sun exposure.

Obesity elevates the risks associated with many types of surgery. If you are obese, you may be advised to lose weight before undergoing elective cosmetic surgery, or special measures (such as overnight hospitalization) may be recommended to help ensure your safety. Weight control and stabilization are important factors in determining patients' readiness for such procedures as liposuction or abdominoplasty and their chances for long-term positive results.

As vital aspects of maintaining optimum health, nutrition and sleep also play a role in a patient's surgical outcome. Both have an impact on your immune system and, therefore, your ability to heal and fight infection.

Tobacco has numerous negative effects on the body, including constriction of blood vessels and binding of oxygen, reducing its availability to the body's cells. When cells have insufficient oxygen following surgery, tissues may not heal as well and scarring may be more significant. In association with certain procedures, smokers have an increased risk and higher rate of infection, skin death (necrosis), wound separation, and anesthesia complications.

"Any patient who smokes runs the risk of a poorer outcome," advises **Steven K. White, Sr., MD**, of Myrtle Beach, South Carolina. "In addition to greater safety risks for smokers, depending on the operation, many patients will simply have a less favorable outcome because of the deleterious effect smoking has on the tissues."

The risk to smokers is so grave that for some procedures — such as face lifts, abdominoplasties, breast reductions and/or lifts — most plastic surgeons insist that their patients stop smoking at least two weeks prior to surgery and for a period following the operation as well. Some surgeons will not perform these procedures on smokers at all.

Alcohol consumption may increase bleeding and reduce your ability to form clots. This can heighten the risk of a hematoma (collection of blood underneath the skin). It would be prudent to minimize these risks by abstaining from drinking alcohol for at least three or four days prior to surgery.

You will be advised, particularly before and after various skin treatments, to avoid tanning and direct exposure to the sun for a certain period of time. Exposure to direct sunlight can cause darkening and thickening of scars for up to a year following virtually any surgery. You should discuss this with your plastic surgeon and follow his or her recommendations to keep wounds covered, using an effective sunblock. When facial surgery is involved, you can further protect your skin with a wide-brimmed hat.

POSTSURGICAL INSTRUCTIONS

Each section of this book dealing with a specific procedure talks about the recovery period and gives general guidelines. It is very important to pay strict attention to the instructions your plastic surgeon gives you following your procedure. Failure to follow his or her guidelines may result in complications or unsatisfactory results. Your plastic surgeon will tell you when you can undertake various activities — ranging from when you can first get out of bed to when you can resume a full course of vigorous exercise.

The amount of activity that is advisable following surgery differs with various procedures. With some procedures, including major operations such as abdominoplasties or lower body lifts, it is very important that patients become ambulatory shortly following surgery. This is crucial, in addition to other measures, in the prevention of blood clots that can lead to deep vein thrombosis (DVT) and pulmonary embolism (PE).

"It is never indicated in any type of aesthetic surgery to lie around the day after the procedure," says Dr. White. "Early ambulation and hydration are the most significant positive factors in reducing lethal blood clots."

Too much activity following a surgical procedure — including lifting, bending, straining or anything that raises blood pressure — can also be harmful. It can result in bleeding and fluid accumulation (hematoma or seroma), reopening of incisions, as well as other serious complications.

It is your surgeon's job to make sure you are well informed about all aspects of your surgery, including the course of action that will lead to the most successful recovery. It is essential, however, that you pay close attention, ask questions about anything you don't understand or that is not clear, and precisely follow the instructions you are given.

MULTIPLE PROCEDURES

While so-called "reality" television shows that promote cosmetic surgery serve the purpose of letting people know that improving themselves with aesthetic surgery is an available option, these shows also may distort the surgical process in ways that can prove damaging.

"On many of the television shows, for example," says Karl O. Wustrack, MD, of West Linn, Oregon, "subjects are specially selected who will achieve the desired results — results that may not be typical. Procedures requiring the work of several surgeons and dentists, long periods of recovery, and results that take several months to fully materialize are condensed into a one-hour show. The results are misleading and can often lead to people forming unrealistic expectations."

John Bruno, MD, of Fort Myers, Florida, adds, "People read and see a plethora of publicity surrounding aesthetic plastic surgery, and not all of it is safe, prudent, or effective. Television shows implying that multiple procedures can be done in one 12-hour operation can be misleading and dangerous."

On the other hand, certain combinations of procedures are frequently and safely performed together during a single surgical session. Other combinations are more often performed in separate or "staged" operations. Whether or not multiple procedures performed together are advisable in any particular case may be determined by patient health factors and surgeon preference. Multiple procedures performed during the same surgical session can increase the risks of surgery, and these risks should be thoroughly discussed with your surgeon.

TRAVEL BEFORE OR AFTER SURGERY

Patients may sometimes select a surgeon who practices in another state or even another country. While there are many advantages to choosing a surgeon who practices in your own geographic area, and there can be significant uncertainties in evaluating the qualifications of surgeons outside the United States and Canada, there are some instances in which patients make the decision to travel for their surgery. Likewise, patients sometimes inquire of their surgeons whether they may travel for business or pleasure soon after a surgical procedure.

Prolonged travel is well known to be a cause of DVT and PE. Lengthy travel by car, train, and especially by air, can significantly increase the risk of these dangerous conditions. If you are traveling a few hours or more to undergo surgery, and your procedure will last longer than one hour, you should not schedule your surgery for the morning after your arrival or plan to return home soon after the procedure. Instead, you should plan on a minimum of one or two days of ambulation time before and after your surgery. For extensive surgeries, this time (especially after surgery) is likely to be longer.

Traveling to a foreign country for plastic surgery may sound exciting, but it can be fraught with difficulties. First and foremost are the concerns about safety. Even if the surgeon is certified according to the standards of his or her country, there may be little guarantee of the quality and safety of the surgical facility. If there should be any complications associated with your surgery, it is essential that you have access to comprehensive medical care — something that may not be readily available in many foreign countries. Late complications or poor outcomes of surgery can occur once you have returned home, and under those circumstances, your options for revisionary surgery with a surgeon in your own community may be limited.

Wherever you decide to undergo plastic surgery, you should be sure that you consider all aspects of your safety, including physician qualifications, facility standards and the risks of extended travel in association with surgical procedures.

"NEW" DOESN'T MEAN "SAFE"

"It's not that there isn't a lot of information out there," says **James D. McMahan, MD**, of Columbus, Ohio, "but rather that much of it is incorrect or misleading. Advertisements, magazine articles, and television shows are repeatedly touting the latest 'miracle treatment' just to make headlines. In actuality, some of these products are unproven, often ineffective, and potentially hazardous."

"I find that there is an absence of accurate and understandable information for the public regarding plastic surgery procedures," says **William G. Armiger, MD**, of Annapolis, Maryland. "Cosmetic procedures are often unrealistically portrayed on television. The real facts of procedures, the seriousness of the decisions being made, and the safety issues need to be clearly understood by the patient."

The desire to cash in on aesthetic surgery's popularity and profitability often motivates individuals and companies to promote materials and devices that are not yet proven effective and, in some instances, may not be safe. The media, always hungry for a story on a popular subject, helps push these products via free publicity on television shows and in magazines. This helps create a demand for them among the public, often before prudent surgeons have even begun to incorporate these techniques into their practices.

No one wants to be a "guinea pig," but that's exactly what some patients become when they subject themselves to new and unproven treatments at the hands of unqualified and untrained practitioners. When considering a "new" type of cosmetic treatment, patients should always find out how long the product or technique has been used, whether results have been reported in a peer-reviewed journal, what complications have occurred and how they were resolved, and how much experience the doctor has had with the treatment. It is wise to find out whether the procedure has been widely adopted by qualified, board-certified plastic surgeons before proceeding.

Plastic surgeons sometimes participate in clinical trials, approved by the U.S. Food and Drug Administration (FDA), for new products and devices. If you consider participation in a clinical trial, you should be provided with all the information you need to make an informed choice.

For any type of cosmetic surgery, whether a new technique or a tried-and-true procedure, you may be asked to sign a document of informed consent. The purpose of this document is to confirm that you completely understand the treatment that will be provided by your surgeon. You should also be informed of and consent to the use of any specific brand of injectable or implantable material. This is to help protect you from unknowingly receiving treatment with a material that is not FDA-approved. You should also be informed if the use of a material is "off label," meaning that the material is FDA-approved but not for specific uses that will be part of your treatment.

YOUR SAFETY, YOUR CHOICE

The chapter in this book, Choosing a Qualified Surgeon, explains the importance of choosing a trained and experienced plastic surgeon for your cosmetic surgery.

Knowing where your procedure will be performed, if the facility is accredited, and if so, by whom, goes hand-in-hand with choosing a qualified surgeon. In the chapter in this book titled The Surgical Facility, we explain the details of facility accreditation and hospital privileges.

"It is very important that cosmetic plastic surgery be performed in an accredited facility, by board-certified surgeons, and that qualified personnel are administering the anesthesia," says **Stephen Goldstein, MD**, of Englewood, Colorado. "In cosmetic surgery, as in all surgery, patient safety comes first."

"The doctor selection process is paramount to patient safety," says **Barbara K. Siwy, MD**, of Carmel, Indiana. "Patients should be diligent in researching their prospective physicians and find out as much as they can about their options and potential outcomes, so they can make the wisest and safest choice."

Aesthetic plastic surgery has an excellent record of safety. Asking the right questions can help you make the right choices — and, ultimately, have the best possible outcome from your cosmetic surgery.

Editor's Viewpoint

Needless to say, patient safety with any type of surgery is of paramount importance. Because aesthetic surgery is totally elective, it is essential that the usual risks of any surgery be reduced to the lowest level possible, and that the safety and effectiveness of selected treatments be well established. Likewise, medical professionals providing cosmetic surgery services must be well trained in the prevention and handling of complications.

The residency programs that prepare a physician for board certification in plastic surgery are among the most extensive of any medical or surgical professional. Plastic surgeons study all major systems of the body, and many plastic surgeons are also fully trained and certified as general surgeons. The course of training for any plastic surgeon includes ample exposure to the prevention of surgical complications, how to promptly recognize them when they occur, and how to most effectively treat them.

Throughout the years, plastic surgery has maintained an impressive patient safety record. Part of the reason is the commitment of our professional societies, such as the American Society for Aesthetic Plastic Surgery (ASAPS) and the American Society of Plastic Surgeons (ASPS), to the continuing medical education of their members, with an appropriate emphasis on patient safety. In 2005, at the start of my term as President, we at ASAPS created the Patient Safety Steering Committee to further focus attention on developing a "culture of safety" at every level of aesthetic surgery practice. Since then, this Committee has developed a number of additional patient safety initiatives, including revised guidelines on prevention of venous thromboembolism (VTE) and new studies focusing on proper patient selection to help minimize surgical risks. The Committee's work is expected to be ongoing. As a result of these and other educational efforts, patients can feel more confident of their safety when undergoing elective cosmetic surgery.

— Peter B. Fodor, MD

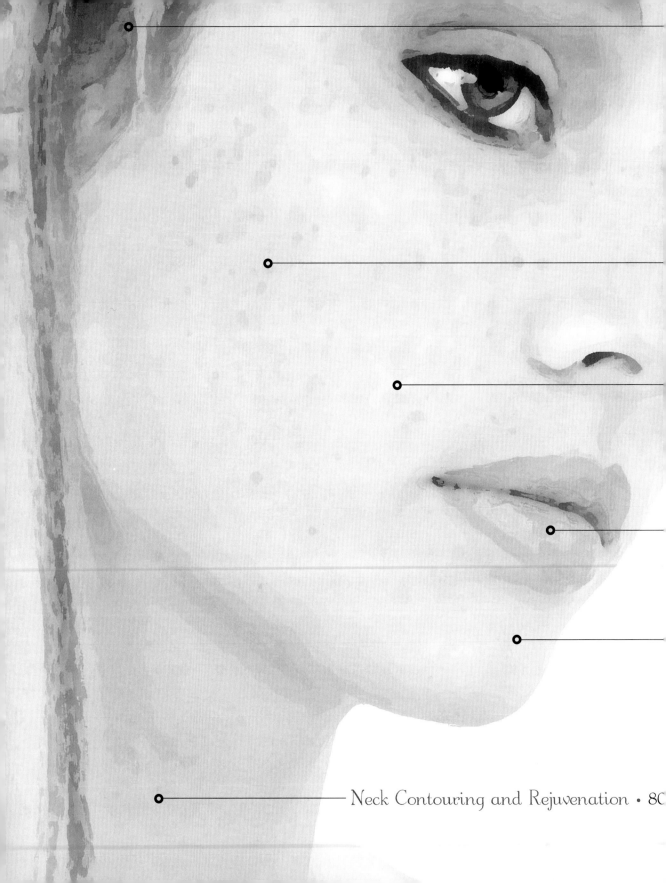

FACIAL
AESTHETIC SURGERY

FACIAL
AESTHETIC SURGERY

Facial aesthetic surgery can be divided into two general categories of procedures: those designed for rejuvenation and those designed to reshape, or recontour, specific facial features.

Among the most common rejuvenative procedures are cosmetic eyelid surgery (blepharoplasty); face and neck lifts; and forehead, or brow, lift. Reshaping procedures include cheek, chin, and lip augmentation; nose reshaping (rhinoplasty); and ear reshaping (otoplasty). It is not uncommon for a combination of rejuvenative and/or reshaping procedures to be performed at the same time (in one surgical session).

FACIAL REJUVENATION

"There has been an evolution over the past 20 years that has led us to think of the face as a number of distinct aesthetic units," offers **Mark P. Solomon, MD**, of Bala Cynwyd, Pennsylvania. "We can treat those aesthetic units either individually or together, depending upon the patient's needs."

Aesthetic analysis of facial aging is often performed by dividing the face into thirds: the upper face is considered to be from the top of the forehead to the level of the eyebrow; the middle face is to the base of the nose; and the lower face is to the bottom of the chin. The neck below the chin line also needs to be evaluated and is an essential "aesthetic unit" when considering overall rejuvenation.

A particular patient's aging process may be more visibly pronounced in certain facial segments or may be relatively uniform in all areas. In either case, the ultimate goal of a treatment plan is to produce a seamless and synchronous rejuvenation throughout the face and neck.

To maintain facial harmony and balance, patients often consider undergoing a forehead lift, eyelid surgery, and a face lift and/or midface lift simultaneously. Other considerations include facial volume, skin wrinkling, and skin texture, which may need to be addressed with additional procedures, often nonsurgical in nature, discussed elsewhere in this book.

The decision to undergo one or more facial procedures is one that should be made in consultation with a board-certified plastic surgeon who can evaluate the degree of facial aging and offer a variety of possible approaches. Remember, facial rejuvenation is designed to restore a more youthful appearance. The goal is not to make you look "different," just firmer, fresher and younger.

RESHAPING PROCEDURES

Facial aesthetic surgery to reshape, or recontour, various facial features may be performed on patients of virtually all ages, depending on the specific procedure. Ear reshaping may be undertaken during the early childhood years or later, while rhinoplasty, or nose reshaping, is performed in both teens and adults. Chin, cheek, and lip augmentation may be performed in patients of many ages and often may be combined with facial rejuvenation.

The goal of these procedures is to reform a specific feature, but this does not mean you will look dramatically different. The degree of change you can expect depends on a number of factors including your personal aesthetic goals, the limitations of your anatomy, and your plastic surgeon's aesthetic and surgical judgment. That is why good two-way communication between you and your plastic surgeon is vital, so that the outcome of your surgery will closely meet your expectations.

Whether performed for rejuvenating or reshaping facial features, facial aesthetic surgery offers you the possibility to improve your appearance in ways that others are likely to notice and appreciate. Nevertheless, the healthiest motivation for undergoing facial aesthetic surgery, like all aesthetic surgery, is to satisfy your own desire to look and feel your very best.

EYELID SURGERY

Blepharoplasty

The eyes are the central focus of facial expression. Eye contact is a primary way people gauge each other's emotions; whether it's looking for love or trying to detect if someone is being truthful, the eyes tell all. Beautiful eyes light up a face. Eyelid surgery, technically called blepharoplasty, can remove excess eyelid skin, correct bagginess and puffiness, and, with related procedures, alter eyelid position, to restore or create a brighter, more rested and alert appearance. Although most candidates for eyelid surgery are over the age of 35, younger patients with droopy or baggy eyelids that are inherited traits can also benefit from this procedure.

"Patients often don't realize the dramatic improvements they can obtain by simply having their eyes 'fine-tuned,'" says **Joseph Michael Pober, MD**, of New York, New York. "Perhaps the fastest way to look younger and more energetic is offered by the eyelid lift, or blepharoplasty."

In aesthetically ideal eyes, no white is seen above or below the iris, the colored ring around the pupil. The upper lid rests just below the top of the iris and the lower lid rests just above the bottom border of the iris.

If the upper lid is too droopy, covering a disproportionate amount of the iris, it can create a tired look and make the eyes appear smaller. A weakness or detachment of the muscle that holds the eyelid open, due to aging or heredity, is the main cause of droopy eyelids (eyelid ptosis).

Eyelid laxity can cause the lower lids to droop, allowing the white of the eye to be seen between the lower lid and the iris (scleral show). This can create a tired, aged appearance (although it also may contribute to the look of so-called "bedroom eyes" that is considered attractive in some popular male actors). Even less severe eyelid laxity, where the lower lid droops but still covers part of the iris, can cause dry eye symptoms. If laxity exists to any degree, it should be corrected. If it is not, symptoms may actually worsen as a result of cosmetic eyelid surgery.

Upper and lower eyelid surgery can correct baggy eyelids caused by excess eyelid skin. In addition, eyelid surgery can remove or reposition herniated fat of the lower eyelids, which can result from aging or genetics and cause bulging and eyelid puffiness. Dark circles under the eyes can result from shadows cast by fat bulges in the lower lids. In these cases, altering the fat, either by removing it or repositioning it, will often improve the appearance. However, your surgeon must determine the actual cause of your eyelid puffiness or dark circles. In some cases, edema (fluid collection) may be the cause of puffiness, or dark circles may be simply skin discoloration. In the latter case, chemical peels or laser resurfacing may help somewhat.

In deciding on the best approach to your eyelid surgery, your surgeon will consider many factors including the skeletal structure around your eyes. In some patients, removing fat from the lower eyelids can create a hollowed-out appearance, and the appearance of dark circles might actually worsen. In such cases, alternative approaches to rejuvenating the eyelid areas, such as repositioning the fat rather than removing it, can be used.

"For much too long, the eyelids were the area most fraught with undesirable aesthetic results. Truly, too much was being done, creating unnatural and unaesthetic results," says **Lawrence S. Reed, MD**, of New York, New York. "Over the past few years, I have been pleased to observe a greater appreciation of the value of preserving the natural aspects of eyelid morphology, preserving fat when necessary or repositioning it to a more desirable location, and the understanding that some fullness in the upper lid and a natural-looking lower lid were a far better ideal than we had previously understood."

"Blepharoplasty may be the most difficult operation because the margins for error are small," says **Rafael C. Cabrera, MD**, of Boca Raton, Florida. "The movements in tissue are measured in tenths of millimeters rather than centimeters, and the stakes are high. The one word I would preach in blepharoplasty is conservatism. I've built my practice on doing the most complicated procedures; I like the challenge, but that doesn't mean I want to take chances with someone's eyes. You can get a very nice result without being aggressive."

Eyelid surgery will not improve the wrinkles around the eyes commonly called crow's feet. Botox and soft-tissue fillers, chemical peels, laser resurfacing, and other skin treatments discussed in later chapters can be used to treat these wrinkles.

When folds of skin appear between the eyebrow and the eyelid at the outside corner of the eye, this is called lateral hooding. Although this condition may be caused by excess eyelid skin, at other times, this may not be the case. Lateral hooding is often caused by droopy brows, and improvement may require some type of brow/forehead lift.

Some people are bothered by a deep groove beneath the lower eyelid, called a "tear trough." A tear trough can contribute to an aged appearance and accentuate the bulging appearance of the lower lids. Fat-repositioning blepharoplasty can often improve this condition and create a smoother transition between the lower eyelids and the cheeks. Sometimes implants or injectables, such as Restylane, can also improve tear troughs.

A thyroid condition called Graves' disease can cause the eyes to bulge. Eyelid surgery will not correct this. Graves' disease is a medical condition that usually requires medical management of the thyroid, which will often restore the eyes' normal appearance. In cases where thyroid management alone does not work, more extensive surgical remedies including bone repositioning may be necessary.

THE CONSULTATION

The consultation is a time for the surgeon and patient to get to know and feel comfortable with each other. The patient should feel completely confident that the surgeon is fully qualified. If you haven't read sections in

PREOPERATIVE APPEARANCE, UPPER EYELIDS. Wrinkled and sagging skin, bulging fat in the soft tissues around the eyes, and lateral hooding at the outer corners of the eyelids can make you look tired and older than you feel.

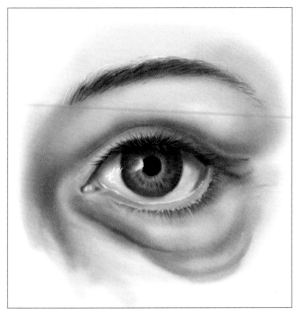

PREOPERATIVE APPEARANCE, LOWER EYELIDS. Laxity of the lower eyelid that exposes too much of the whites of the eyes (scleral show) may be corrected at the same time as puffiness and excess fat.

the beginning of this book about choosing a surgeon who is certified by the American Board of Plastic Surgery, you may want to do so now.

During the initial consultation, a surgeon will often have patients look into a mirror and point out exactly what they find troublesome about the appearance of their eyes. Your surgeon will also study your facial anatomy to determine if eyelid surgery alone will solve your problem, or if you may be better served by performing other or additional procedures. Because eyelid surgery will not correct crow's feet or lateral hooding, in order to best maintain facial harmony, it is often done in conjunction with other procedures, such as a brow lift, face lift, Botox, fillers, or skin treatments.

"The preoperative evaluation is crucial to identify the underlying anatomy of the problem," says **Brian J. Lee, MD,** of Fort Wayne, Indiana. "The eyebrow could be sliding down and crowding the upper eyelid, or there may be excess upper eyelid skin and droopiness that needs to also be corrected. For the lower lid, I need to make sure there's enough support so if I take skin out, the lid won't droop."

Alexander Majidian, MD, of Calabasas, California, agrees. "It is very important to make sure the individual has appropriate skin elasticity and support, so they will have a youthful, smooth result, with a naturally refreshed look. We have to evaluate the patient's anatomy around the eyes and that whole region of the face. Some may have fat that needs to removed, others very prominent eye sockets, which would appear hollowed out if too much fat were removed, while others may need a small cheek lift or fat transfer to really rejuvenate the area around the eyes."

"Lower eyelid aging results from several factors. In addition to excess skin, the muscle loosens, and the junction between the eyelid and cheek separates and becomes visible. In addressing all these problems, the plastic surgeon must do more than just remove skin. Surgery must be comprehensive enough to eliminate excess fat, tighten muscles and lift the cheek moderately," says **Hamid Massiha, MD,** of Metairie/New Orleans, Louisiana.

Your surgeon will determine if you are a suitable candidate for surgery by reviewing your entire medical history, including any medications you may currently be taking, whether you suffer from any allergies, or certain medical conditions, such dry eye, thyroid conditions, Graves' disease, high blood pressure, or diabetes. You should tell your surgeon about any problems you've ever had with your eyes, including whether you tried to wear contact lenses and found it difficult. If you wear glasses or contacts, you should bring them with you. It is extremely important to tell your surgeon if you have had any prior surgeries, any previous plastic surgery — and particularly previous eyelid surgery.

PREPARATION

Your surgeon will give you instructions about how to prepare for surgery. He or she will also give you guidelines on eating, drinking and medications, such as avoiding aspirin or anti-inflammatory medications that promote bleeding, detailed in an earlier section of this book.

As with all surgery in general, whether performed in an outpatient facility or in the hospital, you should arrange to have someone drive you to and from surgery and to assist you for a day or two after you return home.

THE SURGERY

Because each patient is different and has individual needs, your operation will be specifically designed to suit your objectives. Some patients require surgery of the upper or lower lids or both, fat or skin removal or both, fat repositioning, tightening of the lower lids, raising of the upper lids, or a combination of treatments.

The trend in eyelid surgery today is to preserve enough fat for repositioning to provide fullness in adjacent areas. For lower eyelid surgery, additional fullness might be needed in the tear trough area, the groove where the eyelid meets the cheek. In upper eyelid surgery, more fullness in the area beneath the lateral brow may provide a more youthful appearance.

"Blepharoplasty is a procedure that is changing dramatically. With upper eyelids, we are being more aggressive with skin removal, less aggressive with fat and muscle removal. The results are more natural and better than they used to be," says **James D. McMahan, MD,** of Columbus, Ohio. "The approach to the lower eyelid has changed even more dramatically. Instead of just taking out fat, we are repositioning fat and suspending the muscle up to smooth out the area under the eye."

"Historically, surgeons have removed fat," says **George W. Commons, MD,** of Palo Alto, California.

"But think about it — all of us tend to lose fat as we age, and we end up 'fat negative.' Fat loss should not be accelerated by surgery. I tuck the fat back in and secure it, which gives nice correction of puffiness but does not leave the person looking even older and with hollowed eyes later on."

"For eyelids, the key point is centered around preserving and/or restoring volume to the eyelid," agrees **Julius W. Few, MD,** of Chicago, Illinois. "The goal is not to remove all skin, fat, and muscle around the eye but to smooth contours and restore volume to areas that are sunken and which make the person look tired or unhappy. It's helpful to have pictures of the patient from years ago, to be able to maintain anatomical integrity and individuality while restoring a look that the patient liked."

"There's a lot of controversy over whether to leave fat or take fat out of the eyelids," comments **Martin Luftman, MD,** of Lexington, Kentucky. "I feel that taking some fat from the upper lid areas makes the eyes look more youthful and rested. On the other hand, in the lower lids, I do preserve fat. I use a technique that repositions the fat over the bony orbital rim, and then I suture this fat to the cheek fat. This creates a smoother transition between the lower eyelid and the cheek, and a more youthful appearance."

UPPER EYELID SURGERY

The incision for upper eyelid surgery is generally well hidden in the natural crease of the upper eyelid and usually extends as far as the laugh lines at the eye's outer corner. It is virtually invisible once healed. Fat repositioning or removal, where the surgeon usually separates underlying fatty tissue from the muscle and skin, removing any excess, can be accomplished through this incision. Treatment for true droopiness, or lazy eyelids (ptosis), which can occur with aging or from too much rubbing due to allergies, requires tightening part of the muscle and can also be addressed through the same incision. You should discuss whether or not you have this condition with your plastic surgeon. Once completed, the surgeon will close the incisions with very fine sutures.

The removal of too much skin from the upper eyelid can cause lagophthalmos, also called upper lid retraction. This results in the inability to completely close the eye, possibly causing dryness that can damage the cornea.

Asian Blepharoplasty

CREATING AN EYELID CREASE

Approximately half of all people of Asian descent are born without a natural upper eyelid crease. Often, those without the crease may seek double eyelid surgery to give their eyes a more wide-open look. While this procedure shares most aspects of upper eyelid surgery, there are a few differences. An incision is made where the new upper eyelid crease is to occur, usually three to eight millimeters above the eyelashes, and the eyelid skin is surgically attached to deeper structures in order to create the crease. The amount of tissue removed is often less than in other blepharoplasties.

"Many Asians already have a double fold," says **Joseph M. Perlman, MD**, of Spring, Texas. "So I think the term "Westernization" applied to Asian blepharoplasty is a misnomer, because Asians with a single fold do not want to look like a Westerner; they want to look like an Asian with a double-fold eyelid." Dr. Perlman adds that "Asian patients often may have a more significant amount of excess fat in the eyelid areas that requires excision."

This can be treated with additional surgery to the upper lid, but the ultimate aesthetic result may be less satisfactory.

"Patients want to look rested, not operated on," says **Seth R. Thaller, MD**, of Miami, Florida. "We don't take out a lot of fat, and we put a nice sharply defined crease in the upper lid, particularly for women."

LOWER EYELID SURGERY

Two different incision sites can be used to perform lower eyelid surgery. If the patient needs both excess skin and fat removed, the surgeon will use the traditional incision. This is made just below the lower eyelashes and may extend for a short distance along one of the laugh lines at the outside corner of the eye. Excess skin, fat, and muscle, when necessary, can be removed. When needed, muscles can also be tightened through this incision. The traditional incision becomes virtually unnoticeable in a short time.

"What's most important is what you do with the muscle," says **Michael Kane, MD**, of New York, New York. "I don't believe in taking out much skin or fat. I believe that by pushing the fat up and using the muscle to hold it in place, you can improve the appearance today and protect against a hollowed out look in the future. And because the skin is adherent to the muscle and drapes back nicely, you don't have to remove too much of it."

"We have found lower lid rejuvenation is best approached by preserving all possible muscle and fat and adding support when needed," agrees **Peter Johnson, MD**, of Des Plaines, Illinois. "I prefer addressing each component separately, removing skin when in excess and repositioning or conservatively removing prominent fat when necessary. I have found fat transfer deep into the groove between cheek and lower lid to be very effective in improving the hollow, tired look that the thinning out of the natural tissues causes in the lower lid. What may be more 'unique' in our practice is to raise the skin of the lower lid above the muscle, rather than the skin-muscle flap widely practiced. I find this to be very safe, and it allows us to address skin laxity independently and maintain the muscle for contour and support."

Lower lid retraction, or "pull down," can occur and is most often caused by lower lid laxity or removal of too much skin during surgery.

"Even if a surgeon is highly skilled and experienced, it's possible for the muscles of the lower eyelid, which are very sensitive, to lose tone and not function normally," says **David L. Buchanan, MD**, of Santa Barbara, California. "I have found that by just taping and suspending the eyelids and having the patient massage them, usually over a four-to-six-week period, they very often come back to a normal position."

In some instances, however, surgical intervention may be necessary to correct or avoid lower lid retraction. Treatment usually involves tightening the lower lid (canthopexy), or may require more complex surgery. A canthopexy, which is performed at the outer corner of the eyes to tighten and improve lower eyelid tone, and to help prevent droopiness and dry-eye symptoms, may be done at the same time as blepharoplasty to correct a pre-existing problem, or sometimes may be done to help avoid eyelid "pull down" following surgery. The canthopexy usually leaves no additional scars.

An alternative technique may often be used for those patients who need to have excess fat removed or repositioned, or muscles tightened, in the lower eyelids, but do not have a significant amount of excess skin. Fat, but not skin, can be removed or altered through a transconjunctival incision, which is placed inside the lower eyelid. The incision is not visible on the skin, and stitches are unnecessary. The transconjunctival incision is most often used on younger patients whose skin is still firm but who have puffy lower eyelids due to inherited excess fat.

"For the lower lid, I use the transconjunctival approach, pull down the lower lid, and use the laser to make the incision and remove the fat," says **Richard O. Gregory, MD**, of Celebration, Florida. "Virtually 100 percent of my blepharoplasties are done with laser."

"There are two things that happen to the lower lid. The skin loses elasticity, and so it wrinkles, but there is very little redundancy. Also, the supporting structures get weak," says **Donald W. Hause, MD**, who practices in Sacramento, California. "When you surgically open the eyelid, take the fat out, and do all of these complicated things, you run the risk of creating a lower lid malposition. Instead, I do a transconjunctival incision and take fat out if they need it. In some cases, if you just raise the cheek fat pad up with a face lift, you may not need to do surgery on the lower eyelid."

POST OP

Eyelid surgery is an outpatient procedure that generally takes between 30 to 90 minutes to perform, usually under sedation (twilight) anesthesia. Some patients may prefer general anesthesia.

"I do most of my blepharoplasties using a local anesthetic with a pain pill and a Valium. Most patients are surprised at how little pain they have," says Dr. McMahan.

No matter what type of anesthesia you have, you will not feel any pain during the surgical procedure. Although some patients may remain in the facility

The upper lid incision is hidden in the lid crease. The lower lid incision is a few millimeters below the lower lid margin, concealed by the eyelashes. Both incisions follow the natural smile lines at the corners of the eyes.

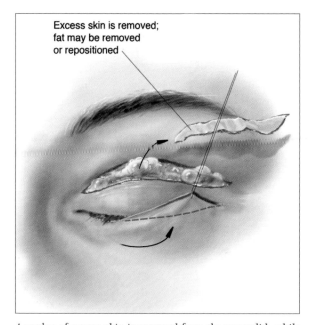

A wedge of excess skin is removed from the upper lid, while fat deposits are removed or repositioned. Excess skin from the lower lid is trimmed, fat is redistributed or removed, and muscles are tightened, as necessary. If you do not have excess skin in the lower lids, you may be a candidate for a transconjunctival incision, which is made inside the lower eyelid and not visible on the skin.

POSTOPERATIVE APPEARANCE. Following surgery of the upper and lower eyelids, the eyes look more rested, alert and youthful.

overnight, most are allowed to return home the same day.

One of the first things you will notice while you are in the recovery area after surgery is temporary blurry vision. This is due to the ointment used to soothe and protect the eyes during the surgery and from routine swelling after the procedure.

Most patients experience only mild discomfort following eyelid surgery. You may feel some tightness and soreness in your eyelids, but this can be easily controlled with oral medication. You must, however, remember to not take aspirin or anti-inflammatory medications that promote bleeding.

You will be instructed to keep your head elevated on the first night and maybe for several days. The degree of swelling and bruising varies between patients, and your surgeon may instruct you to use cold compresses on your eyelids. Some patients will find that swelling lasts several weeks while for others it may subside in less than one week. Likewise, bruising varies from patient to patient. Most find that it disappears within a week to 10 days, yet for some it may last as long as a month. As a general rule, the more

complex the surgery, the longer the swelling and bruising will last.

Your surgeon will allow you to use makeup within the first week, if you so desire, to help camouflage any discoloration. Your eyes may remain somewhat "gummy" for a week or so. You can ask to be shown how to clean your eyes and your surgeon may also recommend eyedrops to relieve any feelings of dryness, burning or itching. You may also experience some continued blurring or double vision, excessive tearing and light sensitivity. You should wear dark sunglasses to help protect your eyes from the elements. Stitches will be removed within a few days to a week following surgery.

You should keep activities to a minimum for several days. Your surgeon may ask you to refrain from strenuous activities, particularly those that raise your blood pressure, such as bending, lifting, straining and rigorous sports, for a few weeks. You can expect to resume most of your normal activities within 10 days or less. Blurry vision may affect your ability to accomplish certain tasks, such as reading or paperwork, even though you might feel quite fit enough to return to work. You should be able to read or watch television after a few days. Contact lenses should not be worn for one or two weeks.

LOOKING AHEAD

The healing process is gradual, and you won't get an accurate picture of the results of your surgery for several weeks. Incisions will fade gradually, and ultimately become barely visible.

The eyes are the most expressive facial feature. They are your windows to the world and also project your inner vision for the world to see. Once you have healed, you should find, as most patients do, that your eyes appear more rested, and that you look alert and refreshed.

Although heredity and lifestyle factors may affect the longevity of your procedure, the results of eyelid surgery are generally long lasting. Of course, as the aging process continues, the skin may once again become lax along with fine wrinkling in the eyelid area. However, if fat was removed to reduce puffiness, this condition usually will not recur.

The aesthetics of the eyes, other than color, are determined entirely by the bony and soft tissue architecture surrounding them. Variations in the bony skeleton, such as underdeveloped cheek bones, when not recognized in advance of blepharoplasty can negatively impact the final aesthetic result.

The upper and lower lids are complex and delicate structures with important physiologic functions essential to the well-being of the eyes. During the past decade, aesthetic plastic surgeons have come to recognize that removing "too much" from the eyelids results in an aged, rather than rejuvenated appearance — especially over time. That is why, as so many of our contributing experts have noted, the current trend in eyelid surgery is preservation of skin, muscle, and fat combined with selective repositioning of tissues and, if indicated, of the outer corners of the lids. For the best result, these surgical alterations are often combined with elevation of the eyebrows, lifting or augmentation of the cheeks, or other related aesthetic procedures.

As the comments by our contributing experts clearly reflect, careful preoperative analysis and alterations in surgical technique to fit each individual patient's needs, avoiding any compromise of eyelid function, are the keys to successful blepharoplasty outcomes.

— Peter B. Fodor, MD

BROW LIFT
Forehead Lift

The brows and forehead, which contribute significantly to a person's facial expression, are often the first areas of the face to show signs of aging. As people age, their skin loses elasticity. Sun damage and repeated muscle contraction form vertical frown lines and horizontal wrinkles across the brow, while the effects of gravity draw down the eyebrows, creating the appearance of increased heaviness.

Deepening forehead creases and low brows often begin to make people look older as early as their 30s, when they may start to notice that their expression always appears angry or worried.

A brow lift, also called a forehead lift, can dramatically affect the appearance of the entire face, providing a more relaxed, refreshed and youthful look. The procedure can improve brow position, raising it to or above the level of the bony rim of the eye socket, which is often considered the ideal position for the eyebrows. A brow lift can also improve lateral hooding. This occurs when there is excess skin near the outside corner of the eye, between the eyebrow and the eyelid, often contributing to an aged and tired look.

When it comes to lifting the brow, determining the best brow position for each individual is a matter of anatomy and personal aesthetics. "The appealing female brow is often high and arched, while the male brow is more transverse," offers **Gary R. Culbertson, MD**, of Sumter, South Carolina.

Herbert H. Bunchman II, MD, of Mesa, Arizona, agrees that male brow aesthetics are significantly different. "Most males have low brows, and my personal opinion

is that men look more masculine with a lower brow. What I usually say to a younger man is, 'What would John Wayne look like with eyebrows up there?' I advise many of my male patients to undergo blepharoplasty to eliminate excess skin of the upper eyelids and to accept the lower position of their brows."

PREOPERATIVE APPEARANCE. Horizontal wrinkling in the forehead and vertical frown lines between the eyebrows produce an angry or worried expression. Eyebrows may sag, creating the look of redundant skin in the upper eyelid area.

Horizontal forehead wrinkles can be improved with a brow lift, which elevates and smoothes the forehead skin. Because the brow lift raises the eyebrows, eliminating the need for someone to frequently lift her or his brow, it allows the forehead muscles to relax and thus may reduce the recurrence of horizontal wrinkles.

Vertical wrinkles or folds between the brows, often called frown lines, can make people appear angry even when they are not. These wrinkles usually form only when someone frowns, but once they have developed from repeated muscle contraction over time, the appearance of frowning is constant. The brow lift may include modification of the muscles responsible for these frown lines, thus diminishing the appearance of these bothersome wrinkles.

"I often recommend that patients first consider treatment with Botox injections. This allows them to reduce the appearance of frown lines and see what they may look like after undergoing a surgical brow lift. The results of Botox can last up to six months. After that, if they like the results, they often may decide on a permanent surgical solution," says Dr. Culbertson.

While the brow lift will lighten a person's expression, removing many elements that contribute to an older, tired or angry expression, it will not do some things people commonly think it will. Neither the brow lift nor eyelid surgery will typically improve the wrinkles on the outside corners of the eyes, also called crow's-feet, although some improvement may be achieved with the lateral brow lift. Crow's-feet must generally be treated with Botox, fillers, or skin treatments discussed later in the book. While for some patients, a brow lift may provide sufficient improvement of excess skin on the upper eyelid, many patients will require upper eyelid surgery (blepharoplasty) to correct excess eyelid skin and eyelid puffiness.

"You have to consider the brows and the eyes together because they influence each other so much," says **Martin Luftman, MD**, of Lexington, Kentucky.

However, combining a brow lift with upper eyelid surgery requires careful surgical planning. "The forehead lift is one of the 'unsung' great operations for facial rejuvenation," says **Walter L. Erhardt, Jr., MD**, of Albany, Georgia, "Many patients will fixate on their eyes and not see the brow as being a contributor to their tired look. The brow affects the eyelids. When I was in practice only about five years, a young lady came in who had undergone a blepharoplasty somewhere else. She complained about still looking 'tired.' I sat her down and pushed the brow up, and she liked what she saw. Her problem was congenital low brows, not redundant skin. Unfortunately for her, because so much skin had been removed with the eyelid surgery, I was not able to offer her a brow lift — she wouldn't have been able to close her eyes."

Alfonso Oliva, MD, of Spokane, Washington, agrees that a brow lift, instead of or sometimes in addition to upper eyelid surgery, is often what's

LENGTH OF SURGERY
Usually between one to two hours.

ANESTHESIA
Typically local anesthetic and intravenous sedation; general anesthesia may be used.

LENGTH OF STAY
Usually outpatient procedure, home the same day.

RECOVERY
Initial mild to moderate discomfort; up and about in one to two days; wash hair in two days; swelling, bruising possible for 10 days; back to work with makeup, two weeks; full effect, four weeks.

SCARS
Minimal visible scarring, virtually undetectable within hairline or can be covered by combing hair forward.

RISKS/POSSIBLE COMPLICATIONS
Serious complications, while possible, are unlikely. Some potential complications can be avoided by carefully following your surgeon's instructions.

In addition to the usual risks associated with anesthesia, other risks include:
- Nerve damage: Occurs in less than one percent of patients; usually temporary, with full motion typically returning within three months.
- Bald spots: May occur at incision lines with either the coronal or endoscopic technique; hair usually grows back.
- Numbness: Numbness of forehead usually temporary, lasting for two weeks to three months; permanent numbness occurs in less than one percent of patients.
- Early relapse: Slight relapse is not unusual; significant relapse is uncommon.

The above-listed risks may be only some of those that your surgeon will discuss with you in greater detail during your consultation.

needed to achieve a patient's goals. "Most patients requesting upper blepharoplasty should first consider repositioning of the brow to a more youthful level. By lifting the brow manually, the surgeon can simulate the final result for the patient and the effect the lifted brow has on the upper eyelid."

CONSULTATION

The consultation is a time for the surgeon and patient to get to know and feel comfortable with each other. The patient should feel completely confident that the surgeon is fully qualified. If you haven't read sections in the beginning of this book about choosing a surgeon who is certified by the American Board of Plastic Surgery, you may wish to do so now.

Your surgeon needs to determine if you are a suitable candidate for brow lift surgery and will need to review your entire medical history, including any medications you may currently be taking. Most candidates for brow lift surgery are between the ages of 40 and 60, although people who have developed frown lines or furrows in their foreheads by the time they reach their 30s also often have the procedure. Whether the brow is furrowed and saggy due to aging or low hanging by heredity, a brow lift can achieve a rejuvenated and refreshed appearance.

During the consultation, patients may be asked to look into a mirror and describe exactly what they find troublesome about their appearance in order to determine if a brow lift will solve the problem or if other (or additional) procedures may be needed. Your surgeon will examine facial structure, skin condition, and the hairline as well as discuss incision placement and the procedural technique he or she recommends.

Do not hesitate to ask any questions or air any concerns you may have. Ask your surgeon to explain his or her proposed technique and how the most natural-looking results can be achieved.

With a brow lift, undesirable results can include an unnatural facial expression, such as a surprised look resulting from eyebrows that are raised artificially high; an angry or sad appearance if the outer half of the eyebrow is raised more than the inner half; or a too-wide gap between the eyebrows. An experienced aesthetic plastic surgeon can usually avoid these problems, creating a brow position that is aesthetically correct for you. The 'ideal' brow position, however, may be a

matter of personal taste and can also vary considerably according to the fashion of the times. For example, today there is a trend toward brows that are placed a bit lower medially with a high lateral arch. You should be sure to communicate to your surgeon the type of brow that you prefer. Your surgeon will then explain what can or cannot realistically be achieved given your particular anatomy.

PREPARATION

Your surgeon will give you instructions about how to prepare for your surgery. He or she will also give you guidelines on eating, drinking and medications, all of which are detailed in an earlier section of this book.

Preparation specific to a brow lift might include letting your hair grow out if it is currently cut very short. Allowing it to grow longer will better enable you to hide the incisions while they heal.

As with all surgery in general, whether performed in an outpatient facility or in the hospital, you should arrange to have someone drive you to and from surgery and assist you for a day or two after you return home.

THE SURGERY

The various techniques used in brow lift surgery are: the coronal, also referred to as the classic or traditional; endoscopic; temporal or lateral; and subcutaneous.

CORONAL BROW LIFT

The coronal brow lift involves an incision that extends from ear to ear all the way across the top of the head within the hair in what has been referred to as an "earphone" pattern. It is sometimes the best choice for patients with severe signs of aging, such as deep horizontal wrinkles and major eyebrow droop. In some patients, the incision may be made just in front of, rather than behind, the hairline.

"Although I have used other techniques, I've largely gone back to the coronal brow lift," says Dr. Bunchman. "I have found it to be longer lasting than the other methods. Of course, with the brow lift or any facial procedure, it's always important to achieve the most natural-looking results possible, which often means doing 'less' rather than 'more.'"

With the coronal brow lift, all muscles that contribute to wrinkles and scowling such as the frontalis, which is responsible for deep horizontal creases, can be altered.

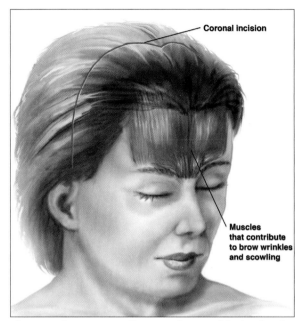

Coronal incision

Muscles
that contribute
to brow wrinkles
and scowling

The coronal incision usually spans the top of the head and is completely hidden within the hair. Another option in patients with an already high hairline is to place the incision at the hairline.

To elevate the brows and forehead, the surgeon will also remove about a 1-2 centimeter strip of the scalp and sew the remaining scalp together. The incision will be closed with stitches or clips, and dressings such as gauze padding and an elastic bandage may be used. Although the coronal lift is the most extensive and invasive of the various techniques, scarring is typically well hidden and undetectable.

"Most people want to get rid of that stern look in the central brow. We can treat that with a brow lift, by modifying the corrugator muscles and the procerus muscles," says Dr. Luftman. "Most surgeons learning today are taught the endoscopic approach, but many of us who first learned the open, or coronal, approach are going back to it. Generally speaking, I feel that I can tailor and shape the brow much better through the open approach. It's a home run for the patient."

Donald W. Hause, MD, of Sacramento, California, explains his preference for the open technique this way: "The open technique allows me to soften the medial brow and then re-drape the lateral brow to frame the eye properly, so you achieve an elegant look — not a surprised one. That's one of the reasons I use

the open approach. With this technique, I have the freedom to change the vectors of pull in certain areas of the brow."

The height of a patient's forehead and position of the hairline is always a consideration in planning brow lift surgery and selecting the appropriate technique.

"If the patient already has a high hairline, I might want to use an open approach with the incision in front of the hairline, to avoid further raising the hairline." explains **Julius W. Few, MD,** of Chicago, Illinois.

When the incision is made in front of the hairline, sometimes called a subcutaneous forehead lift, muscle alterations to improve forehead creases and frown lines are possible, just as with the coronal incision. Unlike the coronal, however, the sensory nerves to the top of the head are not divided, so problems with numbness and itching are less likely. Another advantage for people with high foreheads is that because the incision is made in front of the hairline, the hairline is not raised when the skin is removed.

The location of the incision, at the top of the forehead just where the hairline begins, also spells out a potential problem with this technique, which is a visible scar along the hairline. Although these scars have a good chance of healing very well and becoming virtually imperceptible, this cannot be predicted or guaranteed. As always, the skill and experience of the plastic surgeon is important to the final result.

"I use a hairline incision and never have any problem with it. If it's done carefully, it's virtually undetectable," says Dr. Hause.

Patients can expect excellent aesthetic results with the coronal technique or any variations of the open technique. These methods are considered long-lasting, and they usually will not have to be repeated as the patient continues to age.

"The endoscopic approach, in which the surgery is performed with the aid of an endoscope inserted through relatively small incisions made at or within the hairline, is well-suited for younger patients or those with less brow laxity," offers **Gary D. Hall, MD,** of Leawood, Kansas. "I've found that the more traditional coronal approach seems to provide a long-lasting effect, and for patients with more severe brow ptosis (sagging), the coronal approach achieves an excellent result."

John Bruno, MD, of Fort Myers, Florida, adds, "Like all procedures, the technique must be tailored to the patient's needs. I would use the open approach, with the incision just in front of the hairline, if a patient has a very high hairline, since with this approach I am actually shortening the forehead. In other instances, if a patient primarily needs muscle modification and not a lot of elevation, I might perform an endoscopic procedure."

A technique sometimes used for men who are bald or have a receding hairline, as well as deep horizontal creases in their forehead, is to place the incision within one of the forehead creases. When healed, this incision is usually difficult to detect.

Despite the many benefits of the coronal brow lift, some surgeons prefer other methods, citing such problems as numbness, itchiness, and possible hair loss at the incision site — problems that they say are minimized, if not eliminated, with the endoscopic approach. For more than 10 years, endoscopic forehead lifting has offered an alternative to open techniques, which many surgeons and their patients have found beneficial.

ENDOSCOPIC BROW LIFT

The endoscopic brow lift utilizes an endoscope, which is a slender fiber-optic tube equipped with a tiny

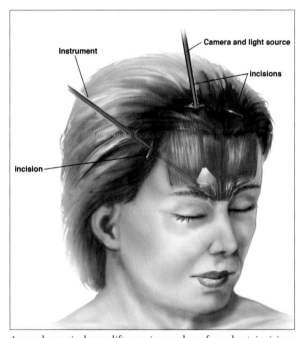

An endoscopic brow lift requires only a few short incisions within the hair. Special instrumentation allows the surgeon to make adjustments to internal structures without the need for a long coronal incision.

video camera and bright light, no larger than a pencil eraser, which allows the surgeon to view the internal structures of the forehead without making a long incision.

Rather than the one long incision used in the coronal lift, the surgeon will make four to six small incisions at or within the hair. Inserting the endoscope through one incision, the surgeon will operate through the other small incisions and work on the underlying tissue and muscles.

"The newest techniques involve the endoscope and offer virtually 'scarless' surgery," says **Joseph Michael Pober, MD**, of New York, New York. "With the endoscope, brow lifts can be performed through several small (fingertip-width) incisions in the scalp, concealed by the hair. With the endoscopic forehead lift, there is less risk of uncomfortable complications such as numbness and itchiness of the scalp and less possibility of hair loss at the incision sites. Just like the open technique, the endoscopic forehead lift can be used to correct frown lines and lift the upper third of the face. Wrinkles of the forehead and brow virtually disappear and the eyebrows are attractively elevated."

With an endoscopic forehead lift, the skin is shifted backward on the head, tightening the brow. Excess scalp cannot be removed using this technique. Some surgeons then place drill holes or small metal or absorbable screws into the skull and place sutures around the screws or through the holes to anchor and support the skin until it has healed in its new location. Other fixation techniques, or no fixation at all, may be used with good results.

"The endoscopic brow lift was a major advance in forehead surgery," offers **Kulwant S. Bhangoo, MD**, of Buffalo, New York, "With the endoscope, we could make small incisions behind the hairline, insert the endoscope, and while protecting the nerves, modify the muscle that causes frown lines. Now, some surgeons are using an even newer technique that involves insertion of the Endotine device, which is a small, dissolvable tined hook, through an upper eyelid incision; and in this way we are able to secure the brow in a higher position. The Endotine dissolves in four to six months, but the eyebrow remains fixed in its newly elevated position."

"I usually prefer an endoscopic approach," says **Michael R. Schwartz, MD**, of Camarillo, California, "but for those patients who are having eyelid surgery, I often will address a limited elevation of the brow and muscle modification through the eyelid incision. This, of course, eliminates potential problems such as a large area of numbness in the scalp incision region as well as the additional dissection that goes along with a brow lift. The recovery is much quicker, and because the muscles have been altered, there is no need for Botox in that area in the future."

In an endoscopic brow lift, the incisions will be closed with stitches or clips. Your surgeon may use dressings such as gauze padding and an elastic bandage. If metal screws were used, they will be removed in the doctor's office after two weeks; absorbable screws will dissolve within a few months.

The endoscopic technique allows the surgeon to accomplish most but not all of the things that can be achieved through a coronal lift. Using the endoscopic lift, the surgeon can weaken the muscles that cause vertical frown lines. Botox may also be recommended as a supplement to soften forehead wrinkles and help prevent further wrinkling from muscle activity.

"To me, the coronal approach always seemed to be too much surgery for the slight elevation of the brow that was really necessary," explains **Leo R. McCafferty, MD,** of Pittsburgh, Pennsylvania. "When patients bring in pictures of themselves from 20 or 30 years ago, we can see that the brows have not fallen that much; they just need to be elevated slightly. The minimally invasive endoscopic approach matches the technique to the problem. I place the incisions right at the hairline, angling them away from the hair follicles. Then, as they heal, hair grows through the scar."

Some surgeons recommend the endoscopic lift only for those with moderate aging of the forehead, advising that patients with deep furrowing might find this technique less effective and shorter lasting than the coronal. Other surgeons feel that the benefits of the endoscopic approach are significant for almost any patient, and this is their preferred technique. Some endoscopic techniques may raise the hairline slightly.

LATERAL BROW LIFT

While the lateral brow lift will not raise the middle of the brow, it does lift the outer third of the brow and is a relatively simple procedure for the patient. Incision patterns may vary. In one method, the incision begins at the hairline from a line directly above the pupil of the eye and extends laterally into the scalp. The surgeon will dissect about one inch of skin on top of the frontalis muscle.

The lateral brow lift allows the outer portion of the eyebrow to be elevated and improves the appearance of the lateral upper eyelid (right), with the incision and skin dissection (left) behind the hairline.

"In general, you don't want to elevate the entire brow the same amount; the medial brow needs less elevation than the lateral brow," says Dr. Erhardt. "I find that patients 50 years old or older usually need more lateral brow elevation than I can achieve with the closed techniques. I often have to combine these techniques with some scalp excision laterally."

Although a limited procedure particularly effective for patients who have droopiness of the brow at the outer edges of the eyes and perhaps some slight skin redundancy in the same area, a number of patients find that this minimal technique is all they need to create a fresher look and rejuvenate their appearance.

"While the lateral brow lift is not appropriate for all patients, this minimally invasive procedure, which usually takes me about 15 to 20 minutes to perform, can provide wonderful benefits to many," offers **Robert W. Bernard, MD,** of White Plains, New York. "Using relatively short incisions, with resulting scars that are virtually undetectable, we can effectively create a very natural elevation of the lateral 50 percent of the brow. This procedure also stabilizes the lateral brow and reduces the skin

POSTOPERATIVE APPEARANCE. A brow lift reduces the appearance of lines and wrinkles, elevates the eyebrows, and creates a more pleasant facial expression. Some techniques may slightly raise the hairline.

redundancy between the eyelashes and the lateral eyelid, which can coincidentally improve the effects of upper eyelid surgery, making it more long-lasting and aesthetically pleasing — all with less surgical time, less recovery time, and less expense for the patient."

Dr. Bruno adds, "I also have used a thread lift technique, a different type of minimally invasive method with barbed sutures, when the primary concern is drooping of the lateral brow."

FROWN LINES

If the primary concern is the vertical frown lines between the brows, an endoscopic procedure may be used or, alternatively, the muscles causing these frown lines can be altered through an upper-eyelid incision. This would make sense particularly if the patient were undergoing eyelid surgery at the same time, since both procedures could be accomplished through the same incision.

"An excellent option for patients who only need a slight lift is a browpexy," says Dr. Few. "With this procedure we go in through the upper blepharoplasty incision, release the brow-retaining ligament, and elevate the brow. And since the eyelids are affected by the position of the brow, this can provide the patient with a very effective and harmonious result."

The advantage of surgery to correct frown lines is that the results are permanent. However, Botox injections are a nonsurgical alternative to temporarily correct frown lines by inactivating the muscles that cause them. Botox can also smooth horizontal forehead wrinkles and improve the appearance of crow's-feet. In the hands of a skilled surgeon, Botox can be used to somewhat alter the position of the brows.

The results of Botox injections are temporary, and the treatment must be repeated periodically to maintain results. In another section of this book, we discuss Botox in more detail.

POST OP

Brow/forehead lifts usually take between one to two hours to perform, often under sedation (twilight) anesthesia, although general anesthesia may be recommended for some patients. Whether you are awake and unaware of what is going on, or you are unconscious, you will not feel any pain during the surgical procedure. Although some patients may remain in the facility overnight, most are allowed to return home the same day.

There will be some swelling and bruising during the first 10 days following surgery. Some patients may experience these symptoms in the cheek and eye area as well as the forehead. Any pain or discomfort will be controlled with a drug such as acetaminophen or a mild prescription pain medication.

Bandages, if they have been used, will be removed in one to three days, and sutures are usually removed within seven to 10 days after surgery. A drain, if your surgeon elected to use one to diminish postoperative bruising and swelling, will usually be removed in 24 to 48 hours after surgery. Your surgeon may advise you to elevate your head to help relieve swelling, and cold compresses may also be advised for the same purpose. As healing progresses, some numbness followed by itching may occur. It is possible for this to continue, to some extent, for as long as six months, and some hair around the incision may fall out or become thinner. These situations are usually temporary, and normal growth typically resumes within a few weeks or months. Permanent hair loss is a rare occurrence.

Although strenuous activities are not recommended for about one week following surgery, you will usually be up and about within a day or two, and able to wash your hair after about two days or when the bandages are removed. Most patients can feel good about appearing in public with the aid of makeup in about two weeks. Patients who have undergone an endoscopic procedure may be ready to venture out sooner.

The final results of the procedure should be evident in approximately four weeks. However, patients are usually advised to avoid any strenuous activity that increases blood pressure, including jogging and sexual activity, and also to use sun protection, for several weeks postoperatively.

LOOKING AHEAD

Most patients are not only happy with their brow lift, a large number are also pleasantly surprised at the improvement in their overall appearance. When the forehead becomes furrowed, the brow droops, and folds form at the outside corners of the eyes, people can appear markedly aged. The result of a forehead lift typically is a more youthful and refreshed appearance.

Of course, having a brow lift does not halt the progression of aging. The procedure will, however, help slow down that process and help minimize the effects of aging in the upper third of the face. Slight relapse in brow position is not uncommon and should be expected, but significant relapse should not occur for many years, if at all.

Because the brow and forehead are seen in the context of the entire facial appearance, it is quite common that patients choose to combine this procedure with a face lift and eyelid surgery in order to maintain facial harmony and balance.

It is not uncommon for the upper eyelid/brow areas to show early signs of aging. Modifying eyebrow shape and position through chemical denervation (Botox) and or brow lift surgery, sometimes combined with conservative upper eyelid surgery, can reverse and retard this aging process. As you can see from the opinions of our experts, the choices of technique are numerous with arduous supporters of each. We mention elsewhere in this book, regarding a variety of aesthetic procedures, that custom tailoring is essential, and good results can be obtained from multiple approaches. While the debate on the relative benefits of open and endoscopic brow lift surgery continues, ultimately what also matters is the experience and confidence of the surgeon with a particular technique. If a patient is adamant about wanting one or another of the various options, it is best to find a surgeon who has ample experience in using that method.

In my view, an endoscopic forehead lift, expertly performed using minimal or no fixation, can provide an aesthetically pleasing and natural result. Having tried all the various fixation methods, I firmly believe that the most critical factors in attaining a successful result from brow lift surgery are the details of surgical dissection — not the specific fixation technique employed. There is a somewhat steep learning curve for performing the endoscopic forehead lift, and this may be a deterrent to its adoption by some surgeons. On the other hand, I agree that there are definitely some, albeit a small percentage, of forehead rejuvenation patients for whom the open approach is a better choice.

Surgical alterations in the shape and position of the brows, as pointed out in this chapter, can also be carried out through an upper eyelid incision. The effect of this approach, however, is limited to the central eyebrow where elevation may not be desirable from an aesthetic standpoint. The temporal approach, which is the simplest and least invasive, may produce sufficient improvement in properly selected patients. In other patients, often those who are younger and whose main concern is frown lines and crow's-feet formation, Botox may be the right choice, either as a temporary measure for the patient to assess the effects, or as an ongoing therapy. As physicians who are expe rienced in administering Botox understand, injections into the frontalis muscle (the primary elevator of the eyebrows) for treatment of horizontal forehead furrows can result in undesirable lowering of the eyebrows. This side effect may be acceptable in some male patients, but seldom in females. Fortunately, there are ways to compensate for this by injecting additional sites. Details such as this may not be fully appreciated by the less trained and experienced injector. Intimate knowledge of anatomy readily acquired by surgeons through their repeated experience with forehead surgery (open or endoscopic) is of the essence for optimal results with Botox injections.

Rejuvenation of the forehead, brow, and upper eyelid areas is a complex process that requires careful patient assessment and meticulous planning by the surgeon — whether a surgical procedure or a nonsurgical alternative is selected. The final results can be among the most satisfying for patients who wish not only to look younger and more attractive but also to soften an angry or frowning appearance.

— Peter B. Fodor, MD

FACE LIFT

Rhytidectomy

As signs of aging begin to appear, the disparity between people's mental picture of themselves and the image in the mirror can be pronounced, even disturbing. The face lift, or rhytidectomy, was among the earliest aesthetic procedures to gain widespread popularity. A face lift affects the lower two-thirds of the face and the neck; it is an indispensable component of facial rejuvenation and can seem to subtract years from a person's appearance. Yet, as discussed earlier in this section, additional procedures are commonly necessary, such as treatment of the forehead and eyelid areas, to achieve optimal rejuvenation of the face.

The face lift can remove excess skin, tighten muscles, and reposition underlying tissues to reduce or eliminate some of the predominant signs of an aged appearance such as sagging, wrinkling, jowls, and excess fat while restoring a youthful, revitalized look.

"A face lift is not a tightening procedure but rather a restoration," says **Bruce Genter, MD**, of Jenkintown, Pennsylvania. "This involves not only getting rid of excess skin but also redistributing soft tissues to a more youthful position."

"When I perform a face lift, I reposition the underlying tissues, tighten neck muscles, and use liposuction to contour the jawline," says **James D. McMahan, MD**, of Columbus, Ohio. "I've seen patients who have gone somewhere else and had one of the 'quickie' procedures. Invariably, they just aren't happy with the results. The face lift technique that I use takes time, but the results are excellent and long-lasting."

The neck is another area that shows distinct signs of aging that can be improved with a face lift.

"During the past 10 to 15 years, so much emphasis has been placed on rejuvenating the midface and cheek areas that the jaw and neck are often ignored," says **Richard P. Rand, MD**, of Bellevue, Washington. "A smooth jawline and a nice angle between the neck and chin are more noticeable, even at conversational distance, than are some of the more subtle changes seen after extensive midface surgery."

Surgery of the lower face and neck can restore a sharper definition to the jawline, repositioning tissues and trimming excess skin, and in conjunction with fat suctioning can eliminate a double chin. It can also correct or improve vertical bands on either side of the neck formed by separation of a muscle called the platysma.

"Some patients are primarily concerned about their neck, but these individuals most often are in need of a more traditional face lift," says **David L. Abramson, MD**, of New York, New York. "Otherwise, with a neck lift alone, certain areas such as the jowls will not be addressed. On the other hand, because everyone ages differently, some people who need face lifts don't need any correction to their neck."

THE CONSULTATION

"People must have a realistic expectation about what to expect from a face lift," says **Jay B. Fine, MD**, of Pembroke Pines, Florida. "There is a lot of advertising about quickie, lunchtime, no-incision, no-scar lifts. Face lifts are real surgery with real risks, but also with real benefits. A face lift can achieve results that are simply not possible with other more marginal procedures. But face lifts, like all cosmetic procedures, have to be individualized."

The consultation is a time for you and the surgeon to get to know and feel comfortable with each other. You should feel completely confident that your surgeon is fully qualified. If you haven't read sections in the beginning of this book about choosing a surgeon who is certified by the American Board of Plastic Surgery, perhaps you should do so now.

Your surgeon will need to determine if you are a suitable candidate for face lift surgery and will want to review your entire medical history, including any medications you may currently be taking. Many factors, such as sun exposure, tobacco use, alcohol consumption, stress, and physical illness, as well as genetics, can cause more pronounced effects of aging in some people. Although the most common age at which people have a face lift is in the 50 to 65-year range, no two people are exactly alike or age in precisely the same fashion. Some individuals as young as 40 may be good candidates for a face lift, and some in their 80s may benefit from the procedure — which may, in fact, be their second or third lift.

"My average face lift patient is in his or her 50s," says **Goesel Anson, MD**, of Las Vegas, Nevada. "That's significantly younger than it used to be. Life expectancy has increased as the medical sciences have become more sophisticated. 'Middle age' is not defined the same way as it was in our parents' or grandparents' generations. As a society, our desire is to have our appearance reflect our inner vitality, health and strength. People have accepted plastic surgery as an effective means of maintaining a more youthful appearance throughout life."

"Typically, if I can catch patients early enough, in their early 50s or mid-50s, we can do extended mini procedures and then three to five years later they can have another mini procedure to refresh everything," says **David V. Poole, MD**, of Altamonte Springs, Florida. "I think a good skin care program before and after surgery is important and helps maintain the improvement we've achieved."

In addition to assessing the wrinkles, folds, and other elements you wish to correct, your surgeon will evaluate several factors, including skin elasticity and bone structure, as well as examine your hairline for incision placement. You and your surgeon will work together to determine the best surgical plan to meet your individual needs.

"Precise diagnosis, appropriate planning, and skillful execution are ingredients of a successful face lift surgery," comments **Fanny dela Cruz, MD**, of West Bloomfield, Michigan.

"One important point sometimes overlooked is the underlying bony structure," says **Steven J. Smith, MD**, of Knoxville, Tennessee. "Sometimes the bony skeleton of the face needs treatment — either augmentation or

LENGTH OF SURGERY
Usually two and a half to four hours.

ANESTHESIA
Local anesthetic and intravenous sedation, or general anesthesia.

LENGTH OF STAY
While usually an outpatient procedure, overnight stays are possible.

RECOVERY
Initial mild to moderate discomfort; up and about within one to two days; wash hair in two days; swelling, bruising mostly gone in two weeks; back to work with makeup, two weeks; full effect, one to four months.

SCARS
Inconspicuous scarring, mostly concealed in the hair or in natural facial creases; scar behind ear may be most visible.

RISKS/POSSIBLE COMPLICATIONS
Serious complications, while possible, are unlikely. Some potential complications can be avoided by carefully following your surgeon's instructions.

In addition to the usual risks associated with anesthesia, other risks include:
- Hematoma: Collection of blood beneath the skin; can be treated without compromising result.
- Skin necrosis: Can occur in front of or behind ear, may result in wound that can leave a more visible scar.
- Facial weakness or paralysis: Caused by injury to facial nerve; usually temporary.
- Infection: Risk less than one percent, but can cause skin necrosis and other complications.
- Ear numbness: Rare; caused by damage to the great auricular nerve.
- Hair loss (alopecia): Usually temporary.
- Pulmonary emboli: Extremely rare; a blood clot that travels to the blood vessels in the lung.

The above-listed risks may be only some of those that your surgeon will discuss with you in greater detail during your consultation.

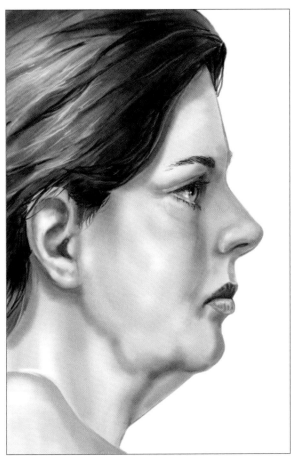

PREOPERATIVE APPEARANCE. Sagging skin and descent of the deeper tissues make the face and neck look aged.

about the full spectrum of possible ways to treat their problem, whether it be lifts, fillers, Botox, peels — basically, we find out where the patient's needs intersect with the options we have available. I do a wide variety of face lifts, including standard lifts, skin lifts, lower face lifts, and upper face lifts. I do some with a laser, but whether or not I do the lift with laser, more than 90 percent of my face lift patients get some laser treatment at the same time."

"I think of a face lift as a sort of puzzle — it is a three-dimensional puzzle that requires innovation, imagination, and skill to find the right solution for each patient," says **Mutaz Habal, MD**, of Tampa, Florida. "I enjoy seeing a satisfied patient and being able to be helpful to others. A well-performed face lift has the potential to truly uplift patients' spirits — if they start with a realistic expectation."

"It's vital to understand the patient's goals and concerns," says **Brian J. Lee, MD**, of Fort Wayne, Indiana, "as well to evaluate their underlying anatomy so I can determine what we can realistically expect to accomplish. It's also very important to explain and point out facial asymmetries to the patient. No one has a face that is exactly alike on both sides. Patients may be unaware of subtle asymmetries before surgery but then discover them after surgery when they are subjecting their face to increased scrutiny. I'm also very adamant about only doing modified types of surgery on smokers because of the risks."

Your surgeon may discuss other procedures that are often done in conjunction with a face lift, such as a brow lift or eyelid surgery, if it appears that those areas also need attention to achieve a truly rejuvenated appearance and maintain facial harmony. As we age, our faces lose fat and, consequently, volume, which can cause an aged, drawn look. Procedures such as injections with soft tissue fillers or placement of facial implants may sometimes be recommended, as well, to address volumetric and contour problems.

"Facial beauty and harmony consists of a combination of contour, shape, and three-dimensional volume," explains **Larry A. Sargent, MD**, of Chattanooga, Tennessee. "Sometimes the three-dimensional aspect is overlooked. The fact that someone has lost cheek prominence or that they would benefit from improving the contour of the chin can be brought to their attention and could make a big difference in the overall aesthetic result."

reduction — in order to achieve an excellent external appearance."

"A natural look is a priority, and a good result is achieved when a patient's beauty is enhanced without evidence of surgery. During the consultation, I spend extra time with patients, analyzing their features both at rest and when they move — for example, when they are speaking or smiling. This gives me a true understanding of how to make surgical enhancements balance with the rest of the patient's face," offers **Fredric Newman, MD**, of Darien, Connecticut. "This also allows me to spend more time communicating with patients and thereby get a better sense of what they want."

"When a patient comes in, I find out what bothers them and prioritize those areas," agrees **Richard O. Gregory, MD**, of Celebration, Florida. "Then we talk

"I don't believe in performing face lift surgeries unless there is a realistic expectation for significant overall improvement," says **James M. Platis, MD**, of Chicago, Illinois. "Until that time I usually recommend minimally invasive or noninvasive modalities such as Botox, Restylane, skin care, and so on. On the other hand, once it becomes apparent that face lift surgery is necessary, I believe that the entire face from the forehead to the collarbone should be treated. Sometimes not all areas need surgical intervention, but there is nothing more disharmonious than a youthful looking midface with a sunken brow or neck. I do agree that returning volume to the face is critical for overall rejuvenation, but it is not the only answer. Atrophy over time can age a face, but gravity has its effects as well, and, almost always, lifting is necessary along with volume restoration."

"I usually don't like to correct only one facial area, because it can look unnatural," offers **Peter Hyans, MD**, of Berkeley Heights, New Jersey. "You need to assess the aesthetics of the entire face to maintain balance and achieve a more pleasing result — so the patient looks refreshed and rejuvenated, not 'operated on.'"

Other nonsurgical procedures, such as laser resurfacing, chemical peel or dermabrasion, may be recommended to address skin-quality issues that a face lift will not correct. These include surface wrinkles, texture problems and color irregularities. Spot resurfacing treatments may be done in conjunction with a face lift, but full-face resurfacing usually is delayed until after the face lift has had adequate time to heal and full circulation has been restored to the skin, generally about three months.

"It's very important for the surgeon to consider the whole package. If someone has had a face lift but still has sun damage or other skin problems, she still doesn't look her best," says **Herbert H. Bunchman II, MD**, of Mesa, Arizona. "I've had great success using the Obaji skin care program, which uses medical ingredients such as Retin-A coupled with other agents that enhance its effectiveness, to achieve outstanding improvement in skin color and texture."

"Both dynamic motion of muscles and the effects of gravity contribute to facial aging," says **Alexander G. Digenis, MD**, of Louisville, Kentucky. "Dynamic aging changes are usually surface phenomena, such as lines etched into the skin, which no amount of pulling and lifting will correct. For these problems, some of the nonsurgical procedures such as skin resurfacing, fillers and Botox, are helpful. The drooping caused by gravity, however — such as jowls or a sagging neck — will not respond to surface treatment and must be addressed through a surgical lifting procedure."

"I like to use a combination of treatments," agrees **David L. Buchanan, MD**, of Santa Barbara, California. "Surgical procedures give structural support; then laser resurfacing refines and enhances the skin. I may augment the soft tissues with fillers such as Restylane, and then maybe very strategically and carefully block some of the muscle actions with Botox to decrease furrows. I find that by treating the different layers of muscle, tissue, and skin, we can achieve the best cosmetic results."

"A face lift should be done in conjunction with a skin care program," says **James Apesos, MD**, of Dayton, Ohio. "Healthy skin is extremely important to a youthful appearance. In addition to sun exposure, smoking, which affects proteins and circulation, definitely damages and ages the skin."

Do not hesitate to ask your surgeon any questions and air any concerns you may have.

"I talk to patients with a mirror in hand, going over what is bothering them," says **Seth R. Thaller, MD**, of Miami, Florida. "Most are troubled by their jowls, jawline, and neckline. To help them get an idea of what to expect from a natural face lift, I have them lie down while holding the mirror. I discuss the incisions with them. I also point out the potential stigmata of a face lift and how we will avoid it."

It is entirely appropriate to ask your surgeon to explain how he or she avoids undesirable aftereffects that can call attention to the fact that a surgical procedure was performed. Among these are the attached earlobe (also called "pixie ear"), the open ear canal, loss of sideburns, the "cobblestone" appearance, and the "wind-tunnel" look.

"It's very important to achieve a result that does not show stigmata of surgery," says Dr. Steven Smith. "Plastic surgeons try to respect the natural anatomy and also adapt to changes in the anatomy at different stages of life — to re-create the natural anatomy of youth. As a result, a woman in her 40s may need a somewhat different surgical technique than someone in her 70s.

All portions of the face should complement each other so that it is pleasing and well-balanced."

The pixie ear results from too much skin being removed in the earlobe area, which pulls the earlobe down and into the surrounding skin. This undesirable result can be corrected with minor surgery.

An ear canal with a normal appearance is partially hidden from view by the cartilage flap in front of the ear. If the face lift results in too much tension on this area, the cartilage can be pulled forward, widening the ear canal. Although this sign may betray surgery, most people do not notice it. The problem is difficult to correct since there is no longer excess or loose facial skin, and revisions might have to wait until the skin becomes somewhat more lax and a secondary face lift procedure is appropriate, perhaps years later.

Most women place little value on sideburns as a facial feature — until they are lost. A face lift can cause sideburns to migrate upward, creating an unnatural-appearing hairline. Ask your surgeon about techniques that can preserve sideburns.

"It is very important also to prevent hair loss during a face lift," says **Alfonso Barrera, MD**, of Houston, Texas. "That can be done by placing the incisions correctly, for example, avoiding hair-bearing skin and placing them horizontally below the sideburn. It is important that incisions be placed in such a way as to not cause the sideburns or the hairline at the back of the neck to be moved upward."

The "cobblestone" appearance can occur when too much fat, which serves as a natural buffer between skin and muscle, is removed from the face or neck.

"Rarely is fat removed from the face in face lift surgery; however, neck fat is routinely removed in a manner that enhances the neck contour and never 'skeletonizes' the neck," says **Steven K. White Sr., MD**, of Myrtle Beach, South Carolina.

The expression "wind-tunnel look" needs little explanation. An appearance of the skin being pulled too tightly announces to the world that a face lift has been performed. This unsatisfactory result is more common following a second or third face lift. Surprisingly, not all patients find an overly tight appearance objectionable. If the patient's skin has lost most of its elasticity and she or he still insists on a very tight and smooth facial contour, a somewhat over-pulled look may be unavoidable.

"People should look well-rested and have a youthful appearance, not a wind-tunnel appearance," says Dr. Abramson. "Some people want to be as tight as possible, but I try to dissuade them of that. The results of a tighter lift might last longer, but it definitely doesn't look natural at the beginning."

And **Edward J. Domanskis, MD**, of Newport Beach, California, adds, "Many patients are afraid that they will not look like themselves after facial surgery, but I reassure them that they will. It is, fortunately, unusual now to see patients who sport the telltale distortions following face lift surgery that were so common in the past. It's really important, though, for patients to look at photographs of their chosen doctor's work to make sure their aesthetic tastes are compatible."

"A specific goal or set of goals should be well thought out by both the patient and the surgeon," says **Zachary E. Gerut, MD**, of Hewlett, New York. "Most patients tell their plastic surgeon what they are unhappy with, such as jowls, a loose neck, and so on. But it is equally or even more important for me to know what patients like and how they want to look after surgery. Just as the same hairstyle or dress would not look good on every patient, the same surgery cannot be done on every patient. Each face is different — different bone structure and soft tissue volume — and we all age differently based on genetics and many other factors. Each face lift should therefore be different."

PREPARATION

Your surgeon will give you instructions about how to prepare for your surgery. Smoking can have a profoundly negative effect on healing and blood flow, and for some procedures including face lift, it can seriously compromise your chances for an optimal outcome. If you smoke, your surgeon may ask you to quit for a while before and after surgery. He or she will also give you guidelines on eating, drinking and medications, such as avoiding aspirin or anti-inflammatory medications that promote bleeding.

Preparation specific to a face lift might include letting your hair grow out if it is currently cut very short, because longer hair will better enable you to hide the incisions while they heal.

As with all surgery in general, whether performed in an outpatient facility or in the hospital, you should arrange to have someone drive you to and from surgery and to assist you for a day or two after you return home.

THE SURGERY

As with many of the sciences, technical advances in surgery have greatly accelerated. Many aesthetic surgical techniques have relatively recent origins. The classic subcutaneous, or skin-only, face lift, was virtually the only type performed until the 1970s. During the mid-70s, doctors developed techniques to reposition and tighten the deeper tissues of the face and neck, the SMAS (superficial musculo-aponeurotic system) and the platysma muscle complex. The debate as to which of many face lift techniques achieves the best and most long-lasting results is ongoing.

"There is no scientific evidence that proves any one technique is better than any other," states **Stanley Klatsky, MD**, of Lutherville, Maryland. "In face lift surgery, it's not how you play the game, but whether you win or lose that counts — that is, what technique works best in your hands. As plastic surgeons, our goal is to design the surgery so that it makes our patients look good but not strangely different. We also want operations that don't cause distortion of the tissues and that allow patients to successfully undergo secondary procedures in the future, should they choose to do so."

"To achieve the highest degree of patient satisfaction, the aesthetic surgeon must be comfortable with a variety of surgical and nonsurgical approaches to facial rejuvenation," points out **Robert Zubowski, MD**, of Paramus, New Jersey. "Patients' desires and expectations differ; therefore, matching the procedure or technique with each patient's expectations for results and recovery is crucial for a successful outcome."

"During my career, I have witnessed the evolution in face lift surgery," agrees **Lawrence S. Reed, MD**, of New York, New York, "starting with the simple skin lift to some highly complex and, in many cases, undesirable approaches and, finally, to an approach that involves a good understanding of the anatomy and restructuring of the underlying foundation. The addition of adjunctive nonsurgical procedures to enhance and maintain results has been important, but perhaps more important is the recognition by patients and physicians alike that a natural result is the best result."

"Today's face lift techniques that deal more with the underlying structures are more complicated but allow us to achieve a very natural-looking result," says Dr. Apesos. "Incisions are placed inconspicuously, and the

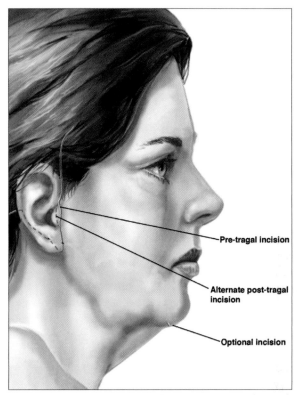

Pre-tragal incision

Alternate post-tragal incision

Optional incision

A common incision pattern for a traditional face lift starts in the temple region within the hair or just under the sideburn, closely follows natural creases in front of the ear (pre-tragal) or, for a short distance, just inside the ear (post-tragal), and continues behind the ear to end in the hair. If necessary, a small incision underneath the chin may provide further access to the neck.

overall result is a healthy, rested appearance that does not look like you've had surgery."

Additional techniques and types of face lift procedures include the subperiosteal face lift, which may be performed using an endoscope, as well as the less extensive short scar technique, and the midface or cheek lift.

"The seemingly endless variety of approaches to correct a specific problem suggests the obvious: any number of techniques properly applied can yield satisfactory results. Whichever method is used, incisions must be placed so that they will heal well, and great attention to technique and detail will result in scars that will be almost imperceptible," says **Jack A. Friedland, MD**, of Scottsdale, Arizona.

"It must be the goal of every face lift to conceal each and every incision, because what has this procedure truly accomplished if a patient becomes burdened by unsightly, visible scars," adds **Jonathan H. Sherwyn, MD**, of New York, New York. "I tell patients during the consultation, as a matter of record, that they will be able to wear their hair in a ponytail or any style they choose, without any evidence that they have undergone facial rejuvenation surgery. Toward this end, incisions are placed along the margin of the ear, as opposed to in front of the ear, and attention given to re-creating the ear's normal architecture as well as to the location of the sideburn, the incision behind the ear, and the quality of the line of closure."

"No one technique is perfect for every patient," says **Rafael C. Cabrera, MD**, of Boca Raton, Florida. "I do my assessment of each patient individually, carefully and thoroughly, to design a customized operation for them using tried and true techniques. The anatomy should be what determines the technique rather than the other way around. What we want is a natural, pleasing result without any stigma of surgery — that classic, freshened appearance that is everybody's goal."

Dr. Anson agrees, "There is no single type of face lift that is suitable for every person. Rather, I utilize a variety of techniques including mini-face lifts, full face lifts, and midface lifts. My technique for tightening the underlying structures of the face beneath the skin will also vary. Each face is unique, and plastic surgeons have a wide range of techniques and procedures from which to choose so that we can treat each patient on an individual basis."

"Face lift surgery has changed dramatically in recent years," says **Mark Sofonio, MD**, of Palm Springs, California. "We specialize in a more natural-appearing face lift — where the tension of the surgery is placed in the deeper muscle layer, not in the superficial skin layer. This allows the face to appear refreshed and youthful without looking pulled. In addition, the nasolabial folds may be treated separately with a midface lift, which gently softens the folds and give the cheeks a fuller appearance."

Craig Dufresne, MD, of Chevy Chase, Maryland, tells us, "With the techniques available today, we can not only manipulate the soft tissues but actually alter the skeleton — which secondarily changes the soft tissue relationships. To me the ideal aesthetic result is based partly on scientific techniques but also on the surgeon's artistic solutions. Actually sculpting the patient's facial skeleton to enhance the beauty, proportion, and facial balance yields an improved but still natural appearance."

Dr. Sargent agrees. "What is often overlooked about the face is that the facial skeleton shape and contour play extremely important roles in facial aesthetics and rejuvenation. Restoring or replacing the volume lost with aging, either with alloplastic implants or some of the newer soft tissue fillers, can have a tremendous benefit."

Most patients favor a natural look. The goal of facial rejuvenation surgery is to offer significant improvement without drastic change. Patients want to hear people comment that they look rested or refreshed. They like to be asked if perhaps they've been on vacation, not if they've had surgery.

"Over the years that I've been in plastic surgery practice, I've witnessed an evolution in technique," says **James L. Baker, MD**, of Winter Park, Florida. "Back in the 60s and 70s, we just pulled skin, and patients looked like they'd had surgery. Now, the ideal is to have a very natural-looking result. When plastic surgeons started working with the SMAS, it changed everything. I generally do a strip SMASectemy, where I just cut a strip of the SMAS and plicate it, or I'll do a SMAS elevation, depending on the patient. These techniques produce an excellent, long-lasting result with minimum downtime."

Chester Sakura, MD, of Albuquerque, New Mexico, adds, "I believe optimal results are achieved by deep tissue support rather than relying on the skin for lifting and tightening. Skin is not designed to remain tight under tension, and it will stretch when pulled. Repeated face lifts that only tighten skin accentuate the loss of skin elasticity, resulting in a drawn or 'wind-tunnel' look. Deep plane face lifts, on the other hand, involve lifting the supporting structures such as the platysma muscle and the SMAS fascia. These tissues are able to remain tight for a prolonged period, and I believe this type of face lift creates a more natural, long-lasting correction."

And **David G. Genecov, MD**, of Dallas, Texas, adds, "I reposition the soft tissues in such a way that patients look rested and refreshed, but not like they've had a face lift. This is possible using a variety of techniques, and I tailor the treatment to the individual. I avoid any technique that puts a lot of tension on the skin. I also use fat to increase facial volume, and in some cases perform bony advancement, such as moving the cheekbones, to create a more sculpted look. For many of my patients, I add laser treatments or chemical peels to improve the texture of their skin."

"Surgeons talk about proper vectors of pull, and I think that's important. The skin and deep tissues should be handled as two separate planes. You want to elevate the deep tissue, but you don't want to pull upward on the skin, which creates a very operated look. There should be a vertical lift of the deep tissue and a natural redraping of the skin over it," says Dr. Rand.

The incisions for a standard face lift usually are hidden in the hairline and begin at the temples. They generally extend down in front of the ear (hidden within natural creases), or just inside the cartilage at the front of the ear, and continue behind the earlobe to the lower scalp. When work is being done on the neck, a small incision may also be made under the chin.

"From patient to patient, there are rather discrete differences in the best location for the incisions, though placement will be more or less similar," says Dr. Fine. "The goal is to camouflage the final scars. I prefer to place incisions within the hair-bearing skin as much as possible."

SUBCUTANEOUS (SKIN ONLY)

Although the number of skin-only face lifts has declined considerably since the introduction of the SMAS technique in the mid-1970s, some surgeons still find this method applicable and effective. The subcutaneous face lift comprises the separation of the top layer of skin from the fat and muscle below. The surgeon then pulls the skin in an uplifted direction, redraping it and removing the excess. If necessary, fat may also be removed or recontoured. The result is a smoother, more youthful facial appearance. Incisions are closed with stitches, sometimes in conjunction with a substance called "tissue glue." Metal clips may be used in the scalp area.

SMAS

The SMAS (superficial musculo-aponeurotic system) face lift addresses not only the superficial top layer of skin but also the deeper tissue layer. In the face, this deeper layer is a sheet of muscle and fibrous connective tissue. A broad muscle, called the platysma, comprises the deeper layer in the neck area. A skilled plastic surgeon who has experience performing this procedure can achieve excellent results while avoiding damage to other even deeper anatomic structures.

"In my opinion, the SMAS is the workhorse of the face lift," says **Michael R. Schwartz, MD**, of Camarillo, California. "It holds the tension so that the skin doesn't have to. If you let the SMAS do the work, it allows the skin to redrape more naturally and prevents tension on the scars so they can heal almost imperceptibly."

"If you pull the skin, you create an artificially tight appearance," agrees **Donald W. Hause, MD**, of Sacramento, California. "The key to a natural-looking face lift is repositioning soft tissue, then re-draping the skin over the new contour, which gives you a much more elegant and sophisticated look. The extended SMAS lift is a powerful technique because it moves the underlying tissues very precisely and in the right direction, or vector, to restore a more youthful facial contour."

"People tend to focus on the skin, but it's really the muscle and fat beneath the skin that descend and thereby pull the skin down," says **Michael Kane, MD**, of New York, New York, "so rather than pulling on the skin to 'tighten' the face, the results are much better by elevating the fat and muscle and then just trimming off the excess skin."

The SMAS face lift repositions and tightens the underlying tissue layers, which tend to grow lax and sag with aging. The skin is then redraped over this rejuvenated framework. This procedure generally produces a natural-looking result that is long-lasting, though the longevity of results for any type of face lift depends to some extent on individual patient factors.

"My technique, which I call the anterior vertical SMAS lift, takes elements of several popular face lift techniques and combines them in a unique way to achieve natural-looking, long-lasting results with fewer scars," says **Robert W. Bernard, MD**, of White Plains, New York. "One of the reasons why SMAS techniques last so well is because the lift is supported by the underlying structures of the face. I achieve this support without undermining the tissues as extensively as with some other techniques, and this increases the safety of the operation while decreasing recovery time."

Dr. Bernard also pays close attention to facial sculpting. "A deep sternomandibular trough — the area of shadow just beneath the curve of the jawline — typically is one of the features that make a model's face look so finely chiseled," he says. "I use a special sculpting technique to contour this area and, in women with poor definition, to create a deeper trough."

Archibald S. Miller, MD, of Tulsa, Oklahoma, explains his approach this way, "I find it very important to use a multi-plane technique, dissecting both skin and SMAS, and to tighten in different directions to avoid that wind-tunnel look. Also, when elevating and tightening the skin, finding the correct angle of pull is critical, and it is different for the facial skin in front of the ear versus the neck skin behind the ear. These details can make the difference between an excellent face lift and a poor one."

Daniel C. Morello, MD, of White Plains, New York, offers this insight about the SMAS. "I use the SMAS as a 'handle' to lift up the soft tissues of the face. Sometimes I may need to dissect the SMAS only one inch to achieve the movement I want, and other times I may need two inches. Every patient is different and requires an individualized approach."

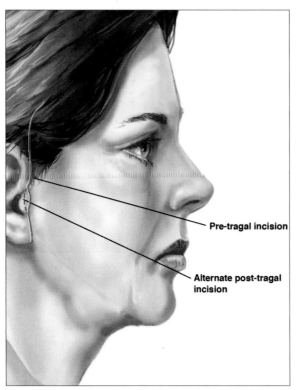

Pre-tragal incision

Alternate post-tragal incision

A typical "short scar" incision is limited to the temple and the ear but may be extended behind the ear as required. Other types of short-scar patterns may be used, depending on the patient's needs and surgeon's preference.

Repositioning of the SMAS layer is one way to add volume to the cheeks, which gives the face a more youthful contour.

"The SMAS can be elevated and positioned according to what each person needs," says Francine Vagotis, MD, of Grand Rapids, Michigan. "Not everyone's facial aging is exactly the same. The beauty of it is that it's not a cookie-cutter operation and can be tailored to each individual."

While the SMAS technique has definite benefits that compare favorably with a skin-only procedure, it is a more extensive operation that may involve a slightly longer recovery.

SHORT SCAR

A short scar lift refers to an incision pattern, rather than a distinct technique. While there are different ways to perform a short scar face lift and different incision patterns, one common approach is to use an S-shaped incision placed at the temple and in front of the ear. Unlike a conventional face lift, the incision does not extend behind the ear.

"Though the 'S' incision is small, we can effectively re-suspend tissues to support the smile lines and jowl and also address the loose skin that accompanies facial aging," says Peter E. Johnson, MD, of Des Plaines, Illinois. "The smaller incisions contribute to reduced swelling and bruising, shorter recovery, and a very safe procedure overall."

Mark P. Solomon, MD, of Bala Cynwyd, Pennsylvania, comments, "With the short scar face lift, we use smaller incisions but do a lot beneath the skin. After all, it is the structures beneath the skin that really define our facial contours and appearance. If we reposition what is underneath, restoring it to a higher and more youthful position, the skin can be nicely redraped to achieve a rejuvenated appearance."

"Using a short scar technique, I can get both a vertical pull and a horizontal pull precisely where they are needed," says Howard Dawkins, MD, of Greenville, North Carolina. "The nice thing about this technique is that one need not worry about scarring behind the ears."

Although the short scar lift allows a woman to wear her hair pulled back without fear of revealing a scar, the surgeon's ability to eliminate loose, sagging skin in the lower face and neck may be limited by this incision placement compared to more traditional lifts. That's why some surgeons reserve this type of lift for younger individuals who have minimal to moderate excess skin and do not need extensive correction of the neck.

"I perform a lot of limited-incision face lifts on women in their 50s. My patients generally want to be back at work in a week or two, and I get a nice result without going behind the ear or significantly into the scalp," says **Malcolm Z. Roth, MD**, of New York, New York.

"I try to use minimal incisions whenever I can," says **Paul. M. Parker, MD**, of Paramus, New Jersey. "The best way to achieve a natural-looking result is by restoring volume, moving fat from where it is now to where it should be, or where it used to be. Recently I had a patient who said that she had chosen not to tell her co-workers about her surgery, and they really couldn't tell. She said that they think she's lost weight, or changed her hairstyle, or just gotten more rest. She just looks better — rejuvenated — and they don't know why. I consider that a success."

Dr. Domanskis says, "Almost none among the myriad of small-incision facial rejuvenation techniques removes excess skin, and patients may have to make a trade-off of less-than-perfect results for a shorter scar. In my experience, patient selection is very important. This procedure is best reserved for someone who does not want the more extensive scars and longer recovery of a traditional face lift and who will be satisfied with less improvement."

"For many younger patients, from the early 40s to mid-50s," says **Robert Anderson, MD**, of Fort Worth, Texas, "the limited-incision face lift can provide significant benefits with fewer complications and less recovery time. In combination with this procedure, I also find it very beneficial to liposuction the jowls, through a small stab incision in the nasolabial fold, which reduces the volume of the jowls and provides for more redraping of the cheek skin to achieve better results in the lower cheek and jowl areas."

Dr. Genter adds, "It's particularly important in the mini, or short scar, face lift to be very careful with the direction and amount of pull in order to achieve a natural-looking result. While too much horizontal pull can result in the undesirable wind-tunnel look, too much vertical pull can create waviness in the lower face. I am also extremely careful to place the incision below the sideburn; this avoids lifting the sideburn above the ear, which can be a telltale sign that surgery was performed."

Another surgical approach for facial rejuvenation consists of using an endoscope. This minimally invasive technology is, in principle, similar to arthroscopic surgery for other body parts such as knee surgery and gallbladder removal. The endoscopic approach works well for patients whose aging is primarily in the upper (forehead) and the middle (midface) facial areas; it is not well suited for rejuvenation of the neck.

Among the many variations of short scar techniques is the MACS lift. "With the MACS lift, the incision stops right at the earlobe. You don't have an incision behind the ear or back into the scalp," says **Karl O. Wustrack, MD**, of West Linn, Oregon. "The vertical pull directly counters the effects of aging and creates a very natural effect. Because there is less undermining and dissection, there is less postoperative swelling and recovery is generally quicker."

ENDOSCOPIC

The endoscope, a pencil-shaped probe containing a tiny camera, transmits video images of the body's internal structures to a television monitor in the operating room. By allowing the surgeon to effectively see beneath the skin, endoscopic surgery can minimize the invasiveness of

Tissue Glue

FIBRIN SEALANT

Tissue glue, a surgical sealant and adhesive, has been used for decades in Europe and was approved by the U.S. Food and Drug Administration (FDA) for use in the United States in 1998. Tissue glue, or fibrin sealant, is derived from human plasma. Fibrin is a natural clotting substance, and most people have observed it in its natural state. When someone scrapes their skin and the wound weeps a substance that forms the scab, that substance is fibrin.

Used with a variety of procedures in aesthetic plastic surgery, including endoscopic and traditional face lifts, brow lifts, abdominoplasties, and laser resurfacing, many surgeons believe that by duplicating the body's normal healing process in an accelerated way, fibrin sealant can aid healing and speed recovery times. In some instances, tissue glue is used in lieu of sutures. Proponents claim that the "pin pricking" and irritation some patients feel as they heal can be eliminated with fibrin sealant.

Tissue glue advocates also claim that using the substance when performing a face lift produces a better-quality scar and assists healing due to an easing of the tension across the incisions. When applied along the incision line, the tissue glue closes off severed or broken capillaries and seals the incision within minutes. Researchers state that about 70 percent of the sealing effect occurs within the first 10 minutes, and full strength is achieved within two hours. The tissue glue is completely absorbed by the body within 10 days, which eliminates the need for suture removal. In addition to acting as a sealing agent, tissue glue helps stop unnecessary bleeding during surgery, which some surgeons say markedly reduces bruising, seroma formation (collection of clear fluid beneath the skin), and speeds healing and recovery times.

Beyond closing incisions and reducing bleeding and bruising, another important use of fibrin sealant is to secure elevated tissues of the forehead, face, and neck in the most favorable position for healing. Fibrin glue is sprayed on and provides even fixation over the entire tissue surface.

Rick J. Smith, MD, of East Lansing, Michigan, uses tissue glue in conjunction with laser skin resurfacing to aid in healing. "I feel that it makes a huge difference as far as healing time, drainage, and crusting," he says. "With laser resurfacing, essentially you are creating a wound over the entire face. Fibrin sealant provides a fibrin clot to seal off the nerve endings as well as the lymphatic vessels, so there's a lot less oozing and much less discomfort because the nerves are not exposed. It promotes the ability of the skin to heal itself."

Although many surgeons are enthusiastic about the benefits of tissue glue, the cost of the material and preparation time may mean additional expense for the patient. And although all fibrin sealants used in the United States are made from blood plasma taken from carefully screened donors and rigorously tested to eliminate hepatitis viruses, HIV-1, and parvovirus, as with all plasma-derived products the possibility for transmission of infectious agents cannot be completely ruled out. Fibrin sealants are generally not advised for individuals who are known to have anaphylactic or severe systemic reaction to human blood products. Allergic reactions, although rare, can occur. These can be mitigated by manufacturing the sealant using the patient's own blood, but this is a complex and even more expensive process.

procedures and reduce the size of incisions. The endoscopic face lift may be an option for patients without a significant amount of excess skin.

"The use of the endoscope and facial lipocontouring has helped extend the benefits of the face lift and forehead lift approaches to younger patients, even those in their late 30s and early 40s," says **Joseph Michael Pober, MD**, of New York, New York. "The best candidates are those with minimal excess skin who have developed drooping brows, sagging or flattened cheeks, or folds around the mouth. Patients in their late 40s (and early 50s) with similar problems as well as early jowls and neck fat also can benefit from the advances of endoscopic surgery. Neck lifts can be performed using a tiny incision underneath the chin and in the posterior scalp, creating no noticeable scars around the ears."

Richard D. Anderson, MD, of Scottsdale, Arizona, adds, "An endoscopic face lift can provide significant, long-lasting benefits, particularly to relatively younger patients without significant skin excess but with upper and middle face changes, including: sagging brows, forehead frown lines, sagging of the midface and cheek areas with prominent cheek folds, hollowing under the eyes, drooping of the lateral corner of the mouth area, and jowl changes along the jawline. By lifting tissues up, rather than pulling back, we can restore a more youthful look with a rested, refreshed, and very natural appearance. I have many patients who demonstrate persistent and lasting improvement for six or seven years and even longer. The endoscopic face lift can also be paired with a neck lift, eyelid surgery, cheek or chin augmentation, skin resurfacing, and other cosmetic facial procedures."

Some surgeons believe that the advantages of endoscopic face lifting include reduced scarring, less risk of facial nerve damage, minimized bleeding and swelling, and a potentially quicker recovery.

Charles Spenler, MD, of Torrance, California, adds, "Endoscopic facial rejuvenation surgeries are becoming more popular, and their popularity will most likely continue to increase."

MIDFACE/CHEEK LIFT

While a face lift will improve the lower third of the face, a midface lift, also called a cheek lift, addresses problems in the middle third of the face. These include accentuated nasolabial folds (creases running from the base of the nose to the sides of the mouth), a hollow

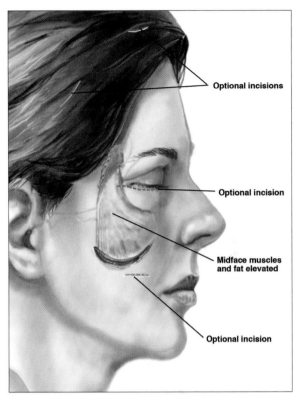

The midface may be elevated, either as a separate procedure or in conjunction with a face lift or other aesthetic procedures. Incisions may be in the temple and inside the mouth, or inside the lower eyelid. The dissection is in a plane deep to the periosteum (the tough layer covering the cheek bone) allowing the midface soft tissues to be elevated and secured in a more youthful position.

appearance between the upper cheeks and lower eyelid, and fatty bags in the upper cheek area just below the lower eyelids.

"When you see a younger person, you see a diamond-shaped face with high cheeks," says Dr. Apesos. "Someone who has aged gracefully still has high cheeks. A flat midface produces an aged-looking face, and pulling the skin back toward the ears and the scalp flattens the midface. With a midface lift, we pull the tissues in a vertical direction, toward the eyes, which gives a high cheek effect."

"The traditional face lift utilizes incisions from the ear into the hairline, and it works well for the lower face, jowls, nasolabial folds, and neck. But there are many younger patients who show aging in their midface, from the corner of their eye socket down to about the base of the nose and the corner of the mouth," agrees **William G. Loutfy, MD**, of Albuquerque, New Mexico. "That whole region is suspended by the zygomatic ligament. A midface lift allows us to pull that ligament vertically, rather than back as with a traditional face lift."

"With aging, the lower eyelid-cheek junction often hollows out as a result of tissue descent in the midface," explains **John P. Zimmermann, MD**, of Napa, California. "Grafting fat or using fillers provides only a temporary solution. Instead, a midface lift using an incision inside the lower eyelid allows us to elevate the cheek fat and use it to fill in this hollowed-out area. If there is any skin excess, it can be trimmed or, if there is only a small amount of excess, it can be lasered to achieve mild tightening."

The cheek lift is perfect for those whose aging has occurred primarily in the midface area and can be performed as an isolated procedure. However, it often is performed in conjunction with a face lift to maintain facial integrity and harmony.

Daniel C. Mills, MD, of Laguna Beach, California, adds, "Patients who may be concerned with deep lines from the nose to the outer corner of the mouth, or with a downturn at the corners of the mouth, or with a bulge of cheek tissue that may have slipped below the cheekbone, may be candidates for a midface suspension procedure with other face lift procedures. The midface suspension I perform is accomplished through a lower eyelid incision, just underneath the lashes, or through an intraoral incision, mobilizing and lifting the cheek tissues, and suspending them with an anchor suture in the temporal hairline."

"There are several approaches to the midface, depending upon the severity of aging," offers **Julius W. Few, MD**, of Chicago, Illinois. "If aging is moderate, I prefer to go in through a lower eyelid incision. In more severe cases, such as when a patient has malar bags that appear as mounds of fat in the upper cheek, I will often combine a cheek lift with a face lift."

The endoscopic technique has become a popular method for performing this procedure. Incisions for the endoscopic midface lift are very small and may be placed inconspicuously within the hairline and inside the mouth.

"Endoscopic midface and brow lifts apply the same principles and are minimally invasive," explains R. Laurence Berkowitz, MD, of Campbell, California. "I prefer performing these procedures endoscopically to avoid possible complications of other techniques."

Sometimes the procedure is performed in conjunction with eyelid surgery, and incisions are placed within the lower eyelids. Using an endoscope, the surgeon works through these short incisions to reposition the cheek tissues up and over the cheekbones, restoring them to their proper position.

Although the endoscopic approach is widely used, many surgeons still prefer an open technique, through which they can gain better access to the face's structural layers. Like a face lift, a cheek lift may be performed in the deeper or more superficial tissue layers.

"The midface lift should be done cautiously and conservatively," offers **Hamid Massiha, MD**, of Metairie/New Orleans, Louisiana. "If you lift too much, gravity may pull the lower lid down. When performing the lift through a lower eyelid incision, you may also perform a canthopexy, which tightens the lower lid and beautifies the eyelid-cheek junction."

"I make a little incision about one inch behind the hairline and come down into the midface, usually right on top of bone," says **Hervè Gentile, MD**, of Corpus Christi, Texas. "I change planes multiple times, which is more complicated than the traditional approach but is an excellent method of improving the cheeks and the area just below the eyes."

"A youthful face is wider at the top and narrower at the chin. As we age, this is reversed; we lose fat in the upper part of the face as it sags and accumulates in the jowls and neck," says **George Marosan, MD**, of Bellevue, Washington. "Rather than the artificial appearance created by many lifting techniques, where the skin is pulled back at a 45-degree angle, the subperiosteal mid-cheek lift restores fullness to the upper part of the face by repositioning the soft tissues over the bony structure. Often, I also do some fat grafting around the lips and nasolabial folds for further volume enhancement."

The subperiosteal cheek lift, usually performed through incisions inside the mouth and/or at the temple or within the lower eyelids, is the deepest lift. The deep tissues are lifted from the cheekbone and re-suspended higher on the bone to restore a more youthful appearance. A trained and experienced plastic surgeon is careful to avoid damage to the delicate facial nerves. Cheek lift techniques are demanding and complex, and recovery for a subperiosteal approach can be significantly longer than for many other face lift techniques.

"A midface procedure gives exceptional results when done properly by an experienced surgeon," says **Edward O. Terino, MD**, of Thousand Oaks, California. "However, the convalescent time to look really good is greater with a midface suspension operation than a standard face lift. This must be taken into consideration by the patient before having the procedure done."

SUTURE SUSPENSION TECHNIQUES

An outpatient procedure usually performed under local anesthetic, the percutaneous cheek lift may be considered less invasive than some other methods of midface lifting. The percutaneous cheek lift uses securely anchored sutures, sometimes with barbs, to elevate and suspend sagging tissues in the cheek area. The sutures are inserted through small incisions in the temporal hairline, passing through the malar cheek pad and exiting through tiny incisions in the nasolabial folds. To achieve a more vertical pull, a suture may also be placed through the lower eyelid.

Kulwant S. Bhangoo, MD, of Buffalo, New York, offers further commentary on the use of Contour Threads. "Although not a substitute for a conventional face lift, the thread lift can provide benefits, with minimal or no visible scarring and very little downtime. The concept of the thread lift has been around for quite some time, but the smooth threads used with older methods did not yield as good results. The breakthrough came in the development of a new type of barbed suture, which I now use. These are inserted through a small incision at the hairline in the temple, snaked through to the areas that needs to be lifted, and then pulled in the opposite direction, which engages the barbs uniformly all along the thread and creates a uniform pull."

Dr. Hyans agrees, "While not equivalent to a full face lift, the thread lift is very efficacious for people who don't need or don't want to undergo a more invasive procedure. It can be tailored to specific areas, such as the midface, brow, neck, or jowls, depending on what the patient's needs are, and all can be done through minimal incisions. It can also be combined with other procedures such as liposuction, blepharoplasty, Botox or Restylane injections."

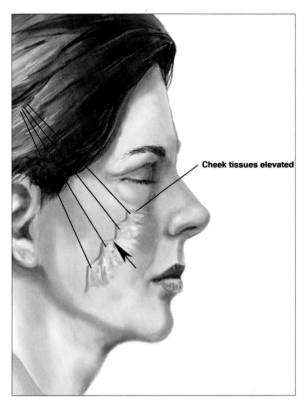

Cheek tissues elevated

Soft tissues of the midface may be elevated and suspended using non-absorbable sutures designed with barbs, cones, knots, or other devices to aid tissue fixation.

While procedures using barbed sutures, or similar devices, may offer patients a relatively quick fix with potentially less downtime and inconvenience, as these board-certified plastic surgeons point out, they are not a substitute for more traditional procedures.

George Sanders, MD, of Encino, California, says, "Patients today have many choices. On one hand, there is the traditional face lift that has long-lasting results, and on the other hand there are nonsurgical procedures such as injectable fillers that are less expensive and may have little or no recovery time but provide only temporary results. And in between we have suture suspension techniques and lasers that allow a certain degree of tightening or lifting of the skin with less inconvenience and downtime than traditional methods."

While there is controversy regarding the benefits of barbed sutures, these techniques seem to have found a following among some surgeons and their patients.

Although not as long-lasting as a more extensive surgical procedures, they can be used as a bridge or stopgap measure to address minimal facial laxity and the patient still has the option of having a full face lift later.

"Once implanted, a thin envelope of scar tissue forms around the sutures," explains Dr. Bhangoo, "and this scar tissue actually helps support the lift. Of course, like any aesthetic procedure, a thread lift may turn back the clock, but it cannot stop it from running. The face will continue to age. And if as a patient grows older they decide they want a surgical face lift, the thread lift will in no way interfere."

John Bruno, MD, of Fort Myers, Florida, finds that the thread lift can sometimes be useful in patients who have had a previous face lift. "Although the technique I use depends completely upon the individual needs of the patient, I have found the thread face lift to be very helpful in a secondary face lift where the patient has had a very good result but years later is having some return of laxity."

Yet not all surgeons are enthusiastic about these devices. As Dr. Vagotis puts it, "The face is not static, and some procedures are. When the face is animated, such as when a patient is smiling, static procedures may become evident."

And even those who find barbed suture, or thread, techniques useful in some cases may find that they have limitations. "My own feeling about using threads in the neck is that they probably will not be very effective if there's much excess skin," says Dr. Bruno.

With some suture suspension techniques, there may be restrictions on facial movement during the initial recovery period. In addition, these "quick" procedures are not necessarily free of complications. Infection, suture visibility and extrusion, to name a few, are not uncommonly reported. While these procedures may be termed "nonsurgical," in fact they require a precise knowledge of the facial anatomy. The skill and experience of your board-certified plastic surgeon are valuable in helping to ensure both the effectiveness and safety of thread lift procedures.

ENDOTINE DEVICE

The Endotine device is yet another method of fixation popular with some surgeons.

"What I consider the next evolutionary phase in midface lifting began with development of a device called the Endotine," says Dr. Loutfy. "After the plastic surgeon has restored the cheek tissue back to a more youthful position, whether through incisions in the temple and the mouth or through a lower eyelid incision, this device secures the cheek tissue in its elevated position until scar tissue forms to hold it in place. The result is a natural-appearing lift that has greater longevity."

"The Endotine for the midface," says **Paul J. LoVerme, MD**, of Verona, New Jersey, "is a unique and effective device that utilizes prong-like tines, providing multiple points of contact, to suspend the delicate midface tissue. The five tines distribute tension over a wide area for increased fullness and less tension. As healing progresses, the Endotine dissolves, leaving an elevated, full, and youthful appearance. A stand-alone procedure in younger people whose primary facial aging may be in the cheek area rather than the lower

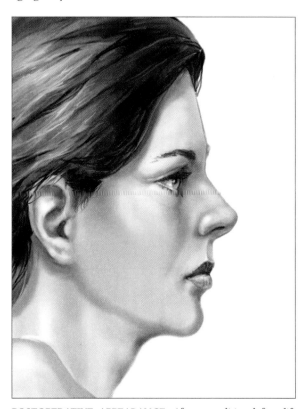

POSTOPERATIVE APPEARANCE. After a traditional face lift procedure, the deeper tissues have been repositioned and the skin trimmed and redraped, restoring a more youthful appearance.

face, this type of midface elevation can be combined with a face lift in patients who also have jowling and neck laxity."

Dr. Zimmermann agrees with the importance of adequate tissue fixation in the midface, "The approach used to be to elevate the soft tissue of the cheek off the bone and use sutures to secure the tissues at a higher level. The idea was correct, but the technique had several problems — mainly, that the sutures would break or pull out of the tissues. The development of absorbable fixation devices for the midface, such as Endotine, has solved this problem. Endotine attaches very securely to the bone and the block of cheek fat that descends with aging. The device absorbs within four to six months and by then the soft tissues have healed securely to the bone."

SECONDARY FACE LIFT

Most face lift procedures are long-lasting, usually seven to 10 years, but this is highly variable and depends on many factors, including the type of lift performed as well as the individual patient's anatomy, heredity, and lifestyle. As a person continues to age, several or many years following a face lift he or she may wish to have a "touch up."

Secondary face lifts usually use incisions similar to the initial operation. Depending on what type of face lift procedure was performed initially, the secondary face lift may not be as extensive as the first.

"If you have had surgery before, you have to work within certain limits. Whether you have a face lift or procedure on any other part of the body, existing scars can limit blood supplies to certain areas — so you have to be more careful when planning the surgery," says Dr. Abramson.

"With a second or third face lift, you may need to modify your technique in order to avoid an 'operated' look," explains **Bruce I. White**, **MD**, of St. Louis, Missouri. "In a first face lift, making the incision in the temporal hairline hides the scar but also widens the space between the lateral eyebrow and the hairline. The second time, it widens that space even further. Of course, each procedure is individualized and depends on the patient, but generally on a second face lift, I would consider making the temporal incision just in front of the hairline. I find that the surgeon's true artistry is most evident not in the first lift, with which most can get a good result, but with the second, third,

or fourth, where keeping the patient from looking like she's had a face lift is much more difficult and requires more skill."

Dr. Genter adds, " I would rather have to do a touch up in six months, to tighten a bit more, than to leave someone looking unnatural for years until the skin loosens up again."

"In some patients undergoing a second face lift, I may put more tension in the neck and temporal area and less in the jawline and nasolabial folds, because putting more tension in those areas will make the face look artificially tight," says Dr. Bruce White.

POST OP

A face lift usually takes from two and a half to four hours to perform. If you are also having additional procedures, such as eyelid surgery or a forehead lift, the total time will, of course, be longer. The procedure can be performed under sedation (twilight) anesthesia, although general anesthesia is frequently used. Whether you are awake and unaware of what is going on, or you are unconscious, you will not feel any pain during the surgical procedure. Most patients are allowed to return home the same day, but an overnight stay may be recommended in some cases.

It is important that your head be kept elevated, cold compresses be applied to your face, and someone stays with you the first night to help you and be alert to any possible problems. A temporary drain, a small, thin tube, may be inserted under the skin behind your ear to draw off any blood that might collect there. You will not feel this at all. Your head may be wrapped loosely in bandages, although not all surgeons believe that this helps minimize bruising and swelling.

Following a face lift, you should limit if not curtail most of your activities and prepare for a few days of pure relaxation. You should continue to elevate your head when you sleep to help minimize swelling and bruising. Most people suffer only mild discomfort. You can anticipate taking pain medication, according to your surgeon's instructions, for about three days; acetaminophen (Tylenol) alone is usually sufficient. Aspirin and certain anti-inflammatory drugs that promote bleeding are to be strictly avoided, as is smoking or exposure to secondhand smoke.

After a couple of days, any drainage tubes and bandages will usually be removed. Don't be shocked by puffiness and discoloration. These are normal. You may also see some unevenness or temporary asymmetry, which is a result of the variance in swelling and bruising and nothing to worry about. Although recovery time can vary greatly among individuals, swelling and bruising usually peak 24 to 48 hours after surgery. While most bruising will greatly improve if not disappear within two weeks, some puffiness may take a while longer to completely resolve. Swelling and bruising will also last longer after a face lift involving the deeper tissues.

"Ideally, you want the minimum of swelling and bruising. You want patients to be able to get back to work and their life as quickly as possible," says Dr. Baker.

"I try to minimize patients' downtime, letting them wash their hair after 48 hours. However, I keep drains in for two to three days, because I think it decreases the amount of edema and swelling," says Dr. Thaller.

"In my experience, patients are most concerned with a rapid recovery," says Dr. Dawkins. "If you choose a technique that has a low risk of complications, little swelling, and allows patients to be back to normal activities in two weeks, they will be much happier."

Although you will be permitted to wear makeup after only a few days to help conceal any discoloration, it will most likely take about two weeks before you will feel comfortable enough with your appearance to go out socially. Some numbness in the facial area may also be present for several weeks or longer. Stitches and staples will be removed usually four to 10 days following your surgery.

You will be instructed to avoid straining, bending, lifting, and any activity that may elevate your blood pressure during the early postoperative period. Typically, but depending on the extensiveness of your procedure, you can expect to resume most of your normal activities within two weeks. You should not begin exercising for at least three to four weeks after surgery, or whenever your surgeon advises. Your surgeon will also advise you to temporarily avoid exposure to direct sunlight, and to use a high-quality UVA/UVB sunscreen for at least six months, (although this is a habit that should really be adopted for the long term). As some minor yet expected "settling" of your lift may occur over time, the final effect will be seen in one to four months.

LOOKING AHEAD

Most patients are extremely happy with their face lift procedure. Beyond being pleased with their more youthful and refreshed appearance, they generally feel revitalized emotionally as well. Whether the results are dramatically apparent or more subtle, confidence is bolstered and spirits are lifted. Not only do patients see a difference in the mirror, but they may have a more positive attitude as well.

This chapter about face lifts includes a tremendous amount of information, which can lead to some confusion in regard to which is the "right" or "best" technique for each individual candidate. The loud and clear message, emphasized by virtually all our experts, is that an individualized approach, custom tailored to each patient, is the key to optimizing the results. There are indeed a multitude of techniques to choose from, and often there is more than one way to obtain a very satisfactory result. For this reason, it is to the patient's benefit to approach his or her face lift consultation with an open mind. Rather than insisting on a particular technique that he or she may have read or heard about, it is often wisest to take into consideration the level of comfort and experience the surgeon has with a given technique. The ultimate result will often be best with a method more familiar to the aesthetic surgeon rather than the one suggested by the patient.

My personal preference, except for patients who require significant rejuvenation of the neck, is an endoscopic approach. This can provide excellent rejuvenation of the forehead and midface and, to a lesser degree, the lower face and neck via a transmitted pull. The incisions are one-half to one-and-a-half inches in length and placed only behind the hairline. The pull is more vertical than with other approaches, recovery is rapid, and results appear very natural. Without getting too technical, the approach I favor is supraperiosteal (above the periosteum) as opposed to subperiosteal, which is one approach mentioned in our chapter. Based on a patient's individual needs, I often combine this technique with the use of cheek and chin implants, soft tissue fillers for volume restoration, and Botox.

I often like to use specially designed barbed sutures for the purpose of fixating the surgically undermined tissues in their elevated position during the healing process. However, the method of the fixation chosen — whether barbed sutures, Endotine, tissue glue or other — is, in my opinion, far less important to the quality of the ultimate result than are many other factors. Specifically, preoperative facial analysis; choice of the appropriate procedure for each candidate, including consideration of extent of tissue undermining and vectors of pull; skillful execution of the surgery; and the surgeon's overall aesthetic sense are critical elements in the entire process of facial rejuvenation surgery. Perhaps even more than for other aesthetic procedures, patients are well served by seeking consultation with more than one qualified face lift surgeon. This can help clarify, for each individual, the various options available to them and also lead to selection of a surgeon who shares their general aesthetic goals and concepts. The likelihood of attaining the desired result is greatly enhanced by this kind of "homework."

— Peter B. Fodor, MD

NECK CONTOURING AND REJUVENATION

If you are bothered by the appearance of your neck, whether because of hereditary fat deposits that create the look of a "double chin" or due to visible signs of aging, there are a number of effective treatments that can help. The neck is often one of the first areas to show early signs of aging. The combination of tissue descent, fat accumulation, and exposure to the elements can have a profound impact on neck contour and skin quality. When the skin becomes slack under the chin, it can create an unattractive "wattle" or "turkey neck." Fat may accumulate in the same area, while the muscles of the neck may become prominent and sometimes appear as vertical cords. Fatty deposits and loose skin can also affect the contour of the jawline. All of these factors contribute to a more aged look.

In many instances, the best and most effective treatment for the neck requires that you undergo a full face lift. That's because so many of the problems of the aging neck are related to the descent of facial tissues, and, in addition, the incisions used for a face lift provide the best access and directional pull to tighten the neck tissues. The face and neck are viewed together and should be in harmony with one another; if there are significant signs of facial aging as well as aging of the neck, correcting only the neck would likely cause your appearance to look "out of sync." Likewise, undergoing a face lift without making corrections to an aged-looking neck would produce a disharmonious overall result.

However, there are some people in whom aging of the neck has occurred at a faster rate than other facial aging. Also, many individuals suffer from hereditary fat

deposits in the neck, which may be apparent even in adolescence. Various surgical procedures, including liposuction to remove excess fat, employing sutures to support the muscles, and excising redundant skin, can give the neck a more pleasing contour and an aesthetically rejuvenated appearance. One or more of these procedures may also be helpful in situations where a significant amount of weight was lost resulting in excess hanging skin which has lost its elasticity and cannot conform to a new, slimmer profile. Neck surgery, often in conjunction with a face lift but sometimes as an isolated procedure, can help to correct this problem and restore a smoother neck contour.

Alexander Majidian, MD, of Calabasas, California, explains, "Many factors can contribute to a fullness of the neck. It can be a combination of muscle, fat, skin, and sometimes glands. As with all procedures, it is important for the surgeon to properly evaluate the patient's condition, understand the underlying causes, and formulate an effective treatment plan."

THE CONSULTATION

The consultation is a time for the surgeon and patient to get to know and feel comfortable with each other. The patient should feel completely confident that the surgeon is fully qualified. If you haven't read sections in the beginning of this book about choosing a surgeon who is certified by the American Board of Plastic Surgery, you may want to do so now. In aesthetic plastic surgery, good communication between surgeon and patient is a vital component of achieving a successful outcome.

Your surgeon will advise you which techniques would be most effective and whether other facial procedures performed in conjunction with treatment of your neck, including a face lift, brow lift, eyelid surgery, or a midface lift, might also help to achieve your overall goals and maintain facial harmony. Frequently, patients who complain of a poorly defined angle between their chin and neck may benefit from insertion of a chin implant to provide greater chin projection.

Your plastic surgeon will need to review your entire medical history, including any medications you may currently be taking, whether you suffer from any allergies or medical conditions, and if you have had any prior surgeries. He or she will examine you to determine the extent of the excess fat and loose skin in your neck and assess the quality of your muscle and skin tone.

Your surgeon should describe the procedure in detail, including where incisions will be placed and how much improvement can realistically be expected. Your surgeon will also discuss anesthesia and where the surgery will be performed.

PREPARATION

Your surgeon will give you instructions about how to prepare for surgery. He or she will also give you guidelines on eating, drinking and medications, such as avoiding aspirin or anti-inflammatory medications that promote bleeding, also detailed in an earlier section of this book.

As with all surgery in general, whether performed in an outpatient facility or in the hospital, you should arrange to have someone drive you to and from surgery and to assist you for a day or two after you return home.

THE SURGERY

LIPOSUCTION (LIPOPLASTY)

If your problem is only excess fat underneath the chin and perhaps along the jawline, you do not have hanging skin, and your skin tone is good, then liposuction alone may be the answer. When liposuction is performed in the area underneath the chin, it is called submental contouring. This procedure may be performed in conjunction with a face and neck lift, or as an isolated procedure. Your surgeon will make one or two small incisions on the underside of the chin and/or in the crease around your earlobes and then insert a thin, hollow tube called a cannula beneath the skin and into the fatty tissue. Using the cannula, the surgeon breaks up and suctions out the excess fat, eliminating your double chin and contouring your neck, with improvement of the angle between your chin and neck.

"I think a well-defined jawline with a sharp line between the face and neck is the hallmark of a youthful face," says **Kulwant S. Bhangoo, MD,**

LENGTH OF SURGERY:
Depending on whether a neck lift alone or in combination with a lower face lift, one to four hours.

ANESTHESIA:
Usually local anesthetic with intravenous sedation, or general anesthesia.

LENGTH OF STAY:
Usually outpatient, home the same day.

RECOVERY:
Initial mild to moderate discomfort; minimal activity for several days; back to work in two to four weeks; swelling and bruising begin to improve in a few days; avoid strenuous exercise for about one month.

SCARS:
Depending on the procedure, scars may be short and nearly undetectable (underneath the chin) or occasionally long and visible but camouflaged (Z-plasty/W-plasty).

RISKS/POSSIBLE COMPLICATIONS:
Serious complications, while possible, are unlikely. Some potential complications can be avoided by carefully following your surgeon's instructions.

In addition to the normal risks associated with anesthesia, other risks include:
• Infection.
• Hematoma: Collection of blood beneath the skin; can be treated without compromising result.
• Seroma: Collection of fluid under skin, usually not severe and does not alter cosmetic result.
• Skin irregularities: Lumpiness or mottling, or relapse of the platysma banding and neck laxity.
• Tightness or numbness: Usually subsides within the first few weeks.

The above-listed risks may be only some of those that your surgeon will discuss with you in greater detail during your consultation.

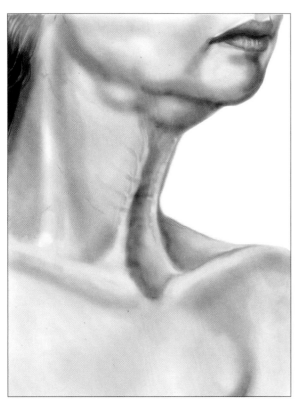

PREOPERATIVE APPEARANCE. Fat deposits beneath the chin, banding in the neck, and a poorly defined jawline may be treated with various surgical approaches, often but not always requiring a lower or full face lift.

of Buffalo, New York. "Even in younger patients, if they have a double chin or a blunting of the angle between the face and neck, it gives them a less aesthetically appealing appearance than somebody with a sharp jawline. With judicious use of liposuction alone, we can contour a well-defined jawline by removing the fatty deposits under the chin, the so-called 'turkey gobbler' neck. In the past, surgeons thought if you just remove the fat there will be a lot of extra skin that would hang, and so they tended to excise the skin directly, creating unnecessary scarring. When you remove excess fat, you actually need more skin to drape around the newly contoured angles of the neck and jaw. So, you can achieve an excellent result without any cutting or removing of skin at all."

Howard Dawkins, MD, of Greenville, North Carolina, cautions that removal of too much fat from the neck can produce unwanted effects. "If a surgeon were to take out too much of the neck fat, the result would be an unhealthy, emaciated appearance. This is an area where the skill and judgment of the plastic surgeon is critical."

PLATYSMAPLASTY

The platysma is a layer of muscle situated on each side of the neck. With age, it can become loose, and "banding," or vertical cords, can occur. Platysmaplasty allows your surgeon to tighten the superficial neck muscles. This can be combined with performing liposuction of the neck to reduce excess fatty tissue. The procedure will create a smoother neck contour and a better-defined jawline.

If platysmaplasty is performed as an isolated procedure, without a face lift, it may sometimes be accomplished through only a small incision on the underside of the chin. However, your surgeon may recommend other minimal incision techniques to improve your results.

"I do what I call a limited-incision neck lift, which recontours the neck and the lower jowls," says Daniel C. Morello, MD, of White Plains, New York. "Neck skin almost always shrinks nicely following fat removal. So I can use a short incision under the chin and a little U-shaped incision hidden where the earlobe joins the face, and remove no skin. I achieve the effect by wide undermining and manipulation of the deep tissues, removing fat above and below the platysma muscle, and then working on the muscle itself. Approximating the central edges of the muscle in what plastic surgeons call a corset technique, I mold the deep tissues, and re-drape the skin, which will shrink to the new neck contour."

"The most important part of the neck lift is addressing the muscle that causes the 'turkey gobbler' neck," agrees Joseph P. Hunstad, MD, of Charlotte, North Carolina. "Working through a small incision under the chin, I bring together the medial borders of the platysma muscle and tighten the underlying tissues. This tightening or repositioning of the underlying tissues provides a dramatic effect without putting tension on the skin and creating a pulled look."

When there is a significant amount of excess skin and a lower face lift is recommended, your surgeon will probably begin by making incisions under and behind the ears to allow repositioning and trimming of saggy skin. The remaining neck skin is pulled up and back, lifting it into place where it is sutured or fixed with tissue glue, leaving a well-hidden, inconspicuous scar.

"I've found that in planning excisional surgery to improve the neck, the direction of skin pull should be more vertical than horizontal," says Dr. Dawkins. "This creates the most natural-looking result."

As discussed above, your surgeon may specifically address the platysma muscle by making an additional small incision beneath the chin to tighten it, then bring the ends together and suture them at the mid-anterior or front section of the neck. The platysmaplasty leaves no visible scars on the neck, only underneath the chin where the scar will be barely perceptible.

SUTURE SUSPENSION

Some surgeons may want to further support the neck with sutures, mesh or even AlloDerm, which is a material created from banked human skin tissue that has been specially processed for safety. Suture suspension techniques may be used in combination with a face and neck lift, platysmaplasty, or sometimes may be used alone to achieve improvement in the neck contour.

Michael Kane, MD, of New York, New York, says, "I do an operation I call a neck suspension. The keys are removing some of the deep fat, not the superficial fat near the surface, then tightening the platysma muscle and also suspending it with sutures to the bone behind the ear. If there's not a lot of extra skin, you can make the neck look a lot better and limit scarring to the bottom of the chin and behind the ear."

"Most people have some subcutaneous fat, which you can remove with liposuction, and some subplatysmal fat, or fat under the platysma muscle, which isn't accessible with liposuction but nevertheless needs recontouring," explains **Walter L. Erhardt Jr., MD**, of Albany, Georgia. "Frequently we do what I call a submental neck lift. We contour the subcutaneous fat and tighten the submental area. The precise approach depends on many individual patient factors, and there are various options, but I often may use sutures to suspend the muscle, creating a better-defined jawline."

Neck suspension procedures use an internal suture, which is usually inserted through an incision just behind the ear and tunnels along the border of the jawline, running underneath and elevating the platysma muscle before anchoring behind the ear on the other side. When used alone, this technique is best suited for

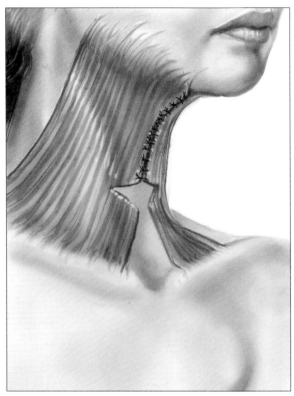

In platsysmaplasty, borders of the platysma muscle, a broad thin muscle lying immediately under the skin, are sutured together, creating a sling to tighten the neck. The only visible scar is under the chin, where it is barely perceptible.

individuals who do not have a significant amount of excess skin in the neck and who may wish to delay having a face lift. The suture is designed to increase jaw definition and create a sharper angle where the jawline meets the neck.

Z-PLASTY OR W-PLASTY

Z-plasty and W-plasty are techniques sometimes used to improve neck contour, usually in mature men who want to correct looseness of the neck without undergoing a face lift.

"For men in their 60s or older who have that 'turkey gobbler' neck," says Dr. Kane, "I may do some direct excision of the skin, and by tilting the scar diagonally with a little Z-shape, it becomes almost undetectable. For these men who don't want a face lift, this is a great procedure that can be done in the office under local anesthesia and once healed, the scars are extremely well hidden."

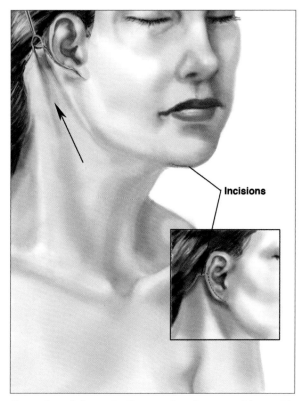

Incisions

Correction of the neck often requires fat removal in combination with muscle tightening and a lower face lift. Once the muscle is tightened, the tissues are repositioned, and excess skin is trimmed. Placement of incisions may vary.

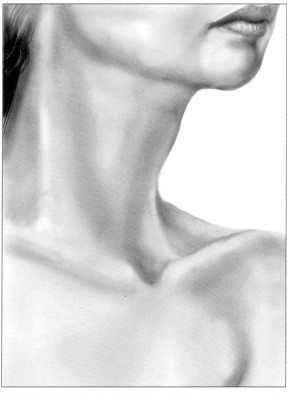

POSTOPERATIVE APPEARANCE. Following surgery, the neck and jawline are better defined, cords are smoothed, and excess fat has been removed from the area beneath the chin.

Z-plasty is performed by creating two triangular flaps of equal dimension that are then transposed to align scars with natural skin folds or the lines of least skin tension. W-plasty is a similar technique used to prevent contracture, (hardening or tightening) of a straight-line scar by trimming the wound's edges in the shape of a W or series of W's. While effective in reducing excess skin, both of these techniques leave a long, visible scar in the front of the neck. That's why these methods have limited application and are generally reserved for men with heavily creased and weathered neck skin, where the scar can blend with existing lines and be somewhat camouflaged. These patients are usually looking for a "quick fix" and are reluctant to undergo a bigger operation associated with a longer recovery.

POST OP

Although there are a number of options for patients seeking improvement to their neck, usually a neck lift is done in conjunction with a face lift, and the total procedure can take between two to four hours. Operating time may be longer if the surgery is done in conjunction with other facial rejuvenation procedures such as a brow lift and eyelid surgery.

If performed alone, treatment of the neck may sometimes be done under sedation (twilight) anesthesia, but general anesthesia is often used. Whether you are awake and unaware of what is going on or you are unconscious, you will not feel any pain during the surgical procedure. These procedures are generally done on an outpatient basis, and patients are allowed to return home the same day.

Immediately following surgery, you will be closely monitored in the recovery area. Generally, you will be wrapped in a gentle pressure dressing, which extends from around the top of the head to underneath the chin. You will most likely still feel quite groggy while in the recovery area, and your neck will probably feel tight and tender as the anesthesia wears off.

You may experience bruising and swelling in your neck, jaw and ears for up to 10 days, and your surgeon will probably advise that you use one or two pillows under your shoulders in bed to slightly extend your neck backward and keep your head and neck elevated (but not bent forward) until the swelling subsides. You might experience some numbness, which is normal and usually lasts no longer than a few weeks. Most people suffer only mild discomfort.

You can anticipate taking pain medication according to your surgeon's instructions for about three days; acetaminophen (Tylenol) alone is often sufficient. Aspirin and certain anti-inflammatory drugs that promote bleeding are to be strictly avoided. If you have undergone a face or neck lift, it is particularly important to avoid smoking or exposure to secondhand smoke. It is normal to experience some mild, periodic discomfort, but any severe pain or excessive swelling should always be reported to your doctor.

The pressure bandage around your head can usually be removed or replaced with an elastic bandage one day following surgery. Your surgeon may instruct you to continue to wear the elastic bandage while you sleep.

You will be advised to avoid straining, bending, lifting, and any activity that may elevate your blood pressure during the early postoperative period. You can expect to resume most of your normal activities within two to three weeks, and you should not begin exercising for three to four weeks after surgery. Although recovery can vary greatly among individuals, you should see early results of your neck contouring within the first week or two, and final results within several months.

LOOKING AHEAD

Most patients who have realistic expectations are highly satisfied with their neck surgery. Of course, the aging process does not stop, and you may at some time in the future decide to undergo a secondary or touch-up procedure. Following platysmaplasty, some surgeons recommend further treatment of the platysma muscles with periodic Botox injections; this helps to keep these muscles relaxed and therefore to prevent a relapse of banding.

Editor's Viewpoint

Customizing the surgical approach for each individual is paramount in achieving the most aesthetic results in neck enhancement. Various choices are available, ranging from liposuction (lipoplasty) with or without chin augmentation to much more extensive operations such as a "corset platysmaplasty" and/or a full face lift. The length of recovery and the extent of scarring vary accordingly, and these are points that require thorough discussion between surgeon and patient during the consultation.

It is also important for patients undergoing some of the more extensive neck procedures to carefully follow postoperative instructions. This can greatly reduce the potential for postoperative complications. If a problem, such as a hematoma (collection of blood underneath the skin), does occur in the immediate postoperative period, the patient should not delay in alerting his or her surgeon. When measures are taken in a timely manner, this type of complication is easily controlled, and the final aesthetic result is not compromised.

Current aesthetic judgment dictates a judicious surgical approach to the neck, which goes a long way toward avoiding an unnatural hollowed-out look or a too-sharp angle of the neck. In general, surgical improvement for sagging neck tissues has shifted in recent years from a backward pull toward a more vertically oriented pull. This evolution in technique has allowed plastic surgeons to produce more pleasing, natural and long-lasting aesthetic improvements for patients seeking neck contouring and rejuvenation.

— Peter B. Fodor, MD

LIP ENHANCEMENT AND PERIORAL REJUVENATION

The sensuality of the lips has been portrayed by artists and hailed by poets for centuries. The facial appearance of many of today's top models and celebrities is characterized by full lips with an accentuated "pout," and this has encouraged greater interest than ever before in a variety of cosmetic procedures to enhance the lips.

Patients who desire lip enhancement fall into two groups; those seeking augmentation of what they feel are genetically thin lips; and those seeking correction of aging changes, including thinning or sagging lips, down-turned corners of the mouth, and other age-associated problems of the perioral (around the mouth) area.

LIP ENHANCEMENT (AUGMENTATION)

Lip augmentation by means of injecting or implanting synthetic or natural products has become a popular way for people to acquire fuller, more pleasantly shaped and sensual lips. Candidates for lip augmentation should be in good physical health, with no medical conditions that would interfere with the procedure's successful outcome. Such conditions might include cold sores, diabetes or lupus, any scarring of the lips, and blood clotting or circulation problems.

INJECTABLES
Among the advantages of injectable soft tissue fillers are minimal downtime and rapid return to normal activity. Injectables provide excellent volume to the lips.

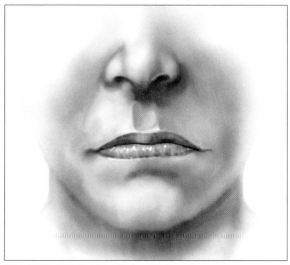

PREOPERATIVE APPEARANCE. Heredity, aging, or a combination of the two may cause thin lips, downturned corners of the mouth, and too wide a space between the base of the nose and the upper lip border.

It must be noted, however, that injectable treatments are very technique-dependent. It is essential that you select a well-qualified and experienced physician to avoid complications and achieve the best possible results.

"For lip enhancement, the ideal injectable material would be safe, relatively permanent, easy to use, require no downtime, and be easily reversed," says **Richard D. Anderson, MD**, of Scottsdale, Arizona. "Unfortunately, the perfect material does not yet exist, but in the meantime, we have several injectables that provide improvement. I recommend that patients first try a temporary injectable such as collagen or hyaluronic acid. The temporary feature of these products actually can be considered an advantage, just in case a patient decides she does not like the result."

Injectable materials commonly used for lip augmentation include collagen, hyaluronic acid products (such as Restylane, Hylaform or Captique), the synthetic filler Radiesse (made from the same mineral compound found in bones and teeth), and fat. The use of bovine collagen requires an allergy test prior to treatment.

"In my practice, the most popular lip injectables are hyaluronic acid preparations. These products are approved for use in the United States and are formulated as injectable gels. They have been used worldwide and do not require skin testing. Their advantage over collagen is a longer-lasting result, which is about six months for lips," says Dr. Anderson.

Mark Sofonio, MD, of Palm Springs, California, adds, "Fillers such as hyaluronic acid (HA), which do not require any tests prior to treatment, provide a simple technique for adding volume to the lips. You may be able to return to work or social activities a day or two after injection with HA; it will take significantly longer for the lips to look 'normal' following fat injection."

Nevertheless, says Dr. Sofonio, many patients like the idea of using fat from their own body to enhance their lips. "A tiny amount of fat is taken from another area of your body, using a small needle attached to a syringe. Sometimes patients who are undergoing liposuction will ask their surgeon to use some of the suctioned fat to augment their lips. After processing to remove excess fluids, the fat is injected to create a fuller, rejuvenated lip "

Injection technique may vary somewhat depending on the product being used. In general, however, the patient should feel little or no discomfort during the procedure.

More details on the nature of the various synthetic and natural substances used in lip enhancement can be found in this book's chapter titled Injectable Treatments for Facial Enhancement.

SURGICAL LIP AUGMENTATION

A surgical technique called V-Y lip advancement is an option for those seeking fuller, well-shaped lips, but is usually preferred for patients who also require correction of a drooping lower lip. You can read about this procedure in this chapter's section on perioral rejuvenation. Most patients seeking lip augmentation opt for injectable soft tissue fillers or surgically placed implants.

Implants used for lip enhancement are inserted through tiny incisions inside the corners of the mouth. Implant materials include products such

LENGTH OF SURGERY
Usually between
30 minutes to two hours.

ANESTHESIA
Typically local anesthetic or local anesthetic and intravenous sedation.

LENGTH OF STAY
Usually outpatient procedure, home the same day.

RECOVERY
Depending upon procedure and individual characteristics, pronounced swelling for one to two days; will be advised to temporarily limit talking or chewing; generally back to normal activities within seven to 10 days.

SCARS
Minimal scarring.

RISKS/POSSIBLE COMPLICATIONS
Serious complications, while possible, are unlikely. Some potential complications can be avoided by carefully following your surgeon's instructions.

In addition to the usual risks associated with anesthesia, other risks include:
• Infection, possibly requiring implant removal.
• Ulceration.
• Asymmetry.
• Numbness or nerve damage, usually temporary.
• Implant hardening, which may require removal.

The above-listed risks may be only some of those that your surgeon will discuss with you in greater detail during your consultation.

as AlloDerm, Gortex, and SoftForm. Another common implant material is dermal fat grafts — excised tissue from the patient's own body often removed in conjunction with another cosmetic procedure such as a face lift. The epidermis is removed, and the fatty tissue layer is inserted as a graft.

"My current favorite implant for lips is AlloDerm, a product derived from human skin and available to doctors through accredited tissue banks," says Dr. Anderson. "This material has been used frequently in burn and reconstructive surgeries and more recently for cosmetic lip augmentation. I have found AlloDerm to provide a natural appearance and natural feel, plus a longer-lasting result, in several hundred of my patients."

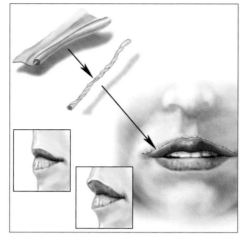

Implants are inserted through incisions inside the corners of the mouth. The implant material, such as rolled AlloDerm, is inserted using a pull-through technique with a specially designed instrument. Alternatively, lip augmentation may be performed using injectable materials.

in conjunction with other facial procedures for which the patient has already been anesthetized. You should plan on having someone drive you home after your procedure.

POST OP

You may experience swelling and some pain immediately following surgery. Oral pain medications will help control any discomfort. Cold compresses used during the first 48 hours will help control the swelling. Talking and chewing should be avoided as much as possible during this period. Your surgeon may also prescribe antibiotics to reduce the possibility of infection.

You will probably feel comfortable returning to your normal activities one to two weeks following surgery. Any non-absorbing stitches will be removed about seven to 10 days after the procedure. Your lips may feel unnaturally stiff for a few days and up to two to three months, depending on the material used for augmentation.

PREPARATION

Your surgeon will give you instructions about how to prepare for your surgery. He or she will also give you guidelines on eating, drinking and medications, such as avoiding aspirin or anti-inflammatory medications that promote bleeding. Because you may have difficulty chewing for a time, have plenty of liquid and soft foods on hand for after your surgery.

THE SURGERY

Implants are inserted surgically through incisions made inside the corners of the mouth. The material is generally made into a tube-like shape and inserted using a needle. Once in place, the implants become integrated with the natural tissues. The outpatient procedure generally takes less than an hour but can range between 30 minutes and two hours, depending on various conditions. Your surgeon will be able to tell you approximately how long your procedure should take. Lip augmentation with implants is usually performed using local anesthetic, although twilight anesthesia, where a sedative is administered along with local anesthetic, is sometimes used. Commonly the surgeries are performed

LIP AND PERIORAL REJUVENATION

Unfortunately, time and natural forces take their toll on the lips and surrounding areas. The area between the nose and the Cupid's bow — the notched center of the upper lip — often elongates with age. In addition to thinning of the lips, people frequently develop a long, sagging upper lip with drooping corners. The lower lip may also sag, revealing the lower teeth when the lips are slightly parted. Various lip-lift techniques can help correct these signs of aging.

Another common problem of the perioral area is vertical wrinkling above the upper lip, creating an aged appearance and causing lipstick to "bleed" onto the skin along the lip border. Perioral rejuvenation often will include not only treatment of the lips themselves, but also techniques to reduce this fine wrinkling. Dermabrasion and chemical peeling of the perioral area are frequently the treatments of choice. You can read more about these methods in this book's chapter, Skin Resurfacing. Botox (botulinum toxin, or BTX) injections may sometimes be used to help smooth wrinkling above the upper lip and, to some extent, to shape the upper lip to create a fuller appearance. It is extremely important that Botox injections of the perioral area be performed by a physician who understands the anatomy of the lip region, since improper placement of BTX in this area can temporarily impair normal function of the lips.

Patients who desire to add volume to the lips may have injections using soft tissue fillers or fat in conjunction with a lip lift. Fillers may also be helpful, sometimes in combination with BTX injections, to soften perioral wrinkles.

"There are several techniques to make the lips look younger, but in general, the fuller the lips, the more youthful the look," says **Steven K. White, Sr., MD**, of Myrtle Beach, South Carolina.

The most common surgical lip lift technique is called the bull-horn lift. In this procedure, a small wedge of skin under the nose is removed to decrease the vertical space between the nose and upper lip. The less commonly performed gull-wing lip lift, often referred to as the vermilion lift, requires an incision along the vermilion border, or the top outline of the upper lip.

Another procedure usually intended to augment or correct drooping of the lower lip is called the V-Y lip augmentation. In this procedure, the surgeon makes one to three small V-shaped incisions in the wet part of the lip inside the mouth.

A relatively simple procedure, called a corner lip lift, can improve what often appears as an angry or extremely taciturn appearance. A corner lip lift creates a more pleasant expression because down-turned corners of the mouth are often associated with aging. This procedure may be performed in conjunction with a face lift or independently. The corner lip lift involves excising a small diamond-shaped piece of the skin just above each corner of the mouth, with incisions made on the exact outer edge of the upper lip. Anesthesia, length of the procedure, recovery and risks are similar as those outlined below for other lip rejuvenation surgeries.

CONSULTATION

The consultation is a time for the surgeon and patient to get to know and feel comfortable with each other. The patient should feel completely confident that the surgeon is fully qualified. If you haven't read sections in the beginning of this book about choosing a surgeon who is certified by the American Board of Plastic Surgery, you may wish to do so now. In aesthetic plastic surgery, good communication between surgeon and patient is a vital component of achieving a successful outcome. Everybody's sense of aesthetics differs. It is extremely important that you tell your surgeon everything that you feel about the appearance of your lips and how you would like them to look, so that you can agree on realistic expectations for this procedure. Your plastic surgeon will need to review your entire medical history, including any medications you may currently be taking, whether you suffer from any allergies or other medical conditions, and if you have had any prior surgeries.

He or she will examine your lips and facial structure and discuss incision placement and the procedural technique he or she recommends.

PREPARATION

Your surgeon will give you instructions about how to prepare for surgery. He or she will also give you guidelines on eating, drinking and medications, such as avoiding aspirin or anti-inflammatory medications that promote bleeding.

THE SURGERY

All of the following outpatient procedures usually take less than an hour to accomplish and can be performed under local anesthesia, although twilight anesthesia, where a sedative is administered along with local anesthetic, is sometimes used. It is a good idea to plan on having someone drive you home after your procedure; this is essential if you have been under sedation.

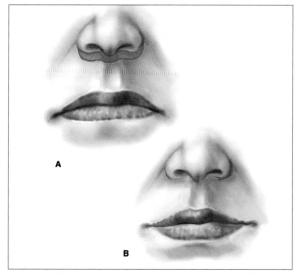

A. One of the more common lip lift techniques, the bull-horn lift removes a wedge of tissue immediately beneath the nose. **B.** The distance between the base of the nose and the upper lip border is reduced, and the incision is closed with very fine sutures, leaving a scar that can be visible in some instances.

BULL-HORN LIFT

The so-called bull-horn lip lift procedure achieves a more youthful upper lip by shortening the space between the lip and the base of the nose, which tends to elongate with age, and by accentuating the Cupid's bow. The incision for this procedure is made directly below the nose.

Before injecting local anesthetic, your surgeon will probably make a series of preoperative markings. These markings create lines of reference that help ensure symmetry and aid in determining the exact dimensions of the incision. Markings often include several points on the base of the nose, from which lines are drawn to the roll on the philtrum, the vertical groove that lies between the base of the nose and the pigmented edge of the upper lip.

The amount of skin to be excised depends on each patient's unique needs. The surgeon usually makes an incision along the curves directly under the nose and excises a portion of the philtrum directly beneath the nose in the shape of a bull's horn.

Post Op

Fortunately, the scars, which can be very well concealed due to the natural folds of the skin below the nose and the shape of the incision itself, are usually very inconspicuous. You may be able to return home as early as one hour after surgery. Discomfort is minimal and can usually be controlled with nonprescription medication. Expect some swelling, peaking in two to three days and subsiding over the following week. Stitches are either dissolvable or will be removed in three to four days. Depending upon your feelings about the visible swelling of your lips, you should be able to return to work within one or two days and resume all activities within one week.

GULL-WING, OR VERMILION, LIP LIFT

While the incision for the bull-horn technique is made directly below the nose, that for the gull-wing lip lift is made directly above the lip, along the vermilion border, at the junction of the colored part of the lip and the philtrum above the top lip. The surgeon excises a strip of skin, suturing the lip to the skin above and thus drawing it upward. The surgeon will usually make a wavy, irregular incision to avoid constriction of the scar. Some surgeons feel that this procedure tends to flatten out the white roll and that it can leave more visible scarring and distortion than the bull-horn technique.

Post Op

There is noticeable swelling for one to two weeks (sometimes more). You may also experience some numbness and difficulty speaking or chewing, which should subside within the first week. Sutures are generally removed within one week of the procedure. Depending on how you feel about your appearance and the degree of swelling, you can usually resume all normal activities within seven to 10 days.

THE V-Y
LIP ADVANCEMENT

This procedure involves one to three small V-shaped incisions made in the wet part of the lip inside the mouth, called the mucosa. The lip lining is elevated and reshaped to enhance the lip contour. Then the incisions are sutured in the shape of a Y, with the V at the top of the Y left open to heal and thus expand the lip. This can be done to either or both the upper and lower lip and results in an advanced "pout" and projection of the lip and or lips.

Post Op

You will probably experience considerable swelling of the lips, which may remain quite pronounced for about

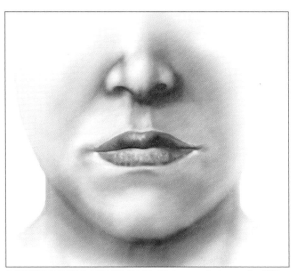

POSTOPERATIVE APPEARANCE. Various techniques for lifting the lips and increasing lip volume can result in fuller lips and a rejuvenated appearance.

two weeks, then subside gradually. Depending on how you feel about your appearance, you should be able to return to your daily activities within seven to 10 days. In some cases swelling, and even numbness, can persist for months.

Editor's Viewpoint

Lip augmentation or rejuvenation procedures are increasingly requested by patients to enhance their overall facial aesthetics. When performing any of these techniques, it is important for the surgeon to exercise good aesthetic judgment in determining the proper amount of augmentation. Over-augmenting the lips, which is not uncommon but is entirely avoidable, invariably creates an unnatural and even "abnormal" appearance. Fortunately in most such instances, the material used for augmentation is absorbable and, therefore, the results are only temporary. However, this is not always the case. Patients seeking lip augmentation may often be well served by starting with a temporary filler to be certain that they are pleased with the amount of volume enhancement before considering longer-lasting or permanent methods.

There are, indeed, significant differences between the various injectable and implantable materials currently available, as well as other surgical options. This diversity is indicative of the fact that the search for an ideal material/method is ongoing. Careful evaluation of the patient's aesthetic goals as well as the perioral anatomy is paramount in selecting the best approach for each individual.

For some patients, recovery time is a major factor in determining which materials or techniques are most appropriate. Duration of postoperative swelling for fat injections and V-Y advancement techniques is often measured in months as opposed to hyaluronic injections and AlloDerm implants where swelling may dissipate in two or three days.

Perioral surgical procedures such as the bull-horn, gull-wing, and corner of the mouth lifts can be effective adjuncts to other facial rejuvenation operations, enhancing overall facial rejuvenation. Meticulous surgical technique is imperative in reducing the visibility of scars when performing these procedures.

— Peter B. Fodor, MD

CHEEK ENHANCEMENT

The cheeks play an important role in defining an attractive face, and well-defined cheekbones have long been recognized as a hallmark of beauty. Sufficient volume of the cheek contour is essential to a youthful appearance. As people age, however, the fat pads that give cheeks their fullness begin to descend, creating a flat visage. In addition, supportive tissue beneath the skin begins to erode, hastening the appearance of lines and wrinkles.

Aesthetic plastic surgery offers various ways to restore a more youthful appearance to the cheeks. In addition to a cheek or midface lift, discussed elsewhere in this book, there are other methods that can enhance cheek volume and improve contour.

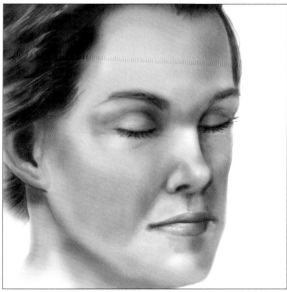

PREOPERATIVE APPEARANCE. Cheekbones that lack projection make the midface area appear flat and long.

The least invasive method of adding or restoring volume to the cheeks is by injections using a biocompatible soft tissue filler or the patient's own fat. Although a pleasing appearance may be achieved, repeat treatments are necessary to achieve or maintain the desired results. For more information on injectables, see the Injectable Treatments for Facial Enhancement chapter in this book.

Implants made of materials such as silicone, Gortex, or AlloDerm can be implanted to add permanent volume and definition to the midface.

Buccal fat reduction is a procedure to remove fat pads from the lower part of the cheeks, achieving a more sculpted look typical of many fashion models. This procedure is generally reserved for individuals with round faces, because removing the fat pads may accelerate an aged look in some individuals.

THE CONSULTATION

The consultation is a time for you and the surgeon to get to know and feel comfortable with each other. You should feel completely confident that the surgeon is fully qualified. If you haven't read sections in the beginning of this book about choosing a surgeon who is certified by the American Board of Plastic Surgery, perhaps you should do so now.

Your surgeon needs to determine if you are a suitable candidate for surgery and will want to review your entire medical history, including your previous dental and sinus history and any medications you may currently be taking. Several factors will be evaluated, including the current contour of your cheeks, your skin texture, bone structure, facial sensation, and muscle function.

"People who would not be suitable for cheek implants are most often those with very round faces or those whose soft tissues are very thick," says

Edward O. Terino, MD, of Thousand Oaks, California. "Cheek implants fill out the face with precision and permanence, so in some cases they may be beneficial for an older patient. But this depends on a variety of factors that need to be carefully evaluated by the plastic surgeon."

Your surgeon will analyze the overall structure of your face and how it can be enhanced, as well as identify and discuss any naturally occurring asymmetries. He or she will explain the details of the recommended procedure, such as incision placement and the type of implants or filler material that will be used. Some implant materials may increase the risk for infection or implant mobility, which in turn may increase the risk of other problems. You should discuss the various types of implants with your surgeon, who will recommend what he or she thinks best meets your overall needs. Your surgeon may discuss other procedures that are often done in conjunction with cheek enhancement, such as face lift, brow lift, or eyelid surgery, if it appears that those areas of your face also need attention to achieve a rejuvenated appearance and maintain facial harmony.

PREPARATION

Your surgeon will give you instructions about how to prepare for your surgery. He or she will also give you guidelines on eating, drinking, and medications, such as avoiding aspirin or anti-inflammatory medications that promote bleeding.

As with all surgery in general, whether performed in an outpatient facility or in the hospital, you should arrange to have someone drive you to and from surgery and to assist you for a day or two after you return home.

THE SURGERY

CHEEK AUGMENTATION

There are a variety of procedures and treatments to enhance your cheeks, and the techniques vary. Some of these involve surgery and some, which use injectable substances to achieve volume, are nonoperative procedures that are discussed in another chapter. The results of soft tissue fillers, whether pharmaceutical fillers or fat, differ from those achieved by facial implants, the latter providing permanent structural changes.

Implants used for cheek augmentation are usually made of medical-grade silicone or another material such as Gortex. They can be placed either over (malar) or under (submalar) the cheekbones. A malar implant will create a heightened curve of the cheekbone, while a submalar implant is generally used to correct a sunken, or hollow looking, midface. Implants are available in a wide variety of sizes and shapes, which allows the surgeon to custom-fit the implant to each patient's face. They may be used in conjunction with facial surgery to correct congenital deficiencies or to rejuvenate or beautify the facial contour.

LENGTH OF SURGERY
Usually 30-90 minutes.

ANESTHESIA
Local anesthetic and intravenous sedation, or general anesthesia.

LENGTH OF STAY
Outpatient procedure, home the same day.

RECOVERY
Initial mild to moderate discomfort; up and about first day; back to work within one week if swelling permits; swelling, bruising mostly gone in two to three weeks; full effect in two months.

SCARS
Undetectable within mouth or behind the lower lid.

RISKS/POSSIBLE COMPLICATIONS
Serious complications, while possible, are unlikely. Some potential complications can be avoided by carefully following your surgeon's instructions.

In addition to the usual risks associated with anesthesia, other risks include:
- Sensory changes: Numbness, pain, and tingling common for two to six weeks; permanent or delayed numbness rare but can result from implant shifting.
- Asymmetry.
- Infection.
- Implant displacement.
- Bone erosion: Rarely a problem.
- Extrusion of implant: Usually requires implant removal.

The above-listed risks may be only some of those that your surgeon will discuss with you in greater detail during your consultation.

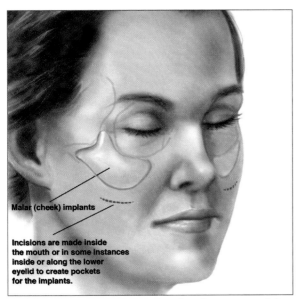

Implants may be positioned either directly on or just below the cheekbone, depending upon the cosmetic goal. Here, implants have been inserted into pockets that are accessed through small incisions inside the mouth to achieve a fuller cheekbone.

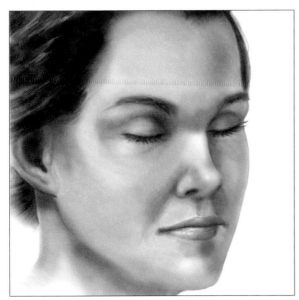

POSTOPERATIVE APPEARANCE. Following surgery, implants fashioned to fit the cheekbones add attractive definition and projection to the midface area.

The incision for cheek implantation usually is made inside the mouth between the cheek and gum. If the procedure is done in conjunction with a face lift or eyelid surgery, the surgeon most often will use the same incisions for insertion of a facial implant.

"Cheek implants are most often inserted through an intra-oral approach, but they can be inserted through a lower eyelid incision," says Dr. Terino. "This approach, however, requires greater experience and expertise on the part of the surgeon. That's because the lower eyelid, generally speaking, is a structure that has to be treated very delicately or it can develop scar tissue leading to complications. If an eyelid incision is used, the surgeon will also need to perform a very secure canthopexy technique to tighten the corner of the eye, preventing the lower lid from pulling down during the healing process."

To insert the implant, the surgeon stretches the tissue to form a pocket in front of the cheekbone and places the implant into the soft tissue, creating the cheek's desired contour. Most surgeons feel that using judicious techniques to develop the proper size and location of the implant pocket is sufficient for securing implants in place. Some may add fine sutures, or specially designed screws may be used to hold the implants in place.

POST OP

Cheek implantation usually takes about 30 to 90 minutes. The procedure can be performed under sedation (twilight) anesthesia although general anesthesia is sometimes used. Whether you are awake and unaware of what is going on, or you are unconscious, you will not feel any pain during the surgical procedure. Cheek implant surgery is an outpatient procedure and patients are generally allowed to return home the same day.

You can expect some tenderness and a tight, stretched feeling for several days. Pain medication, according to your surgeon's instructions, may be needed for about two to three days; acetaminophen (Tylenol) alone is generally sufficient. Aspirin and certain anti-inflammatory drugs that may cause bleeding are to be strictly avoided. Your surgeon will instruct you concerning oral hygiene and very likely put you on an initial diet restricted to liquids and soft foods following surgery.

Bruising may be minimal, but expect swelling to last for two to three weeks. Keeping your head elevated and applying ice frequently can help reduce swelling. Although rigorous activity should be avoided for the first few weeks, you can resume most normal activities in about a week to 10 days. You should protect your skin from the sun while tissues are healing. If skin incisions were used — usually in conjunction with another procedure — stitches will be removed in five days; absorbable stitches used for intra-oral incisions will dissolve by themselves.

You should feel able to return to work within two to five days, however, the degree of your swelling may be a determining factor. Although recovery can vary greatly from individual to individual, and for some, swelling may not completely subside for as much as six months, your final result should usually be evident within two months.

Following intraoral placement of cheek implants, transient reduction of sensation of your upper lip can occur, but this is rarely permanent.

BUCCAL FAT PAD REDUCTION

The buccal fat pad lies beneath the cheekbone. Buccal fat pad reduction enhances the midface area by reducing rather than adding volume. An intra-oral incision, similar to that used for placement of an implant, is made between the cheek and gum. The surgeon will remove buccal fat through this incision to achieve a more refined, sculpted cheek contour. As mentioned earlier, this surgery is recommended primarily for patients with decidedly round, full cheeks. As aging generally causes a certain amount of thinning of the cheeks, excessive removal of the buccal fat can actually accelerate an aged appearance.

There will be some brief swelling after buccal fat reduction, as well as difficulty chewing. And because the patient has undergone surgery involving an intra-oral incision, he or she should generally follow the same postoperative course of care as discussed for cheek augmentation.

LOOKING AHEAD

Most patients are extremely happy with the results of cheek enhancement, whether they have added height and volume to their cheekbones or reduced their "pudgy" cheeks. Even when the change in facial contour is subtle, as is often the case when cheek augmentation is performed to correct a flat malar eminence in a male, this type of surgery nevertheless can produce a significant change in facial aesthetics. Beyond being satisfied with your more aesthetically pleasing appearance, you might feel a surge in self-confidence and a new freedom to experiment with your new "look" by trying a swept-back hairstyle or more dramatic makeup.

Editor's Viewpoint

A younger face is more triangular in shape with the chin representing the tip of the triangle. With aging, as the malar areas descend, jowling occurs and the facial shape becomes more rectangular. In individuals whose facial contours have changed as a result of advancing age, as well as in individuals who have congenitally flat cheek areas, malar augmentation can offer significant enhancement of facial aesthetics. Though implants offer the advantage of a permanent structural change, injectable materials may be a good alternative when a lesser degree of augmentation is sufficient and permanency of the result is not mandatory. In the future, with ongoing evolution of soft tissue fillers, injectable treatments may become an even better option with long-lasting results.

Over-augmentation of the malar area, unfortunately, is not uncommon. Old photographs that illustrate how a patient looked in younger years, before aging impacted the facial contours, may be helpful in determining the optimal enhancement. Similarly, images from beauty magazines can be useful tools for the prospective patient to communicate her or his aesthetic goals to the plastic surgeon during a consultation. Injection of saline, which will absorb quickly and harmlessly, into one side of the face is a further technique that can be useful to more accurately define a patient's desires. When considering modifications to the cheek contour, and especially those that are to be relatively permanent, careful preoperative evaluation and good communication between surgeon and patient are essential components of a happy outcome.

— Peter B. Fodor, MD

CHIN AUGMENTATION AND REDUCTION

The chin and nose are the facial features that most clearly define your profile. An aesthetically pleasing profile is generally considered to be one in which the chin is located 2-3 millimeters behind an imaginary vertical line that extends downward from the foremost point of the upper lip. A chin that projects past this point may be regarded as a "strong" chin, while one that falls far short of this line may be referred to as a "weak" or receding chin.

Since a strong chin and jawline are often identified as signs of masculinity, men may be especially concerned about a receding chin. While in women a chin positioned slightly behind the imaginary vertical line may be acceptable and even sometimes preferred aesthetically, one that recedes too far creates a less flattering profile. A receding chin can also make an otherwise average size nose appear too large.

In some instances, increasing the chin's projection can bring the entire profile into harmony, even eliminating the need for rhinoplasty. In other cases, your surgeon may suggest rhinoplasty in addition to chin augmentation. Chin augmentation is generally performed only after the facial bones are fully developed, usually not before the age of 15 in girls and 17 in boys.

Chin augmentation with implants, genioplasty (where the patient's own chin bone is shifted forward and secured into a new position), or chin reduction surgery can recontour the lower face to create a more pleasing profile.

Chin augmentation can also be achieved through injections of fat or other soft-tissue fillers. For information about these procedures, please see the chapter titled Injectable Treatments for Facial Enhancement.

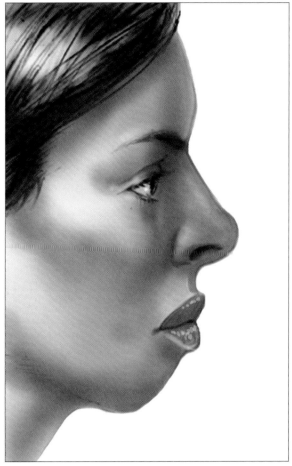

PREOPERATIVE APPEARANCE. A recessive chin causes the lower face to appear underdeveloped and out of harmony with other facial features.

THE CONSULTATION

The consultation is a time for you and your surgeon to get to know and feel comfortable with each other. You should feel completely confident that the surgeon is fully qualified. If you haven't read sections in the beginning of this book about choosing a surgeon who is certified by the American Board of Plastic Surgery, you may wish to do so now.

A board-certified plastic surgeon will determine if you are a suitable candidate for surgery and will want to review your entire medical history, as well as any medications you may currently be taking. Your surgeon will evaluate several factors, including the size and shape of your chin, the angle between your chin and neck, your bite and the condition of your teeth and gums, your skin texture, bone structure, facial sensation, and muscle function. It is also important that any pre-existing asymmetries of your chin or jawline are identified and addressed.

Your surgeon will discuss the overall structure of your face and how modifications to your chin would affect your facial balance. He or she will explain the details of the procedure, such as incision placement and whether or not an implant will be used.

Your goals and the aesthetic judgment of your surgeon are both important factors in determining how your chin contour will be modified. In some cases, the jawline may need to be reshaped, and there are special implants that may be used for this purpose.

"A young female patient I saw in my office, who had a very narrow face, had undergone previous chin augmentation that really had not achieved an aesthetic result. In fact, I felt that her prior surgery had actually made her lower face look more out of balance with her other features," says **Craig Dufresne, MD**, of Chevy Chase, Maryland. "I ultimately removed the chin implant and, instead, recontoured her jawline to give it more prominence, which significantly improved her facial balance."

You and your surgeon will work together to determine the best surgical plan to fulfill your desires and meet your individual needs. If appropriate, your surgeon may discuss with you other procedures that are often done in conjunction with chin augmentation, such as rhinoplasty and liposuction to reduce fatty deposits that can create the appearance of a "double chin."

PREPARATION

Your surgeon will give you instructions about how to prepare for your surgery. He or she will give you guidelines on eating, drinking, and medications, such as avoiding aspirin or anti-inflammatory medications that promote bleeding.

As with all surgery in general, whether performed in an outpatient facility or in the hospital, you should arrange to have someone drive you to and from surgery and to assist you for a day or two after you return home.

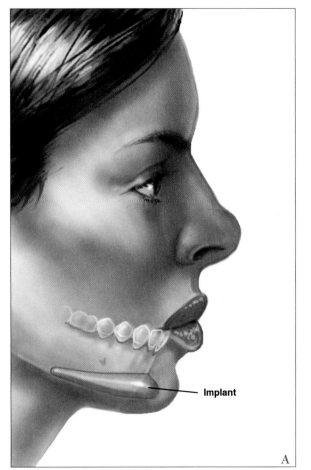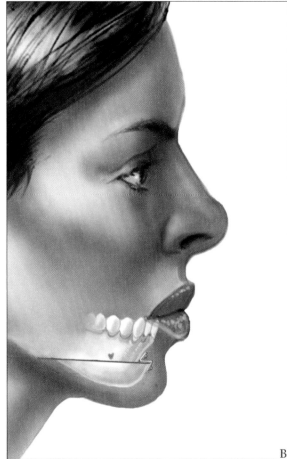

Implant

A. The more common approach to augmenting the chin uses an implant inserted through a small incision underneath the chin or inside the mouth. **B.** In an alternative technique to increase chin projection, the surgeon makes a cut (osteotomy) through the lower jaw below the roots of the teeth. Access to the bone is through a small incision inside the lower lip. The lower segment of bone is advanced a precise amount and held in place permanently with a small plate and screws or wires.

THE SURGERY

Chin augmentation is performed either by inserting an implant or, less often, by reshaping the existing bone and/or adding the patient's own cartilage or bone. Implants may be made of silicone or Gortex. They are available in a wide variety of sizes and shapes, which allow the surgeon to custom-fit the implant to the configurations of the patient's face.

"I think the implant materials that plastic surgeons use today are approaching the ideal," says Dr. Dufresne. "They are biocompatible and easily sculpted. With my preferred implant, the patient's own soft tissue

eventually grows into the material so that the implant becomes truly integrated with the facial skeleton."

The incision for inserting a chin implant can be made either inside the mouth, where gum and lower lip meet, or under the chin. When the procedure is performed in conjunction with a face lift that already requires an incision beneath the chin, the surgeon will usually use the same incision for both procedures. While placing the incision inside the mouth leaves no visible scars, the beneath-the-chin incision is inconspicuous.

"Generally, I use a submental incision, which is located under the chin," says **Edward O. Terino, MD,** of

Thousand Oaks, California, "because scarring is not noticeable in that area. Moreover, this provides a more direct approach, making it easier to place the implant properly and avoid injury to the nerves that give sensation to the lower lip. By using the submental incision, one can also fasten the implant in a position that ensures that it does not shift."

The surgeon makes an incision, going deep into the tissues to create a pocket into which the implant will be placed, creating the chin's desired contour. The implant is held in place either by fine sutures or by positioning it beneath the fibrous protective layer, called the periosteum, connected to the jawbone.

Joseph Michael Pober, MD, of New York, New York, adds that further research may provide additional choices for surgeons and patients in the future. "Having performed many different types of plastic surgery procedures of the chin, I am very interested in developing even simpler and safer techniques for chin enhancement. Some of the most exciting research I am doing is studying ways to actually induce new bone growth. This is a more natural approach to enhancing facial features such as the chin, jawline, and malar regions, and I think in the future this method could replace facial implants of silicone or other currently used materials for augmentation."

An alternative to implants is a procedure called sliding genioplasty, where the patient's chin bone is surgically cut, moved forward and secured with wires or screws. For genioplasty, the patient's own cartilage or bone, from another part of the body such as the hip, may need to be added to give the chin more projection.

Using the patient's own bone reduces the small risk of infection and absorption associated with implantation. However, the operative time to perform the procedure is increased, as is the length of the recovery. Additionally, genioplasty is more difficult to modify than chin augmentation with an implant, should the patient be dissatisfied with the result, since the bone would have to be re-cut and moved again. Sliding genioplasty may be used if the patient's chin is too small for an implant or if there are complicating factors such as problems with the patient's bite or deformities of facial bones. A dental history and X-ray studies may be necessary to determine the appropriate treatment, and some patients with severe jaw irregularities may require even more complex reconstructive surgeries.

In chin reduction surgery, the surgeon will also use incision points either inside the mouth or under the chin to gain access to the chin bone, which he or she then sculpts to the desired size and shape. Alternatively, reduction may be achieved by a procedure similar to a sliding genioplasty for augmentation, except that the chin bone is moved backward rather than forward.

POST OP

Chin augmentation by implantation, the most common technique, usually takes about 30 minutes to perform. The procedure can be done under sedation (twilight) anesthesia or general anesthesia. Whether you are awake and unaware of what is going on, or you are unconscious, you will not feel any pain during the surgical procedure. Chin surgery, when performed alone, is an outpatient procedure, and patients are generally allowed to return home the same day.

Immediately following surgery, your surgeon will apply a dressing that will remain in place for two to three days. You can expect some tenderness and a tight, stretched feeling for several days.

You can anticipate taking pain medication, according to your surgeon's instructions, for about three days;

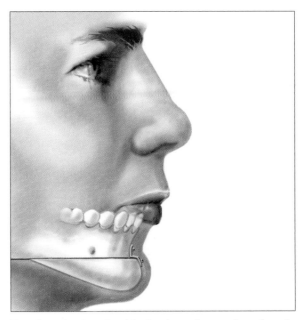

To reduce the size of a chin that is too long, and needs to be shortened vertically, the chin bone may be cut. After a portion of bone is removed, the rest is repositioned and secured in place.

acetaminophen (Tylenol) alone is usually sufficient. Aspirin and certain anti-inflammatory drugs that may cause bleeding are to be strictly avoided.

Areas of black and blue might be visible around the face and neck, and swelling, which should peak during the first week, could be evident. Chewing causes discomfort and should be limited. Your surgeon will instruct you concerning dental hygiene and very likely put you on a diet restricted to liquids and soft foods for the first few days following surgery.

Most swelling should be gone after approximately two weeks. Although rigorous activity should be avoided for the first week, you can resume normal activities in about a week to 10 days. If the incision was

placed beneath the chin, sutures will be removed within five to seven days; sutures for intra-oral incisions will dissolve by themselves.

"Since the body heals best with rest, inactivity, and an environment of moderate temperature, the patient should observe these conditions to achieve optimum, rapid healing," says Dr. Terino. "Too much motion of the head and neck can definitely create problems. Turning over or putting pressure in the area of the cheek, chin, or upper midface after chin augmentation can cause bleeding or push an implant out of position, especially within the first five days after surgery."

You should be presentable, with bruising gone and swelling greatly reduced, and able to return to work 10 to 14 days following surgery. Although recovery can vary greatly from individual to individual, and for some patients swelling may not completely subside for as much as six months, your final result should usually be evident within three to four weeks. When the surgery involves reshaping of the bone, rather than insertion of an implant, recovery is prolonged.

LOOKING AHEAD

Most patients are extremely happy with the appearance of their chin following surgery. Beyond being satisfied with their more aesthetically pleasing appearance, they often feel more self-confident about how they look. Whether the results are dramatic or subtle, recontouring of the chin can make a significant contribution to overall facial harmony. People who may have been self-conscious about being viewed in profile find that, after undergoing chin surgery, they no longer have feelings of embarrassment and don't mind being seen from any angle.

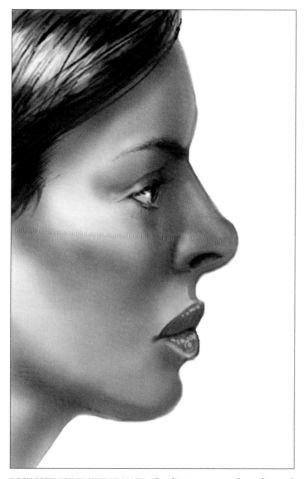

POSTOPERATIVE APPEARANCE. The chin is augmented or advanced to achieve better facial balance and a more pleasing profile.

Chin augmentation, performed by itself or often in combination with other surgeries such as liposuction of the neck, face lift and rhinoplasty, is a procedure with significant aesthetic benefits. Especially from a profile view, the chin is a defining aesthetic component of the lower third of the face. Its vertical projection ideally is at about the level of the forehead, with the forehead and chin framing the nose. In a pleasing profile, these three facial elements are in harmonious balance, and their relationship to one another has a tremendous impact on whether an individual is seen as being attractive.

Aesthetic enhancement of the chin, especially through adding to its projection, has been performed in various ways for a long time. Earlier and unfortunately ill-conceived methods included injection of substances such as paraffin and implantation of materials far less well-tolerated by the body than those commonly used today.

Until about a decade ago, the emphasis in chin enhancement was primarily on augmenting the center of the chin only. This tended to produce a "cherry on the chin" appearance still not uncommonly seen by plastic surgeons in older patients coming in for face lift and other surgical consultations. More recently, the aesthetic superiority of an extended "wrap around the chin" implant has been recognized. Such implants are now commercially available in a wide variety of sizes and shapes from which the surgeon may choose. Primarily made of medical-grade silicone, the implants can be further trimmed and custom-shaped before insertion. This implant design can also improve on the "marionette folds" (the vertical indentation that runs from the corner of the mouth to the jawline).

Bone reshaping procedures are significantly more complicated to perform and require a longer recovery. Nevertheless, they may be a better choice for some patients. The training and clinical experience of the plastic surgeon enables him or her to make a determination of which method will produce the most satisfying results for each individual patient.

— Peter B. Fodor, MD

NOSE RESHAPING

Rhinoplasty

We've all heard the expression, "The truth is as plain as the nose on your face." When it comes to what makes a nose attractive, however, the "truth" may not be so obvious. That's because many types of noses — whether long, short, narrow or wide — can be considered attractive. Rather than its particular size or shape, the most important aspect in judging the aesthetics of your nose is whether it fits your face in a complementary way.

A nose that is in harmony with other facial features seems to blend in. One that is not, no matter what its size or shape, can become the central focus of your face and draw attention away from your other attractive features such as expressive eyes and a bright smile. Profound dissatisfaction with a nose that is clearly out of sync with the rest of the face can negatively affect self-image, emotional development, and psychological well-being.

"The Indian surgeon, Sushruta, in about 500 BC, said, 'Of all the organs of the body, the nose is considered the organ of respect and reputation,'" says **Jack A. Friedland, MD**, of Scottsdale, Arizona. "Every plastic surgeon soon learns that the nose deserves respect. Rhinoplasty is a challenging operation, and the results achieved may significantly impact a surgeon's reputation. From its early origins as a reconstructive procedure to restore, or augment, a nose that had been amputated, often as punishment for a crime, rhinoplasty subsequently became a reduction technique for those who considered their noses too large. It then progressed full circle to its current role as both a reduction and augmentation operation."

R. **Laurence Berkowitz, MD**, of Campbell, California, says the evolution of rhinoplasty has made it the most valuable operation that plastic surgeons perform. "Rhinoplasty has changed most dramatically over the last 20 to 30 years; before then, it was a highly unpredictable procedure designed for the patient who wanted to reduce the size of an exceptionally large nose. Today, it has become a highly individualized aesthetic procedure that can achieve multiple goals, giving people the opportunity to have not just a smaller nose, but a better nose."

Zachary E. Gerut, MD, of Hewlett, New York, notes, "The nose is the centerpiece of the face. More than with any other facial feature, small changes can greatly alter the overall facial appearance. My primary goal in rhinoplasty is to achieve a natural look that fits the patient's face." Dr. Gerut says that even if major changes are made to the appearance of the nose, if these changes are in harmony with other facial features, they can be hard to pinpoint. "People may see that there is something different about the way an individual looks, but they often can't identify what the difference is."

Fereydoon S. Mahjouri, MD, of Fridley, Minnesota, echoes the belief that rhinoplasty is among the most difficult procedures performed by an aesthetic plastic surgeon. "No other operation in plastic surgery requires as much from an experienced plastic surgeon in terms of combining innate artistic talent with his or her surgical skills, both of which are necessary to deliver results that will bring a patient's features into pleasing harmony. Failure to do so is invariably due to improper analysis of the anatomical imbalance and how to correct it with minimal disturbance to the delicate structures of the nose."

"The goal of rhinoplasty is a nose that looks natural and blends harmoniously with your other facial features," agrees **Richard D. Anderson, MD,** of Scottsdale, Arizona. "This operation is often regarded as the most difficult of all aesthetic procedures performed by plastic surgeons, and the most comprehensive training and experience possible are vital to success."

Nose reshaping, called rhinoplasty, can modify the bone, cartilage, and soft tissue of your nose to change its appearance in a multitude of ways. Noses can be lengthened, shortened, widened, narrowed, straightened, lifted, and the tip reshaped. Although aging can affect the nose, causing it to droop, most people who are unhappy with the appearance of their nose feel that way from quite an early age. Rhinoplasty can be performed throughout the adult years or in adolescence. Plastic surgeons, however, usually recommend postponing cosmetic rhinoplasty until at least the age of 14, and sometimes longer for boys, because the nose may not be fully developed before then.

Surgeons are also careful to consider a teenager's motivation for having the procedure and want to make sure that it is the teen's own decision and not one being imposed from an outside source. It is also important to assess a young person's attitudes and certainty about how they want to look, since the changes resulting from rhinoplasty are permanent. Maturity is important, since recovery from rhinoplasty requires careful adherence to the surgeon's postoperative instructions for limiting physical activity and avoiding injury to the nose. Although there is no upper age limit for having rhinoplasty, some surgeons believe that younger patients, and particularly those under 30, may adjust more easily to a significant change in the appearance of their nose.

"A rhinoplasty on a 16-year-old can be very different from one on a 36-year-old," says **Fredric Newman, MD,** of Darien, Connecticut. "Usually I will be much more inclined to make dramatic improvements in a younger patient, with little in the way of social attachments other than parents, who is committed to making a significant change. On the other hand, patients in their 30s or 40s generally are married, have children and various stable relationships, and they don't want to look dramatically different. I've spoken with many patients who, even though they have the same nose they had at 16, say they don't want as dramatic as change now as they would have back then."

The skill of the plastic surgeon is the key factor in achieving the type of result that each patient desires. In many instances, the best results are those that are subtle.

"Implicit in a surgeon's ability to correct nasal deformities are the development of a personal sense of aesthetic beauty of the nose and the

FAST FACTS

LENGTH OF SURGERY
Usually one to three hours.

ANESTHESIA
Local anesthetic and intravenous sedation or general anesthesia.

LENGTH OF STAY
Usually outpatient procedure, home the same day.

RECOVERY
Initial mild to moderate discomfort; one day of bed rest, minimal activity for a few days; bruising gone in one to two weeks, some swelling for several weeks, residual swelling up to one year; back to work in seven to 10 days; avoid strenuous activities for three to four weeks.

SCARS
No external scars with closed procedure; small scar between nostrils, often virtually imperceptible, with open procedure.

RISKS/POSSIBLE COMPLICATIONS
Serious complications, while possible, are unlikely. Some potential complications can be avoided by carefully following your surgeon's instructions.

In addition to the usual risks associated with anesthesia, other risks include:
- Severe bleeding. Occurs in less than two percent of rhinoplasties.
- Infection.
- Sinusitis: Can occur within weeks of surgery, usually caused by internal swelling and can be treated with medication.
- Bumps and irregularities in cartilage or bone structure.
- Nasal breathing obstruction: If caused by collapse of cartilage or over-narrowing of bones, may be improved with revision surgery.
- Graft/implant migration: Grafts and implants can resorb, shift or extrude; can often be revised and stabilized.

The above-listed risks may be only some of those that your surgeon will discuss with you in greater detail during your consultation.

maturity to vary this concept to the individual patient. An optimal result demands a sense of beauty, art, and aesthetics in addition to a detailed knowledge of the complex anatomy and physiology of the nose, familiarity with different surgical techniques, persistent self-discipline in applying the technique, and constant self-criticism in evaluating the results," says Dr. Friedland.

"Today, there's less removal of tissue and more preservation of structures, a decided tendency toward under-operation rather than over-operation," adds Dr. Friedland, "and always an effort for total correction of all the problems at one time."

"Rhinoplasty techniques have become much less 'destructive' in that we don't take out as much; instead, we use sutures to reshape or reconstruct what's already there," agrees George Sanders, MD, of Encino, California.

"I don't like to 'overdo' the nose. I've had the opportunity to see the results of rhinoplasty 20 or more years later, and the surgeries where less was done seem to hold up the best over time," says Joel B. Singer, MD, of Westport, Connecticut.

Surgery of the nose can solve a wide variety of problems. Reconstructive nasal surgery addresses problems caused by birth defects, injury or disease. Breathing problems caused by abnormalities of the internal nasal

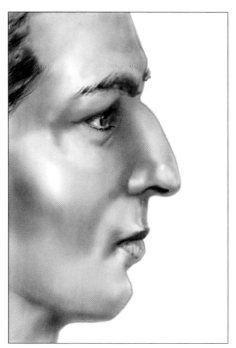

PREOPERATIVE APPEARANCE A pronounced nasal bridge, or hump, and a drooping nasal tip are common problems that can be effectively corrected through cosmetic rhinoplasty.

structures can be corrected in conjunction with cosmetic surgery of the nose.

It is important to note that both reconstructive surgery and the correction of breathing problems related to the internal structures of your nose may be covered by insurance. Your surgeon can help you determine this, and you will need approval from your insurance company before surgery. Cosmetic rhinoplasty, which is performed to enhance the outward appearance of your nose, is not covered by insurance. If surgery to improve your breathing function is performed at the same time as cosmetic alterations to your nose, only the noncosmetic portion of the operation is eligible for insurance coverage.

"Surgeons have to be prepared to deal with both the aesthetics of the nose and its function as a unit," says Jay B. Fine, MD, of Pembroke Pines, Florida. "A plastic surgeon must be able not only to make a nose look good, but also to make sure it works as it should. It is philosophically incorrect to sacrifice one element — either form or function — for the other."

While rhinoplasty can help you achieve your goals for a more attractive nose, there are some limitations. Just how these apply to you will be determined by the size, shape, and structure of your nose as well as the texture and thickness of your skin. For example, if you have thick skin, it may be more difficult to create a well-defined nasal tip. Other factors that will be considered in planning your rhinoplasty are the shape and contour of your face including the angle where the nose meets the forehead, the slope of the forehead, and the projection of the chin and lips.

"I can sum up the results of a successful rhinoplasty in two words: facial balance," says Frederick N. Lukash, MD, of Manhasset, New York. "When a person comes to me for rhinoplasty, it's usually not just the nose that needs to be made smaller. Some patients also may need a bigger chin, others may need a fuller midface. My job is to tell the patient what I believe he or she needs, based both on personal aesthetics and on the goal of achieving optimal facial balance."

The chin can be particularly important. A receding or weak chin can make an appropriately sized nose appear too large. In some cases, chin augmentation will alleviate the need for rhinoplasty. In other instances, where rhinoplasty is called for, correcting a receding chin at the same time may enhance facial harmony. If these are factors in your situation, your surgeon will discuss this option with you.

"When I do a consultation, I have the patient, and sometimes the entire family, sit down in front of my computer, and I use imaging software to illustrate what could be done to the patient's nose, often including modifications to the chin and midface," says Dr. Lukash. "This facial balance analysis is extremely important because it helps them truly understand how the face is the sum of its parts and that, for example, a reduction in the size of the nose alone often isn't enough to achieve the desired result."

If you are having rhinoplasty to correct signs of aging, such as a drooping tip, it can often be accomplished in conjunction with a face lift or other facial aesthetic surgery.

THE CONSULTATION

The consultation is a time for the surgeon and patient to get to know and feel comfortable with each other. The patient should feel completely confident that the surgeon is fully qualified. As the experts note, many plastic surgeons consider rhinoplasty to be the most difficult of all cosmetic surgeries. Patients would be well advised to only consider a surgeon who has extensive experience with this procedure. If you haven't read sections in the beginning of this book about choosing a surgeon who is certified by the American Board of Plastic Surgery, you may want to do so now.

Good communication between you and your surgeon is vital to a satisfying outcome. It is essential that you know exactly what bothers you about your nose's appearance and that you can specifically describe the problem to your surgeon.

"When a patient comes in for a rhinoplasty," says Jonathan R. Berman, MD, of Boca Raton, Florida, "I first ask them what they like about their nose. I believe it's important to start by emphasizing the positive rather than the negative aspects of their appearance, because that's the best way to convey that I'm here to help them and always to look at them in a positive way. So I give them a mirror, and after they have told me what they like about their nose, they can then tell me what they dislike. I understand that when people talk about their nose, they also are essentially talking about their inner self and how they think, so I listen very carefully."

Aesthetics are subjective judgments; factors such as your personal concept of attractiveness as well as your ethnicity and cultural norms all come into play. No matter how technically proficient the surgery may be, it will not be a success unless it meets your goals and expectations. When you express these openly and precisely, your surgeon can better give you an accurate idea of what you can realistically expect.

"I find computer imaging to be a great advantage because you can take a patient's photograph and show what that individual would look like with different surgical approaches to changing the appearance of the nose," explains George Sanders, MD, of Encino, California. "Imaging is very helpful in communicating to patients what cannot be accomplished, so they will have more realistic expectations."

"Digital imaging with photography has been a true asset for nose surgery," says Dr. Berman. "I have a good idea what I can do technically by looking at how I can augment or reduce the nose on a computer. It also gives me a good feel for what the patient really wants. When we're done with the imaging session, I write down what we've talked about, and I usually feel that we've established a mutually agreeable direction for surgery."

Sometimes patients will bring in photographs, often of celebrities or other well-known people, and request to have "the same nose" as these individuals. However, a nose that looks good on your favorite actor may not be appropriate for your face. Your surgeon may use computer imaging to show you both what can and cannot be done to enhance the appearance of your nose. No matter how much you may like what you see, remember that what appears on an inanimate computer screen cannot be guaranteed as an actual result of surgery on living tissues. Likewise, some surgeons may not be as proficient at using a computer as they are at achieving outstanding results in the operating room. Never make your decision based solely on a computer image; you must also consider your overall communication with the surgeon, his or her training and experience, and examples of actual surgical results.

In determining if you are a suitable candidate for surgery, your surgeon will review your entire medical history. This will include discussion of any medications you may currently be taking, whether you are a chronic

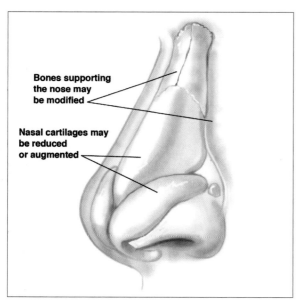

Structures creating the framework of the nose that may be surgically reduced or augmented include the nasal bones and cartilages.

user of nasal spray, or if you suffer from allergies that can cause nasal stuffiness. You should also be honest with your surgeon about any cocaine use, past or present. If you are a current user of this drug, your surgeon will want you to stop, most likely for at least one year prior to surgery.

Every nose is asymmetrical to some extent. For example, everyone's nose has a long and a short side. Asymmetry is often difficult to detect, and it is likely that you have never noticed any differences between the two sides of your nose. During the consultation, your surgeon will probably discuss this with you and help you to identify any pre-existing asymmetries so you don't mistakenly think they have resulted from the surgery.

"Everybody's nose is different, and you have to keep that in mind. You need to be conservative and to respect the limitations of the operation as well as the patient's wishes," says Dr. Berman, who adds, "The bottom line about rhinoplasty is: The less you do, often, the better results you get."

When performed by a qualified surgeon, rhinoplasty is an extremely safe operation and the vast majority of patients are very satisfied with their outcomes.

However, because healing is not totally predictable, minor revisions are often necessary to achieve an optimal result. Do not hesitate to ask any questions and air any concerns you may have about your surgery.

PREPARATION

Your surgeon will give you instructions about how to prepare for surgery. He or she will also give you guidelines on eating, drinking and medications, such as avoiding aspirin or anti-inflammatory medications that promote bleeding.

As with all surgery in general, whether performed in an outpatient facility or in the hospital, you should arrange to have someone drive you to and from surgery and assist you for a day or two after you return home.

THE SURGERY

"A successful rhinoplasty is the product of a pre-conceived outcome, a specific operative plan, and meticulous technique," says **Robert Brink, MD**, of San Mateo, California.

"The 'art' of plastic surgery is what separates this specialty from the science of medicine. And if there's any part of the body where the surgeon's artistic sensibilities are critical, it's the nose," observes **Guy Stofman, MD**, of Pittsburgh, Pennsylvania.

Your surgeon will design your rhinoplasty to achieve results that are consistent with your goals and possible within the limitations of your specific nasal structure and skin quality.

He or she will accomplish this by sculpting the underlying bone and cartilage of the nose. In some cases, to narrow the base of the nose or reduce the width of the nostrils, your surgeon will also remove small wedges of skin.

The bone structure may need to be reduced, augmented or refined. Bone reduction usually involves fracturing and repositioning the bone. Augmentation can be accomplished using tissue harvested from the nose or from another part of your body. Alternatively, allo-plastic material can be used. The latter prevents the need for "harvesting" from another area of your body and may sometimes be recommended. However, using your own tissue is preferred as this lowers the risk of infection and may provide a more stable result. If your nose requires augmentation, your surgeon will most likely use cartilage harvested from your own nose, ear, or rib.

If your nasal septum, which is on the inside of your nose, interferes with your ability to breathe, your surgeon may perform a surgical procedure, called septoplasty, to straighten it. This procedure does not alter the appearance of your nose. It is performed through an incision made within the nose and can be accomplished in conjunction with cosmetic rhinoplasty or by itself.

"Rhinoplasty surgery is unique in that the shape of the nose is not only important cosmetically, but also functionally," says **James M. Platis, MD**, of Chicago, Illinois. "No matter how good a patient's surgical result might look, if they can't breathe well through their nose, the surgery was not a success. The reverse is true as well."

The specific rhinoplasty technique your surgeon will use depends on many factors including your goals, your anatomy and the degree of difficulty of the correction required. There are two main options for incision placement, often called the "closed" approach or the "open" approach.

CLOSED RHINOPLASTY

"I perform most rhinoplasties using a closed technique," says **Csaba L. Magassy MD**, of McLean, Virginia. "The key to an attractive nose is a well-formed nasal tip. Using the closed technique, I can preserve the blood supply that goes to the tip and to the supratip area. Achieving optimal shape in the tip has to do with projection, the way you bring the domes together, and how the soft tissue drapes on top of the nasal structure. It's a question of balance, both within the nose itself and with the face, creating a more pleasing shape while preserving individuality."

With the closed technique, also called endonasal rhinoplasty, all incisions are confined to the inside of the nose. This results in no external scarring, but it can limit the surgeon's view of and access to the cartilage and bone and, for this reason, surgeons may sometimes choose an open technique.

"Due to certain circumstances, I feel that some rhinoplasties must be done open, but I prefer to use a closed technique whenever possible," says **Alfonso Barrera, MD** of Houston, Texas. "Although the scar resulting from the open technique is fairly insignificant, with a closed procedure there is no visible scar and the recovery is quicker."

"I use the open technique on secondary procedures, which often present unique difficulties," says **David G. Genecov, MD**, of Dallas, Texas, "but I think closed

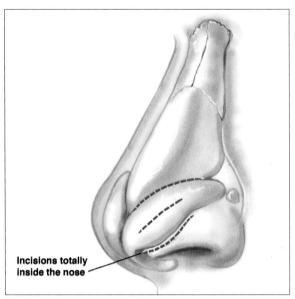

Incisions totally inside the nose

Closed rhinoplasty uses incisions that are placed inside the nose, leaving no visible scars.

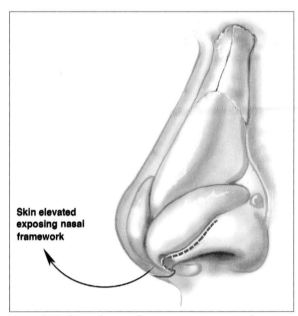

Skin elevated exposing nasal framework

Open rhinoplasty also involves an incision across the center column between the nostrils (columella). The resulting scar usually fades and becomes barely perceptible.

rhinoplasty is a very good operation, and I use it on many of my primary cases." Dr. Genecov acknowledges that the closed approach to rhinoplasty reduces visibility, but he emphasizes what he feels are the positive aspects of the technique, such as elimination of visible scarring and greater ease in adding cartilage to the nasal tip: "Especially in cases where I am going to augment the tip, I prefer the closed technique."

OPEN RHINOPLASTY

Many surgeons prefer open rhinoplasty, particularly for more complicated problems, because it affords them a clear view of the underlying cartilage and bone and greater access to some portions of the nose. In the open technique, a tiny incision is made across the columella, the vertical strip of tissue that separates the nostrils. Although usually almost imperceptible once healed, there will be a small scar where the incision was made.

"I think the open approach is much more predictable and precise for shaping the nose, especially the tip. You can see the framework and set everything exactly where you want it to be, thus leaving much less to chance," explains **Alexander Majidian, MD**, of Calabasas, California.

"The open technique increases my ability to determine exactly what's going on inside," agrees **Rick J. Smith, MD**, of East Lansing, Michigan, who adds that he finds the open technique to be very compatible with the use of cartilage grafts "Gaining access to the various structures using a closed approach requires distortion of the nose. I find that the open approach aids me in preserving the nose's structural integrity."

Kaveh Alizadeh, MD, of Garden City, New York, adds, "I try to preserve as much of the patient's own tissues as possible while restructuring his or her bony architecture. I feel open rhinoplasty achieves the most reliable and long-lasting results."

"I use the open technique for most secondary procedures," says Dr. Friedland, "especially if the first surgery was performed elsewhere and I need to really see what was done before."

Hamid Massiha, MD, of Metairie/New Orleans, Louisiana, offers this opinion, "I believe the technique of open rhinoplasty has made it possible, in many cases, to achieve better results. I still use the closed method in cases where the tip does not require correction, and it's

only a matter of adjusting the bone that is too wide or reducing the nasal hump. But when there is a problem with the tip, which is the most important part of the nose, I always use the open technique."

Clearly, there are differences of opinion among the experts with regard to the relative benefits of closed and open rhinoplasty techniques, though many surgeons utilize both methods. In selecting a rhinoplasty technique for you, your surgeon will weigh the benefits and drawbacks of each method in your particular case and may also consider his or her personal preference — the technique that, in your surgeon's hands, produces the best and most consistent results.

In the past, rhinoplasty was more about making a nose larger or smaller, rather than refining its appearance. As the procedure evolved and surgeons learned how to reshape the nasal tip, it was not uncommon for doctors to create a similar look for all their patients, so that frequently one could tell from looking at the results of rhinoplasty exactly which doctor had performed the operation.

This was because, at the time, the importance of preserving the individuality of the nose was not fully recognized, either by doctors or their patients, most of whom were very happy with their reshaped noses. Today, individuality is key.

"A unique aspect of rhinoplasty surgery deals with individuality," says Dr. Platis. "I believe that a person's nose is their most uniquely individual physical feature. This is why, in my opinion, it is so important for rhinoplasty surgery to be individualized to the patient's specific needs and appearance."

"No one wants to hear, 'Gee, who did your nose? It's beautiful,'" says **Joseph Michael Pober, MD**, of New York, New York. "I work to bring out the hidden beauty of a person's entire face, so the end result is total beauty and not just a pretty nose. I want my rhinoplasty patients to be told, 'Gee, your face looks beautiful.'"

'No one wants a 'signature' nose anymore," agrees Dr. Newman. "When I was 16 years old, there were two plastic surgeons in my community, and whenever a girl from my school had her nose done, I could tell which doctor she'd gone to. Each surgeon had his own 'style' and his patients' noses all looked the same."

The nose's size and shape, as well as its ethnic character, are carefully considered so the results of surgery will enhance each patient's unique facial appearance. In most instances, rhinoplasty isn't about drastic changes, instead, it is about enhancing the natural contours of the nose.

Robert Wald, MD, of Fullerton, California, agrees that both surgeons and patients have changed their expectations about rhinoplasty, "The procedure has evolved considerably over the years, with much more emphasis now being placed on individuality. The goal is to make the nose blend harmoniously with the rest of the face. Rhinoplasty is, ideally, a refinement of the nose."

"Rhinoplasty has really become an operation for people of all racial and ethnic backgrounds," says **George Sanders, MD,** of Encino, California. "Some may want a limited and subtle result, retaining their ethnic characteristics, while others may want a dramatic change that impacts their overall appearance to a greater extent."

Gary R. Culbertson, MD, of Sumter, South Carolina, adds, "A person's heritage or ethnicity often may be a significant component of his or her nasal structure. I believe that, in such cases, straying too far from the natural appearance of the nose may result in an artificial appearance."

Gender is also an important consideration in determining aesthetic corrections of the nose. "Female and male noses differ considerably," says **Herve` Gentile, MD,** of Corpus Christi, Texas. "The female nose, in addition to being generally smaller and having a thinner skin covering than that of the male, has other more subtle structural differences. These differences affect the way in which I shape the nose and particularly the tip, which should have a more triangular shape viewed from the front and below and should also have a gentler, softer look from the profile."

Taking your goals and his or her experience into consideration, your surgeon will recommend and explain the technique that he or she believes will afford you the best results.

"I perform rhinoplasty based on each patient's unique needs," says Dr. Berman. "Whether I use an open or closed technique, I always tailor each operation to the specific patient. I know the anatomy and what I can and can't do in each case."

It is important that you have confidence in your surgeon and feel comfortable enough to ask to see photographs of prior results and to ask questions about why he or she is recommending one method over another.

"Today, patients can generally feel comfortable that plastic surgeons are taking a more measured, rational, and aesthetically sound approach to nasal surgery with respect for the functional aspects of nasal physiology and structure," says **Lawrence S. Reed, MD,** of New York, New York. "The rhinoplasties one sees today are more natural and more consistent with the patient's facial features."

POST OP

Rhinoplasty is an outpatient procedure that generally takes between one to three hours to perform, under sedation (twilight) anesthesia or general anesthesia.

"I prefer to perform this operation without putting the patient to sleep. In addition to other benefits, they get a chance to see the final results in the operating room before any swelling settles in," says **Fereydoon S. Mahjouri, MD,** of Fridley, Minnesota.

No matter what type of anesthesia you have, you will not feel any pain during the surgical procedure. Although some patients may remain in the facility overnight, most are allowed to return home the same day.

You will most likely experience moderate discomfort: your nose may ache, you may suffer a slight headache,

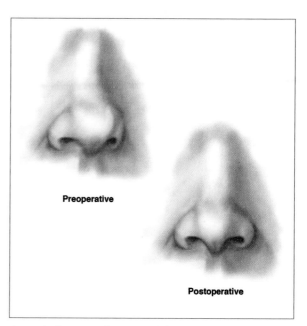

Preoperative

Postoperative

A crooked nose, often caused by injury, interferes with facial symmetry as well as normal breathing.

and portions of your face will be swollen and bruised. Pain will be controlled by medication. Following surgery, a splint may be placed on the bridge of your nose. This will allow the tissues to stabilize and also protect your nose, particularly while you sleep. Any nasal packing that may have been placed inside your nose will self-dissolve or be removed within three to seven days after surgery. Your stitches may also be removed at that time. The nasal splint may have to remain in place for up to a week, and your surgeon will instruct you on its care, such as the importance of keeping it dry. Except for getting up to go to the bathroom and take short walks around the house with the help of a care-giver, you will spend the first day at home in bed with your head elevated. This will help control swelling and bruising as well as

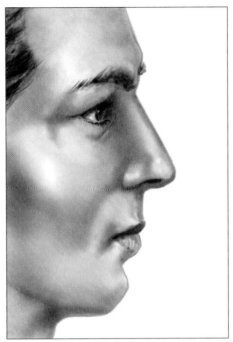

POSTOPERATIVE APPEARANCE. Following surgery, the nasal hump has been reduced and the tip elevated, balancing the nose with other features for a more harmonious facial appearance.

minor bleeding that often occurs within the first few days. Your surgeon will have instructed you not to take aspirin or certain anti-inflammatory drugs that can aggravate bleeding. You should continue to limit your activities, sleep with your head elevated for the first few days, and apply cold compresses to provide comfort and help to reduce swelling. Avoid bending or heavy lifting. It is important to remember that recovery time can vary greatly between individuals, but even if you are feeling better than expected, you should not try to do more than your surgeon has advised.

Don't be concerned if the swelling and bruising around your eyes and cheeks actually increases during the first two or three days; after that, it should begin to dissipate, with most discoloration disappearing within a week or two. If you wish, you can begin using makeup to conceal some of the bruising within a few days. Some swelling may last for several weeks or longer. It is not uncommon for the nasal tip to be affected by some residual swelling for up to one year.

However, this is usually so minor that it will be apparent only to you. Your surgeon will most likely instruct you not to blow your nose for the first week to give the tissues time to heal.

Although you will most likely be able to return to work within a week to 10 days following surgery, you should avoid strenuous activities for three to four weeks that could increase your blood pressure or cause injury to your nose. These include rough sports, swimming, jogging, bending, and sexual relations. You should take special care to protect your nose: wear sunblock for at least eight weeks and do not expose it to direct sunlight for a few months. Be careful washing your face and applying cosmetics, and particularly avoid rubbing your nose. While contact lenses can be worn as soon as you feel like it, if bones were altered during your rhinoplasty, you may not be able to place glasses on your nose until it is completely healed or for about six or seven weeks. They will have to be propped on your cheeks or supported with tape.

LOOKING AHEAD

You will most likely be very pleased and be able to enjoy your new look within a few weeks, although the final results may not be completely stabilized for up to one year. The results of rhinoplasty are usually permanent, although minor changes in the appearance of your nose may occur over time. Some of these changes may be related to your rhinoplasty surgery, while others are a natural part of the aging process.

REVISION RHINOPLASTY

As mentioned earlier, because rhinoplasty is not as predictable as many other cosmetic surgeries, it is not uncommon for patients to require minor revision of results. In fact, this is estimated to occur in about 20 percent or more of rhinoplasty cases. If you and your surgeon agree that adjustments are desirable, he or she will explain the type of reversionary procedure needed. Usually, this will not be nearly as extensive as your original surgery.

If your surgeon is experienced in revision rhinoplasty surgery, agrees that your expectations were realistic but that your results are unsatisfactory, and has a plan to fix the problem, there is no reason you shouldn't have the same surgeon perform the revision.

It is also a good idea to allow some time to pass before considering revision rhinoplasty. Since the appearance of your nose can still change over time, it is usually necessary to wait at least six months to a year before attempting a second operation.

Editor's Viewpoint

Interestingly, the word "rhinoplasty" originates from the word "rhinoceros." As the experts agree, reshaping of the nose is clearly one of the most difficult procedures an aesthetic plastic surgeon performs. Perhaps more than any other type of cosmetic surgery, rhinoplasty requires a blend of impeccable aesthetic judgment and technical finesse. Open and thorough preoperative communication between the patient and surgeon is essential and can be aided by drawings or computer-generated images that illustrate possible adjustments of the nasal appearance. Pre-existing characteristics of the nose, which vary greatly among individuals, have a significant bearing on what can be surgically accomplished in any particular case. This is one reason why the experts stress the importance of discussing the limitations, as well as the expected benefits, of surgery during the preoperative consultation. Photographs of noses that the patient considers ideal can serve as a useful starting point for discussion and can also provide a "signal" of how focused the patient really is with regard to his or her desires and expectations. For example, I have occasionally had a patient bring in several photographs of noses, each of which looked entirely different from the next. When this happens, it clearly indicates that a patient is confused about his or her aesthetic goals, and it is necessary to sort this out before proceeding with surgery.

Revision surgery, as described in this chapter, often may consist of minor surgical adjustments and is not an uncommon occurrence. In fact, any surgeon who suggests that there is never a need to perform revisions on his or her work either does not perform rhinoplasties or is being less than candid. More extensive secondary surgery to improve on over-operated, and particularly an over-reduced nose, is often extremely challenging but can also be very rewarding for the patient and surgeon alike. It has been said this type of rhinoplasty "redo" surgery may be 10 times more difficult than a primary surgery. The choice of surgeon is imperative and consulting with several experienced surgeons before proceeding is wise.

It is wonderful to watch how patients of all ages truly "blossom" following successful rhinoplasty surgery. The change is a combination of their improved appearance and the sometimes dramatic emotional relief that they feel as a result of having a more normal-looking or aesthetically balanced nose. Makeup and hairdos no longer need to be attempts to hide or de-emphasize the nose, glasses are traded for contact lenses, cosmetic dental work may be undertaken to enhance the smile, and weight control programs are often adopted. When plastic surgeons see these far-reaching positive changes in our patients, it is our best possible reward and certainly justifies the many years of training and experience that go into achieving outstanding results from rhinoplasty.

— Peter B. Fodor, MD

EAR SURGERY
Otoplasty

Ear surgery, called otoplasty, is most often carried out to reposition protruding ears closer to the head or, less frequently, to reduce the size of large ears. It is, however, also possible for a plastic surgeon to reshape the ears.

Ears that are too prominent or "stick out" too far from the head can be the cause of great psychological distress. Since this is most often a hereditary or congenital condition, and the ears are generally almost fully formed by age four or five, otoplasty is typically performed on children between the ages of 4 and 14. However, there are no additional risks associated with otoplasty for adults, who may also be good candidates for this procedure.

"Otoplasty, performed at any age, can allow patients to wear their hair at whatever length they like without the need to cover up protruding ears," says **Laurie Casas, MD**, of Glenview, Illinois.

In addition to protruding ears, other problems that can be helped with surgery include ears where the tip seems to fold down and forward, where the curve in the outer rim and the natural folds and creases are missing, or where the overall size is too small. These may be called "lop ears," "cup ears," "shell ears," or "constricted ears," depending on the specific ear configuration. Other even more severe ear deformities, including congenital or traumatic absence, may also be corrected with reconstructive plastic surgery.

"The goal of this surgery is to produce symmetrical, natural-looking ears with no obvious signs that surgery has been performed and minimal complications, in spite of patient differences in age, gender, or magnitude of defect. More than 200 techniques have been described in the medical literature," says **Jack A. Friedland, MD**, of Phoenix, Arizona.

In addition to procedures to reshape the ears, there are also aesthetic surgical techniques that address only the earlobes. Large or stretched earlobes, earlobes with deep creases and wrinkles, or torn earlobes can be improved or corrected through relatively minor procedures, which can be performed alone or in conjunction with other facial rejuvenation surgery.

If you are interested in ear surgery for your child, you should know that most surgeons believe parents should be sensitive and alert to their child's feelings about protruding ears but should not insist on surgery if the child seems unconcerned about the condition. However, many children do feel uncomfortable about ear abnormalities, particularly if they are subjected to teasing by classmates or even by well-meaning adults. Children who are presented with the option and welcome the surgery are usually very cooperative during the process and happy with the outcome.

THE CONSULTATION

Whether the surgery is for you or your child, the consultation is a time for you and the surgeon to get to know and feel comfortable with each other. You should feel completely confident that the surgeon is fully qualified. If you haven't read sections in the beginning of this book about choosing a surgeon who is certified by the American Board of Plastic Surgery, perhaps you should do so now.

When surgery is to be performed on a child, extreme care is needed to be certain that both the physical and psychological needs of the child are met. The initial evaluation phase may involve several specialists including a plastic surgeon, pediatrician, and mental health professional. Your selected plastic surgeon should be one who is comfortable and experienced with children.

Whether it is you or your child who is undergoing ear surgery, the surgeon will need to review the entire medical history, including any current medications. Your surgeon will evaluate several factors, including the current size and contour of the ears and the skin texture.

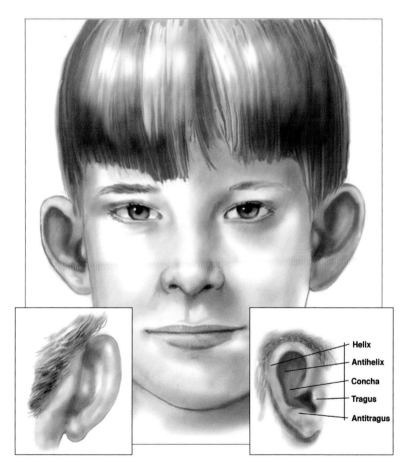

Helix
Antihelix
Concha
Tragus
Antitragus

PREOPERATIVE APPEARANCE. Typical appearance of prominent ears before surgery; the fold is missing and the bowl of the ear is deep. Asymmetry is not uncommon.

LENGTH OF SURGERY
Usually two to three hours for purely cosmetic surgery. Complex ear reconstructive surgery is longer and/or performed in stages.

ANESTHESIA
Local anesthetic and intravenous sedation, or general anesthesia, especially for young children.

LENGTH OF STAY
Usually outpatient procedure, home the same day.

RECOVERY
Out of bed first day; some discomfort for few days; resume normal activities within one week, and avoid contact sports for one month.

SCARS
Scars behind ears fade over time.

RISKS/POSSIBLE COMPLICATIONS
Serious complications, while possible, are unlikely. Some potential complications can be avoided by carefully following your surgeon's instructions.

In addition to the usual risks associated with anesthesia, other risks include:
• Infection: Some patients develop an infection in the cartilage; this can cause scar tissue to form. Usually can be treated with antibiotics; in rare cases, surgery is necessary to drain the infected area.
• Hematoma: Collection of blood beneath the skin; can be treated without compromising result.

The above-listed risks may be only some of those that your surgeon will discuss with you in greater detail during your consultation.

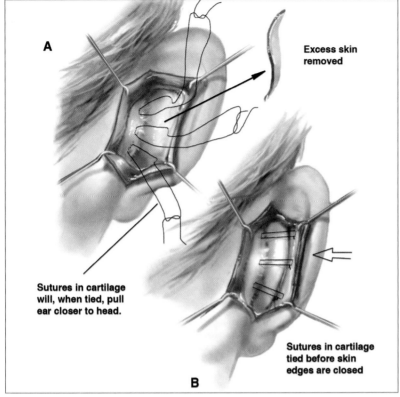

A. In one common technique, the incision is made and the ear cartilage is sculpted. Permanency of the result is sometimes aided by the use of folding sutures. **B.** Once these sutures are tied, a more defined central (antihelical) fold is created, and the ear is set back to its natural position.

Your surgeon will discuss the overall structure of the face and how the ears should be sized and shaped to achieve the proper balance. He or she will explain the details of the procedure, including the type of anesthesia to be used and the various techniques used in ear surgery.

You and your surgeon will work together to determine the best surgical plan to fulfill your desires and meet your individual needs.

"I think the most important step in performing otoplasty is making the correct analysis of the ear deformity," says **Larry A. Sargent, MD**, of Chattanooga, Tennessee, "This careful analysis allows the surgeon to choose the proper procedure that will best create a normal-looking ear — not a pinned-back or plastered-back looking ear. For example, if the concha (the bowl part of the ear) is very large, it needs to be reduced. A

technique I've used for a number of years that has been extremely effective and successful is a combination of concha resection and suture shaping — that is, placing sutures in the cartilage to re-create the fold in the ear. But for each individual patient, whatever is abnormal needs to be addressed in order to achieve a natural appearance of the ear."

Frederick N. Lukash, MD, of Manhasset, New York, agrees that careful evaluation by the surgeon is the key to planning the right operation for each patient. "Analysis is important when it comes to otoplasty because not every child has the same problem. For example, some children have an exaggerated concha, while others have an underdeveloped antihelical fold (the incurved rim of the ear). I'm a believer that with prominent ears it's not just one thing but a combination of things that need to be addressed. That's why in most otoplasties, I do a combination of procedures that have been developed by plastic surgeons. First, I make an incision behind the ear. Then I weaken the cartilage of the antihelix (the curved elevation within or in front of the helix). After I fold the helix back and suture it in place, I trim the extra skin in the back. The result is a very natural-looking ear."

PREPARATION

Your surgeon will give you instructions about how to prepare for surgery. He or she will also give you guidelines on eating, drinking and medications, such as avoiding aspirin or anti-inflammatory medications that promote bleeding, also detailed in an earlier section of this book.

As with all surgery in general, whether performed in an outpatient facility or in the hospital, you should arrange to have someone drive you to and from surgery and to assist you for a day or two after you return home.

THE SURGERY

Among many and varied techniques to treat protruding ears, one of the more common involves a small incision made in the back of the ear to expose the ear cartilage. The surgeon will then sculpt and shape the cartilage, curving it back toward the head. Sometimes, the ear is also secured with non-removable stitches to help maintain its new shape. In some cases, in addition to sculpting, the surgeon will remove a larger piece of the cartilage if doing so will provide a more natural looking fold.

In a somewhat different technique, the surgeon works through a similarly placed incision to remove skin and, rather than removing cartilage, uses stitches to fold the cartilage back on itself, thus reshaping the ear.

The surgery usually results in a scar in the back of the ear that will fade over time. To achieve and maintain proper balance, this surgery is generally performed on both ears, even when only one appears to protrude.

POST OP

Ear surgery usually takes about two to three hours. Complicated reconstructive procedures may take much longer and often must be done in stages. The procedure can be performed under sedation (twilight) anesthesia although general anesthesia is often used, particularly for younger children. Whether you are awake and unaware of what is going on, or you are unconscious, you will not feel any pain during the surgical procedure. Ear surgery is usually an outpatient procedure and patients are generally allowed to return home the same day. In some cases, your surgeon may recommend that the surgery be performed as an in-patient procedure, which would entail an overnight stay in the hospital. Oftentimes, when the patient is a young child, the parents prefer an overnight hospital stay to be sure all the effects of general anesthesia have worn off.

The patient's head will be wrapped in a turban-like bandage immediately following surgery. This bandage will help to protect the ears in the initial stages of healing and also contribute to proper healing. There may be some throbbing or aching of the ears for a few days, but patients are usually up and around within a few hours of surgery. Any discomfort can be relieved with medication. A lighter head dressing, similar to a headband, will replace the full-wrap bandage within a few days. The surgeon will instruct you in the wearing

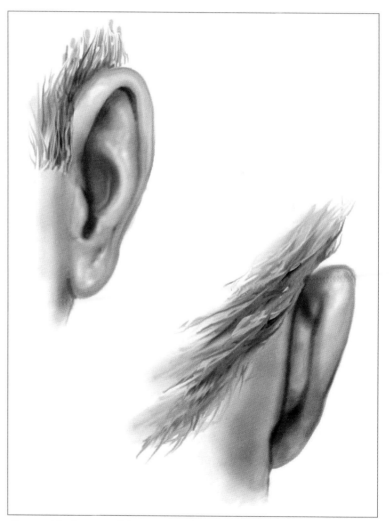

Front and back views of the ear in a normal position with a well-defined central (antihelical) fold and only an inconspicuous scar in the back.

of this lighter dressing; it is important that it also be worn at night to help prevent inadvertent tugging on or playing with the ears while sleeping. Stitches will usually dissolve or be removed about one week following surgery.

Patients can usually resume normal activities within one week; adults return to work within five days and children, with a strong admonishment to be careful on the playground, may return to school about seven days following surgery. Contact sports or any activity in which there is a danger of the ear being bent forward should be avoided for about one month.

Although recovery can vary greatly from individual to individual, ears should look "normal" within 10 to 20 days.

LOOKING AHEAD

Most patients are extremely satisfied with their ear surgery. Beyond being happy with their more aesthetically pleasing appearance, they generally feel relieved to be rid of a stressful emotional problem. However, it is impossible to guarantee perfect results, and any type of surgery may require minor revisions to achieve an optimal final outcome. Because cartilage is living tissue, the results of reshaping are not always predictable. There is a possibility that the ears may heal in an over-corrected or under-corrected fashion, or there may be some asymmetry. In the case of asymmetry, it should be remembered that all of us have normal asymmetries in our facial features and, unless severe, it most likely will not be noticeable to the casual observer.

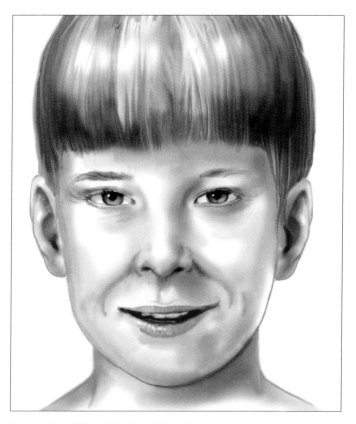

POSTOPERATIVE APPEARANCE. After surgery, the ears are set back in a more normal position closer to the head, and natural folds in the cartilage are present.

Body image and concerns about one's appearance are developed as early as 2 to 3 years of age. What is considered a normal appearance of the ears can depend on racial or cultural norms. For example, smaller ears are often seen in people of African descent, while in Ireland and parts of Scotland, protruding ears are quite common and not considered objectionable. However, when children are perceived to have deformities of the ears, they are often subjected to naive but, nevertheless, cruel teasing. They may be called names such as "antenna ears," "telephone ears," "Dumbo ears," and so on. As a result, children as young as 4 to 5 years of age frequently are very determined to undergo ear surgery, and such children typically are good and cooperative patients.

Until the 20th century, corrective surgery focused solely on removal of skin from the back of the ears. It was not understood that the abnormal appearance of the ears stemmed from a deformity of the cartilage. With the earlier skin-removal technique, the correction, if any, was of course only temporary, and excessive tension on the skin resulted in significant scarring. Once the role of cartilage reshaping was recognized, a variety of surgical techniques emerged, many producing excellent results.

As our experts have noted, the well-trained aesthetic plastic surgeon will carefully analyze the ear deformity in order to select the best technique from the many available methods for each individual patient. Complications from otoplasty are rare and, as a general rule, the results of this surgery are quite rewarding.

— *Peter B. Fodor, MD*

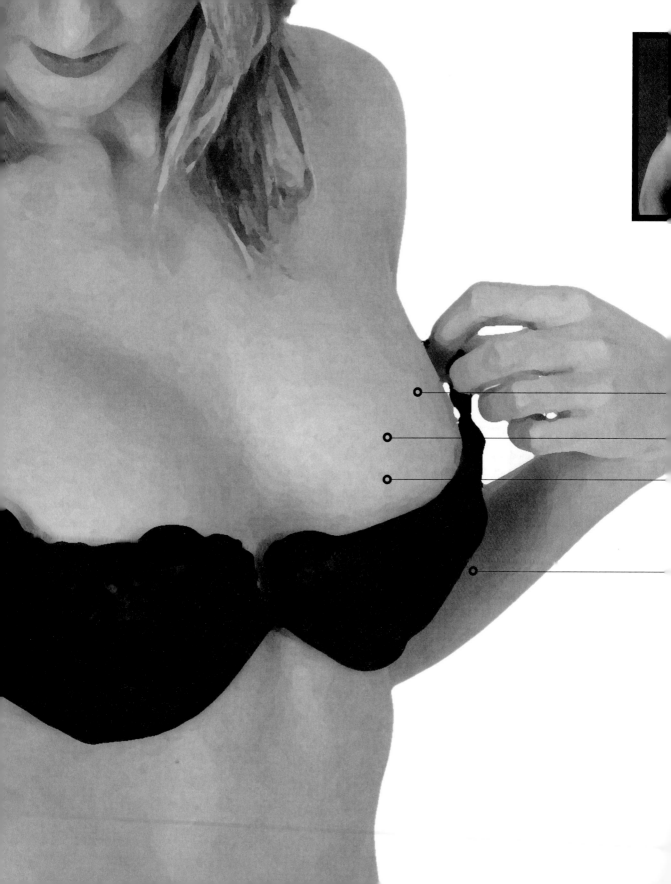

BREAST
SURGERY

BREAST SURGERY

Perhaps nothing better defines the female form than the breast. In primitive sticklike sculptures, breasts are often the only feature distinguishing women from men. Breast imagery can be seen throughout all cultures of the world. In art, as in our own psyches, breasts often symbolize femininity, nurturing, sexuality, and power.

Breasts that are well-shaped and sized in proper proportion to the body also play an important role in modern fashion's presentation of the female silhouette. But beyond fashion, a woman's breasts often are an important part of her personal identity. When a woman feels uncomfortable about the appearance of her breasts — whether she perceives them as being too small, too saggy, or too large — it can impact her self-confidence and even her intimate relationships.

"In my experience, no surgery is more directly associated with a woman's self-image and self-esteem than breast enhancement," states **James M. Platis, MD**, of Chicago, Illinois. "This includes breast augmentation, lift, and reduction surgery. That is why I feel it is so important for my patients to try and disregard expectations of others when they contemplate breast enhancement surgery. Ultimately, what is going to matter most to them is how they feel when they look at themselves in the mirror."

Michael A. Marschall, MD, of Wheaton, Illinois, believes, "The defining feminine nature of the breast means appropriate expectations must be aligned with the appropriate surgical technique to obtain the optimal enhancement. This goal is best achieved with the experienced plastic surgeon and his or her extensive surgical repertoire."

Today's women have a variety of choices when it comes to enhancing the appearance of their breasts. They can feel confident that aesthetic surgery offers effective solutions to problems such as large, heavy breasts that cause physical discomfort, underdeveloped breasts that cause some women to feel less feminine than they would like, and breasts that have lost their youthful contours as a result of childbirth and aging. Both tried-and-true techniques and newer variations are available to address the specific aesthetic goals and concerns of every woman seeking breast enhancement surgery.

Charles Spenler, MD, of Torrance, California, puts it simply, "With the latest advancements in breast surgeries, patients can achieve more natural-looking breasts."

This section deals with all kinds of breast enhancement surgery — breast augmentation, breast lift, and breast reduction. Whichever of these procedures may be most relevant to your specific needs, you'll find in these chapters valuable information and fascinating insights from our plastic surgery experts.

BREAST AUGMENTATION
Augmentation Mammaplasty

$Breast$ augmentation, technically known as augmentation mammaplasty, is a surgical procedure to enhance the size and shape of a woman's breasts. Many women find that breast augmentation not only enhances their appearance but also contributes to their quality of life. Women decide to have breast augmentation for a variety of reasons. For many, it is an opportunity to improve their body contour and achieve the more proportional figure they always wanted. Some women view breast augmentation as an option for taking control of their lives and changing their appearance to better reflect how they feel about themselves.

THE CONSULTATION

One of the first things for you and your plastic surgeon to determine is whether you are a good candidate for breast augmentation. In some cases, women may seek breast augmentation to restore breast volume lost as a result of having children. Weight loss can change the size and shape of the breasts, and breast augmentation (alone or in conjunction with a breast lift) may be recommended to improve these problems. Another reason for undergoing breast augmentation may be to equalize the size of the breasts if one is larger than the other. Perhaps most commonly, women simply feel that their breasts are too small; their clothes fit well around the hips but are often too large at the bust line, making it difficult to wear the styles they prefer. They may feel self-conscious about wearing a swimsuit or form-fitting top, or they lack confidence about their body in intimate situations.

"When I began performing breast augmentations in 1971, we didn't know what questions to ask to best determine which women were good candidates for the surgery," says **James L. Baker, MD**, of Winter Park, Florida. "I teamed up with a psychiatrist and conducted a psychological study, which was published in 1974 under the title, *Psychosexual Dynamics of Breast Augmentation.* Patients selected at random were evaluated prior to surgery and then at three months and one year after surgery. Our findings included that, for many of these patients, their low self-esteem began when their breast development fell behind that of their peer group during adolescence. We also found that women were internally motivated — they wanted breast augmentation for themselves, not to please others. Studies conducted during the 1990s and in 2000 validated our choice of questions and corroborated our findings that after breast augmentation, more than 90 percent of patients were satisfied, had increased feelings of self-worth, and considered themselves happier."

A woman should decide whether to have breast augmentation surgery after careful study and after all aspects of surgery are seriously discussed and considered.

"Every patient is unique, bringing different desires and expectations to the plastic surgeon's office about how they would like their appearance to be improved," says O. **Allen Guinn, III, MD**, of Lee's Summit, Missouri. "Although two women may have very similar appearing chests, they may have vastly divergent opinions about how they want to look after breast enhancement surgery. In my practice, significant time is spent preoperatively to determine the patient's aspirations — for both the anticipated size and shape of her enlarged breasts — so that we can determine the 'best' method to accomplish that dream."

In addition to the patient's personal goals for surgery, there are physical considerations that must be carefully assessed in developing the surgical plan. These include factors such as the patient's body type and proportions, the base diameter of her breasts, the amount of breast tissue, the size and position of her areolas (the pigmented skin surrounding the nipple), and whether there is existing breast asymmetry (one breast is larger than the other).

"When I evaluate patients for breast augmentation surgery, I use a number of objective criteria," explains **Mark P. Solomon, MD**, of Bala Cynwyd, Pennsylvania. "What I've learned over the years is that collecting the necessary data allows me to make decisions that result in an augmentation that is proportionally correct for each individual patient. Within any limitations imposed by these objective criteria, I can offer patients selected alternatives while providing them with the information they need to make an informed choice. I am comfortable with all the technical approaches and have used all implant types, so I can truly tailor the best procedure for each individual patient."

J. Vicente Poblete, MD, of Avon Lake, Ohio, points to one of the anatomical limitations that may govern a woman's choices: "A significant factor with augmentation is the amount of skin laxity. Someone who has no skin laxity would not be a good candidate for a large augmentation. On the other hand, many patients are women who are finished with their childbearing, and the effects of pregnancy and breast-feeding have naturally stretched out, or expanded, the skin — often making them very good candidates. These women want to restore their 'before-baby' bodies, so to speak."

"It's very important to educate breast augmentation patients about the limits of their anatomy," agrees **Alexander G. Digenis, MD**, of Louisville, Kentucky, "specifically, how much skin they have to work with. We do a lot of breast augmentation for young women who have not yet had children. Typically, they are thin and rather small breasted, with much less droop or sag in their skin compared with women who have had several children and whose skin has stretched out. Most patients want to look natural and proportional; the key is to guide the patient regarding the appropriate shape and size for her individual anatomy."

Michael R. Schwartz, MD, of Camarillo, California, also stresses the importance of individualizing the approach to breast augmentation. "I think the most important thing is tailoring the operation to each individual patient's wishes, as much as possible. At the same time, I don't believe in large augmentations that are out of proportion with the rest of the patient's body. An essential aspect of achieving the best result is to work with the

LENGTH OF SURGERY
Usually one to two hours.

ANESTHESIA
Usually local anesthetic with intravenous sedation, or general anesthesia.

LENGTH OF STAY
Usually outpatient procedure, home the same day.

RECOVERY
Initial mild to moderate discomfort; minimal activity for several days; back to work in three to 10 days; swelling, bruising improve in three to 10 days; avoid strenuous exercise for about one month.

SCARS
Minimal scarring, concealed in the dark area surrounding the nipple, the crease beneath the breast, the armpit, or the belly button; firm and pink for at least six weeks; fade after six weeks; usually inconspicuous.

RISKS/POSSIBLE COMPLICATIONS
Serious complications, while possible, are unlikely. Some potential complications can be avoided by carefully following your surgeon's instructions.

In addition to the usual risks associated with anesthesia, other risks include:
- Capsular contracture: The scar around the implant can contract months or years after the procedure; does not have to be treated unless patient is troubled by breast firmness or distortion; treatment usually involves surgical removal of scar tissue and implant replacement.
- Nipple problems: Numbness or loss of sensation; usually temporary, permanence is rare.
- Implant displacement: Implants can displace upward, drop or rotate.
- Implant deflation: Saline implants can develop leak and deflate, not harmful; saltwater is absorbed by the body; deflated implant should be removed and, if desired, replaced. A leak in a silicone-gel implant may be less readily detectible; treatment varies.
- Sloshing and rippling: Liquid can move within the implant causing small ripples; can result in an unnatural appearance; moving fluid can cause sloshing sensation.
- Infection.
- Hematoma: Collection of blood beneath the skin; can be treated without compromising result.

The above-listed risks may be only some of those that your surgeon will discuss with you in greater detail during your consultation.

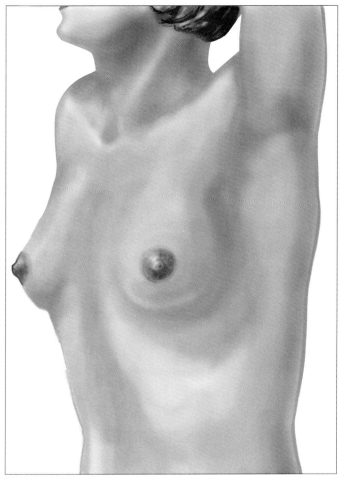

PREOPERATIVE APPEARANCE Some women are bothered by a lack of breast volume. Some have always had a minimal amount of breast tissue while others have lost breast volume as a result of having children.

"In the initial consultation, I want to find out if breast augmentation is really the right step for each particular patient," says **Laurie Casas, MD**, of Glenview, Illinois. "I think many patients approach the surgery without giving a lot of thought to what it means to have a foreign material in their body. A breast implant is not a lifetime device; it is likely, at some point, to require reoperation and replacement. If a patient cannot accept this, then breast enlargement is not the right operation for her. The decision for this surgery cannot be simply an emotional one."

"The outcome a patient achieves from breast augmentation is directly related to the decisions she makes, emphasizes **Carl Williams Jr., MD**, of Henderson, Nevada. "Make sure you are well informed about the procedure, the physician, and the long-term care and maintenance of your breasts. Do your homework. Be physically, emotionally, and financially prepared for your surgery. Breast implants do not last forever; are not perfect, and may require replacement. Like any surgical procedure, breast augmentation has associated risks and trade-offs."

The doctor-patient consultation offers the opportunity to discuss all of your concerns, desires, and expectations. You should tell your surgeon the breast size you would like to achieve and discuss all your feelings about the appearance of your breasts. Some women seeking breast augmentation may have breast sagging that requires additional surgical techniques in order to achieve a fuller and more rejuvenated breast contour.

"Whether a patient needs an augmentation, a mastopexy (breast lift), or both, depends on a variety of factors, the patient's goals being primary among them," offers **Paul M. Parker, MD**, of Paramus, New Jersey. "When I see patients in consultation and do an examination, I try to get a sense from them of how much volume they have, how much they had when they were younger, and how much they're seeking. I want a clear understanding of their goals, and then we talk about how to achieve them. I don't just describe the different techniques and possibilities; I get the patient

patient to agree upon reasonable goals. The same procedure; the same implant, incision site, or technique simply doesn't work for every patient."

Part of the patient education process for breast augmentation includes helping prospective patients understand the significance of having a foreign material in their body and the responsibility this entails. Like any device, breast implants require "maintenance." This may include using various methods to keep the breasts mobile, wearing a specific type of bra, or self-massaging the breasts. It definitely should include annual check-ups with your plastic surgeon to assess long-term results.

involved. We use computer imaging to convey visually what they might look like and show them PowerPoint presentations of similar patients to see the results of a lift, augmentation, or both. Then we work out a plan together."

"Breast augmentation should not be viewed as a method to drastically alter the overall shape of the breast," adds **Brian K. Howard**, MD, of Roswell, Georgia. "Breast implants add fullness and can provide a small degree of a breast lift; the overall appearance of the breast will remain essentially the same but on a larger scale."

Otis Allen, MD, of Bloomington, Illinois, comments, "Breast augmentation is one of the most common procedures that I perform on women in their 20s and 30s. It is my philosophy to educate the patient so she can make intelligent decisions regarding implant (bra cup) size, choice of incision for insertion, choice of location of the implant (above or below the muscle), and type of implant. I have found that this has led to patient satisfaction rates in excess of 99 percent."

"We always talk to patients about achieving more ideal proportions," offers **Onelio Garcia**, MD, of Hialeah, Florida. "Most patients would like to be able to buy clothes off the rack. If they try on a bathing suit and the bottom fits but the top is too large, then their breasts are generally too small; if the bottom fits and the top is too tight, then their breasts are too big. It's important to aim for aesthetically correct proportions. I tailor the technique for the patient's individual needs. I select incision placement on the basis of what will work best for the patient's anatomy — my thinking is that the patient shouldn't see their incisions, even when they're unclothed."

Selecting the right implant size is a crucial part of the process, both before and during surgery. Most surgeons engage patients in this process during the preoperative consultation so there is a clear understanding by both surgeon and patient regarding the expected breast size. Once in the operating room, it is up to the surgeon to come as close as possible to meeting those expectations. The goal remains patient satisfaction with the procedure.

James Apesos, MD, of Dayton, Ohio, offers this on helping patients determine their proper size: "I don't take chest measurements. Instead, one of the techniques that I've found to be extremely helpful is to ask patients to buy a non-stretch cotton bra, and we fill it with a breast sizer that lets them see exactly the size they would be after surgery. So we have a very high success rate as far as patient satisfaction is concerned."

Michael Horn, MD, of Chicago, Illinois, adds, "I think it's very important that the patient joins in the decision process concerning the procedure, beginning with breast size. We generally let patients try implants in a bra to be able to better decide what they want. That way they can look in the mirror and both see and sense what feels right for them. I generally find that it's good practice to narrow it down to a couple of sizes and then suggest that they choose the larger of the two. I like them to have input into selection of the incision site, too. I show them pictures of other patients, ones who had a similar breast formation before augmentation, to give them examples of the various choices. Most patients seem to favor the inframammary incision, which is placed at or just above the breast crease."

"I strongly advocate the sizing system we use in our office," says **Herluf Lund**, MD, of St. Louis, Missouri. "It's one I have used with great success for breast reconstructions. The patient simply wears a bra with a pocket into which she can insert sizers until she finds one that looks right. I do think it's important to spend time with the patient and develop an understanding of the results you hope to achieve."

Lee H. Colony, MD, of East Lansing, Michigan, prefers showing before and after photographs to help patients determine the size they would like to be. "While some surgeons will insert implants into a sizing bra to help patients determine size, we find that most patients tend to underestimate their implant size with this method. We prefer to have patients view before and after photos of similar patients who have had surgery to identify the appearance they like. Knowing the size of the implants used by the patients in the photos, we gain an understanding of a relatively suitable implant size. We further refine this during surgery by inserting a temporary implant into the newly created pocket and filling it to various sizes to determine what will best match the patient's wishes. Only then is the sterile implant package opened for placement."

Otto Placik, MD, of Arlington Heights, Illinois, offers this perspective, "There's a chasm between surgeons' jargon and patients' expectations. When surgeons talk about breast volume, we talk in terms of cc's (cubic centimeters), while patients talk cup sizes.

It's best if patients can actually see what a particular size will look like. Some doctors let patients try implants on under a bra in the office; the shortcoming of this approach is that patients can't take the implants home, show them to friends and family, or try them with different outfits. The surgeon might tell them to use a zip lock bag filled with 300 cc's of oatmeal or something else, but the shape is wrong. That's why I developed a patented sizing device that patients can take home with them to try out the recommended size, and it's hygienically safe, rather than an implant that others have touched."

"In helping patients to determine the size implant they want," comments **Herbert H. Bunchman II, MD**, of Mesa, Arizona, "I find it much better to have them look at many pictures that approximate their breast size with the addition of various size implants, rather than having them 'try on' an implant inside their bra. Once an implant is placed inside the body, it has a very different shape and projection than it does inside a bra."

Steven J. Smith, MD, of Knoxville, Tennessee, points out, "Patients need to know that an implant size they see on the Internet or on another patient may not achieve the same result for them. There are many variables, including pre-existing breast volume, chest wall shape, and tissue elasticity. I use a dimensional method to determine optimal implant size, which considers the patient's height, weight, and body frame, including their ribcage shape. Then I show before and after pictures of other patients. I organize the photos according to cup size and try to point out to patients examples of other patients with a similar shaped chest to their own in terms of the bony structure, muscle structure, skin envelope, and the size and location of the nipple-areola complex."

"Choosing an implant that the patient's breast tissue will accommodate is vital," advises **Gene Sloan**, MD, of Little Rock, Arkansas. "I measure the diameter of the breast, the thickness of the tissues, and the tissue mobility. My goal is to fill the skin envelope rather than stretch it out. Stretching weakens the skin, and over time it may not be able to support the implant as well."

"In breast augmentation, bigger is not necessarily better," adds **Alexander G. Nein, MD**, of Nashville, Tennessee. "The larger the breast, the less natural the appearance, and the larger and heavier the implant, the greater the risk of long-term skin stretch and sag."

"I end up several times a year operating on women who have had unfavorable results from breast augmentation, usually performed by physicians without formal plastic surgery training who used implants that were simply too large," offers **Walter L. Erhardt Jr., MD**, of Albany, Georgia. "All this accomplishes is to add projection and weight to the breasts — not to improve the breast shape and contour. After a year or even less, the breasts are sagging even more and the woman is very unhappy."

Robert Zubowski, MD, of Paramus, New Jersey, points out, "The primary goal of breast enhancement must always be to create a breast with natural shape and contour. Ultimately, most patients will be happiest with this kind of a result, even if it means compromising on size."

However, **Malcolm Z. Roth, MD**, of New York, New York, makes this interesting observation, "Society has reached a point at which many women actually may not want a natural-looking result from breast augmentation. Younger people have essentially grown up seeing models and actresses with surgically enhanced breasts, oftentimes without realizing it. Because breast implants tend to be fuller above the nipple than they would be without an implant, many people are now conditioned to think of that type of breast shape as natural. As plastic surgeons, we have to be mindful of this fact and listen to what our patients want."

Your plastic surgeon will evaluate your expectations and determine if they are realistic. The clearer you are in your own mind about your personal goals for breast augmentation, the easier it will be for you to convey your desires and for your surgeon to understand how best to assist you.

Some prospective patients have expectations or ideals that the surgery cannot achieve. That's why it is vital that patients are completely forthcoming and honest. Good communication between patient and surgeon is essential to achieving the best possible result.

"During the consultation I go over all the different options and help patients choose what would be best for them," says **Christopher Morea, MD**, of Raleigh, North Carolina. "Although certain aspects of the patient's anatomy can be altered to achieve her goals, I think it is important to point out the features that cannot be altered. I'm always very honest with patients to help them form realistic expectations, and I go over the major foreseeable risks of the surgery."

"I've found it very helpful to have patients bring in photographs of someone of the same size and weight, whose breast size looks good to them," offers **David L. Buchanan**, **MD**, of Santa Barbara, California. "If I have a patient who I feel just wants to be too big, and I am unable to convince her that is not in her best interests from an aesthetic standpoint, I'll explain to her that I simply cannot perform the surgery for her. If she wants me to refer her elsewhere, I am happy to do that. It's important to be able to say no, for both the doctor and the patient."

Your surgeon will examine your breasts and evaluate your breast anatomy because this is a determining factor in deciding what can or cannot be accomplished. There is a wide variety in natural breast shape, which can be altered somewhat but usually not dramatically by breast augmentation alone.

Patients will often assume that larger breasts automatically translate into increased cleavage. This may not be so if your breasts are naturally spaced far apart. No matter what size implant is used, it is likely that this space will remain. For a woman whose breasts connect to the chest wall more closely to each other, cleavage may be achieved by using the proper size and width implant.

Abnormal breast shape, such as a tubular breast — in which the base of the breast is quite narrow, giving the breast a tubular appearance — is difficult to correct and often requires additional techniques. Results are seldom perfect.

"We can usually improve breast shape by adding some volume in breadth, width, and projection," says **Bruce Genter**, **MD**, of Jenkintown, Pennsylvania. "Tubular breasts, however, may need additional procedures, such as scoring the breast tissue so it splays out over the implant, or removing a ring of tissue from around the areola (the pigmented skin surrounding the nipple), which helps create a round, rather than pointy, breast shape."

Asymmetry, where one breast is larger than the other or nipple height is different, is very common. In fact, virtually all women have some degree of breast asymmetry, though it may not be readily noticeable. Patients may be more aware of how their breasts look after an augmentation and sometimes only notice these slight variations following surgery. That's why most plastic surgeons are careful to point out asymmetries prior to breast augmentation, so patients will understand that these differences were present before surgery and are not the result of breast implants. In some cases, asymmetry can be improved by breast augmentation. If there is size asymmetry, breasts can be made more similar with the use of different size implants. However, if the inframammary creases, where the bottom of the breast meets the chest, are at different heights, the breasts will generally remain at different heights following an augmentation. This condition is not unusual, and a one- to two-centimeter difference is fairly common. The plastic surgeon may be able to equalize crease height somewhat but probably cannot achieve perfect symmetry.

Improving asymmetry in the position of the nipples can be done at the time of the implant surgery and requires an incision around the areola. Most patients are willing to accept a slight difference in nipple height, which is usually not noticeable to anyone else. Far more bothersome is the situation of nipples that are too low on the chest.

"I feel that optimal results require attention to detail," states **Chester Sakura**, **MD**, of Albuquerque, New Mexico. "For example, I look carefully at the position, size and shape of the nipple-areola. I consider the amount of upper breast fullness and lateral breast curve. Naturally, breast size and symmetry are important, but breast shape is just as important as size. I believe the careful formation of the implant pocket, accurate filling of the implants, internal or external breast lifting, and small adjustments of the nipple-areola, as needed, will produce an outstanding cosmetic result."

PREPARATION

Once you and your surgeon have decided that breast augmentation is appropriate for you, he or she will advise you on the procedural details. In addition to examining your breasts and possibly taking photos for your medical record, your surgeon will interview you about your medical history. It is important to provide a complete history of medical procedures and illnesses you have had, as well as medications you have taken or are taking currently. Be sure to include any information concerning a family history of breast cancer. Although no scientific evidence suggests that breast augmentation increases the risk of breast cancer, the presence of breast implants can make mammography more difficult. Women with implants, who are of the age to undergo mammographic screening, require additional X-ray views in order to visualize as much breast tissue as possible.

Depending upon your age, your surgeon may also recommend a mammogram before surgery.

Tell your doctor if you plan to lose a significant amount of weight, since your plastic surgeon may recommend that you stabilize your weight before having the procedure. There is no evidence that breast implants affect pregnancy or the ability to breast-feed; however, pregnancy does affect breast size, and this could impact the long-term results of your breast augmentation. You should tell your surgeon if you might plan to become pregnant at some time in the future. Many women decide to proceed with breast augmentation even if they anticipate future pregnancy, feeling that they can deal with the possible need for secondary surgery to restore their desired breast contour at a later time.

As **Fredric Newman, MD**, of Darien, Connecticut, reports, many of his patients who seek breast augmentation when they are finished bearing children are also good candidates for a tummy tuck. "I am doing more and more breast augmentations in conjunction with tummy tucks. A lot of women who are coming in for a tummy tuck also have involution of the breast as a result of childbirth, and these two procedures go very nicely hand-in-hand. One, in fact, complements the other, not only in restoring natural contours but also in one contour actually enhancing the other. You go from having a protuberant abdomen and a flat chest, where one accentuates the other negatively to having a nicely projecting chest and a flat abdomen. The hills and valleys complement and enhance each other."

Breast augmentation can be performed with local anesthetic and intravenous sedation or with a general anesthesia, which allows you to sleep through the surgery. Your surgeon will discuss and explain the type of anesthesia to be used. He or she will give you guidelines on eating, drinking, smoking, vitamins and medications prior to surgery. It is important to follow these guidelines precisely to avoid the possibility of drug interactions or other potential complications associated with anesthesia.

"Breast augmentation can generally be performed safely as an outpatient procedure in an accredited ambulatory facility or office surgical setting," says **Jay B. Fine, MD**, of Pembroke Pines, Florida. "I usually use general anesthesia, administered by an anesthesiologist, and I am assisted by a highly trained operating room staff. As with any surgery, there are risks involved with this operation. But it is extremely rare for a patient to experience serious complications that might require transport to a hospital."

Unsatisfactory results or complications of breast augmentation can include infection, bleeding, marked asymmetry of the breasts, loss of nipple sensation, breast firmness (called capsular contracture), and implant deflation or rupture. Although serious conditions rarely occur, you need to be aware of the risks involved and how your surgeon plans to handle complications if they occur. There is no way to predict which patients will experience breast firmness, but in some cases this problem may necessitate reoperation and may reoccur.

There is a variety of techniques and options in breast augmentation your doctor will discuss with you. As mentioned earlier, if you want to increase your breast volume but your breasts are sagging, your surgeon may recommend that a breast lift be performed in conjunction with augmentation. If your only concern is droopy breasts and you have no desire to increase breast size, then a breast lift alone, without implants, is most appropriate.

"Patients who want a breast lift are usually trying to regain something they once had, but augmentation patients are seeking something they haven't had — an amount of breast volume that they feel comfortable with," offers **Julio L. Garcia, MD**, of Las Vegas, Nevada.

"Without question, the combination of augmentation and mastopexy is one of the most difficult procedures in plastic surgery," says **Scott Holley, MD**, of Portage, Michigan. "The inherent challenge lies in combining augmentation of breast volume with lifting and enhancing breast shape during the same operation. Fortunately, recent advances in implant design and refinement of traditional shaping techniques have helped plastic surgeons deliver consistent results, often with smaller scars. I have found augmentation/ mastopexy to be truly transforming for the post-partum or weight-loss patient who wants to get rid of her 'deflated' figure."

THE SURGERY
IMPLANT PLACEMENT
The methods for positioning implants include subglandular placement (directly beneath the glandular tissue of the breast) or submuscular placement (beneath

the glandular tissue and the pectoral muscle). There are advantages and disadvantages of each method. Your plastic surgeon will discuss these with you and, based upon your anatomy and desires as well as his or her relevant clinical experience, will make a recommendation.

"Cosmetic breast surgery has moved away from the 'cookie-cutter' approach, where the surgeon learns one way to do the procedure and does it the same way for every patient," says **Michael Rose, MD,** of Shrewsbury, New Jersey. **Andrew Elkwood, MD,** also of Shrewsbury, agrees and adds, "Now, we have a wide range of techniques to choose from, and it behooves every plastic surgeon to be able to apply the right procedure to the right patient and thus achieve an optimal result for that patient."

Rosellen Meystrik, MD, of Springfield, Missouri, explains it this way, "We individualize the procedure for each patient. For example, if a patient has had several children and her breasts have gone through an involutional change and lost volume, there is a mismatch between the amount of breast tissue and the size of the skin envelope. In that case, I would recommend that we use a subglandular approach so we can balance the amount of skin she has with the amount of breast volume. Another patient may be very small and have very little breast tissue. Since the implant will make up a significant portion of her breast, I would recommend a submuscular approach, which would make the implant less visible."

David V. Poole, MD, of Altamonte Springs, Florida, agrees, "Implant placement depends on the patient. If a woman is thin, I generally put the implant under the muscle, since there is usually insufficient tissue to adequately cover and hide it if placed on top of the muscle. The incision site also depends on the patient's individual needs and desires. Although I have used the transaxillary (armpit) incision site, I most often use the periareolar (around the lower portion of the areola) or the inframammary (just above the breast crease) incision. Sometimes conditions dictate the site, but it's usually based on patient preference. I explain the differences to patients and show them pictures of augmentations I've done with scars in the different locations."

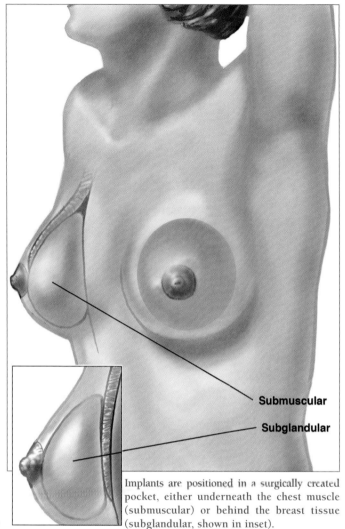

Submuscular

Subglandular

Implants are positioned in a surgically created pocket, either underneath the chest muscle (submuscular) or behind the breast tissue (subglandular, shown in inset).

Subglandular placement generally means less recovery time with less postoperative discomfort and pain, since only skin and fat are cut and the muscles are left intact. However, any pain or discomfort following a submuscular augmentation can easily be controlled with medication in the typical patient.

"I feel that implants should go on top of the muscle, except for breast reconstruction," says Dr. Baker. "Studies show that there is no difference in the occurrence of capsular contracture with subglandular or subpectoral placement. The problem with subpectoral placement is that it distorts the breast when the muscle is tightened.

It also involves a more painful recovery, and I think it looks less natural. Plus it weakens the muscle by about 20 percent. A study of female body builders showed that after subpectoral placement they were not as proficient at bench presses and butterflies."

Clearly, there are strong opinions on both sides of the issue of implant placement. Some surgeons feel that submuscular, rather than subglandular, placement provides a more natural look, but it is advisable for patients to review before and after photographs illustrating the results of both methods.

"I recommend placing the implant under the muscle," says **Gloria A. de Olarte, MD**, of Pasadena, California. "The muscle will in effect create an internal brassiere, which supports the implant and helps prevent sagging. When a patient has the implant placed over the muscle, the implant is more conspicuous. If there are ripples in the implant, they will be noticed as well."

Gary D. Hall, MD, of Leawood, Kansas, also favors submuscular placement, "Except in cases involving certain deformities of the breast, or if the patient expresses a strong desire for subglandular placement, I place implants beneath the muscle. It has been my experience that it gives more tissue coverage and support for the implant. I also believe that submuscular place-ment reduces the incidence of complications such as infection or capsule formation. I've found in my practice that there is less chance of noticeable rippling or future sagging of the breasts. I've had a less than one percent rate of capsule formation, and I've never had an infection. Also, if a patient is having a breast lift in addition to augmentation, I always recommend putting the implant beneath the muscle. It helps preserve the blood supply to the nipple, and I believe it reduces the risk of complications from the combined procedures."

It is generally thought that submuscular placement causes less interference with mammography. Yet, a woman who works out with weights may feel that placement under the muscle creates an unnatural appearance when the muscle is flexed. Some surgeons adopt a method that, to some extent, combines elements of each approach.

"I think it's a very straightforward operation," com-ments **Donald W. Hause, MD**, Sacramento, California. "In my opinion, the bi-planer method, where the pectoral muscle covers the upper portion and the lower plane is left open, is probably the best way to go. You get advantages of being both above and below the muscle."

"My goal with all procedures is to make the end result look natural," says **Brian J. Lee, MD**, of Fort Wayne, Indiana. "I personally like placing implants under the muscle, which I believe creates a more natural appearance and reduces complications. Because it is beneath the muscle, everyday movements massage the implant, which I believe helps to lessen the chance of developing capsular contracture and thus increases the longevity of optimal results."

Linda Leffel, MD, of Bend, Oregon, also likes to put implants beneath the muscle, "With saline breast augmentation, I prefer a submuscular approach. This minimizes the visible and palpable wrinkling under the muscle, decreases the risk of infection, and most importantly, over the last 14 years of following my patients, I have seen excellent longevity of breast shape. The pectoralis muscle helps support the implant, and there is less sag of the breast skin over time."

And **Joel B. Singer, MD**, of Westport, Connecticut, adds, "Of course each case is different because each patient is different, but the technique I generally use with saline implants is to do a periareolar incision, and then a total submuscular placement, making a pocket that's totally surrounded by muscle. I don't cut any muscle. Sometimes I'll stretch the muscle if it's really tight, but I don't cut the muscle fascia. Then I leave the muscle space open when I finish the procedure. I've done it this way for years and get very good results."

"I began putting implants behind the pectoralis and seratus muscles in 1981, which totally reversed what until then had been a significant problem, namely capsular contracture," says Dr. Bunchman "Since then I have rarely had an incidence of capsular contracture. I believe the majority of surgeons are doing it that way now. My reason at first was to avoid implant wrinkling in thin people, but in doing so I also achieved the reduction in the incidence of capsular contracture."

Alexander Majidian, MD, of Calabasas, California, says, "I go to great lengths to minimize capsular con-tracture, or hardening of the breast. We use a no-touch technique protocol, where everybody involved in the surgery wears two pairs of powder-free gloves; implants are touched only by the surgeon who changes gloves before and after each handling, the implant doesn't touch the patient's skin even though the skin is sterilized; and, rather than filling the saline implants from a basin, they are filled through a closed system of tubes, avoiding all environmental exposure."

Mokhtar Asaadi, MD, of West Orange, New Jersey, adds, "The goal of breast augmentation is a natural-looking breast with no long-term problems, especially capsular contraction, and easy follow-up with mammograms and breast evaluation. We use saline implants under the pectoralis muscle through the submammary, or inframammary, approach. Finesse in surgical technique and attention to detail enable us to achieve the results we want for our patients without complications."

IMPLANT TYPES

For some time, saline-filled implants, which comprise a silicone shell filled with sterile saltwater, have been used in all patients undergoing primary breast augmentation surgery. 1n 1992, because of concerns that there was insufficient information demonstrating the safety of silicone gel-filled breast implants, the U.S. Food and Drug Administration (FDA) took gel-filled implants off the market. Surgeons have been permitted by the FDA to use silicone gel-filled implants for post-mastectomy breast reconstruction, certain cases of congenital deformity, replacement of already existing gel implants and situations where saline implants have proven unsatisfactory. Since the ban on silicone gel-filled implants, a great deal of additional scientific research has been compiled and analyzed in support of their safety, and manufacturers have recently won FDA approval for marketing current models of silicone gel-filled implants. Your plastic surgeon can update you on the currently available choices for implant types and styles.

"Silicone implants have never stopped being used for breast augmentation," comments Dr. Apesos. "They've been used continuously for the past 20 years throughout Asia, Africa, South America, and Europe. The only place there was a moratorium was in the United States, which really puts the silicone implant issue into the political realm rather than the scientific realm. There has been no scientific evidence that silicone caused problems. The biggest problem with silicone breast implants, and the heart of the controversy, is that they can break, and detection is not as easy as with saline implants. When a saline implant deflates, it becomes flat. A silicone gel implant usually requires clinical diagnosis to determine rupture. If a silicone gel implant ruptures, the gel can 'bleed' into surrounding tissues,

causing contracture, or firmness of the breast. Nevertheless, gel implants have never been shown to be harmful from a health standpoint."

John P. Zimmermann, MD, of Napa, California, has this to say about silicone gel-filled implants: "There is no scientific evidence that silicone implants cause disease. As far as rupture, most modern gel implants are extremely cohesive. If you cut them in half, they will remain solid and not push out of shape or leak. In thin women, I find that gel implants have the most natural look and feel."

Dr. Fine feels that saline implants deliver excellent results for his patients. "All implants are silicone bags, which can be divided into categories based on what they're filled with: some have silicone gel, and some are filled with sterile saltwater. The gel-filled implants have been off the general market for more than 10 years, but saline-filled implants have been in use for 40 years or so and are generally available to us. They're safe and produce consistently good results, and because they are inflated after insertion, they can be placed through a much smaller incision."

"With saline, if it should leak, which doesn't happen very often, the sterile solution is harmlessly absorbed by the body," says Karl O. Wustrack, MD, of West Linn, Oregon. "The implant goes flat, so the surgeon removes it and puts in a new one. When a saline implant is placed underneath the muscle and the pocket is sufficiently stretched out, it is very soft and natural appearing."

The silicone shell of a breast implant may be smooth or textured. Some surgeons believe that textured-surface implants help to reduce the incidence of capsular contracture. However, studies have been inconclusive, and there is insufficient evidence to conclude that either textured or smooth implants offer a definitive advantage in reducing the risk of breast firmness. Breast implants also come in different shapes — round or shaped to resemble the natural curve of the breast. There is disagreement among surgeons as to which of these shapes is more anatomically correct, but either one can provide an excellent result. In fact, it may be very difficult to determine which type of implant has been used when viewing a patient in the standing pose.

More recently added to the variety of implant models are those offering added projection. The suitability of such implants for a particular patient can be determined by careful preoperative evaluation as well as consideration of the patient's aesthetic goals.

INCISION OPTIONS

There are several options for incision placement in breast augmentation. One incision, called the inframammary, can be located in or just above the crease beneath the breast.

"I think a lot of emphasis has been placed on keeping the incision off the breast mound," says **Robert Anderson, MD**, of Fort Worth, Texas. "In my view, a 'good' scar — that is, a normal, well-healed scar — is inconspicuous no matter where it's located. The thing I tell patients is that 99 percent of patients have 'good' scars. But if you happen to be in the one percent that gets a thick, red, angry scar, I don't think you'd want it in your armpit, where it's going to show when you wear a bathing suit, tank top, or T-shirt. The second least favorable place would be around your nipple. If you

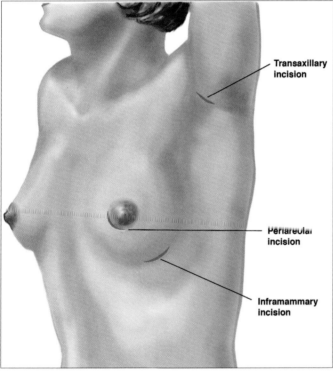

The incisions for placing breast implants are generally small and can be placed inconspicuously in one of several locations: underneath the breast (at or just above the breast crease), called the inframammary approach; around the areola (the pigmented skin surrounding the nipple), called the periareolar approach; or under the arm (in the armpit), called the transaxillary approach. A less common technique, the transumbilical approach (not shown), places implants through an incision in the navel (belly button).

end up with an unfavorable scar, the best place would be under the breast."

"I prefer the inframammary incision," agrees **John Burnett, MD**, of Fresno, California, "which with saline implants can be less then two and a half centimeters long. When there's need for some revision, such as replacing a deflated implant or making a size adjustment, I find it easier to go back in from below, through the inframammary incision, rather than having to go through all the breast tissue and muscle. In my experience, there is a higher degree of alteration in nipple sensation going back in through the periareolar incision. I find with the inframammary incision, revisions are a simpler operation requiring less anesthesia."

"While I tailor the surgery for each patient, most of my breast augmentation patients choose, and I favor, a small inframammary incision," says **Stephen Goldstein, MD**, of Englewood, Colorado. "I find that this allows me to place the implant with more precision. I place most implants in the submuscular plane. Having more natural padding over the implant tends to serve the patient best in the long run."

Another choice is to make the incision around the dark skin surrounding the nipple (areola), called a periareolar incision. "One of the advantages of augmentation using saline implants is that the incisions are small, about three centimeters," adds **Daniel C. Morello, MD**, of White Plains, New York, "which is slightly over an inch. When such a small incision is placed around the edge of the areola, it is virtually undetectable.

"I find that about 90 percent of my augmentation-lift procedures can be approached fully through a periareolar incision," says **Francine Vagotis, MD**, of Grand Rapids, Michigan. "The scar from this incision fades and becomes very hard to distinguish."

George Sanders, MD, of Encino, California, adds, "I have always found that the incision around the areola is the most versatile. If you need to go back in for additional surgery, it can be done through the same site. If you make the incision in a careful way and repair it in a careful way, you will have a scar that's very difficult to detect, and the chances of numbness of the nipple are minimal. In fact, it's not clear that the risk of altered nipple sensation is any greater with the periareolar approach than with other approaches, because subsequent numbness is primarily a result of how the nerves were impacted when creating the pocket for the implant."

Steven K. White, Sr., MD, of Myrtle Beach, South Carolina agrees. "Nipple sensation is not related to the incision made on the breast but rather to the pocket made for the implant."

Fereydoon S. Mahjouri, MD, of Fridley, Minnesota, also prefers the periareolar incision site, "In my hands, placing implants through incisions around the areola produces the most pleasing results. The inframammary fold (where the breast meets the chest wall) is left untouched; therefore the chance of an unsightly "bottoming out" is reduced. With the periareolar approach, the nipple-areola complex can be adjusted and placed at the peak of the breast mound. Excess skin of the breast envelope, in some patients, can be trimmed above, below, or around the areola. Loss of sensation in the breasts has not been any different with this approach than with others."

Archibald S. Miller, MD, of Tulsa, Oklahoma, is another advocate of the periareolar incision. "The periareolar approach is a minimal incision technique that provides a maximum result with practically no noticeable scarring. If you make the incision directly in the areola and just about an inch long, it is virtually undetectable after about six months to a year. You can use that incision for both submuscular and subglandular techniques."

Alternatively, the incision can be placed in the armpit. Called axillary or transaxillary, this technique may use an endoscopic method of placement, where the surgeon employs a tiny camera and very slender instruments to guide the implant into place.

Although transaxillary placement, with or without use of an endoscope, doesn't leave any scarring in the breast area, there is a scar in the armpit, which may be visible with sleeveless clothing.

"Although we tailor each surgery for the individual, I generally prefer the armpit incision. This avoids having a scar on the breast where it could be seen in an intimate situation," says Dr. Julio Garcia.

"I specialize in transaxillary subpectoral augmentation," says Daniel C. Mills, MD, of Laguna Beach, California. "With this surgical technique, the incision is made in the axilla, or armpit. The implant is placed under the breast tissue and beneath the pectoralis or chest muscle. I prefer this approach because there are no scars directly on the breast, there is less chance of nipple-sensation loss, and the submuscular approach allows for better mammogram reading."

"After having done breast augmentations for a quarter of a century, I have found that the ideal situation is endoscopically placing a saline breast implant through a small incision under the armpit," says R. Laurence Berkowitz, MD, of Campbell, California. "Endoscopy affords the ability to control the size and shape of the pocket. It is minimally invasive, simple with predictable results, takes less than an hour for the procedure and three to five days to recover. I prefer saline implants because each is simply a bag of sterile water placed in a pocket — the biggest challenge is achieving symmetry. Silicone gel implants have more shape and are easier to control, but in my view they are not worth the potential complications associated with rupture."

Alfonso Oliva, MD, of Spokane, Washington, also likes to use the transaxillary incision when appropriate, "Although not applicable in all patients requesting augmentation mammaplasty, placing a saline implant under the pectoralis muscle via an axillary incision has several advantages. The biggest advantage is that the incision is completely hidden and heals well. The endoscope provides magnification, clear visualization of the dissection planes, and precision in elevating the pectoralis muscle. The operation is best suited for patients with good breast shape but who require an increase in volume without much manipulation of the muscle-breast parenchyma interface."

Mario Loomis, MD, of Middletown, New York, adds, "Most of our patients' breast enlargements are performed endoscopically through the axilla since this avoids scars on the breast and dissection through breast tissue. I place saline implants under the muscle because I feel this provides for a more natural appearing breast augmentation with greater camouflage of the implant."

Another option for breast augmentation is the TUBA, or transumbilical breast augmentation technique, which involves inserting the implants through an incision in the belly button. Using the TUBA technique, a surgeon makes a small incision in the inner folds of the belly button, guiding an endoscopic tube that transports the implant from the navel to the breast pocket.

"The choice of incision site depends on the patient's goals," says **Lawrence Rosenberg, MD**, of Lutherville, Maryland. "Incisions are only about an inch long, so they will not be very noticeable regardless of their location."

Paul J. LoVerme, MD, of Verona, New Jersey, adds, "Everyone wants the perfect breast, with little or no scarring. There are choices, so it's important for patients to discuss with their surgeon and fully understand the advantages and disadvantages of each approach."

Once an incision is made in the location that you and your surgeon have agreed upon, the breast tissue is lifted to create a pocket. If the procedure is subglandular, this is done directly behind the breast tissue; if submuscular, the pocket is created underneath the pectoral muscle. A deflated breast implant is then placed in the pocket, inflated with sterile saline to the appropriate size, and positioned optimally. In the case of a transumbilical procedure, the unfilled breast implant is rolled into a tubular shape, inserted through the tunnel and into the pocket.

Eric Mariotti, MD, of Concord, California, uses a couple of techniques to help ensure the proper positioning of breast implants. "I almost exclusively use a technique of suturing the bottom of the pocket to itself, creating a strong sling, which holds the implant in the correct position. This, along with having the patient wear an underwire bra with the cup cut out, provides excellent support where needed while the breast heals in the correct position."

Breast augmentation surgery usually takes between one and two hours to complete. Stitches are used to close the incisions; tape may also be used for greater support. A gauze bandage may be applied over your breasts to help with healing.

POST OP

When surgery is completed, you will be taken into a recovery area and closely monitored. Unless you have previously determined that you will stay in the hospital or surgical facility overnight, you should be able to go home after a few hours.

One of the things that many breast augmentation patients are concerned about is postoperative pain.

Dr. Lund says, "Most of my patients are back to work the next day. In the past, when surgeons were performing augmentations, they were very rough with the tissues. Now, by treating the tissues much more tenderly and creating a pocket with much greater precision, trauma is minimized. Patients experience much less pain and can recover more quickly. In my practice, I also use pain pumps, which help patients feel more comfortable and avoid the side effects of pain medications."

"I don't use pain pumps, yet when I speak with my patients on the night after their surgery, almost all report feeling no substantial pain from this procedure," says Dr. Morello, "and that's without taking narcotic pain medication. I accomplish this in several ways. Pain in surgery is directly related to how much surgical trauma is inflicted. If surgery is done delicately and very precisely, there is less trauma and less pain. I do all augmentations under general anesthesia and have muscle relaxation administered by the anesthesiologist. I retract the pectoral muscle very gently and divide it sharply from below to release it and accommodate the implant, thus inflicting minimum trauma. Additionally, patients are treated for five days with muscle relaxant. If the operation is done on Thursday, patients are back to work by Monday."

"One of the things I do that dramatically reduces pain," offers **James D. McMahan, MD**, of Columbus, Ohio, "is to inject tumescent fluid, which already contains a short-acting anesthetic and to which I've also added a long-acting anesthetic, around the breast right after the patient goes to sleep. Then, after making the incision, I lift up the corner of the muscle and inject more of that diluted local anesthetic before starting the dissection. The effect is dramatic, and patients come out of anesthesia feeling much more comfortable."

And **Robert Lowen, MD**, of Mountain View, California, comments, "A rapid recovery with return to normal activity, including driving within four days, can be obtained for 95 percent of patients by using specific techniques and instrumentation. Using monopolar forceps cautery and fiberoptic illumination, a bloodless dissection under direct vision is done which results in no trauma to the chest wall, no tissue staining with blood, minimal to no bruising, and no need for drains or special bras. In addition to rapid recovery, using this technique there has been no incidence of capsular contracture in my last 250 patients."

Dr. Sloan adds, "In my practice most of my breast augmentation patients are women who've had at least two children, and they just want to restore some of their lost breast volume. With precise surgical technique and a specific recovery protocol, which includes prescribing mild analgesics rather than strong narcotics, I can perform an augmentation on Friday, putting the implants under the muscle, and patients can be back at work on Monday."

Your preparations for surgery should include arrangements for someone to drive you home after your surgery and, if needed, to help you out for a few days with household tasks. Women with small children should avoid lifting them or other strenuous activities as advised by their surgeon.

Dressings, if you have them, will be removed within several days. If you were fitted with a support bra directly after surgery, you will probably be told to continue wearing it, or you may now be instructed to wear one. You will probably be permitted to shower between three and seven days after the surgery, and the stitches will be removed in about a week. Some doctors encourage patients to regularly massage their breasts during the early post-operative period.

"I use no dressings after the surgery, just a Band-Aid or a tiny piece of gauze on the incision," says Dr. Morello, who adds, "While the formation of scar tissue around the breast implant is a normal process after surgery, controlling the scar, keeping it mobile and moving rather than fixed, accomplishes a more natural result. I start early motion exercises and implant massage within the first five days."

There will be some discoloration and swelling, but this will quickly disappear. You may also experience a burning sensation in your nipples for about two weeks, but this will subside as bruising fades. Some residual swelling will probably continue but should completely resolve within one month.

It is often possible to return to work within a few days or a week following surgery; however, vigorous activities, particularly arm movement, may be restricted for two to three weeks. You should abstain from sexual activity for at least the first week following surgery. Care

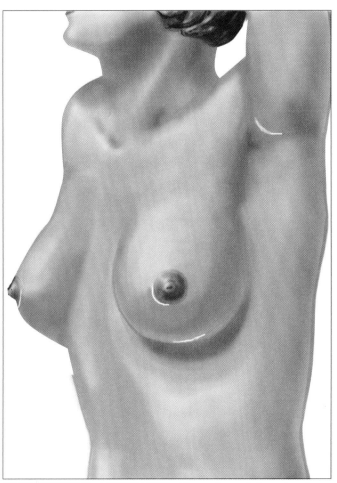

POSTOPERATIVE APPEARANCE. The enhanced breast volume achieved by breast augmentation surgery often helps women feel more satisfied and self-confident about the way they look. Depending on the selected incision option, scars are inconspicuous, either underneath the breast, around the areola, or in the underarm area.

must be taken to be extremely gentle with your breasts for at least the next month.

Your scars will be firm and pink for six weeks or longer. After several months, your scars will begin to fade, and most likely will be inconspicuous.

LOOKING AHEAD

Most women are very happy with the results of breast augmentation. It is not unusual for them to feel a real sense of excitement about their new figure and a boost in self-confidence.

"Breast augmentation can be a dramatic, life-changing procedure, although no one can promise that it will be," says **David J. Levens, MD**, of Coral Springs, Florida. "Some women start out somewhat shy and reserved, and after the procedure they really come out of their shell — their posture is better or they may enjoy wearing a different style of clothing. Depending on the individual, this 'coming out' can be very public or a more private event."

This doesn't mean that women who seek out breast augmentation naturally suffer from low self-esteem or lack of self-confidence. The decision to have breast augmentation is a highly personal one, and most women who choose breast enlargement say that they are doing it to please themselves. In fact, many women decide to have the procedure despite objections or even criticisms from others. On the other hand, family and friends are often extremely supportive of a woman's choice to enhance her breasts, and if a woman is in fact a good candidate for breast augmentation, this kind of support is always beneficial.

"Sometimes a patient will come in with her husband or a friend and ask their opinion," says **Gustavo Galante, MD**, of Munster, Indiana. "But it's the patient's desires that are important. In these cases, I bring this to the patient's attention, telling her, 'This is your body, these are your breasts, and you are the one who has to be happy with them.'"

Women who seek breast augmentation usually are fairly well informed about the procedure prior to consulting with a plastic surgeon. They have explored and researched the surgery through authoritative sources such as the official Web sites of the American Society for Aesthetic Plastic Surgery (www.surgery.org) and American Society of Plastic Surgeons (www.plasticsurgery.org). After they have consulted with a qualified plastic surgeon and reviewed the options, risks, and benefits associated with breast augmentation, they are ready to make a decision that is right for them. Your chances of feeling wonderfully fulfilled will be greatly enhanced by educating yourself well regarding breast enlargement surgery and by communicating honestly and openly with your plastic surgeon.

You will have an ongoing relationship with your plastic surgeon, including follow-up care and postoperative evaluations.

"We want to see patients frequently during those first three months, and then yearly. I never charge for postoperative visits because I want patients to come back, and I want to encourage them to guard against complications," says Dr. Goldstein. "It's my experience that if capsular contraction will be a problem, it will occur in the first three months," he adds.

"The success of this procedure lies in good patient education and evaluation, meticulous operative planning and surgical technique, and conscientious postoperative management," offers **Fanny dela Cruz, MD**, of West Bloomfield, Michigan. "Breast implants are not lifetime devices: they have the potential to leak or rupture, and they do not change as a woman's body ages over time. There is no way to predict how long the implants will maintain their softness, appearance and function. That's one reason it is important to have an ongoing professional relationship with your plastic surgeon."

Your health and satisfaction are your surgeon's primary concerns. Never hesitate to contact him or her with any questions you may have before or after your procedure.

Historically, conceptions of the "ideal breast" — size, shape, and even nipple characteristics and position — have varied across time and cultures. Efforts to enlarge the breast have included injections of paraffin, silicone, and other substances, which produced catastrophic outcomes. Sometimes the disastrous consequences of these methods are not apparent until years later. Unfortunately, plastic surgeons continue to see women who have undergone such ill-advised treatments, the results of which are generally irreversible.

The first recorded surgical breast augmentation, performed by Czerny of Heidelberg, Germany, in 1895, was an attempt to correct breast asymmetry by transferring a large lipoma from the buttock to the breast. The first reported use of silicone breast implants was by Cronin and Gerow in the early 1960s. Their work began the era of modern breast augmentation, a procedure that has been among the most commonly performed cosmetic operations for many years, according to statistics from the American Society for Aesthetic Plastic Surgery. A temporary dip in the popularity of breast augmentation, fueled in no small measure by the press and subsequently by the "ambulance chasing" tactics of trial attorneys, occurred after a sensationalized television news report on breast implants by Connie Chung in December 1990. Ultimately, in 1992, stating that there was insufficient scientific evidence confirming the safety of silicone gel-filled breast implants, the FDA banned the use of gel implants for breast augmentation. (Their use was permitted, however, for breast reconstruction and other exceptional situations.) Since that time, saline-filled breast implants have been the only option for American women seeking breast augmentation, and they have generally been quite a satisfactory product.

With the collection of additional scientific proof of implant safety, however, the FDA has recently approved new varieties of gel-filled implants for breast augmentation. These additional options will give women and their surgeons more choices and, presumably, further increase patient satisfaction with the results of breast enlargement.

Today, the news about breast augmentation is quite positive. As a result of expanded scientific and clinical research, we now know a lot more about breast implants and how to best use them. The search for even better implant designs and filler materials continues. We also are taking a new look at nonsurgical alternatives. Fat injection for breast enlargement, condemned for almost two decades primarily because of its potential to obscure the results of mammography, is being reinvestigated in light of advances in cancer detection methods as well as our ability to transfer fat with better long-term survival. However, more research is needed before this approach can be considered safe and effective.

Breast augmentation, like liposuction, is a procedure that has increasingly been promoted by physicians without extensive enough training. Many such physicians hope that by reducing the fees they charge for the procedure, patients will overlook their lack of relevant credentials. Fortunately, most patients recognize that breast augmentation surgery requires a high level of skill and experience, beginning with the quality of preoperative evaluation and surgical planning through the actual details of the surgical procedure and postoperative care. Board-certified plastic surgeons have been performing breast augmentation for more than 40 years, and it continues to be one of the operations that brings our patients the greatest satisfaction. Our expert surgeons' personal preferences regarding technique are based not only on their training but also their experience — in general, what works well in their hands. Once again, as with most other aesthetic surgical operations, there is more than one way to achieve a great result.

Studies have shown improvement in body image, self-confidence, and sexuality resulting from breast augmentation, and the vast majority of women who undergo this procedure say they would make the same choice again. It is important, however, for any woman considering breast augmentation to be well aware of the potential risks and side effects associated with the procedure. The fact remains that breast enlargement requires the insertion of a medical device and conscientious follow-up throughout a woman's life. If all this is well understood before surgery, patients have an excellent opportunity for a happy outcome.

— Peter B. Fodor, MD

BREAST LIFT

Mastopexy

A breast lift, or mastopexy, is designed primarily to elevate and recontour rather than to increase the size of the breasts — although a breast lift can be performed in conjunction with breast augmentation if greater breast volume is desired. Candidates for breast lift surgery are women who have droopy or saggy breasts and would like to have them restored to a more youthful position. Additionally, almost all breast reduction operations also combine an element of breast lifting.

"Unfortunately, until the law of gravity is repealed, all breasts are going to droop over time," says O. **Allen Guinn, III, MD**, of Lee's Summit, Missouri, "and the larger the breast, the faster it will happen. A breast lift removes the excess skin that is responsible for the droopy look, placing the breast in a higher position on the chest, with a more youthful shape. Implants alone may help temporarily by filling out a 'deflated breast,' but the sagging returns rapidly, leaving the patient with a larger drooping chest. Several operations are available to lift the breast, with or without the addition of implants, and the procedure chosen is based on the desires and needs of the individual patient."

"The patients I see most often for breast enhancement surgery are women who have lost a lot of volume and elasticity in their breasts after childbirth," explains **Peter Hyans, MD**, of Berkeley Heights, New Jersey. "This usually requires an implant for volume and various techniques for lifting. My goal is to create natural-looking, not overly large, breasts. I usually use a dual plane technique, where the majority of the implant is beneath the muscle but the lowest part may not be. I find this delivers a more natural-appearing result. A vital aspect of a successful procedure is for the patient to have realistic expectations, and it is up to the surgeon to help her understand the process so she has a good idea of what to expect."

"The joys of childbirth often bring excess skin of the breasts with loss of breast volume," says **Linda Leffel, MD**, of Bend, Oregon. "My patients complain of a 'deflated' breast and want to restore the fullness of youth. An implant will increase the breast volume, and a lift will remove the extra skin. I prefer a natural appearance, so I most commonly place incisions around the areola (which will move the nipple higher on the chest wall, and narrow the diameter of the areola). If a woman has significant excess skin, then a vertical incision, similar to a dart that serves to tailor a piece of clothing, will remove additional skin. The implant is first placed under the muscle, followed by redraping of the skin over the implant. Generally the scars are quite minimal; however, if scars become raised or widened, there are options for improving them. A majority of women retain nipple sensation and the ability to breast-feed following a breast lift."

As mentioned earlier, while the use of implants is an option for increasing volume at the time a breast lift is performed, a traditional mastopexy procedure elevates without enlarging the breast.

"Combining mastopexy and augmentation can work well, but often a woman simply doesn't want larger breasts," says **Martin Luftman, MD**, of Lexington, Kentucky. "In such cases, reshaping the breast requires working with the breast tissue. Breast shape is all about the breast base diameter. If you have a woman with a large, flat, sagging breast and you try to reduce the excess, you will just end up with a large, flatter breast unless you can reduce the diameter of the breast base and increase breast projection. The technique I use allows me to use the breast tissue to form the base of a cone with the center projecting out into a peak, providing a more youthful and aesthetically pleasing breast shape."

Lawrence Rosenberg, MD, of Lutherville, Maryland, adds, "Plastic surgeons often perform lifts in conjunction with augmentation, but for some patients it isn't appropriate. Patients for mastopexy are often older than augmentation patients and have different goals for their surgery; they've finished their childbearing and seek to regain their earlier shape."

"Of course, breast lift, or mastopexy, can be done without placement of breast implants," offers James M. Nachbar, MD, Scottsdale, Arizona. "A breast lift elevates the nipples, along with tightening of the skin in the breasts' lower portion to achieve better shape and positioning of the breasts. However, a breast lift alone will not restore the loss of fullness of the breast, especially the upper breast, which occurs following pregnancy. Therefore, when a breast lift is done following pregnancy, I find that it is most often combined with the placement of breast implants, although relatively small implants may be used if desired. I place the implants under the muscle (pectoralis major), which helps to avoid sagging."

Richard P. Rand, MD, of Bellevue, Washington, offers this perspective on combining breast lift and augmentation, "Some surgeons believe you can't do a lift without an implant. Yet some patients feel that their breasts are large enough. For those women, I perform a complete lifting and reshaping procedure to elevate the nipple and areola well above the inframammary crease, tighten the skin envelope, restore support to the breast, and remove any excess skin. This involves actual sculpting of the breast. If a surgeon is comfortable with this method (I use the central pedicle technique) of sculpting and shaping the breast tissue, excellent results can be achieved for patients who feel they already have enough volume."

Several factors may contribute to the loss of breast volume and tone, breast sagging, and down-turned nipples. These factors include large breast size, aging, gravity, the effects of pregnancy on the body and, in some cases, significant weight loss. The skin of the breasts is the "envelope" that holds them in position. As the skin ages and loses elasticity, breasts can begin to sag. The larger the breast, the more forceful gravity's downward pull, stretching the skin and causing breast laxity, loss of tone, and droopiness. The process may be accelerated by pregnancy. During pregnancy, breasts enlarge, causing the skin to stretch. After pregnancy, breast size diminishes, but the overlying skin may remain stretched.

LENGTH OF SURGERY
Usually one and a half to three and a half hours.

ANESTHESIA
Usually local anesthetic with intravenous sedation, or general anesthesia.

LENGTH OF STAY
Usually outpatient procedure, home the same day.

RECOVERY
Initial mild to moderate discomfort; prescription pain medication for two to seven days; minimal activity for several days; back to work in seven to 10 days; swelling, bruising improve in three to 10 days; avoid strenuous exercise for about one month.

SCARS
Usually visible but undetectable when wearing clothing or most swimwear.

RISKS/POSSIBLE COMPLICATIONS
Serious complications, while possible, are unlikely. Some potential complications can be avoided by carefully following your surgeon's instructions.

In addition to the usual risks associated with anesthesia, other risks include:
- Infection.
- Hematoma: Collection of blood beneath the skin; can be treated without compromising result.
- Skin necrosis: Extremely rare; would cause an open wound usually beneath nipple, will frequently heal within weeks, final appearance is unpredictable but often completely satisfactory.
- Changes in nipple sensation: Loss of sensation, usually temporary, permanence is rare.

The above-listed risks may be only some of those that your surgeon will discuss with you in greater detail during your consultation.

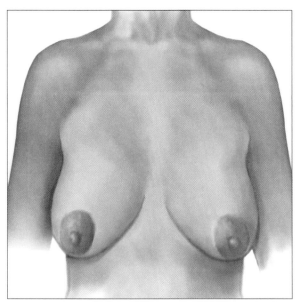

PREOPERATIVE APPEARANCE. Childbirth, weight loss, gravity, and aging all take their toll on a woman's breasts. Loss of breast volume, stretched skin, sagging breast tissue, and down-turned nipples often are the result.

"My most common patient for mastopexy is a married woman who has had a couple of children and wants to restore or improve her breast shape," says **Walter L. Erhardt Jr., MD,** of Albany, Georgia. "They often come to their consultation thinking they want an augmentation but when they describe their breasts, they use words like 'saggy' or 'droopy.' They often are also dissatisfied with their breast shape. Implants alone will provide fullness and some projection, but they won't significantly affect shape. To adjust breast shape, a mastopexy is needed. If the patient is happy with her breast size, I will simply lift the breasts; if she would like more volume, I will perform the breast lift in combination with an augmentation."

There are no age restrictions for having a breast lift. However, plastic surgeons usually recommend waiting until after the breasts have completely developed and often advise waiting until after women have had their last pregnancy.

Alexander G. Nein, MD, of Nashville, Tennessee, offers this about the timing of breast lift surgery, "Breast sag caused from pregnancy is best corrected after the woman has finished having all her children. Future pregnancies can degrade the quality of the result."

Breast lift surgery can restore a more youthful look to a woman's figure. In addition to repositioning breast tissue to a higher level and elevating the nipples and areolas (the dark skin surrounding the nipple), the surgery can reduce the size of areolas that have been stretched over time.

"Breast lifting is a complicated subject," says Dr. Rand. "I always tell patients that breast lifting is to restore the proper position of the nipples and areolas. It can rejuvenate and reshape the breasts but does not add extra volume. It is important for the patient to understand the difference between what a lift and an augmentation will accomplish."

Mastopexy has been shown to have positive psychological effects. Women often feel better about their body image and enjoy increased self-confidence, which can enhance other areas of their lives.

THE CONSULTATION

The consultation is a time for the surgeon and patient to get to know and feel comfortable with each other. The patient should feel completely confident that the surgeon is fully qualified. If you haven't read sections in the beginning of this book about choosing a surgeon who is certified by the American Board of Plastic Surgery, you may want to do so now.

In aesthetic plastic surgery, good communication between surgeon and patient is a vital component of achieving a successful outcome. Everybody's sense of aesthetics differs. People have varying opinions of what is desirable for the size, shape, and position of breasts. It is extremely important that you tell your surgeon everything that you feel about the appearance of your breasts and how you would like them to look.

Also tell your doctor if you are planning to lose a significant amount of weight, since your plastic surgeon may recommend that you stabilize your weight before having the procedure. If a woman becomes pregnant after having a breast lift, the results of breast lift surgery may be altered or lost completely. Yet for a variety of reasons, some women do decide to undergo breast lift surgery prior to having children, understanding that they may have to deal with ensuing changes sometime in the future. Mastopexy usually leaves the milk ducts and nipples intact, and breast lift surgery normally will not affect the ability to breast-feed. This, however, is something that should be fully discussed between patient and surgeon if there is a possibility you may wish to breast-feed in the future.

Your surgeon will examine and measure your breasts to gauge the degree of sagging. This is determined by nipple position relative to the crease beneath the breasts, called the inframammary crease. Ideally, the nipple should be positioned above this crease, but time, age, and gravity cause the breast to descend. Your surgeon will also examine you to assess variables that may affect the procedure; these include skin condition, the size and shape of your breasts, and the size of the areolas. All variables will be discussed with you. You and your surgeon will also talk about whether a breast augmentation procedure, in addition to mastopexy, is necessary to fulfill your desires and meet your expectations.

"I find there are very few women in whom either an augmentation alone or a lift alone will suffice," states **Rafael C. Cabrera, MD**, of Boca Raton, Florida. "Most women have too much tissue in one place and not enough in another, and fighting gravity is always a losing proposition. The operation I find to be the most satisfying for my patients is a combination mastopexy-augmentation, where the augmentation is used to create volume in the upper portion of the breast while the mastopexy may remove some of the excess tissue in the lower portion that, because of gravitational pull, can't be effectively suspended, or tightened. Of course, the nipple must be restored to its proper position. When you achieve harmony of the various aspects of the breast — breast volume, nipple position and skin envelope — you achieve an aesthetically attractive breast."

If your goal is both to lift and enlarge your breasts, discuss how your surgeon prefers to do this — with a combined procedure or with two separate procedures performed at different times. Many surgeons will perform mastopexy and breast augmentation procedures concurrently. Some surgeons, however, prefer to perform them separately. "I believe it is safer not to perform breast augmentation and mastopexy at the same time. Also, stretching of the skin from breast augmentation places tension on the mastopexy incisions; by performing the operations separately, you avoid this problem, and the appearance of scars is better," says **Daniel C. Mills, MD**, of Laguna Beach, California.

Gary D. Hall, MD, of Leawood, Kansas, says, "Many patients require both an augmentation and a breast lift, and in these cases, I do the majority as a combination procedure. There are several advantages for the patient, such as not needing to recover from two surgeries, which minimizes downtime and cost. I can also better gauge how much skin to excise once I have the implant already in place."

"While some surgeons prefer to perform mastopexy and augmentation in two stages, citing a possible loss of accuracy due to the manipulation of two independent variables during the same procedure, I believe that accuracy need not be sacrificed," explains **Jonathan H. Sherwyn, MD**, of New York, New York. "I accomplish this through the use of a technique referred to as 'tailor-tack.' With this technique, the augmentation is performed first. Next, the operating table is brought to a fully upright position, and temporary sutures are placed to provide the uplift, such as a tailor altering a garment. In this way, the breast mound is brought into harmony with the underlying implant. Should the temporary sutures prove satisfactory, they are delineated, the lift is definitively performed and permanent sutures placed."

"In my patient population, I've seen many women in their 30s or 40s who have postpartum involution of their breasts," says **Joseph M. Perlman, MD**, of Spring, Texas. "Approximately 50 percent of these patients have enough ptosis, or sagging, to warrant consideration for a mastopexy at the time of breast augmentation. I used to perform these as staged procedures, but over the last five years I have performed them in a single stage. It is necessary to be somewhat conservative with the breast lift to allow for final positioning of the implant. For that reason, I explain to patients that they may need some small degree of adjustment of the lift, which is usually a minor procedure."

According to **D'Arcy A. Honeycutt, MD**, of Bismarck, North Dakota, "In the past there were some serious wound healing problems when augmentation was combined with mastopexy, mainly because of compromising the blood flow. Nowadays, however, I think the majority of plastic surgeons are placing implants partially or completely under the pectoral muscle, preserving the blood vessels that travel from the muscle into the breast and, therefore, maintaining a good blood flow to the tissues. I've had excellent results performing both the lift and augmentation at the same time. An additional benefit of combining the procedures is being able to use smaller implants to achieve the patient's desired size rather than filling out loose skin with a too-large implant."

Your surgeon should describe the procedure in detail, including the specific technique he or she plans to use and the scars that will result from breast lift surgery, which can be extensive. Although many patients have resultant scars that fade to fine white lines and become nearly undetectable, others have scars that become wide and raised. How scars will finally appear cannot be predicted before surgery. Scars will be permanent, and although they will be either at the nipple or below it, and not visible in clothing or most swimwear, most will be noticeable without clothing. Although there have been tremendous technical advances in aesthetic plastic surgery, it is a fact that whenever an incision is made, there will be a scar. Sometimes a woman will have to choose between the extent of scarring she is willing to accept and the quality of the result she desires.

"As far as incision sites, we tailor the surgery for the individual's needs and desires," says **Onelio Garcia, MD,** of Hialeah, Florida. "I never sacrifice shape for the sake of keeping the incision shorter. Implants, which I almost always use, also help to keep incisions shorter because the increased volume keeps skin removal to a minimum."

"The high-profile implant that came out four or five years ago has completely changed my approach to augmentation-mastopexy procedures," comments **Francine Vagotis, MD,** of Grand Rapids, Michigan. "It allows us to augment and lift the breasts while minimizing incisions and scarring. The high-profile implant has more interior projection with a narrower base diameter and this has several advantages. It fits the body and the chest wall better, provides a more forward projection and more cleavage. It fills out the skin envelope so we don't have to remove as much skin, therefore minimizing incisions."

"Women undergoing breast surgery tend to have more or less tolerance for scars depending on the initial circumstances," says **David J. Levens, MD,** of Coral Springs, Florida. "Breast reduction patients plagued by back pain and heavy breasts are more willing to accept scars as a necessity. Women who had shapely breasts originally and come in for augmentation or a breast lift may be less tolerant of scars. As plastic surgeons, we always try to limit scarring, but there is a balance or compromise between the extent of the procedure to achieve good results and the size and appearance of the scar. The scar is an essential part of the procedure, and there will always be a certain degree of trade-off."

Otis Allen, MD, of Bloomington, Illinois, also mentions the patient's need to reconcile trade-offs, "Mastopexy can be a source of great satisfaction to the patient provided she understands the alternatives in the types of breast lift procedures, including the inevitable trade-offs involved in each one — such as scars in exchange for improved shape and nipple position." Dr. Allen adds, "Most women seeking mastopexy really suffer from a combination of loss of breast volume as well as ptosis (sagging) of the breast. In addition, it is necessary for them to appreciate that lifting the breast may make it seem smaller. This is why breast augmentation is so often done in association with mastopexy."

"Although I am supremely concerned with limiting visible scars when performing

| Inverted T | Vertical | Periareolar |

Various techniques for a breast lift: In addition to the traditional technique that results in an "inverted T" or "anchor-shaped" scar (incision around the areola, down the lower portion of the breast, and horizontally underneath it), limited-incision methods include the vertical technique (incisions around the areola and down the lower portion of the breast) and the periareolar technique (incision around the areola only). The selection of technique depends on individual patient characteristics, the surgeon's recommendation, and patient preference.

breast enhancement surgery," agrees **James M. Platis, MD**, of Chicago, Illinois, "I have found that if it requires more incisions to significantly improve the shape of the breast, it is well worth it. A well-shaped breast with some small but visible scars is always more attractive than a poorly shaped breast with no scars."

Your plastic surgeon will thoroughly review your options and help you decide what best meets your needs.

"The goal is to minimize the scars for each patient, dependent upon the needs of each individual," explains **Michael R. Schwartz, MD**, of Camarillo, California. "We try to use the smallest incision possible to make the most attractive breast in each patient, but ultimately, in my opinion it comes down to trying to make sure the breast is the correct shape and will stay well-positioned and well-shaped, as opposed to making short incisions that will not maintain the breasts' shape in the long run."

"I always try to minimize scarring, but will never compromise results to achieve a shorter scar," agrees Dr. Rosenberg.

Your surgeon will need to review your entire medical history, including any medications you may currently be taking, whether you suffer from any allergies or medical conditions, and if you have had any prior surgeries.

During the consultation, do not hesitate to ask any questions or air any concerns you may have. It is important for your surgeon to help you understand what to expect from breast lift surgery. Although the vast majority of patients are very satisfied with their breast lift surgery, results are not always perfect.

Poorly healed scars are the main undesirable outcome associated with breast lift surgery. As mentioned previously, it is impossible to predict how scars will appear, since each patient heals differently. However, you should discuss the placement of incisions with your surgeon so you will know exactly what to expect regarding the location of scars. Ask to see photographs that show examples of breast lift surgeries the surgeon has performed on other patients.

Be sure to discuss nipple position with your surgeon, as well as how he or she expects your results to look over time. Realize, however, that everyone ages differently, and long-term results of cosmetic surgery are not entirely predictable.

"It's important for patients to know that the results of a breast lift are long-lasting but not permanent. Gravity will continue to affect them, and they may need a touch-up sometime in the future," says Dr. Onelio Garcia.

The breasts may not be perfectly symmetrical, or nipple height may vary slightly. However, natural breasts usually show some variation; in fact, your surgeon may point out the asymmetry of your breasts prior to surgery. If there is asymmetry before your mastopexy, there is likely to be asymmetry afterward as well.

PREPARATION

Your surgeon will give you instructions about how to prepare for surgery. He or she will also give you guidelines on eating, drinking and medications, such as avoiding aspirin or anti-inflammatory medications that promote bleeding.

Breast lift surgery will not increase your risk of developing breast cancer; however, based on your age and whether you have a family history of breast cancer, your surgeon may recommend a mammogram before surgery to be followed by another some months after to help detect any changes in breast tissue and establish a baseline for future breast X-rays.

Your plastic surgeon may also advise you, depending upon your age, to continue a regular course of cancer detection following your breast lift, including routine mammograms and breast self-examination, neither of which will be affected by breast lift surgery.

As with surgery in general, whether performed in an outpatient facility or in the hospital, you should arrange to have someone drive you to and from surgery and to assist you for a day or two after you return home.

THE SURGERY

Because each patient is different and has a different degree of breast sagging, your operation will be specifically designed to suit your anatomy and personal objectives. Various techniques are available, some of which have been discussed above, and your individual factors and preferences will help to determine the technique used by your surgeon. Of course, your surgeon's familiarity with specific techniques is always an importat consideration.

Mark P. Solomon, MD, of Bala Cynwyd, Pennsylvania, adds, "I am very fond of the periareolar, or so-called 'purse string' method, but I can perform all the techniques available. It's important to be able to use the technique that best suits what the patient wants. It's usually a

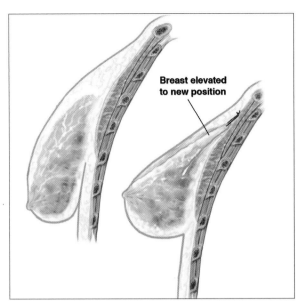

Breast elevated to new position

Shown from the side view, a mastopexy enhances breast shape and nipple position, resulting in a more youthful and attractive contour.

trade-off between scars and the maximum amount of shape and elevation. As with breast augmentation, I spend a lot of time to give patients all the information I can to help them make an informed decision."

Breast sagging is caused by loose or stretched skin, and its treatment is to remove excess skin. With the slack removed, the remaining skin is tighter and holds the breast in a higher, or uplifted, position. The amount of skin that must be removed depends on the amount of sagging. The more pronounced the sagging, the more skin that must be removed. Generally speaking, the larger the skin excision, the more extensive the scarring will be.

A frequently used technique involves what some refer to as an anchor-shaped incision. With this technique, one incision is made around the areola, one extends from the areola's bottom edge to the inframammary crease beneath the breast, and another runs horizontally, following the natural curve of this crease. The surgeon removes excess breast skin and shifts the nipple and areola to a higher position.

"If a woman is a good candidate for a breast lift, I will determine which approach would be best based upon how much her nipple needs to be lifted and how much upper pole fullness is needed," says Dr. Mills. "Typically, I make an incision around the nipple-areolar complex,

down the lower portion of the breast and in the crease just under the breast. I reposition the nipple-areolar complex higher and remove any excess skin, reshaping the breast's contour. If more volume is desired, and more upper pole fullness, I will consider using an implant."

More modified procedures, which can eliminate some of the incisions and thereby lessen scarring, can be used in some cases and are generally most effective when there are lesser degrees of breast sagging. Other factors that determine the technique your surgeon might choose as the best for you include the size and shape of your breasts, size and position of your areolas, and both the degree of skin elasticity and the amount of skin to be removed.

"The eventual shape of the breast is dependent on the tissue rather than the skin," says **Julio L. Garcia, MD,** of Las Vegas, Nevada. "Similar to the evolution in face lifting, where the most natural result is achieved by re-suspending and shaping the underlying tissue and then draping the skin over it, the most natural result in breast lifts is also obtained by repositioning the underlying breast into an aesthetic cone shape with good projection, and redraping the skin over it. That's what the skin is, a cover. It is stretchy, will not hold, and shouldn't be relied upon to support the breast. We've learned to be able to accomplish this through relatively small incisions."

Breast sagging can sometimes be corrected using only an incision around the nipple. The resulting scar is visible but relatively inconspicuous.

Robert Lowen, MD, of Mountain View, California, agrees. "The periareolar mastopexy-augmentation provides consistently good results while avoiding any noticeable scars on the front of the breast. We have obtained long-term results that offer excellent control of breast shape, areolar size, and reduction of excess skin without skin pleating around the areola. Meticulous surgical technique contributes to this outcome. Although time-consuming, these techniques have made periareolar mastopexy the preferred option for my patients and me."

Some surgeons may approach sagging with a technique using an incision around the nipple and in a vertical line from the bottom of the areola to the inframammary crease, still avoiding the horizontal crease underneath the breast that is required for the more commonly performed "anchor" technique.

"The problem with the circle, or doughnut, mastopexy," states **William G. Loutfy, MD**, of Albuquerque, New Mexico, "is that it removed the excess skin and brought it together to meet the areola, like a purse string. Over time, this would cause the areola to stretch out significantly. The newer short scar techniques combine aspects of the doughnut mastopexy with those of the traditional anchor scar, to remove the excess skin while cutting down on the total length of scars and keeping the areola from stretching out too much."

Peter E. Johnson, MD, of Des Plaines, Illinois, adds, "In the past, two issues made breast lift an unpopular option — the scar and relapse of the droop. Now, however, we have applied the vertical pattern or 'lollipop' incision to breast lifting. The shorter scar and the durable result have been very attractive to patients. With vertical mastopexy, we can raise the nipple two inches or more, adjust the nipple size, reduce the "bottoming out" of the breast beneath the breast fold, correct asymmetry with a small implant or small reduction of the breast, or augment the breast if our patient wants a larger breast size. The flexibility and durability of the result has brought mastopexy back as a sought-after procedure, especially after weight loss or multiple pregnancies."

It's important to remember that while you would naturally like to have the least visible scarring possible, there are many considerations when selecting the mastopexy technique that is right for you. Some surgeons, including some of our experts, feel that minimal-incision techniques do not always achieve the best result in terms of breast shape. These surgeons maintain that drawbacks of the so-called "purse-string" or concentric mastopexy, in which only an incision around the areola is used, may include a flattening of the breasts, widening of the areola and development of stretch marks. Many surgeons believe that the more traditional anchor technique produces the best results in the majority of cases.

"In breast surgery, the trend is toward shorter and fewer scars, but many of the new short-scar techniques have higher patient dissatisfaction rates and higher reoperation rates than the more traditional techniques," states **Michael Rose, MD**, of Shrewsbury, New Jersey. **Andrew Elkwood, MD**, also of Shrewsbury, agrees. "Since patient safety and satisfaction are our main goals, the new techniques should supplement but not replace the more traditional techniques until they prove consistently to be better procedures."

James A. Matas, MD, of Orlando, Florida, adds "There's been a move to try to limit the length of the horizontal scar underneath the breast, but I'm not comfortable with that. Maybe it's because I have an engineering background. I mark the position of the nipples very precisely, and I carefully measure distances in order to create the most aesthetically pleasing and symmetrical result possible."

There is, however, a wide range of opinions concerning mastopexy techniques and patient selection. As stated many times in this book, there is no single technique that is right for every patient. Clearly, breast lift techniques utilizing shorter scars have found a place in plastic surgery because some patients prefer them. Many surgeons stress that one of the keys to satisfactory results in mastopexy, whatever incision pattern is used, is proper support of the reshaped and repositioned breast tissue.

"I tend to be in the camp for smaller scars," says **Donald W. Hause, MD**, Sacramento, California, "but I think it's very patient dependent. For patients who don't have a lot of weight in their breasts, I use the Lejour technique. Instead of creating a 'brassiere' out of the patient's skin to hold up the breast, the breast tissue is molded into a conical shape to reform the breast, and then the skin is draped over it. Since skin stretches over time, using it to support the breast isn't a very good idea. Reforming the breast tissue also creates more volume and projection, so I don't have to excise as much skin."

"With a breast lift, or mastopexy, it is extremely important that enough attention is paid to repositioning and creating proper support for the breast tissue," says **Robert Anderson, MD**, of Fort Worth, Texas. "I use a technique that actually uses some of the excess breast skin to create a kind of 'sling' or 'hammock' to support the breast from the bottom. I suspend the upper breast tissue to the pectoralis muscle fascia using permanent sutures, use the dermal sling and then wrap the skin around it to support the breast in three ways, instead of just one. Using this method, I can achieve excellent symmetry and well-shaped breasts with results that are very long-lasting."

"One of my areas of interest involves treating patients who have had problems from a previous augmentation-mastopexy, which may include unsatisfactory scars or implant malposition," says **Kaveh Alizadeh, MD**, of Garden City, New York. "The problem is usually caused by too large an implant that was placed under the breast tissue. In these cases, I use a variation on a vertical mastopexy. One thing I do that really helps these women is to use their own tissue — a dermal flap that we pull from the underside of the breast — to act as a brassiere-like support for the breast. I also reshape the breast, making it possible to use a smaller implant to achieve the woman's desired breast size with less burden on the breast."

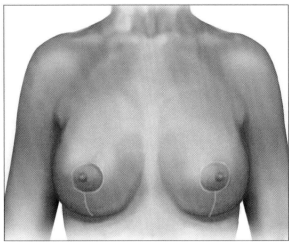

POSTOPERATIVE APPEARANCE. A breast lift, called mastopexy, restores sagging breasts and nipples to a higher position. A breast lift alone will not increase breast volume, although women desiring breast enlargement may often have an implant inserted at the time of mastopexy or as a staged procedure. Scars resulting from a breast lift are permanent. The scars illustrated here are typical of those resulting from the traditional "anchor" incision pattern.

Your best approach is to talk with your surgeon about the various options and view several examples of patient results using the technique that is being recommended for you.

POST OP

Mastopexy is an outpatient procedure that usually takes one and a half to three and a half hours to perform, often under general anesthesia; however, sedation (twilight) anesthesia is also frequently used. No matter what type of anesthesia you have, you will not feel any pain during the surgical procedure. Although some patients may remain in the facility overnight, most are allowed to return home the same day.

Following surgery you will be closely monitored in a recovery area. Your breasts will be covered with gauze dressings over which you will wear an elastic bandage or surgical bra. Unless you and your plastic surgeon have decided that you will remain in the surgical facility or hospital overnight, you will probably be allowed to go home after a few hours.

Your breasts will be swollen and bruised, and you will experience some discomfort for a few days. It shouldn't be severe, and your surgeon will prescribe medication to relieve any pain. Although you may be encouraged to spend short periods of time out of bed the day after surgery, and will be able to move about more freely within several days, you must avoid any straining, bending or lifting, which might increase swelling or cause bleeding.

Your dressings will be changed after a few days, any surgical drains that were inserted to avoid accumulation of fluid will be removed, and the surgical bra or bandages will be replaced by a soft support bra, which you will wear until the swelling and discoloration of your breasts lessens, usually in a few weeks. Usually, some stitches will be removed about a week after surgery, with the balance removed in stages over the following two weeks.

You will likely notice a temporary loss of sensation in your nipples and areolas. This should dissipate as swelling subsides. This numbness is usually temporary, but it may take several weeks, months, or up to a full year until feeling returns to normal. Permanent loss of sensation does occur, though rarely. Incision sites will remain reddish or pink in color for several months. It may also take some time for your breasts to fully assume their new shape.

Depending on your job and how you feel in the days following surgery, you will probably be able to return to work within a week or so. You will most likely be allowed to return to most of your normal activities over the next several weeks, including mild exercise; however, lifting anything over your head should be avoided for three to four weeks. You may periodically experience mild discomfort throughout this period. This is normal. Severe pain or unusual symptoms should be reported to your doctor. You will usually be advised to abstain from sexual activity for a minimum of one to two weeks, and to be gentle with your breasts and avoid strenuous exercise for about a month.

LOOKING AHEAD

The healing process is gradual and your final result won't be evident until your scars have matured, which will take six months or longer. The vast majority of women who undergo breast lift surgery are very happy with the results. Your breasts will be firmer and higher, giving your figure a more youthful appearance. As discussed earlier in this chapter, your new breast contour should be long-lasting, but results are not permanent due to the continued effects of gravity and aging. When mastopexy is performed in conjunction with augmentation, the weight of implants may be an additional factor in the longevity of results.

"Realistic expectations with a breast augmentation-mastopexy include the understanding that revision surgery will most likely be necessary at sometime in the future," says Dr. Loutfy. "Patients should understand that what we are doing is taking skin that's already been stretched out, inserting an implant which stretches it some more, and then removing skin to make this 'envelope' even tighter. Weight and gravity will continue to affect the breast tissue, which will stretch and settle. Since weight is a factor, choosing a reasonably sized implant may help increase longevity of results."

Women who discuss the issues of scarring, breast size, surgical technique, and duration of results with their surgeon and develop a clear understanding of how these factors relate to their personal goals for surgery have an excellent chance of achieving a satisfying outcome.

Editor's Viewpoint

Mastopexy performed by itself or in combination with breast reduction or augmentation rejuvenates breast shape. Selecting the best technique can be challenging; the quality (thickness) of skin, amount of breast (glandular) tissue, skin envelope to glandular ratio, breast shape, symmetry, and nipple position all play a role. As our experts have pointed out in this chapter, no matter which procedure is utilized, the aging process continues relentlessly. Therefore, a secondary surgical procedure may be necessary at some time in the future to maintain a pleasing long-term result. This is especially true when breast implants are also present because their weight contributes to the downward force of gravity.

It is my personal preference to take a conservative approach when performing a breast lift. I have found that not inserting an implant, or using a small implant placed submuscularly when it is absolutely necessary for extremely volume-deficient breasts, has a better chance of achieving a good long-term result. Consequently when applicable, instead of implants, I favor techniques in which the excess skin or ptotic portions of the gland are surgically repositioned to increase breast volume. An exception to this is in small breasts with less severe sagging where good results can be obtained by using an implant only, placed in a "dual plane" partly below the muscle and partly below the breast gland. The resultant scarring is minimal and similar to that produced by breast augmentation alone.

As described by our experts, there are a number of surgical options in mastopexy, each with potential advantages and disadvantages. This is why it is particularly important for patients to fully discuss with their surgeon the approach he or she recommends, assuring as much as possible that the anticipated results meet the patient's personal aesthetic goals.

— Peter B. Fodor, MD

BREAST REDUCTION
Reduction Mammaplasty

Unlike most other procedures discussed in this book, breast reduction surgery is seldom performed for aesthetic reasons alone. Nearly all patients who seek breast reduction suffer from a variety of physical challenges and medical problems brought about by breasts that are disproportionately large for their body frame.

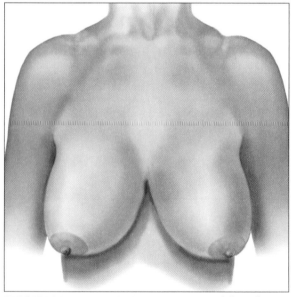

PREOPERATIVE APPEARANCE. Large, pendulous breasts can be the cause of numerous health conditions including back, neck, and/or shoulder pain; skin rashes beneath the breasts; grooves in the shoulders from bra straps; and postural problems. They may also restrict or impair physical activity.

"Breast reduction surgery is generally recommended for women experiencing health problems associated with very large, heavy breasts," offers O. Allen Guinn, III, MD, of Lee's Summit, Missouri. "Several medical conditions have been associated with large breasts, or macromastia, including back and neck pain, skin irritation, skeletal deformities, breathing problems, shoulder indentations from tight bra straps, and poor posture. Excessive breast size has also been associated with a decreased sense of attractiveness and self-confidence. The goal of the surgery is to provide a woman with better-shaped breasts that are proportional to the rest of her body, with improvement or elimination of the health problems associated with macromastia."

Because breast reduction is usually performed to relieve physical symptoms, unlike most other procedures covered in this book, it is sometimes eligible for insurance coverage. However, insurance companies frequently mandate trying other remedies, including diet and exercise, powders for rashes, and even chiropractic care, before approving breast reduction surgery. In addition, many companies specify a minimum volume of breast tissue that must be removed in order to qualify for coverage. This volume amount may or may not fall within the range that would give you the best aesthetic result as determined through consultation with your plastic surgeon. In all instances in which there is a possibility of insurance coverage, this should be explored well in advance of your desired surgical date.

"Breast reductions may sometimes be covered by your insurance carrier as a medically necessary surgical procedure," explains **Gary R. Culbertson, MD**, of Sumter, South Carolina. "Documentation of symptoms such as persistent neck and back pain that is unresponsive to conservative treatment by your family doctor, shoulder pain and grooving, and severe rashes more common in the summertime will assist in the pre-approval process for your surgery."

While breast reduction is often performed to relieve physical problems, it also provides the aesthetic benefits of improving breast shape and tone. In addition, like cosmetic breast surgery, it usually offers a profound psychological benefit. Women who undergo breast reduction surgery generally gain self-confidence and an enhanced body image. Overly large breasts can create the impression of being heavier than you are or even "matronly." Following breast reduction, it should be easier for you to find stylish clothing that fits properly and flatters your figure. For many women, breast reduction surgery enables them to be more physically active, enjoying sports and feeling good about the way they look on the tennis court or at the beach.

Usual candidates for breast reduction surgery are women who are not massively overweight but who have very large, pendulous breasts that cause them physical discomfort, or women who have one breast that is significantly larger than the other. Breast reduction can be performed at any age, but surgeons generally recommend waiting until breast development is complete; this most often occurs by the late teens. If a younger teen is severely handicapped, either physically or emotionally, by overly large breasts, and she has the maturity to understand the choices and responsibilities associated with undergoing the procedure, it may be appropriate to perform surgery now even if later surgical revisions are required to address further breast development. Although many women elect to proceed with breast reduction surgery before they have had children, the results of surgery may be altered by pregnancy, weight gain, and breast-feeding. Candidates who anticipate having children at some time after surgery must understand and accept that nipple sensation may change and the ability to breast-feed may be impaired. However, with the most commonly performed techniques, there is a good possibility that both normal or reasonably normal nipple sensation and the ability to breast-feed will be maintained.

Breast reduction surgery creates one of the most immediate and dramatic changes in body image. Your breasts will be smaller, lighter, firmer, and in better proportion to the rest of your body. The physical discomfort associated with having too-large breasts will be eliminated, and your clothing choices will be expanded. The surgery can also reduce the size of your areolas, the darker skin surrounding the nipple, which may have been stretched as a result of breast development. It can elevate your breasts and nipples to a more youthful and attractive position.

FAST FACTS

LENGTH OF SURGERY
Usually two to four hours.

ANESTHESIA
Typically general anesthesia.

LENGTH OF STAY
Sometimes home the same day, but frequently overnight stay.

RECOVERY
Initial mild to moderate discomfort; prescription pain medication for seven to 10 days; minimal activity for several days; back to work in two to three weeks; swelling, bruising improve in three to 10 days; avoid strenuous exercise for about one month.

SCARS
Usually visible on the breast surface but covered when wearing low-cut clothing and most swimwear; poor healing may result in thick, raised scars that may require revision.

RISKS/POSSIBLE COMPLICATIONS
Serious complications, while possible, are unlikely. Some potential complications can be avoided by carefully following your surgeon's instructions.

In addition to the usual risks associated with anesthesia, other risks include:
- Infection: Generally controllable with wound hygiene; additional surgery seldom is necessary.
- Hematoma: Collection of blood beneath the skin; can be treated without compromising result.
- Seroma: Collection of fluid under skin can usually be painlessly removed in doctor's office and does not alter cosmetic result.
- Loss of sensation: Numbness or loss of sensation in breast, usually temporary.
- Nipple problems: Loss of sensation; change of color; partial or complete loss of nipple.
- Pulmonary emboli: Extremely rare; a blood clot that travels to the blood vessels in the lung.

The above-listed risks may be only some of those that your surgeon will discuss with you in greater detail during your consultation.

Reproductive Endocrinology

AND BREAST REDUCTION

Plastic surgeons are sometimes called upon to correct deficiencies and deformities that may be associated with medical syndromes, growth disorders, genetic diseases, and hormonal problems. Reproductive endocrinology is one of the specialties consulting closely with plastic surgeons on difficult cases of abnormal breast growth.

The average breast size is about 150 to 850 cc's. The majority of breast reductions are for the diagnosis of macromastia, or very large breasts of up to 1,500 cc's in size. These cases are usually not caused by an underlying medical condition, but rather result from familial history or obesity, and no hormone consultation or therapy is needed.

Approximately two percent of breast reduction cases involve gigantomastia, or extremely large breasts, characterized by breast growth up to 80 pounds and associated with difficulty walking and sleeping, chronic skin rashes and ulcerations, and social disability. Although breast reduction surgery alone may be all that is needed for most of these patients, about one percent of all patients seeking breast reduction surgery may require hormone therapy in addition to breast reduction surgery.

"The most severe form of breast enlargement, gigantomastia, can develop during puberty or pregnancy, or can present as a rare side effect of some medications," says reproductive endocrinologist H. Randall Craig, MD, of Tempe, Arizona. "Women with breasts that weigh 20 to 80 pounds have difficulty performing routine tasks, sleeping comfortably, or even standing or walking. In the past, many women with gigantomastia required multiple breast reductions or even resorted to mastectomy to obtain relief. Fortunately, recent advances in the field of reproductive endocrinology have provided effective hormone therapy for this disorder."

There are various types of gigantomastia including Gestational Gigantomastia — huge breast enlargement up to 80 pounds that develops during pregnancy — and Adolescent Breast Hypertrophy (Virginal Hypertrophy) — rapid, massive breast growth up to 60 pounds beginning around age 10 to 16. For most cases of gigantomastia, preoperative and/or postoperative hormonal therapy can be used to stop breast growth and reduce mammary blood supply. This makes subsequent breast reduction surgery easier with reduced blood loss, achieving a better cosmetic result.

If your breasts are asymmetrical, with one breast significantly larger than the other, breast reduction on one side can help equalize your breast size. However, there is likely to still be some asymmetry. This often can be improved by performing a breast lift on the smaller side.

THE CONSULTATION

Tell your doctor if you plan to lose a significant amount of weight, since your plastic surgeon may recommend that you stabilize your weight before having the procedure. Although the nipple and areola most often remain attached to the breast mound during surgery and sensation in these areas is usually preserved, the ability to breast-feed cannot be guaranteed. This is something that should be discussed fully between patient and surgeon, so you need to tell your surgeon if you think you may want to become pregnant at some time in the future. "One risk associated with breast reduction is loss of ability to breast-feed, but this is a small percentage of cases," says David L. Abramson, MD, of New York, New York. "For most women seeking this operation, the idea that they might want to breast-feed at some point in their lives is less of a concern than the back pain and other health problems that hinder their quality of life now."

Your surgeon will examine and measure your breasts and evaluate variables that may affect the procedure, such as your age and skin condition and the size and shape of your breasts. Photographs may be taken for your medical records and to help with processing any insurance preauthorization.

The procedure should be described in detail, including the technique your surgeon plans to use and where the nipple and areola will be positioned. In most cases, they will be moved higher during the procedure; an ideal position is approximately even with the crease beneath your breast, which is called the inframammary crease. Your surgeon will also discuss the scars that will result from breast reduction surgery, which most often will be visible on the surface of your breast. Although many patients find that their scars fade and eventually become only thin white lines, other patients do not heal as well, and their scars may become wide and raised. How your scars will finally appear cannot be predicted before surgery. Scars will be permanent, and although they will not be visible in clothing or most swimwear, the scars from most breast reduction procedures will be noticeable when your breasts are uncovered. With some surgeries, breast reduction among them, there is often a trade-off between the length of scars and the quality of the end result.

"The biggest issue with this procedure is scarring," says Dr. Abramson. "As a result of surgery, the patient will have smaller breasts that are lifted up into a better position, but she is going to have scars — and most patients require techniques that produce significant scars. So an acceptance of scars is crucial and something that needs to be discussed beforehand. But for most people, especially those who undergo surgery because of back pain, the more prominent scarring doesn't matter as much as the improvement in their health and overall appearance."

Various techniques are available for breast reduction, some of which utilize incision patterns that are less conspicuous than the traditional inverted T approach. Most surgeons agree, however, that the limited incision techniques are not for every patient. Most women want breasts that are well shaped and symmetrical, even if it means that incisions must be placed more conspicuously. Your surgeon will discuss the options available to you

and, considering your needs and goals, help you make the best decision. It is important that you understand how the scars from breast reduction surgery are likely to appear. During the consultation, ask to see photographs showing examples of breast reduction surgeries the surgeon has performed on other patients.

"In breast reduction, never sacrifice shape for limited scars," advises **Jonathan Freed, MD**, of Auburn, California. "Scars will fade and get better over time, but shape will only get worse over time. You can never make skin just magically disappear; you have to do something with it. To achieve good shape, you are going to need incisions and, hence, there will be some scarring."

During the consultation, your surgeon will need to review your entire medical history, including any medications you may currently be taking, whether you suffer from any allergies or medical conditions, and if you have had any prior surgeries.

The results of reshaping living tissue are not always completely predictable. Following breast reduction surgery, your breasts may not be perfectly symmetrical or nipple height may vary slightly. Remember that natural breasts usually show some variation; in fact, your surgeon may point out any naturally occurring asymmetry of your breasts prior to surgery. As with any plastic surgery, minor revisions may sometimes be necessary.

"While there's no question that the breast is a symbol of femininity in our society, large breasts can be problematic, both physically and psychologically," says **Frederick N. Lukash, MD**, of Manhasset, New York. "Patients who come to me for reduction mammaplasty usually have one main motive: They want normal proportions. The plastic surgeon needs to carefully analyze the patient's body type so the result is a feminine, proportional silhouette."

PREPARATION

Your surgeon will give you instructions about how to prepare for surgery. As covered in an earlier section of this book, smoking can have a profoundly negative effect on healing and blood flow; with some procedures, it can seriously compromise your chances for a successful and safe surgery. If you smoke, your surgeon may ask you to quit before he or she proceeds. He or she will also give you guidelines on eating, drinking and medications, such as avoiding aspirin or anti-inflammatory medications that promote bleeding.

Breast reduction surgery will not increase your risk of developing breast cancer; however, depending on your age and other factors, your surgeon may recommend a mammogram before surgery to be followed by another some months after to serve as a baseline for comparison of any future changes in breast tissue. Your plastic surgeon may also advise you, again depending upon your age, to continue a regular course of cancer detection following your procedure, including routine mammograms and breast self-examination, neither of which will be affected by breast reduction surgery.

Breast reduction surgery may be performed in an outpatient facility or in the hospital. You may need to stay in the hospital or surgical facility overnight; however, whether you go home the day of surgery or the next day, you should arrange to have someone drive you to and from surgery and to stay with you for a day or two after you return home.

THE SURGERY

Because each patient is different, your operation will be specifically designed to suit your objectives. Your individual factors and preferences, as well as the professional advice of your surgeon, will help determine the specific technique used in your case.

Most breast reductions are performed using pedicle techniques, in which the nipple remains attached to its blood supply while excess breast tissue is removed. Pedicle techniques preserve the nerves attached to the nipple and thereby increase the likelihood that your nipples will maintain normal or near normal sensation following surgery. A frequently used incision pattern for pedicle techniques involves what some refer to as the inverted T or anchor-shaped incision. With this technique, one incision is made around the areola, another extends from the areola's bottom edge to the crease beneath the breast, and another runs horizontally beneath the breast, following the natural curve of this crease. Different pedicle techniques can be performed through this sort of incision and leading to an anchor-shaped scar.

"I find the anchor incision to be the most predictable," says **Eric Mariotti, MD**, of Concord, California. "I use certain techniques to preserve cleavage and prevent the 'bottoming out' sometimes seen with this technique." Dr. Mariotti adds, "Most plastic surgeons find that breast reduction patients are some of the happiest we

have. The relief from back and neck pain and no longer having to bear the weight of such large breasts are tremendous benefits."

Malcolm Z. Roth, MD, of New York, New York, who generally prefers the inverted T incision, shares his experience. "I still perform the majority of breast reductions using the inverted T pattern. Many of my patients need significant reduction, and the inverted T delivers the best breast shape in such patients. I have found that, even in cases where scars have not healed optimally, the excellent breast shape makes women happier than when scars are less conspicuous but breast shape is not as good. Breast reduction patients are so pleased to relieve symptoms and have symmetrical, well-shaped breasts, that they are willing to incur the necessary scars."

During the procedure, your surgeon will remove excess glandular tissue and fat, which reduces breast size and removes skin. This results in a breast that is held higher and tighter on the chest wall, restoring a more youthful appearance and shape. Your surgeon will then move the nipple and areola to their new, higher position. The areolas in large breasts have usually been stretched, so the surgeon can also reduce their size. He or she then takes skin that was previously located above the nipple and brings it down around the areola to reshape the breast.

"The important thing is not how much you remove but how much you leave," offers **Brian J. Lee, MD**, of Fort Wayne, Indiana, "because that's what you have to mold and shape into the breast mound. One of the common problems in breast reduction is 'bottoming out,' which is when, over time, the central mass of the breast droops but the nipple remains at the higher position where it was repositioned. One modification I generally make that helps maintain breast shape and prevent bottoming out is to dissect the upper flaps and leave more volume at the base, which increases projection. Then I secure the pedicle in such a way as to keep it elevated during the healing process."

Although the anchor-shaped incision is the most commonly used, there are variations. In some circumstances, techniques can be used that eliminate the horizontal incision along the crease beneath the breast, or both the horizontal and the vertical incision, by using an incision around the areola. You and your plastic surgeon will determine the best alternative

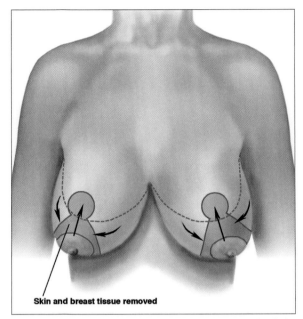

Skin and breast tissue removed

The "inverted T" pattern, also called the "anchor" or "keyhole" incision, remains one of the most commonly used surgical techniques to reduce breast volume and enhance shape. Incisions are made around the areola, vertically down the lower portion of the breast and horizontally along the crease underneath the breast. Excess fat, glandular tissue, and skin are removed, and the nipple, still attached to its blood supply, is elevated into the "keyhole."

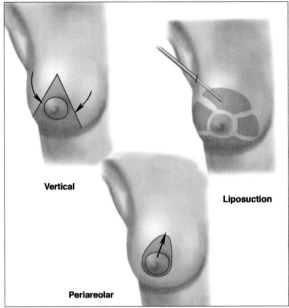

Vertical

Liposuction

Periareolar

Limited incision techniques for breast reduction may involve an incision just around the areola (periareolar technique), eliminating both the vertical and horizontal incision; or around the areola and vertically down the lower portion of the breast (vertical technique), eliminating the horizontal incision in the breast crease. Alternatively, for carefully selected patients, liposuction of the breast may be effective (lipoplasty-only breast reduction, or LOBR), leaving only very small and barely detectable scars.

after evaluating the mitigating factors, such as the size and shape of your breasts and the desired amount of reduction.

Jonathan H. Sherwyn, MD, of New York, New York, explains, "The vertical mammaplasty, or Lejour technique as it is often called, entails an incision around the areola with a vertical limb only. It eliminates the traditional horizontal incision that traces along the inframammary fold, and there is no incision beneath the breast mound. This distinguishing feature, as well as the creation of a final breast shape that is consistently conical, make this technique preferable, in my opinion, to the traditional approach. Many plastic surgeons do not perform this procedure, possibly due to the relatively steep learning curve; familiarity with the nuances inherent in this technique is essential to achieve optimal results."

George Marosan, MD, of Bellevue, Washington, agrees that limited incision breast reduction techniques offer advantages. "I use a short scar technique for breast reductions and breast lifts. Also called the lollipop incision, it goes around the areola and vertically down the breast, avoiding any scar under the breast. These scars usually fade very nicely. I use internal suturing of the breast tissue to create the form, actually increasing volume and projection. There is no tension on the skin, which is just draped over the tissue, and the breast holds its shape very well. I also use tumescent solution, just like with liposuction, so there's almost no bleeding and much less discomfort."

"While the vertical reduction technique can be more challenging to perform with larger reductions," says Mario Loomis, MD, of Middletown, New York, "it still can be used with certain modifications even in patients with very large breasts. I offer it to the vast majority of my breast reduction patients for the benefit of the markedly reduced scars."

Your surgeon may also use liposuction as part of your breast reduction procedure to help shape the breasts or reduce fatty tissue near the underarm area. There are some patients for whom liposuction may, in fact, be the only treatment needed for breast reduction.

The advantage of lipoplasty-only breast reduction is that it leaves very tiny, virtually undetectable scars. Liposuction may be an adequate treatment for a small to moderate breast reduction when the skin has good elasticity and if limited elevation of the nipple is acceptable. Women with dense, fibrous breast tissue are not good candidates, but postmenopausal women, whose breasts tend to have more fat, may be well suited for this procedure. Very large breasts, however, generally require the more traditional methods to achieve adequate volume reduction and nipple elevation.

"I use liposuction for a small portion of my breast reduction patients who have the appropriate tissue composition and are not willing to accept scars," says **Michael R. Schwartz, MD**, of Camarillo, California. "It's very reasonable to reduce one or two cup sizes with virtually no scarring using this method."

In unusual cases in which the breasts are extremely large and pendulous, the nipples and areolas may have to be completely removed and grafted to a higher position. This will result in a loss of sensation to the nipple and areola area. For this reason, nipple grafting is usually avoided except when absolutely necessary to achieve an acceptable breast size and shape, or if there are questions concerning nipple survival using a pedicle technique. The scars for this procedure are essentially the same as for an anchor, or inverted T, pedicle procedure.

POST OP

Breast reduction surgery is usually performed under general anesthesia; you will sleep throughout the procedure. Although some patients return home the same day, many remain in the hospital or surgical facility overnight.

Following surgery you will be closely monitored in a recovery area. A small drainage tube may be placed in your breasts to prevent fluid accumulation for the first day or two. Your breasts will be covered with gauze dressings over which you will wear an elastic bandage or surgical bra.

You will probably feel some pain for the first few days, particularly when you move around or if you cough. Some discomfort will persist for a week or more, and your surgeon will prescribe medication to help control the pain.

"Breast reduction surgery is not as painful as one might think," says Dr. Roth. "Most of my patients are only taking acetaminophen (Tylenol) after the first night."

Although you may be encouraged to spend short periods of time out of bed the day after surgery and will be able to move about more freely within several days, you must avoid any straining, bending, or lifting that might increase swelling or cause bleeding.

Your dressings will be changed after a few days, any surgical drains that were inserted to avoid the accumulation of fluid will also be removed, and a soft support bra will replace the surgical bra or bandages. You will wear the support bra until the swelling and discoloration of your breasts decrease, usually in a few weeks. Usually, some stitches will be removed about a week after surgery with the balance removed in stages over the following two weeks.

You will likely notice a loss of sensation in your nipples and areola areas. This numbness is usually temporary; however, it may take several weeks, months, or a full year until feeling returns to normal. Permanent loss of sensation can occur, but with most reduction techniques the incidence is low. Incision sites will remain reddish or pink in color for several months. It may also take some time for your breasts to fully assume their new shape.

Depending on the type of work you do and how you feel, you will probably be able to return to your job within two weeks or so following surgery. You will most likely be allowed to return to most of your normal activities over the next several weeks, including mild exercise. Lifting anything over your head, however, should be avoided for three to four weeks. You may periodically experience mild discomfort throughout this period. This is normal. You may experience some random, shooting pains over the first few months following surgery, and your breasts may swell and feel tender during your first menstruation after undergoing breast reduction surgery. Any severe pain or unusual symptoms should be reported to your doctor. You will usually be advised to abstain from sexual activity for a minimum of one to two weeks and to be gentle with your breasts and avoid strenuous exercise for about a month.

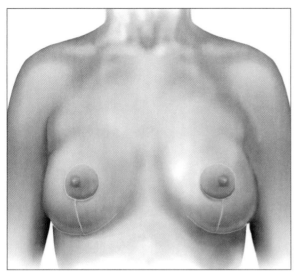

POSTOPERATIVE APPEARANCE. Following breast reduction surgery, in addition to relief from physical symptoms, the breasts are smaller, better shaped and in better proportion to the rest of the body. The position of the nipples is elevated, and the areola size is reduced.

LOOKING AHEAD

The vast majority of women who undergo breast reduction surgery are very happy with the results. The change in body image is immediate and dramatic. On the other hand, it may take a little while for you to become accustomed to and comfortable with the way you look and feel. You should also remember that the appearance of scars immediately after surgery is more intense than it will appear later on. In most cases, scars will fade and become less conspicuous over time.

Unless you experience a major change in body contour through significant weight gain or pregnancy, your new breast size should remain stable. Yet, due to the effects of gravity and aging, the appearance of your breasts will change over time, as do every woman's. Some years in the future, you may decide to undergo a breast lift to restore a more youthful figure.

Editor's Viewpoint

Breast reduction surgery usually involves both lifting and reducing the size of the breasts. The amount of size, or volume, reduction varies greatly. The selection of an appropriate surgical technique for any specific patient depends on a number of individual factors including breast size, shape, skin thickness, laxity of the breasts, and composition of the breast tissue.

There are many breast reduction techniques; in fact, breast reduction probably is among the plastic surgery procedures with the greatest number of possible approaches. In most instances, a very pleasing result can be obtained by selecting any of several methods.

Limited incision pattern techniques have gained popularity in recent years. Although excellent results can be obtained in many surgeons' hands, these techniques can produce less-than-optimal postoperative breast shape. Therefore, any patient considering a limited scar method should give consideration to the individual surgeon's comfort level with a particular technique and may consider asking to see photographic examples of his or her postoperative patients in whom the technique being considered has been used.

The most minimally invasive, and in my opinion still highly underutilized, technique is lipoplasty-only breast reduction (LOBR). Rapid recovery, virtually undetectable scars, and no sensory changes or loss of ability to breast-feed are some of the major advantages. Though not all women seeking breast reduction are good candidates for LOBR, I believe this approach could be selected for many more patients. In women for whom nipple/areola position is not sufficiently improved through LOBR, a lift procedure of a lesser magnitude than previously would have been necessary can be carried out at a later time. In my experience this happens much less often than anticipated. LOBR also serves well for the older patient group, many of whom for health or other reasons prefer to have a smaller operation, even with the trade-off of some residual droopiness. A significant disadvantage of LOBR is that, in most instances, medical insurance companies do not provide coverage.

Whatever technique is employed, breast reduction surgery has far-reaching benefits, aesthetically as well as functionally, and is associated with a very high patient satisfaction rate.

— Peter B. Fodor, MD

BREAST RECONSTRUCTION

Although not strictly an "aesthetic" procedure, and therefore not comprehensively discussed in this book, breast reconstruction can be one of the most aesthetically challenging operations performed by board-certified plastic surgeons.

Breast reconstruction is an operation to rebuild breasts that have been removed as a result of mastectomy for breast cancer, lost or damaged by injury, or are congenitally abnormal. As its name implies, breast reconstruction is reconstructive plastic surgery; however, it also has a significant aesthetic component since the goal is to achieve the most natural-looking breast possible. When only one breast has been lost, the surgeon has the further challenge of creating a new breast that matches, as closely as possible, the remaining breast on the opposite side.

The most common technique involves insertion of an implant. Often, it is necessary to first expand the skin to form a pocket into which the implant can be inserted. In such cases, the surgeon will insert a balloon expander beneath the skin and chest muscle. Over the next several weeks or months, the surgeon will periodically inject a saltwater solution into the expander through a tiny valve buried beneath the skin. When the skin over the breast area has expanded enough, the surgeon will perform a second operation to remove the expander and replace it with an implant. Some expanders are designed to be left in place to serve as the implant, eliminating the need for the second procedure.

An alternative to implants is known as flap reconstruction. Tissue flap reconstruction transposes skin, muscle, and fat from an adjacent donor site, often the abdomen or the back, to reconstruct the breast mound. The tissue flap remains connected to the blood supply of the donor site. Free flap reconstruction is a somewhat more complex procedure in which skin and fat are taken from another, more distant part of the body, usually the abdomen or buttocks, and moved to the chest. The transferred skin and fat are completely removed from their original donor site and connected, using microvascular techniques, to the new blood supply at the recipient site. A nipple and areola can be reconstructed at the same time or at a later stage.

"If you were to ask a hundred women, the majority of them would not be familiar with breast reconstruction using tissue from their own body instead of an implant," says **Peter R. Ledoux, MD**, of San Antonio, Texas. "The breast is basically skin and fat, so ideally you want to replace it with skin and fat. Instead of throwing away the tissue removed during a tummy tuck, you can use it to create a new breast. It's much more natural looking and feeling than an implant, and, unlike an implant, there is no possibility of shifting, leaking, or breaking."

Alfonso Oliva, MD, of Spokane, Washington, adds, "Many women faced with the prospect of a mastectomy choose breast reconstruction that utilizes their own tissues in lieu of using breast implants. The difference between the use of breast implants for primary breast augmentation versus breast reconstruction lies in the fact that following mastectomy there is only a thin layer of skin to cover the implant, which may become firm and unnatural in appearance. By using abdominal skin and fat in the form of a muscle-sparing TRAM flap or a DIEP flap, patients can achieve a natural, mature breast appearance. At the same time, they receive a tummy tuck as a bonus. A procedure to lift the opposite normal breast may be required to achieve symmetry."

Women can achieve satisfactory results from either implant or flap procedures, depending on their individual needs. Not all women are good candidates for flap reconstruction, particularly if they have very little body fat.

For more information on breast reconstruction, visit the Web site of the American Society of Plastic Surgeons at www.plasticsurgery.org.

MALE BREAST REDUCTION
Treatment of Gynecomastia

Gynecomastia, excessive fat or glandular tissue in the male breast, is a much more common problem among adolescents and older men than its lack of publicity would indicate. An estimated 40 to 60 percent of men suffer from this condition, which can occur in either one or both breasts, at some time in their lives. The cause of gynecomastia is not well understood, but it is suspected that hormonal changes often play a role. Anabolic steroids that contain estrogen, marijuana use, and prescribed hormones are a factor in some instances. Massive weight loss can also result in hanging breasts that detract from a man's appearance.

Plastic surgery offers a solution for men who are troubled by this embarrassing condition. Through the use of liposuction, which alone may be adequate to reduce breast size in many male patients, and surgical procedures to remove skin or skin and glandular tissue in other cases, plastic surgeons can create a firmer, flatter, and better-contoured male chest.

"Men rarely speak about their breasts," says **Paul J. LoVerme, MD**, of Verona, New Jersey. "It's

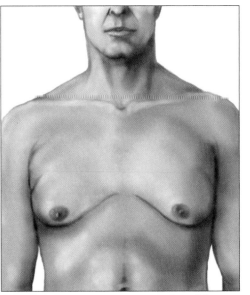

PREOPERATIVE APPEARANCE. Enlarged breasts in a male, a common problem in both adolescents and adults, often causes embarrassment and inhibits exposure of the chest during athletics or at the beach.

an area of embarrassment if they are larger than normal. Most of the men that I treat have long wanted to reduce their breast size but find it difficult to admit, even to a surgeon, that there is a problem."

The best candidates for gynecomastia treatment are healthy, emotionally stable adolescent and adult males whose condition has been persistent and stable for a significant period of time. This surgery is not intended as a weight-loss method, and surgeons may discourage obese or overweight men who have not first tried dieting and exercise from undergoing the procedure. Candidates whose condition may be related to marijuana or anabolic steroid use should stop using these substances; in some cases, though not always, discontinuance may cause breast fullness to diminish.

THE CONSULTATION

Tell your doctor if you are planning to lose a significant amount of weight, since your plastic surgeon may recommend that you stabilize your weight before having the procedure.

Your surgeon will also need to review your entire medical history, including any medications you may be taking, whether you suffer from any allergies or medical conditions, and if you have had any prior surgeries.

In addition to examining your breasts, your plastic surgeon will want to determine whether your gynecomastia might be related to a medical problem, such as impaired liver function or the use of medications or other drugs. In cases where a medical problem is the suspected cause, your surgeon will refer you to an appropriate specialist for further diagnosis. Your surgeon also may advise a breast X-ray, both to rule out the remote possibility of breast cancer and to obtain data concerning the breast's composition. The amount of fat and glandular tissue within the breasts is a factor in determining the best surgical approach to address your problem.

PREPARATION

Your surgeon will give you instructions about how to prepare for surgery. He or she will also give you guidelines on eating, drinking and medications, such as avoiding aspirin or anti-inflammatory medications that promote bleeding.

Breast reduction surgery to treat gynecomastia is usually performed as an outpatient procedure. In some cases, however, your surgeon may recommend an overnight hospital stay. Whether you go home the day of surgery or the next day, you should arrange to have someone drive you to and from surgery and to help you out for a day or two after you return home.

THE SURGERY

The correction of gynecomastia is frequently performed under general anesthesia and sometimes under sedation (twilight) anesthesia, in which both a local anesthetic and sedation are used so the patient is awake but largely unaware of what is going on. The surgery usually takes about an hour and a half to perform; more extensive surgery can take significantly longer. No matter what type of anesthesia you have, you will not feel any pain during the surgical procedure.

In cases where the breast enlargement is primarily caused by excess fatty tissue, liposuction may be the only treatment necessary. Surgeons may use traditional liposuction, also called suction-assisted lipoplasty (SAL), or related techniques such as ultrasound-assisted liposuction (UAL), Vaser-assisted liposuction (VAL) or power-assisted liposuction (PAL). Some surgeons find these newer techniques sometimes offer an advantage in treating fibrous tissue, which may be present in the male breast and other select areas of the body. UAL, VAL or PAL can be used alone or in combination with SAL.

"I find that for male gynecomastia, as well as for treating the back and areas of liposuction revision, I have better results when I add either

LENGTH OF SURGERY
Usually one and a half to three hours.

ANESTHESIA
Twilight (sedation) anesthesia, or general anesthesia.

LENGTH OF STAY
Frequently home the same day, but sometimes stay overnight.

RECOVERY
Initial mild to moderate discomfort; prescription pain medication for two to seven days; back to work in two to three days; swelling, bruising generally subsides in two weeks; avoid strenuous exercise for about one month.

SCARS
Although scars are permanent and can remain noticeable, most scars fade over time; poor healing with raised or wide scars is a possibility.

RISKS/POSSIBLE COMPLICATIONS
Serious complications, while possible, are unlikely. Some potential complications can be avoided by carefully following your surgeon's instructions.

In addition to the usual risks associated with anesthesia, other risks include:
- Infection.
- Hematoma: Collection of blood beneath the skin; can be treated without compromising result.
- Seroma: Collection of fluid under skin can usually be painlessly removed in doctor's office and does not alter the final cosmetic result.
- Pigment changes: Although rare, permanent pigment changes in the breast area can occur.
- Loss of sensation: Numbness or loss of feeling, usually temporary.

The above-listed risks may be only some of those that your surgeon will discuss with you in greater detail during your consultation.

ultrasound or power-assisted liposuction," says **Malcolm Z. Roth, MD**, of New York, New York.

"Newer techniques such as ultrasonic liposuction have made male breast reduction a reliable procedure with a low complication rate and natural-appearing results. I use a device called the Vaser to emulsify and remove the unwanted fat," says Dr. LoVerme.

In situations where only liposuction is necessary, usually a small incision of less than a half-inch in length is made around the edge of the areola, the dark skin that surrounds the nipple. The surgeon then inserts a cannula, which is a very slim hollow tube attached to a suction device, usually a vacuum pump. Using his or her surgical and artistic skill, the surgeon uses the cannula to break up the fatty tissue and literally vacuum it out, decreasing breast fullness. Skin that is healthy and elastic will then "shrink" to the new chest contour. However, if very large quantities of fat have been

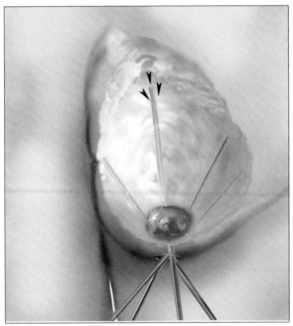

If the tissue excess is primarily fat, liposuction alone may be used to recontour the chest. A liposuction cannula is inserted through a small incision under the breast, in the armpit, and/or at the edge of the areola, and the fat is suctioned out. If a significant amount of fat must be removed, some form of excision of overlying skin may be necessary. When breast enlargement is due to glandular tissue, removal may be accomplished through an incision at the edge of the areola or in the underarm area (not shown). For skin excision, incisions may be larger.

removed, some skin may also have to be excised to create a new, tighter contour. This may be done at a later time, after the initial results have been evaluated.

If, rather than fatty tissue, the primary component of your gynecomastia is dense glandular tissue, your surgeon may need to remove it using an excisional technique, often combined with liposuction to eliminate any excess fat.

To excise glandular tissue, your surgeon will make an incision, usually at the edge of the areola or in the underarm area. He or she will then work through the incision to remove excess glandular tissue, fat and skin.

"In my practice, about 65 percent of men also need excision of glandular tissue to prevent a protruding nipple," says Dr. LoVerme. "The incisions are in the armpit or sometimes around the areola, which is the pigmented skin surrounding the nipple. I have never had a conspicuous areolar scar in a male patient."

In cases where a very large quantity of skin needs to be removed, additional or larger incisions that could result in more noticeable scars may be necessary. This could include an incision in the crease underneath the breast.

A small drain is often inserted to prevent the build-up of excess fluids. The incisions will be closed and most likely covered with a dressing. Your surgeon may also wrap your chest with an elastic bandage to help keep the tissues firmly in place as they heal.

POST OP

You can expect to feel mild to moderate discomfort for a few days after the surgery, which your surgeon will alleviate with prescription medications. Swelling and bruising are normal, and the worst of it should dissipate within the first few weeks following surgery, although it may not completely disappear and final results of your surgery may not be apparent for three or more months. Your surgeon will probably instruct you to wear an elastic pressure garment continuously for the first week or two and to continue wearing it at night for even longer. This will help reduce swelling. Any stitches will be removed about one to two weeks following the procedure.

Although you will probably be advised to refrain from sexual activity for a week or two, strenuous exercise for up to three weeks, and any activity that may risk a blow to the chest area for at least four weeks, it is important for your recovery that you resume some activity almost immediately. You will be encouraged to begin walking around on the day of your surgery and should be able to return to work as early as a day or two after surgery if you feel well enough. You should be able to resume all of your normal activities about one month following your surgery. However, you should refrain from exposing your surgical scars to the sun for at least six months.

LOOKING AHEAD

Correction of gynecomastia eliminates a significant source of embarrassment and anxiety for a young or adult male. Enhanced self-confidence and a greatly improved body image can be expected. The results of surgery are usually permanent. However, if an adolescent is treated prior to stabilization of his condition, and additional breast development occurs, reoperation may be necessary. In addition, in some instances significant weight gain can lead to recurrence of the condition. Asymmetry, a difference in volume between the two breasts, if significant, may require revision.

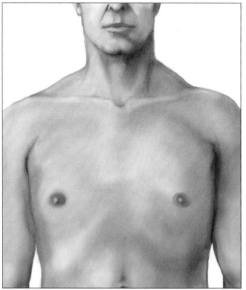

POSTOPERATIVE APPEARANCE. After surgery, excess fat and/or glandular tissue has been removed from the breasts, restoring a more masculine contour of the chest.

Editor's Viewpoint

Gynecomastia, a term derived from the Greek words "gyne" (woman) and "mastia" (breast), is indeed a more common condition than generally realized. Many men affected with gynecomastia are very self-conscious about their condition and go to great lengths to camouflage it. For the most part, it affects males at both ends of the age spectrum: puberty and male menopause, each characterized by significant hormonal changes.

The possibility of male breast malignancy or a hormone-producing testicular tumor, albeit rare, should not be ignored and must be ruled out as an underlying cause of breast enlargement prior to proceeding with plastic surgery.

The advent of liposuction (lipoplasty) revolutionized the treatment of gynecomastia by offering an alternative to excisional surgery for a significant percentage of patients. Liposuction allows the surgeon to achieve not only flattening of the chest but actual sculpting, including a better definition of the pectoral muscle edge. Usually only one or two incisions, one-eighth inch in length, are needed, which eventually heal with barely visible scars. Rarely, in very severe cases, significantly more complicated surgical approaches are required.

The surgical techniques currently available for the treatment of gynecomastia make it possible to alleviate this embarrassing problem, benefiting patients both physically and psychologically.

— Peter B. Fodor, MD

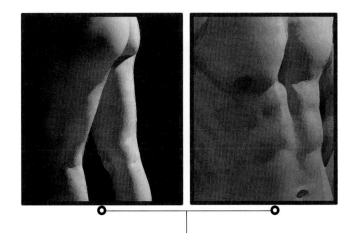

❧ BODY
CONTOURING

BODY CONTOURING

Aging, pregnancy, heredity, and massive weight loss or fluctuations are among the factors that can lead to dissatisfaction with your body contour. Body contouring surgery is designed to address problems such as bulges caused by localized fat deposits in the hips, thighs, buttocks, and other areas; a protruding or wrinkled abdomen; sagging thighs; loose upper arms; and drooping buttocks.

While body contouring procedures such as liposuction and abdominoplasty remove fat from specific body sites, they are not intended for patients seeking an overall reduction in their weight. In fact, such patients may often be advised to lose weight before undergoing these procedures.

"It should be remembered that body contouring surgery is not weight-loss surgery," explains **Andrew Elkwood, MD**, of Shrewsbury, New Jersey. "The purpose is to change the shape of the body to one that is more cosmetically pleasing. A patient who is anticipating getting on the scale and seeing a new, lower number after surgery will be sorely disappointed," says **Michael Rose, MD**, also of Shrewsbury.

"I direct all of my patients to implement appropriate lifestyle changes before they undergo body contouring surgery," says **Samuel Shatkin, MD**, of Amherst, New York, "not only to get the best end results but to help them maintain those results over their lifetime. It is important for patients to maintain proper fitness and nutrition, including avoidance of high glycemic index foods such as white flour and foods high in sugar."

"We have always counseled body contouring patients about diet and exercise," says **Paul M. Parker, MD**, of Paramus, New Jersey. "We have a personal trainer design a specific plan for each patient, which they can carry out under supervision in our own gym. This is great for helping them reach their best body weight and condition prior to surgery, and ideal for helping them maintain the good results they've achieved."

Proper diet and adequate exercise are important to everyone's general health and may be successful in helping you to lose weight and tone muscles. However, good candidates for body contouring surgery are individuals for whom diet and exercise alone are not enough. That is because, in many cases, the stubborn lumps and bumps caused by hereditary fat accumulations are unaffected by overall weight loss, or even a targeted exercise regimen. Likewise, no amount of dieting or physical activity can tighten loose skin or lift sagging body parts.

For properly selected patients, body contouring surgery — whether with liposuction to remove fat or with excisional techniques that also remove excess skin — offers the opportunity for a firmer, more shapely, and better proportioned body that, with adequate attention, can be maintained for many years. As **Alexander G. Nein, MD**, of Nashville, Tennessee, points out, undergoing body contouring surgery can be an incentive for a lifetime of better health. "Many of my patients who have had an abdominoplasty or liposuction become significantly motivated to continue to improve their health and figure following surgery."

LIPOSUCTION
Lipoplasty

Liposuction, also called lipoplasty, the most popular aesthetic procedure performed in the United States, is also perhaps one of the most misunderstood. Although the procedure involves the removal of fat, it is not a replacement for dieting and exercise, and liposuction is not a treatment for generalized obesity.

"Liposuction should not be viewed as a means for weight loss," says **Brian K. Howard, MD**, of Roswell, Georgia. "Liposuction is a tool for aesthetically sculpting the body. Although some weight loss may be noted after healing is completed, this is not the reason for having the procedure."

Otis Allen, MD, of Bloomington, Illinois, adds, "Liposuction remains one of the most commonly requested procedures in all adult age groups and for both sexes. Why? Quite simply, it works — as long as the patient understands that it is best used as a method of 'spot reduction' for areas that do not respond to diet and exercise."

Although adopting a healthy diet and engaging in regular exercise is always a good idea, it is a fact that localized fatty deposits in areas such as the hips, thighs, and abdomen often may be inherited traits that simply cannot be corrected by an improved lifestyle alone. Liposuction can be used to target and reduce unsightly bulges that do not respond to usual weight-loss methods, and to effectively sculpt and recontour various areas of the body.

Alexander G. Nein, MD, of Nashville, Tennessee, also emphasizes that liposuction is not a substitute for weight loss: "Liposuction is ideally suited to treating focal areas of fat accumulation — those lumps and bulges that can make it difficult to wear certain styles of clothing and can cause self-consciousness or even lack of self-esteem. Whole body liposuction is generally impractical."

"I prefer the term 'liposculpting' rather than 'liposuction,'" offers **William G. Armiger, MD**, of Annapolis, Maryland. "The word 'suction' implies simply sucking off a glob of fat from a certain area. In reality, liposculpting is a technique to optimize your particular body form. Everyone's result is different. However, the vision that the physician has initially, before the operation begins, is the key. Your doctor must be able to see the three-dimensional you and devise the most appropriate sculpting procedure to smoothly transition to each of those regions of concern."

Liposuction is sometimes used in conjunction with surgical procedures that entail skin and/or tissue removal, such as a face and neck lift, breast reduction, and abdominoplasty. The procedure can also be used for removal of benign fatty tumors.

Perhaps because it seems like a relatively simple operation, liposuction has attracted a wide range of practitioners with varying backgrounds. However, liposuction is serious surgery, and it is essential to verify that your doctor has accredited training that qualifies him or her to perform this procedure. A physician who is certified by the American Board of Plastic Surgery has completed an accredited residency training program in plastic surgery and should be well qualified to perform liposuction of the face and all body areas. In some cases, dermatologists have received additional training in liposuction; the procedures they perform usually are limited to very small areas of localized fat. A facial plastic surgeon, whose primary specialty is otolaryngology, is also trained to perform liposuction of the face and neck. Your choice of physician should always be based on training, qualifications, and experience. Also important, however, is the fact that a board-certified plastic surgeon has the range of training and experience to be able to advise you on whether liposuction or perhaps some other surgical procedure may be best suited to achieving your goals.

"Because liposuction is practiced by specialists other than plastic surgeons, not all of whom have the same wide range of surgical training, patients can be misled," says **Otto Placik, MD**, of Arlington Heights, Illinois. "A plastic surgeon can appropriately advise them as to whether they are a good candidate for liposuction, or whether a different surgical procedure such as abdominoplasty, brachioplasty, breast reduction, or thigh lift may be a better option to achieve the results they are looking for."

Robert Wald, MD, of Fullerton, California, adds, "Liposuction is a procedure that requires a lot of artistry and experience. The purpose of this procedure is to contour the body. The surgeon is sculpting and shaping. He or she must develop a well-designed surgical plan and mark the patient properly before beginning to operate. The surgeon's good clinical judgment, based on training and experience, is a vital component of successful liposuction."

People at a normal, stable weight, with firm and elastic skin tone who have excessive fatty deposits limited to specific body areas are the ideal candidates for liposuction.

"If the patient's weight remains stable, the results from liposuction will be permanent," says **Alexander G. Nein, MD**, of Nashville, Tennessee.

Good physical health is also very important. Although in the hands of an experienced and qualified surgeon, serious complications are rare, the risks increase significantly for people with medical problems, such as heart or lung disease, poor blood circulation, and diabetes. Those who have recently had surgery near the area they want contoured also may run a greater risk of complications. Age is not necessarily an important factor in considering safety, yet if older patients have reduced skin elasticity, their results may not be as good as those achieved in younger patients with better-quality skin. That's because liposuction removes only fat and not loose, excess skin which may require another type of procedure such as a tummy tuck or a lower body lift, discussed elsewhere in this book.

"Patient selection is probably more important in liposuction than any other procedure," comments **James D. McMahan, MD**, of Columbus, Ohio. "The ideal patient for liposuction is young, healthy, close to their ideal body weight with very elastic skin and just a few bulges they want to

FAST FACTS

LENGTH OF SURGERY
30 minutes to five hours, depending on extent of fat removal.

ANESTHESIA
Local anesthesia, intravenous sedation, epidural block, or general anesthesia.

LENGTH OF STAY
Usually outpatient procedure, home the same day; overnight stay usual with large-volume liposuction.

RECOVERY
Initial mild to moderate discomfort: pain medication; early ambulation but minimal activity for a few days; back to work in few days; normal activities in one to two weeks, strenuous activities in one month.

SWELLING/BRUISING
Most subsides within a week to 10 days, mild residual up to three months.

SCARS
Tiny and inconspicuously placed.

RISKS/POSSIBLE COMPLICATIONS
Serious complications, while possible, are unlikely. Some potential complications can be avoided by carefully following your surgeon's instructions.

In addition to the usual risks associated with anesthesia, other risks include:
- Fluid imbalance, shock, pulmonary emboli: Can be fatal; appropriate safety measures can greatly reduce these risks.
- Hematoma: Collection of blood beneath the skin; can be treated without compromising result.
- Numbness or discoloration: Usually temporary; some lack of sensation and skin discoloration may persist.
- Contour irregularities: Dimpling, depressions, wrinkling, or unevenness of the skin; additional treatments can improve results.

The above-listed risks may be only some of those that your surgeon will discuss with you in greater detail during your consultation.

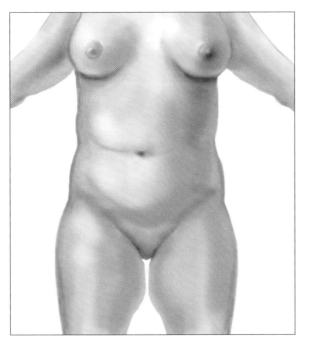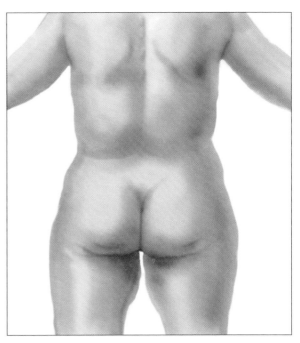

——— FEMALE ———

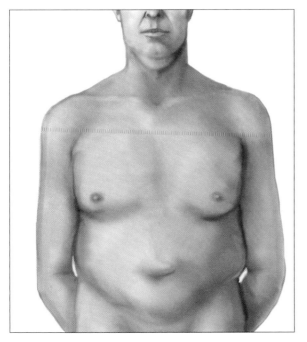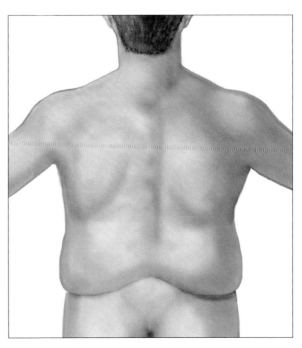

——— MALE ———

PREOPERATIVE APPEARANCE. Ideal candidates for liposuction are women and men in good health and of generally normal weight, with localized fat deposits that have failed to respond to diet and/or exercise.

remove. Those patients do extremely well. Their skin looks great and it looks like they never had the operation, which is what you want. But it really depends on the individual patient. I've had 70-year-olds who did phenomenally, and I've seen people in their 20s who were not good candidates because their skin quality was so poor."

Andrew Elkwood, MD, of Shrewsbury, New Jersey, says, "My general feeling is that, in women, liposuction is well-suited for body contouring in an individual who has not yet had children." "After child-bearing, the skin-reduction techniques such as abdominoplasty and body lifting are usually necessary," adds **Michael Rose, MD** also of Shrewsbury.

In addition to good physical health, realistic motivations and expectations about what the procedure can accomplish contribute to a patient's chances of achieving a satisfying outcome.

Provided you are a good candidate for the procedure, liposuction can eliminate or lessen fatty deposits in problem areas of the body. These include the abdomen, hips, buttocks, back, thighs, knees, calves, ankles, upper arms, jowls, cheeks, and neck ("double chin"). Liposuction can also be used, either alone or with skin excision surgery, to reduce enlarged breasts in men (gynecomastia), which is a common condition among adolescent and adult males, and for breast reduction in women. (Liposuction-only breast reduction is discussed in the chapter on Breast Reduction in this book.)

Liposuction can be performed on several areas of the body at the same time, and it can also be done in conjunction with certain other aesthetic plastic surgery procedures. Depending on the amount and type of surgery you will undergo, your surgeon may suggest performing it in one, two, or more sessions.

As stated previously, liposuction is not a method for weight loss, and it should not be used as a treatment for obesity. Liposuction will not remove cellulite and in some instances could worsen its appearance. That's because fat deposits targeted by liposuction are beneath the cellulite. When the fat volume is reduced, the cellulite "dimples" may be more noticeable.

Skin tone is one of the most important aspects that can affect the quality of liposuction results. The fat cells targeted for removal by liposuction are immediately beneath the skin and above the muscle. The better the skin tone, the more readily skin will contract to fit the newly contoured body shape. There are several factors that influence skin tone quality; these include tightness, thickness, stretch marks, prior sun exposure, and the patient's age.

Some areas of the body may not respond to liposuction as well as others. The inner thighs, calves, and areas with natural skin creases, such as the buttock crease, are more likely to yield less satisfactory results. However, this is not always the case. In addition to the surgeon's experience in treating difficult or delicate areas of the body with liposuction, there are many other factors that must be considered — for example, the degree of correction needed, the quality of your skin, and your expectations for results.

THE CONSULTATION

The consultation is a time for the surgeon and patient to get to know and feel comfortable with each other. The patient should feel completely confident that the surgeon is fully qualified. If you haven't read sections in the beginning of this book about choosing a surgeon who is certified by the American Board of Plastic Surgery, you may want to do so now.

In aesthetic plastic surgery, good communication between surgeon and patient is a vital component of achieving a successful outcome. Everybody's sense of aesthetics differs. It is extremely important that you tell your surgeon exactly how you perceive your appearance problem and how you would like to look.

"A lot of patients come in with a set idea that they want a specific procedure, such as liposuction or abdominoplasty," says **Rosellen Meystrik, MD,** of Springfield, Missouri, "but I always ask them to start by articulating to me what their goals are — or, stated another way, what is it they like and don't like about their body. Because if they come in wanting liposuction but the problem is that they've had a few kids and now have a little sagging on their lower abdomen, liposuction is not going to be the answer. By first clearly understanding their goals, I can devise and recommend the best way to achieve them."

Your surgeon needs to determine if you are a suitable candidate for surgery and will need to review your entire medical history, including any medications you are taking, information about previous surgeries or medical treatments, and any medical conditions you may have such as diabetes, high blood pressure, blood clots, or heart disease.

Your current weight and whether you plan to lose or gain weight in the future are also important factors you should discuss with your surgeon.

"I had a patient recently who said that liposuction did not help her at all and she still wears the same size clothing," recounts **Edward J. Domanskis, MD**, of Newport Beach, California. "After I explained to her that was an impossibility and reminded her how many pounds I had removed, she was still in disbelief. I told her that either she was mistaken or she had gained weight since the operation. She denied both until she stepped on the scale and saw that she was 20 pounds heavier than her preoperative weight. If a patient maintains an appropriate regimen of diet and exercise, and stabilizes his or her weight, the fat will not return."

Patients who gain a significant amount of weight following liposuction sometimes find that fatty deposits appear in new areas or that their previously treated areas appear somewhat lumpy. This can occur because, although fat cells removed by liposuction are gone forever, the remaining fat cells can become larger if you gain weight.

If you've tried dieting or lost weight in the past, your surgeon may ask what effect it had on the areas you now wish to contour. This is to help determine whether these bulging areas of excess fat are resistant to other methods of reduction, in which case liposuction is really the only way to get rid of them. If you have had good results in the past from nonsurgical methods of reducing unsightly bulges, your surgeon may recommend that you try these methods again.

Your surgeon will examine you to evaluate the extent and quality of fat deposits and assess the condition of your skin. In patients with excess fat and skin, it is often necessary to remove both — something that liposuction alone cannot do. Excisional techniques such as abdominoplasty or a lower body lift may be indicated. Your surgeon will discuss with you the various body contouring methods available and those that would be most appropriate in your case, depending on your physical condition and expectations for your final appearance.

"It's important during the consultation to tell the patient if liposuction will do a fantastic job for them or if other procedures, such as a tummy tuck, are also needed," says **Alexander Majidian, MD**, of Calabasas, California. "The surgeon must be experienced with different surgical procedures and techniques in order to be able to design the best procedure for each individual patient."

Surgeons agree that, in addition to anatomy, patient goals are a key factor in designing the correct procedure and maintaining the results of liposuction.

"Patient input is very important," states **David L. Buchanan, MD**, of Santa Barbara, California. "During the consultation, I ask patients to show me their areas of concern. I like to mark and draw a topographical map on those areas, with the high point being the top of the mountain and then tapering off in concentric circles to flatter areas. Then I have the patient look in the mirror and say, 'Yes, I like that,' or 'Be sure to include this or that.' I mark them again on the morning of surgery because it's more difficult to discern the high points once they lie down on the table and after infusion with wetting solution, and I have them look in the mirror and approve the areas we are going to treat."

David J. Levens, MD, of Coral Springs, Florida, agrees that patients must become involved in their surgery and take responsibility for maximizing their results. "Liposuction is a very good procedure for the right person," he says. "It can have very subtle or very dramatic results. The most dramatic results occur when the surgeon uses liposuction to reshape the body, and then patients do the rest. They're motivated by the procedure and go on to lose weight on their own. Liposuction is not a replacement for weight loss and other healthy activities, and if the patient is not expecting to participate in the recovery and improvement process, that's a problem."

PREPARATION

Your surgeon will give you instructions about how to prepare for surgery. These may include guidelines on eating, drinking, smoking, and medications, such as avoiding aspirin or anti-inflammatory medications that promote bleeding.

As with all surgery in general, whether performed in an outpatient facility or in the hospital, you should arrange to have someone drive you to and from surgery and to assist you for a day or two after you return home.

THE SURGERY

First developed in Europe, liposuction was introduced in the United States in the early 1980s. Since then, technological advances and ongoing physician experience with the technique have continually made the surgery safer and more effective.

WETTING SOLUTIONS

One of the major early advances in technique was the development and use of wetting solutions. Prior to this time, when liposuction was routinely performed using a "dry" technique — that is, without the infusion of fluids prior to fat removal — it resulted in significant blood loss and bruising. In fact, when fat was suctioned from the body, the fat aspirate might be as much as 45 percent blood. The expectation of this degree of blood loss severely restricted the amount of fat that could be withdrawn in any single surgery and also limited the quality of surgical results.

All of this changed with the introduction of pre-surgical infiltration with saline solution, which today typically contains epinephrine and local anesthetic to reduce blood loss and decrease pain. With the so-called "wet technique," blood loss was reduced to 15 to 30 percent of the aspirate volume. Later, the "superwet technique" was developed, which required pre-infiltration of even larger amounts of fluid — essentially at a one-to-one ratio with the amount of aspirate to be withdrawn during the procedure. With the superwet technique, blood loss generally dropped to less than one percent, which contributed enormously to increased operative safety.

The tumescent technique carries the principles of the superwet technique even further. Using this technique, the surgeon may infiltrate generally from three to six times as much fluid as the volume of aspirate he or she intends to remove. This has the effect of dramatically swelling the tissues, which proponents of the technique say further facilitates fat removal. However, when used improperly, the tumescent technique can result in serious complications such as fluid overload and anesthetic toxicity — problems that began to appear with increasing frequency in the second decade of liposuction's popularity.

"Over the course of nearly three decades now, liposuction has generally been a very safe procedure," explains **Robert W. Bernard, MD**, of White Plains, New York. "There was a period of time, however, during which there was a greater number of reported complications.

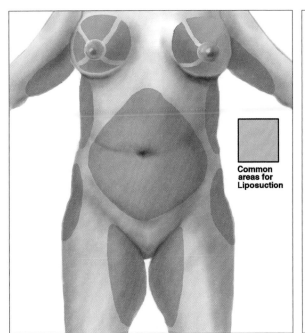 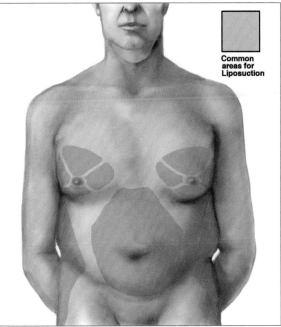

The shaded areas illustrate most of the common sites for liposuction.
In addition to the highlighted areas, the face, back, buttocks, calves, and ankles also can be contoured with liposuction.

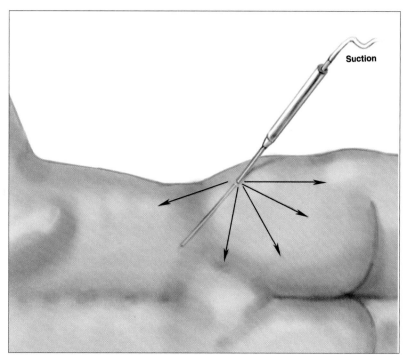

Suction

In traditonal lipoplasty, the surgeon inserts a long, hollow tube, called a cannula, through a tiny incision. The cannula is used to disrupt the fat underneath the skin so it can be removed from the body by suction. Multiple incision sites are needed, depending on the areas to be suctioned.

Many of these stemmed from improper use of the tumescent technique or from poor management of large-volume procedures. Understandably, this created concern about the safety of liposuction and, for a time, gave the procedure somewhat of a black eye. Since then, many of the earlier practices that tended to create problems have been modified or abandoned, which has significantly reduced the number of complications and restored liposuction's excellent safety profile."

"I predominantly perform a variation of the superwet technique, using about a one-to-one ratio," says **Gary D. Hall, MD**, of Leawood, Kansas. "I add one liter of fluid and suction off one liter. I found that using more liquid, as in the traditional tumescent technique, isn't necessary; it can accentuate swelling and make it harder to judge the accuracy of your end result."

Large-volume liposuction, the removal of more than five liters of fat and fluid, involves longer operating times, the infusion and suctioning of greater fluid volumes, increased blood loss, higher doses of anesthetic, and increased surgical risks. It generally requires an overnight stay in a hospital or recovery facility. With proper patient selection and necessary precautions, large-volume liposuction can be a safe and effective procedure.

Many highly experienced surgeons simply choose not to perform large-volume liposuction, preferring to remove smaller amounts of fat and, if necessary, staging procedures to increase patient safety.

"Liposuction can be an effective part of improving overall appearance, but I personally don't perform large-volume liposuction," says Dr. Galante. "I just feel there are too many risks."

Lee H. Colony, MD, of East Lansing, Michigan, observes, "Each surgeon tends to have an individual philosophy as to how liposuction is incorporated into his or her practice. Some will focus on limited fat removal, which is less time-consuming and allows for a rapid recovery. Other surgeons with a stronger emphasis on liposuction will opt for a more aggressive intervention with more extensive fat removal. Although this approach is more physically demanding for the surgeon and challenging from a recovery standpoint (pain, swelling, and bruising), I feel it can better achieve the results that most patients request."

"With larger volume liposuction, fluid management is vital," cautions **Csaba L. Magassy, MD**, of McLean, Virginia, "but it can be done safely in the proper surgical environment and with an experienced team."

George W. Commons, MD, of Palo Alto, California, says, "When performing large-volume liposuction, we carefully measure the fluid that goes in and the fluid that comes out — fat, fluid, and also urine output." He notes that "if you take out 10 liters of fat, at least 15 to 20 percent of that is fluid."

If you choose to undergo large-volume liposuction, it is essential that your plastic surgeon have considerable experience with the procedure and that your surgery is performed in an accredited facility, most likely a hospital where you will stay overnight following the procedure.

CANNULA SIZE

Another factor contributing to the enhanced safety and effectiveness of today's liposuction procedures — regardless of the extent of fat removal — is the use of smaller-diameter cannulas. A cannula is the instrument used to dislodge fat before it is removed from the body. Generally, it is a long, hollow instrument that is connected to a suction device, which allows the surgeon to literally vacuum away excess fat. With the original, larger-diameter cannulas, trauma to the tissues and blood vessels invariably caused a high degree of bruising.

"I was fortunate enough, in 1981, to go to Paris and see first-hand what was then a new technology," says **James L. Baker, MD**, of Winter Park, Florida. "It was fascinating. Of course, back then liposuction was a painful procedure with tremendous bruising. In 1987, plastic surgeons started developing wetting solutions and using smaller cannulas, both of which made the operation much less traumatic. By the late 80s, surgeons were achieving good, predictable results in the majority of patients."

"The way plastic surgeons performed liposuction even as recently as 1992 has completely changed," says **Jonathan R. Berman, MD**, of Boca Raton, Florida. "The evolution of this procedure has been phenomenal. Instead of a 'dry' technique, we now use a 'wet' technique. We use much smaller cannulas requiring only small incisions. Overall, it is a 'gentler' surgery causing less trauma to the patient, providing much more precise surgical results, and allowing removal of more fat in less time with less blood loss. All of this makes liposuction a very safe and effective procedure."

Joseph P. Hunstad, MD, of Charlotte, North Carolina, agrees, "One of the biggest innovations in liposuction has been the use of smaller cannulas. Cannula diameters have been reduced from 10 or 12 millimeters down to three millimeters."

TRADITIONAL LIPOPLASTY, OR SUCTION-ASSISTED LIPOPLASTY (SAL)

In traditional suction-assisted lipoplasty (SAL), the surgeon will insert a cannula through tiny incisions to vacuum the fat layer beneath the skin, thus removing fatty deposits from specific areas of the body to achieve a recontoured silhouette. The incisions are often no more than one-quarter inch in length and frequently can be strategically placed in inconspicuous places, such as in skin folds. Scarring is minimal.

In performing the basic technique, the surgeon energetically guides the cannula back and forth through the fat layer to break up the fat cells, which are then suctioned out. A vacuum pump or a large syringe may provide the suction. If a syringe is used, the fat that is withdrawn may later be injected in other areas of the body, such as the face, to fill in depressions, lines or add volume.

SAL is still the most commonly used technique. Although ultrasound-assisted and power-assisted liposuction may also be used, the final results of your liposuction should be the same or very similar no matter which of these techniques is employed. Surgeons generally use whichever techniques work best in their hands and are best suited for each individual patient.

"When it comes to the procedure itself, I think the surgeon's artistic sensibility is crucial," says **Gustavo Galante, MD**, of Munster, Indiana. "The object is to contour the body. This requires the ability to determine and achieve the best proportions for each patient's individual anatomical structure."

UAL, VAL AND PAL

As liposuction technology continued to advance, new devices were developed to compete with, or complement, the traditional suction-assisted lipoplasty (SAL) instrumentation. Among these are ultrasound-assisted lipoplasty (UAL), Vaser-assisted lipoplasty (VAL), and power-assisted lipoplasty (PAL).

According to the American Society for Aesthetic Plastic Surgery (ASAPS), in 2005 only 21 percent of liposuction procedures utilized the newer ultrasound technologies. Clearly, many surgeons believe that traditional SAL delivers the results they and their patients are looking for. Even those surgeons who have enthusiastically embraced newer technologies, as some of our experts have, generally agree that the most important factor in the success of liposuction is the training and experience of the surgeon — not the particular technology used. Nevertheless, proponents of UAL, VAL and PAL all feel that these devices offer benefits either when used exclusively or in combination with SAL.

"It's interesting that so many different technologies are available now for liposuction," notes **Malcolm Z. Roth, MD**, of New York, New York. "I find that for male gynecomastia (enlarged breasts), for backs, and for areas of revision, I achieve better results when I use either an ultrasound or power-assisted device, but for most of my lipoplasties I still use the standard cannula and suction techniques."

Michael R. Schwartz, MD, of Camarillo, California, agrees, "Most surgeons use all types of liposuction — standard SAL, power-assisted, and ultrasound. I've found that there's definitely a role for ultrasound in treating gynecomastia in males and the back, flank, and abdomen areas in all patients. Because the tissue can be denser in those areas, ultrasound, which liquefies the fat, is much more successful at removing it. The ultrasound is also beneficial in secondary patients because it is able to penetrate the scar tissue left from previous surgeries. Ultrasound has also been shown to be more effective at shrinking the skin, and I like it for that reason, too."

Ultrasound-assisted liposuction, or UAL, uses a special cannula that emits ultrasonic energy. This energy assists in breaking apart fat cells and may make them easier to remove. Some surgeons find that this technique can enhance their precision, minimize trauma to the tissues, reduce bruising and swelling, and help improve recovery times. UAL can be beneficial in more fibrous areas of the body, such as the back and the male chest, as well as in secondary liposuction procedures.

"Ultrasonic liposuction transmits ultrasonic energy through the cannula's tip at a frequency that only affects the fat cells," explains Dr. Baker. "Muscles, bones, and tendons are all at a higher frequency of response and are not affected, so the ultrasonic energy produces less trauma and blood loss."

Julio L. Garcia, MD, of Las Vegas, Nevada, agrees, "Ultrasonic liposuction is a very powerful tool that requires even more concentration on the part of the surgeon. I have found that, in my hands, using the new ultrasonic technology allows me to sculpt and contour the body better and with less blood loss than with traditional liposuction. UAL also allows us to get a little better skin retraction than traditional liposuction, which makes it more effective on older patients whose skin has lost some of its elasticity."

"Ultrasound helps me sculpt and contour better, since I can emulsify the fat and be more precise in where I remove it, and it helps with larger volume liposuction," says Dr. Magassy.

Charles Spenler, MD, of Torrance, California, is also enthusiastic about UAL. "Ultrasonic liposuction has proven to be a most effective way to remove unwanted fat and get the most skin contraction."

Linda Leffel, MD, of Bend, Oregon, adds, "I have been impressed with the minimal bruising and minimal pain patients have after ultrasonic liposuction. The majority of patients return to work and their regular routine in 48 hours. I prefer ultrasonic liposuction for the tough fibrous areas of the chest, male breasts, and back fat rolls."

As Dr. Baker puts it, "I always say, if you're holding an ultrasound cannula, it's like the bow on a violin; you guide it with your fingers. Using a conventional cannula, on the other hand, is more like playing tennis; it requires more work and arm movement."

UAL may take somewhat longer to perform than traditional liposuction, and it can pose additional risks. While appropriate training and experience are important to any liposuction procedure, the surgeon using UAL must also know how to avoid certain complications associated with the UAL device, such as burning or blistering of the skin.

"A disadvantage of the ultrasonic equipment is that you can get a blister or burn on the skin's surface," says Dr. Baker. "But in all the years I've been using it, I've never had a blister. You have to know what you're doing."

A more recent refinement of ultrasound technology is Vaser-assisted liposuction, which reportedly reduces the risk of burning the skin.

"Today's ultrasonic technology for liposuction, such as the Vaser, is a great improvement over the old 1990s devices," points out **Stephen Goldstein, MD**, of Englewood, Colorado. "It uses lower energy, which helps reduce the risk of burn wounds. This lets us work closer to the skin's surface, which improves our ability to sculpt and contour as well as reduce complications. Further helping to reduce complications, the Vaser is selective, breaking up the fat and leaving behind nerve cells, blood vessels, and the connective tissue going from muscle to skin. That the fat cells are emulsified rather than torn free means they can be extracted more easily, which aids our ability to contour as well as reduces trauma, which, in turn, reduces downtime and discomfort for the patient."

J. Vicente Poblete, MD, of Avon Lake, Ohio, shares the enthusiasm for Vaser technology. "I'm very happy with the Vaser, which is the most recent development in delivering ultrasonic energy. The Vaser probe selectively emulsifies the fat cells while leaving the connective tissue matrix intact. Traditional liposuction relies on mechanical trauma to break up the fat cells, which are then removed by suction. With the Vaser, because fat cells are emulsified before being extracted, there is less trauma, more even and accurate contouring, and less bruising."

Gene Sloan, MD, of Little Rock, Arkansas, has also been impressed with the new Vaser ultrasonic technology, "This system is selective for fatty tissues. At first I thought it was just a 'sales pitch,' but I've had opportunities to elevate a flap and see blood vessels intact. By not damaging the blood vessels, patients have much less bleeding. In my experience, there is definitely less postoperative swelling, bruising, and discomfort. I am able to achieve better contours using the Vaser, and my revision rate is lower."

"The Vaser Liposelection has the advantages of the ultrasound without the negatives of the first- and second-generation ultrasound equipment," agrees John Bruno, MD, of Fort Myers, Florida. "It has been very helpful, and patients are very satisfied."

"My interest in noninvasive procedures with minimal downtime carries over to body contouring," states Diane Duncan, MD, of Fort Collins, Colorado. "I find that with the Vaser, patients heal more quickly than with traditional liposuction and with less postoperative pain and swelling."

Mokhtar Asaadi, MD, of West Orange, New Jersey, also endorses the benefits of ultrasonic liposuction using the Vaser device. "With the Vaser, I get better skin retraction, especially with hanging skin. It also improves my ability to treat more difficult areas, such as the back and the lower part of the love handles, and to break down scar tissue for those patients who have had liposuction before."

George W. Commons, MD, of Palo Alto, California, says, "We use Vaser ultrasonic liposuction in routine face lift procedures to remove excess, unwanted fat. We've found that it works very well for contouring the submental (beneath the chin) or mandibular (beneath the jawline) angle and for contouring the cheeks. Previous ultrasonic techniques were questionable in those areas, but the Vaser is much more accurate."

"Vaser liposuction has enabled us to contour the torso much more effectively," states Rodger Wade Pielet, MD, of Chicago, Illinois. "Our patients are extremely happy."

"Using Vaser-assisted ultrasonic liposuction, it is possible to achieve a smooth surface and avoid depressions and irregularities in areas such as the medial and lateral thighs, which may be prone to such complications using standard liposuction," offers Robert Lowen, MD, of Mountain View, California. "Careful, incremental liquefaction of the fat and gentle aspiration are obtained with this technology. Using this latest generation ultrasonic technology, I find that revisions are rarely needed."

"My preferred way to perform liposuction is to use a tumescent technique followed by Vaser ultrasonic energy and then Vaser small cannula techniques," offers John R. Moore, MD, of Franklin, Tennessee. "It is not unusual for me to do the lateral thigh and hip areas, abdomen, medial (inner) thighs, and upper arms in one session. For patients with flattening of the gluteal area (buttocks), I may contour the upper back, hips, flanks, and lateral thigh and then transfer some of the fat to the upper gluteal region. This process has given patients very good, long-term results."

"I feel strongly that the latest generation of ultrasound technology has revolutionized the way we perform liposuction," offers Onelio Garcia, MD, of Hialeah, Florida. "The results are much more precise, and the postoperative course is significantly improved. This technology has also broadened the patient population that can benefit from liposuction treatment, such as older patients and overweight patients for whom additional general weight loss is not feasible for one reason or another."

Power-assisted lipoplasty, or PAL, uses a motorized cannula to assist in breaking up fatty tissue for removal by suction. While the skill and artistry of the surgeon still is important in guiding the cannula, much less physical effort is required because of the mechanically powered back and forth motion of the cannula tip. Some surgeons feel that PAL enhances their precision and ability to sculpt, minimizes trauma to the tissues, reduces bruising and swelling, and helps to improve patient recovery times.

"I've tried ultrasonic devices and found that my results were not as good," says D'Arcy A. Honeycutt, MD, of Bismarck, North Dakota. "I prefer the power-assisted device. Because of the reduced physical effort required, I find I can easily perform a four-hour liposuction in which I may contour a number of areas — the abdomen, flanks, hips and circumferential thighs, for example — and get very good results."

Like all cosmetic plastic surgery, the technique selected in any particular case often depends on individual patient factors as well as surgeon preference. Your surgeon will advise you about the various options and techniques and explain which one he or she feels is best for you.

SUPERFICIAL LIPOPLASTY

Some surgeons employ a technique called superficial lipoplasty to remove fat that lies closer to the surface of the skin. This superficial fat layer serves as a cushion under the skin. That's why superficial fat removal has the potential to cause irregularities such as dimpling and puckering of the skin, especially in areas of the body that have only one layer of fat. However, superficial lipoplasty used by a skillful surgeon in appropriate areas can achieve excellent skin contraction and sometimes works particularly well in older patients with inelastic skin for whom traditional liposuction techniques might produce suboptimal results.

Lipoplasty may sometimes be combined with fat grafting not only to reduce areas of excess fat but also to further enhance contours of the face and body. **Joseph Michael Pober, MD**, of New York, New York, talks about the ever-refining developments in liposuction methods. "Lipocontouring combines multilayer tumescent liposculpture with multilevel fat grafting (microlipoinjection), and can be used for enhancement of both the face and body. Using these techniques in the facial regions, we can achieve higher cheekbones, a better-defined jawline, flattening of the nasolabial folds around the mouth, forehead enhancement, and lip enhancement. Although the technique of lipocontouring might appear 'easy,' a satisfactory three-dimensional result depends on the surgeon's sound anatomic knowledge, refined aesthetic and surgical judgment, precise technique, and stamina to carry out what is a very meticulous and painstaking procedure."

POST OP

Liposuction can take anywhere from 30 minutes to five hours to perform, depending on the size of the area, the amount of fat to be removed, and the type of anesthesia and technique used. Usually an outpatient procedure for small and medium volume procedures, large-volume liposuction generally requires that a patient remain in the hospital or surgical facility overnight.

Liposuction is performed using local anesthesia, intravenous sedation, epidural block, or general anesthesia. No matter what type of anesthesia you have, you should not feel any pain during the surgical procedure.

Following surgery, you will continue to be closely monitored in a recovery area. Blood-tinged fluid may drain from the incisions. While this can be disconcerting to a patient, in actuality this drainage serves to lessen postoperative bruising and swelling. You may feel some discomfort, including pain, burning, swelling and temporary numbness. Your surgeon will prescribe medications to control your pain. He or she may also prescribe antibiotics to prevent infection.

A snug-fitting elastic garment or other compressive dressing may be placed over the treated area to control swelling and help your skin better adapt to its new contours. Your surgeon will instruct you on its removal for bathing purposes and how long it should be worn.

"Your results are dependant on many factors. Wearing the recommended garment and allowing the skin to shrink are essential," says **Carl Williams Jr., MD**, of Henderson, Nevada. "The healing takes time, and I always tell my patients that they will need to have patience."

"Everyone wears their garment until I feel it is okay for them to take it off — usually about two to three weeks," says Dr. Berman. "I see patients frequently in the first three to five weeks after surgery to monitor the wounds and the healing process. We encourage massage and recommend deep massage, if necessary. But usually patients or their spouses can simply 'knead' the areas to break up the scar tissue, which helps eliminate any potential lumps and bumps."

Healing takes time and can vary greatly from individual to individual; it is a gradual process. From the first day following surgery, your surgeon will tell you to move around some to help reduce swelling, aid circulation, and prevent blood clots from forming in your legs. Although if your surgery lasted an hour or longer, you will most likely have worn mechanical anti-embolism devices during the entire procedure, in some cases drugs may be administered following surgery to further protect you from potential blood clotting complications.

"The most serious complication that can result from many types of surgery, including liposuction, is venous thromboembolism (VTE)," says **Germán Newall, MD**, of Houston, Texas. "This may take the form of deep venous thrombosis (DVT) and cause pulmonary embolus

(PE), which can lead to death. For our large-volume liposuction patients — and any patients whose procedures involve extensive undermining and prolonged operating time — we incorporate the use of a low molecular weight heparin (Enoxeparin) into our postoperative protocol. Our experience, which comprised a study that included 296 cases and represented more than 12 years of experience by surgeons and staff handling these types of cases on a daily basis, indicated a zero percent incidence of VTE, DVT, and PE with the prophylactic use of Enoxeparin."

You will probably feel stiff and sore, and your surgeon will advise you to restrict yourself to very limited activities for the first few days. It is important to remember not to take aspirin or certain anti-inflammatory medications that promote bleeding. If you smoke, ask your surgeon how long you should abstain.

Your surgeon will examine the treated areas within several days, and you will notice that they are swollen and bruised. Swelling and bruising usually begin to subside a week or so following surgery, although either may last up to three weeks or longer. You may also feel numbness in some areas, and it may take up to several weeks before feeling returns completely. Stitches, if any were used, typically will be removed or dissolve on their own within 10 days following surgery.

"There is usually very little pain associated with this procedure," says **Gloria A. de Olarte, MD**, of Pasadena, California, "but some bruising and swelling can be seen afterward. Although liposuction offers some immediate results, it will take four to six months for the skin to shrink and before final results can be seen."

Depending on the extent of your liposuction, you may be able to return to work within a few days following surgery, resume most of your normal activities within one to two weeks, and engage in some moderate exercise shortly thereafter. Your surgeon will probably advise you to avoid more strenuous activities for about a month. He or she will schedule follow-up visits to monitor your progress. Of course, if you experience any unusual symptoms, including heavy bleeding or a sudden increase in pain, you should contact your plastic surgeon immediately.

LOOKING AHEAD

Recovery time varies greatly, depending on the amount of fat that was removed, the areas treated, and your individual healing characteristics. For everyone, however, recovery is a gradual process. Improvements in your contour will appear in stages; first after about four to six weeks when most swelling has subsided, and then after about three months when any mild, residual swelling has disappeared, your final contours should begin to be visible.

"I warn patients that although they can see some results early," says **Eric Mariotti, MD**, of Concord, California, "within the first week not only will they think that I didn't take anything out, they may think I put something in! Then after two to three weeks, their new figure starts to take shape, but I remind them that they will continue to see further results for up to several months as the swelling continues to subside and the skin continues to shrink. To speed this process and significantly reduce postoperative pain, I encourage patients to come in frequently for external ultrasound treatments. I believe this stimulates the lymphatic flow, reduces bruising, and softens the feeling of tightness often encountered immediately after liposuction."

Most liposuction patients are extremely pleased with their results, which reduce those unflattering bulges created by areas of fatty deposits. They find that clothing fits better and more comfortably, they are less self-conscious, and often they have an increased sense of confidence.

As long as you maintain your postoperative weight through proper diet and exercise, the results of liposuction will be permanent. For many patients, the results of liposuction are an incentive to make even more improvements in their body through proper diet and exercise.

What if you do gain weight? Even if you gain a few pounds, your weight may be more evenly distributed than in the past, and your previous problem areas won't be as apparent. However, as mentioned earlier in this chapter, there is the possibility that weight gain could result in localized fatty deposits in different areas than those corrected with liposuction.

Because liposuction involves very precise sculpting of the body, it is not unusual for patients to require some minor revisionary procedure to further enhance their results. "Complications from liposuction are rare when the surgery is performed by a qualified and experienced plastic surgeon," says Dr. Leffel. "However, there can be contour irregularities, rippling of the skin, or depressions.

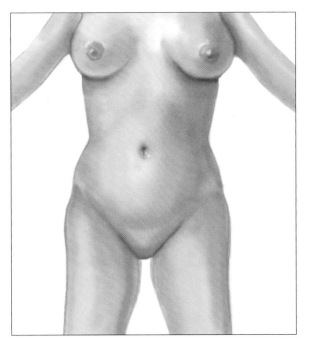
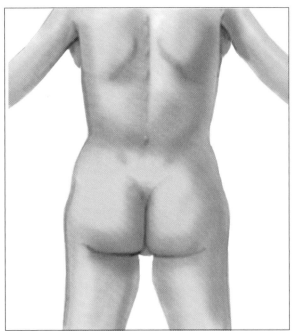

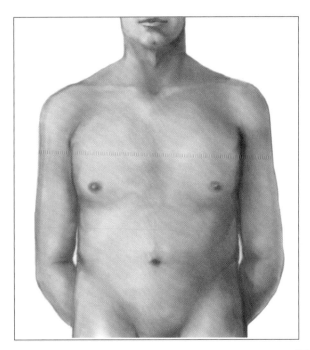
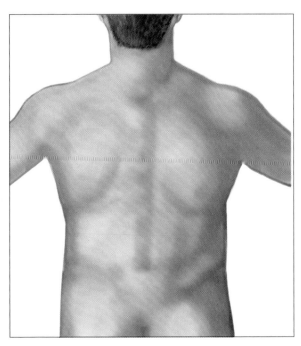

POSTOPERATIVE APPEARANCE. Following liposuction, areas that previously had unsightly bulges caused by localized fatty deposits now appear smoother and more proportionate. The overall effect is a healthier and fitter appearance.

Treatment of visable depressions includes fat grafting into the depression."

Depending on the extent of refinements needed, touch-up procedures can sometimes be performed under local anesthesia in your plastic surgeon's office.

Researchers continue to investigate other potential methods of fat reduction. One of these is injectable, fat-dissolving "mesotherapy," which is not approved by the U.S. Food and Drug Administration and, so far, has no widely recognized scientific validity. Although such treatments may hold promise for the future, currently there is no standardization or quality control of mesotherapy formulas and no oversight of practitioners performing mesotherapy injections.

Liposuction is the only treatment proven to be safe and effective for permanent removal of localized fat deposits. With selection of a trained and qualified surgeon, and realistic expectations of results, patients are likely to achieve highly satisfying results that can last a lifetime.

Editor's Viewpoint

It is no surprise that liposuction, or lipoplasty, has had a meteoric rise to become the most frequently performed aesthetic procedure in the United States and worldwide. Yet the public remains confused about the benefits and safety of liposuction. This stems partly from "mixed messages" conveyed by the media, ranging from unbridled enthusiasm to fearful condemnation and often representing a biased or oversimplified view of what people really need to know about the procedure.

The enthusiasm for liposuction is understandable. Liposuction comes closer to seeming truly "magical" than perhaps any other aesthetic procedure. Access incisions generally produce inconspicuous, if not imperceptible, scars. Recovery is usually very straightforward and uneventful. And the major improvement in those unsightly localized fat deposits that can be present in various areas of the face and body is a result that, for many people, is simply unattainable by dieting, exercise, or any other means.

Placing lipoplasty in a historical context is helpful in gaining an overall perspective on liposuction safety as well as understanding why the training and competency of your plastic surgeon is so important to the successful outcome of this seemingly "simple" procedure.

The first official report of liposuction was from Dr. Joseph Schrudde of Germany in 1972. Even though the dry technique and a sharp curette-like cannula were used, the procedure clearly had the potential to be an important new modality for body sculpting. Dr. Yves-Gerard Illouz of France made a very significant contribution to the further development and popularization of liposuction by advocating the blunt-tipped, and therefore less traumatic, cannula. The dry technique was gradually replaced as surgeons began using wetting solutions with epinephrine. As described in our chapter, the result was a dramatic reduction of the amount of blood loss associated with the procedure.

With the tumescent technique, blood loss was further reduced, allowing for removal of greater amounts of fat. However, infusion of massive volumes of wetting solution and excessive amounts of local anesthetics, as well as removal of larger and larger volumes of fat, turned out to greatly increase the risks for patients. This contributed, for a time, to the image of liposuction as a "risky" procedure — an image not supported by the vast majority of our experience with the technique.

continued on page 180

Around 1986, I coined the term "Superwet" to describe it and introduced the technique of infiltrating approximately as much volume of wetting solution as the estimated volume of fat and aspirate to be removed (1:1 ratio). Blood loss was reduced to less than one percent of the total aspirate, comparable to (if not better than) the tumescent technique. Unlike the tumescent technique, however, Superwet infusion did not have the effect of excessively distending the tissues (which I believe makes sculpting less precise), and it also avoided the hazardous aspects of over-infusion that can include anesthetic toxicity.

Today, even the formerly enthusiastic proponents of the tumescent technique have generally modified their approach to more closely resemble the Superwet technique, or 1:1 ratio, which has proven both safe and effective over many years of use.

Another gradual but significant change has been the introduction of smaller diameter cannulas as well as technologies such as PAL and UAL, rendering the operation less traumatic and hastening recovery.

Superior to earlier generation UAL equipment is the newest VASER, which offers precise instrumentation and a more selective targeting of fat cells. Rightfully so, it has been enthusiastically endorsed in this chapter by a number of our contributing experts. I have enjoyed assisting in the refinement of this technology for clinical applications, beginning with its inception in 1997 to the present.

These new modalities, as well as the development of superficial lipoplasty, have allowed us to achieve better skin retraction. As a consequence, lipoplasty can now be used more successfully in older patients with less elastic skin quality. Technically accomplished plastic surgeons also are able to treat many additional areas of the body with greater precision and finesse, producing results simply not obtainable in the past.

New terms such as "liposculpture," "lipostructure," "microliposuction," and so on have come into use in recent years. While these terms may be meaningful to the practitioners who use these techniques, and such terms also have a certain marketing appeal, unfortunately they tend to be confusing to patients. It is important for patients to ask questions about whatever technique is being recommended and to understand how it differs, if at all, from the more conventional approaches.

In this chapter, our contributing experts have provided insightful commentary on a variety of techniques and have stated reasons for their personal preferences. While there is indeed more than one way to achieve a good result, it should not be overlooked that the different modalities can frequently be used in a complementary manner, each enhancing the overall aesthetic result. In my practice, for example, I routinely use Superwet fluid infusion followed by VASER for fat emulsification, then a combination of PAL for debulking and SAL (using fine instrumentation and suction) for final sculpting.

Looking to the future of fat reduction and related technologies, there are two developments of great personal interest to me.

One is the clinical application of adipocyte stem cell research. The implications of this research for long-term survival of fat injection in secondary, re-do lipoplasty as well as for breast and buttock augmentation are far-reaching. We know that liposuction aspirate is abundantly rich in adipocyte stem cells. The technique of isolating these cells and storing them for future use, not unlike the concept of a blood bank, is already available today. Even now, many of my lipoplasty patients request that, rather than discarding their suctioned fat, we store it for their possible use at a future time when stem cell science has further evolved.

The other developing technology that has particular interest for me is High Intensity Focused Ultrasound (HIFU), which holds the future promise of body sculpting without surgery. HIFU is expected to have more limited results than lipoplasty and, therefore, it is unlikely to replace lipoplasty in the foreseeable future. However, pending FDA approval, a multicenter clinical study will be launched imminently to follow up the results of the very exciting laboratory HIFU research that has already been conducted.

One final and important word on liposuction safety. On the surface, liposuction may appear to be a rather simple operation to perform. As a result, physicians of varying backgrounds and training — some with no surgical residency training — have chosen to incorporate this procedure into their practices. Improper patient selection, excessive volumes of wetting solutions, too much local anesthetic in an attempt to avoid using other forms of anesthesia (general or epidural), inappropriate surgical instrumentation and extraction of excessive volumes of fat aspirate — all are factors that can lead to complications and poor aesthetic outcomes.

Consequently, many board-certified plastic surgeons routinely see patients in need of secondary or re-do operations. In my own practice, at least 50 percent of the patients consulting with me about lipoplasty are seeking corrective surgery. Many, but unfortunately not all, such patients can be helped and their results can be improved. However, it is important for these patients to have realistic expectations; an outstanding outcome from a re-do is less likely, even in experienced hands, than if the procedure were being performed for the first time.

Secondary surgery usually is performed with the goal of treating asymmetry, surface irregularities, and/or contour problems caused by excessive fat removal. Treatment often consists of additional strategically planned suctioning and selective re-injection of the patient's own fat (autologous fat transfer, or AFT).

When properly performed, lipoplasty is indeed a wonderful body sculpting modality. I consider myself very fortunate to have had the opportunity to learn this procedure directly from the lipoplasty pioneers and to play a role in its further development.

— *Peter B. Fodor, MD*

TUMMY TUCK

Abdominoplasty

Substantial weight loss, muscle weakness following multiple pregnancies, or heredity can all cause or contribute to loose, wrinkled abdominal skin and excess fat in the lower abdomen. If your only complaint is the appearance of a protruding abdomen, and if your skin tone is good, it may be that liposuction is the only treatment you'll need. But if you also have loose skin and lack of tone in the abdominal area, then an abdominoplasty, commonly called a tummy tuck, may be recommended for you.

"Abdominoplasty has become one of the most popular procedures I perform," says **Chester Sakura, MD**, of Albuquerque, New Mexico. "Today, the modern woman wants to regain her figure after childbearing, wear fitted clothing and look natural in her overall contour, both sitting and standing. The optimal results in abdominoplasty are achieved by careful attention to incision placement, skin and fat removal, re-creating a natural umbilicus (belly button) and proper but not excessive tightening of the loose stomach muscles."

"This is a wonderful operation for women who, following pregnancy, have developed loose abdominal skin and abdominal wall weakness," says **Alexander G. Nein, MD**, of Nashville, Tennessee. "Our patients appreciate the fact that we can help them get rid of the excess skin of the stomach that is unaffected by diet or exercise. The fact is that diet and exercise simply cannot remove the skin laxity that comes from pregnancy and/or weight fluctuations. An abdominoplasty, on the other hand, can return the abdomen to a beautiful shape that looks great in slacks and swimwear."

"Tummy tucks are very commonly requested following childbirth or weight loss," agrees **Otis Allen, MD**, of Bloomington, Illinois. "This procedure is not a substitute for weight loss but is very useful for tightening muscles and restoring contours. Patients are often surprised to learn that the removed skin and fat usually weigh less than three pounds. Often this surgery results in clothing fitting better, rather than a smaller dress size."

Abdominoplasty is a major surgical procedure that tightens the skin and, when necessary, can reduce fat and modify muscles. A full abdominoplasty generally requires a horizontal incision just above or within the pubic area. The length of the incision and the resulting scar, which extends laterally toward the pelvic bones, depends largely on the amount and location of the skin to be removed. The contour of this incision will vary somewhat according to abdominal structure and personal preferences — such as the style of swimwear or undergarments that you typically wear. Based on these and other factors, your plastic surgeon will discuss with you the incision length and contour that he or she recommends for achieving the best result in your particular case.

Men and women who are not obese but are troubled by a bulging abdomen that won't respond to diet or exercise and by loose skin in the abdominal area may be good candidates for an abdominoplasty.

"Patients for abdominoplasty range from those who just need some tightening of the skin, without any muscle plication, to those who have excess skin and fat, and considerable muscle laxity," says

William H. Huffaker, MD, of St. Louis, Missouri. "What we are able to accomplish makes a significant difference in their appearance and their lives. The results of their abdominoplasty can often inspire them to take better care of themselves. Many of these patients begin to eat better and exercise regularly, which of course adds further improvement to their health and appearance."

Women who have had multiple pregnancies are the most likely to have a condition called diastasis in which the muscles of their abdominal wall have separated vertically and cannot return to normal; this condition can be successfully treated at the time of the abdominoplasty.

"The effects of pregnancy on the abdomen are fairly obvious," says James M. Nachbar, MD, of Scottsdale, Arizona. "The uterus is usually about the size of an orange. During pregnancy, however, the growth of the baby stretches the uterus, which then presses on the inside of the muscle wall of the abdomen. At the front of the abdomen, the two vertically oriented rectus muscles (the 'six-pack' muscles) get pulled apart, and actually separate. Once that has happened, nothing other than surgery can bring these muscles back together. Exercise can't do it, since there is no muscle in the midline for you to exercise."

"Tummy tucks are performed to correct problems with the abdomen resulting from pregnancy, weight loss, or weakened muscles. The muscles and skin become stretched and can't return to their normal position. Unfortunately, sit-ups and leg lifts don't correct the problem," agrees O. Allen Guinn, III, MD, of Lee's Summit, Missouri. "Weight loss helps, but usually the problem is an excess of skin and muscle length. The muscles need to be tightened and the excess skin and fat surgically removed. The operation is tailored to the individual needs of the patient, from where the incision is placed, to whether it is a mini, moderate or full tummy tuck."

An abdominoplasty, or tummy tuck, can effectively remove loose skin and excess fat from the abdominal area, tighten the underlying structure, and restore a more youthful body contour. It can also remove stretch marks in the lower abdomen. By horizontally tightening the fascia (a sheet of connective tissue extending from the rib cage to the pubic bone between the layers of fat and muscle), an abdominoplasty may somewhat narrow your waist. The procedure will leave the skin tighter, effectively making the body look leaner and more youthful. An abdominoplasty will, however, produce a permanently visible scar. This scar can usually be positioned so that it remains completely hidden by your usual style of swimwear and undergarments.

"Body contour surgery has entered a new era in which the simple removal and 'tightening' of the skin is no longer the end point. What is critical is restoring youthful contour in the areas of the abdomen, buttocks, hips and thighs," says Lawrence S. Reed, MD, of New York, New York.

LENGTH OF SURGERY
Generally two to five hours.

ANESTHESIA
Usually general anesthesia, local anesthetic with intravenous sedation in some cases.

LENGTH OF STAY
Overnight stay may be recommended, but frequently home the same day.

RECOVERY
Intial mild to moderate discomfort; prescription pain medication for two to 14 days; minimal activity for several days; back to work in one to four weeks; swelling and bruising improve in three to 10 days, can take months to fully subside; avoid strenuous exercise for about one month.

SCARS
Visible but usually undetectable when wearing clothing or most swimwear; poorly healed scars may, however, appear raised or widened.

RISKS/POSSIBLE COMPLICATIONS
Serious complications, while possible, are unlikely. Some potential complications can be avoided by carefully following your surgeon's instructions.

In addition to the usual risks associated with anesthesia, other risks include:
- Tissue loss: Rarely occurs but usually involves skin above pubic hair; smoking, poorly controlled diabetes, being over weight, and previous abdominal surgery increase risk.
- Infection.
- Hematoma: Collection of blood beneath the skin; can be treated without compromising result.
- Seroma: Collection of fluid under skin, can usually be painlessly removed in doctor's office and does not alter cosmetic result.
- Pulmonary emboli: A blood clot that travels to the blood vessels in the lungs.

The above-listed risks may be only some of those that your surgeon will discuss with you in greater detail during your consultation.

"This understanding of form has been too long overlooked. As body sculpture continues to rise in popularity, we can expect an even greater appreciation of restoration of contour and volume, which is a critical part of the overall rejuvenation process."

Any stretch marks in the upper abdomen, higher than the belly button, will not be improved by an abdominoplasty. A tummy tuck will not narrow your hips. If you have localized fat deposits in your hips, your plastic surgeon may recommend liposuction of these areas in order to improve your body proportions. In some instances, for safety reasons, it may be recommended to postpone liposuction and perform it separately from your abdominoplasty. The

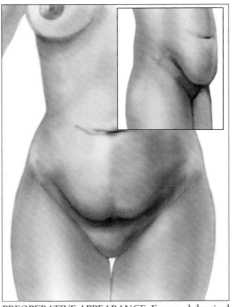

PREOPERATIVE APPEARANCE. Excess abdominal skin and fat, as well as loose abdominal wall muscles, result in the loss of a youthful abdominal contour.

determination of when such combined procedures are appropriate will be made by your plastic surgeon after evaluating your medical history, current health and the extent of surgery required in your particular case.

"Very often, women who come in after their childbearing is finished need both a breast augmentation with some lift and come abdominal work," says **Peter Hyans, MD**, of Berkeley Heights, New Jersey. "If they are of relatively normal weight and their abdominal problem is mainly confined to skin laxity, I combine the procedures. If they need a significant amount of liposuction, however, I will not combine them. I usually keep these patients in the hospital overnight."

"Abdominoplasty is an outstanding technique for restoring or improving the contour of the abdomen following pregnancy or massive weight loss. Because it most frequently involves dealing with changes of the abdomen as a consequence of pregnancy, I often combine it with other procedures — whether it is restoring the size and shape of the breast, or liposuction of the inner and outer thighs," agrees **Otto Placik, MD**, of Arlington Heights, Illinois.

"Although I rarely suggest surgery on areas a patient does not mention, I feel it is very important in patients seeking an abdominoplasty to evaluate their upper outer hips or flanks. For a number of these patients, liposuction of these areas is essential to achieve balance and proportion with their new figure," says **Eric Mariotti, MD**, of Concord, California.

"Combining flank and hip contouring of the back with liposuction can give these abdominoplasty patients a beautiful outcome," agrees **John R. Moore, MD**, of Franklin, Tennessee.

"Ninety percent of my patients undergoing abdominoplasty also have liposuction of the sides and around the back. This is by far the most significant aspect in narrowing the waist," says **Steven K. White, Sr., MD**, of Myrtle Beach, South Carolina.

Liposuction of the abdominal region itself is often performed in conjunction with abdominoplasty and is considered by some surgeons to be an intrinsic part of the procedure.

"Many people require some liposuction as part of this procedure, and this can be done at the same time without doing two separate procedures. It's less costly and the patients have one recovery period," says **David L. Abramson, MD**, of New York, New York.

"The two most important questions about tummy tuck are: How much liposuction can we safely do with a tummy tuck procedure and still provide a safe operation, and what roles do factors like a patient's age, hormonal replacement therapy, and weight play in the safety of tummy tuck procedures?" says **George Sanders, MD**, of Encino, California. "More and more patients in their 60s are requesting abdominoplasty. We want to provide the safest procedure possible and minimize the risk of blood clots. One approach I use is to avoid, as much as possible, tightening the abdominal muscles. Basically, the less surgery one does, the safer the patient is."

"I will not do very much liposuction at the same time as I perform an abdominoplasty," says **Gene Sloan, MD**, of Little Rock, Arkansas. "I place the patient's safety first, and I'm very conservative in my approach."

"I think liposuction is an invaluable adjunct to abdominoplasty," says **D'Arcy A. Honeycutt, MD**, of Bismarck, North Dakota. "I've had some great results by the judicious use of liposuction. I limit my undermining, however, so that I avoid any possible wound healing problems. I also may liposuction the anterior hips, the flanks, and the waist. So that the mons pubis maintains its correct position, I always sew it into place before performing liposuction. These patients will often have back rolls and hip rolls, and I turn them from side to side on the operating table in order to effectively reach these areas with the liposuction cannula."

"An abdominoplasty shouldn't just be viewed as just removing excess skin and fat from the abdomen," agrees **Jonathan Freed, MD**, Auburn, California. "I like to contour everything from the breast down to the pubic bone, and on the back to the back of the hips. It's important to include as much liposuction as possible. However, I perform 75 percent of my abdominoplasties as two-stage procedures. The second stage comes about four months later when I do a small, 30-minute touch-up liposuction on the lower abdomen."

"I use a combination of liposuction and skin excision to tailor the surgery to the patient's physique," adds **Kaveh Alizadeh, MD**, of Garden City, New York.

"I combine all my abdominoplasties with a little bit of liposuction in the waist area so the abdomen and waist flow together and form a natural contour," says **David V. Poole, MD**, of Altamonte Springs, Florida. "That way you don't end up with a flat tummy and a wide-looking hip or waist area. I won't do liposuction above the incision, on the abdominal flap, as I think you risk having some healing problems."

THE CONSULTATION

Depending on your expectations, desires, and the extent of your fat deposits and excess skin, your surgeon will advise you whether a full abdominoplasty, a limited abdominoplasty, liposuction alone, or a combination of abdominoplasty and liposuction will yield the best result.

"Determining the correct abdominoplasty procedure requires an accurate analysis of the underlying muscular and skeletal structures, fatty deposits and skin condition. People think of a tummy tuck as a way of eliminating fat, but more often it is a way of correcting loose muscle and skin tone," says Dr. Placik.

"It is essential that the doctor assess the muscle tissue layer, fatty tissue layer, and the skin to properly individualize the procedure for each patient," says **Stephen Goldstein, MD**, of Englewood, Colorado. "After a woman has had children, the layer of connective tissue between the muscle and the skin loosens and the muscles drift. The essential job of an abdominoplasty is to bring these back together. I am fastidious in how I bring the muscles back together, doing it multi-dimensionally by performing a vertical and horizontal tightening. Because we are treating the whole torso, we almost always incorporate ultrasonic liposuction, and the combination provides excellent results."

"Today's abdominoplasty procedures range from a mini to a full," explains **Daniel C. Morello, MD**, of White Plains, New York. "The mini has a shorter incision, lower muscle plication, some liposuction, and a float of the umbilicus where it's transected and moved down a little. The components of a full abdominoplasty vary between individual patients, and this highlights the need for a good surgical plan ahead of time. A full abdominoplasty, however, always includes excision of skin and subjacent fat, liposuction of fatty deposition, and muscle repair below and/or above the umbilicus."

"Gone are the days of offering only a 'standard' tummy tuck or liposuction. The wide range of abdominal contouring procedures now available requires a more complex individualization for each prospective patient," agrees **Lee H. Colony, MD**, of East Lansing, Michigan. "Sometimes, patients are best served with a circumferential approach to body contouring that addresses the back, flanks, and buttocks along with the abdomen, including both liposuction and skin tightening. These procedures may also create recovery challenges that must be addressed. Conversely, for patients interested in limiting recuperation time, tummy-contouring procedures can be modified to provide acceptable results with less interruption to activities. It is our job as plastic surgeons to understand patient goals and guide patients in choosing the options that best suit their specific needs."

"Abdominoplasty with combined body lift procedures can be performed successfully and safely in one stage, provided they are conducted by an experienced surgeon who performs these procedures regularly and who works with a highly competent team that implements a strict and well-conceived protocol in a fully accredited surgical facility equipped to provide a comprehensive level of care," agrees **Christopher K. Patronella, MD**, of Houston, Texas.

"Abdominoplasty is one of the most dramatic procedures we do. A major change in the patient's shape can be created because we have the advantage of cutting and tightening excess skin, tightening muscle, and combining that with liposuction. I do all three in contouring the trunk; the procedure is circumferential and can improve the waist and the entire midsection," says **David J. Levens, MD**, of Coral Springs, Florida.

Your surgeon will ask if you are planning to lose a significant amount of weight or might become pregnant in the future. Patients who realistically think they will be successful in achieving their desired amount of weight loss may be advised to postpone surgery.

"I won't perform this procedure on patients who are more than 50 percent above their ideal body weight," says Dr. Sloan. "Patients need to be in good health, and they have to quit smoking. The risks increase greatly if these conditions aren't met, and I believe it is the surgeon's responsibility to educate patients about these risks."

Since vertical abdominal muscles that can be tightened during an abdominoplasty may separate again during pregnancy, your surgeon may advise you to delay surgery until you have had your last pregnancy.

"Patients should avoid any large flux in weight after abdominoplasty," says Dr. Abramson. "Gaining weight after surgery can compromise results, and if someone loses weight after surgery, they may have extra skin. So a patient should be at a weight they can maintain before they have surgery, and maintaining an exercise program after surgery is also helpful."

Your plastic surgeon will need to review your entire medical history, including any medications you may currently be taking, whether you suffer from any allergies or medical conditions, and if you have had any prior surgeries. He or she will examine you to determine the extent of the excess fat and loose skin in your abdominal region, assess the condition of your abdominal muscles and evaluate the quality of your skin tone.

"The principles of functional anatomy that plastic surgeons have developed to more effectively rejuvenate the face have now been applied to the abdomen, torso, and extremities, allowing us to achieve improved results," says **Steven J. Smith, MD**, of Knoxville, Tennessee. "One thing we have learned is that the muscle structure needs to be respected and not altered, so the normal function of the muscles is actually enhanced by improving their direction of pull. For instance, when fascia becomes irreversibly stretched with pregnancy, it must be reconstructed to approximate a more youthful anatomy."

"Abdominoplasty must be tailored to the individual patient," says **Fereydoon S. Mahjouri, MD**, of Fridley, Minnesota. "Aging, obesity, and pregnancies can stretch the abdominal skin in horizontal dimensions, vertical dimensions or both. This can be assessed by examining patients in different positions — standing, diving, sitting, and lying on their back or sides. The shape, location, and length of incisions should therefore be adjusted accordingly. Our patients are encouraged to bring their preferred underwear or swimwear for individual tailoring of the incision lines."

"Abdominoplasty begins with a thorough examination and assessment of each patient," agrees Dr. Moore. "I consider the whole patient — overall health and anatomical structure — to determine if he or she is a good candidate for the procedure. If they are in good health, I then examine them from all perspectives. I analyze the full body from the front and back, assessing the upper back, the flank area, hips, and saddlebag areas. I also assess the degree of skin elasticity, muscle laxity, and stretch marks. We check many factors, including if they have intra-abdominal fullness, or masses, and if they have significant intra-abdominal fat versus subcutaneous fat, to accurately plan our course of action."

Patients whose abdominal fullness is primarily due to intra-abdominal fat (fat that surrounds or forms a protective cover over the internal organs) most likely will not be good candidates for abdominoplasty. In fact, such patients will be probably be advised to work on their diet and exercise, since these are often the only solutions to reducing intra-abdominal fat. Patients with intra-abdominal fat often present with a large, distended belly. This condition is far more common in men and commonly referred to as "beer belly."

If you have scars from previous abdominal surgeries, your surgeon will discuss how this may impact the placement and final appearance of your abdominoplasty incisions. Depending on the situation, he or she may recommend against abdominoplasty. On the other hand, your surgeon may feel that your previous scars can be revised and improved upon by undergoing a tummy tuck.

"Abdominoplasty can sometimes be used to eradicate unsightly scars and transform them into inconspicuous ones," states Dr. Placik. "People may have vertical scars beneath the umbilicus (belly button), appendectomy or hernia scars, or they've had multiple procedures resulting in numerous scars. I have often been able to eliminate these scars, leaving patients with one scar that can be hidden below the bikini line. The vast majority of stretch marks located on the lower abdomen can also usually be eliminated."

Although designed to follow natural skin creases and to fall within bikini lines, the length of scars will vary from patient to patient. Your surgeon should describe the planned procedure in detail, including the surgical technique and where resulting scars will be placed. Placement of scars cannot always be ideal, depending on each patient's anatomy and the amount of correction required.

"The abdominoplasty procedure may influence skin tightness, fatty contour of the abdomen, muscle position, or all three of these variables, depending on the individual. As with any surgical procedure that excises skin, there is a necessity of scars. Surgical incisions are designed to end up in the least conspicuous positions," says John E. Hamacher, MD, of Madison, Wisconsin.

"Occasionally, abdominal appearance can be improved with just liposuction," adds Stephen A. Bernsten, MD, also of Madison. "A surgical plan should be clearly outlined during the comprehensive preoperative consultation and evaluation with your aesthetic surgeon."

"In an abdominoplasty, it is important to pay attention to waistline and hip shape and the amount of skin and fat to be removed. Also, the position and length of the scar must be carefully considered," agrees Gloria A. de Olarte, MD, of Pasadena, California.

"Nearly all patients requesting an abdominoplasty benefit from liposuction of the hips," adds Alfonso Oliva, MD, of Spokane, Washington. "The length of the abdominal incision should be commensurate with the amount of lipectomy performed. Patients tolerate long incisions with good contour much better than short incisions with contour irregularities."

"Abdominoplasty is a great procedure for patients who may have achieved their ideal body weight but are still troubled by loose, excess skin, stretch marks, and laxity in the abdominal wall, which frequently occurs as a result of pregnancy. It is, however, a procedure with trade-offs. Patients have to understand that even though the scar can usually be hidden within the bathing suit or underwear line, there is a permanent scar involved, and this is major surgery," says Robert Wald, MD, of Fullerton, California. "Safety is key. I require that my patients spend at least one night in an aftercare facility with nursing care following surgery, and that they adhere closely to the guidelines they are given to help ensure a safe recovery."

In a limited abdominoplasty, incisions frequently do not extend beyond the pubic area. In a full abdominoplasty, they generally span the hips and, in some cases, may even extend toward the back. To remove loose skin above the navel may require another incision around the belly button. The visibility and appearance of scars can vary greatly from person to person. Depending upon an individual's healing characteristics, the final scars may be flat and almost invisible or noticeably raised and wide.

"There is no scar that is more feared preoperatively by patients and less of a concern postoperatively than the abdominoplasty scar," offers James M. Platis, MD, of Chicago, Illinois. "The wonderful thing about abdominoplasty is that visible, unattractive skin that may be loose or may have stretch marks can be traded for a beautifully contoured abdomen and waistline with a hidden scar below the panty line. It always seems to be such a big concern for patients before surgery, but it never seems to be a problem afterward."

Although the vast majority of patients are very satisfied with their abdominoplasty surgery, it is impossible to guarantee perfect results. Any type of surgery may require minor revisions to achieve an optimal final outcome. In addition, abdominoplasty carries certain risks that should be explained in detail by your surgeon. You will want to ask what measures your surgeon and or anesthesia provider plans to take in order to minimize these risks as much as possible.

"For the most part, patients love the operation," states Seth R. Thaller, MD, of Miami, Florida. "However, there are risks, and patients need to know what the potential complications are. One of the risks of this type of surgery is blood clots. What we do to minimize this type of complication is give our patients pre- and peri-operative blood thinners. We also use compression stockings on our patients and, following surgery, keep them ambulated and well hydrated."

PREPARATION

Your surgeon will give you instructions about how to prepare for surgery. As covered in an earlier section of this book, smoking can have a profoundly negative effect on healing and blood flow; with some procedures, it can seriously compromise your chances for a successful and safe surgery. If you smoke, your surgeon may ask you to quit before he or she proceeds. He or she will also give you guidelines on eating, drinking and medications, such as avoiding aspirin or anti-inflam-matory medications that promote bleeding.

As with all surgery in general, whether performed in an outpatient facility or in the hospital, you should arrange to have someone drive you to and from surgery and to assist you after you return home.

"I like to do a tummy tuck as an outpatient procedure in the office," says Dr. Sanders. "When you do additional and more extensive procedures along with the tummy tuck, you increase the risks and for safety reasons, the operation should be done in the hospital. We try to give patients a nice tummy and an attractive torso, but we avoid doing liposuction of the upper abdomen or legs at the same time, because it increases the risk of blot clots."

"An abdominoplasty can be an extensive surgical procedure," says **Gary R. Culbertson, MD**, of Sumter, South Carolina. "Unlike many other forms of plastic surgery, you most likely will require assistance for several days following your procedure. Preparation in advance of this aesthetic procedure is essential for a good outcome. Discuss with your plastic surgeon the necessary preparation for your pre- and postoperative care."

Original incision

New opening for navel

Excess skin pulled down and trimmed

A flap of excess skin and fat is pulled down and excess soft tissue removed. Internally, the abdominal wall may be tightened with sutures. A new opening is made for the navel and all skin edges are closed. The position of the original navel is unchanged.

THE SURGERY

Although incision length depends in large part on the amount of skin to be removed, the most common surgical technique for a full abdominoplasty involves a long incision from hip bone to hip bone made within or just above the pubic area. As mentioned earlier, your surgeon will place this in the natural skin folds and within the bikini line whenever possible.

"The final aesthetic contour of the abdomen should not be restricted by the length of the incision," offers Dr. Patronella. "Proper planning to ensure, as much as possible, an ideal location of the abdominal incision is critical to the concealment of the scar in a swimsuit."

Dr. Steven Smith adds, "It's very important to mark people standing before surgery. You need to be able to judge from this position the amount of tissue that you will resect during surgery, so you can achieve symmetry in the final scars. Marking the patient is like creating a map for the surgery. If you turn the patient side to side during surgery without having these preoperative markings, it is much more likely that the final scar may not be symmetrical."

In most cases involving a full abdominoplasty, a second incision is made all the way around the navel to tighten loose skin above. The belly button remains attached to its blood supply, and its position will not be changed by the surgery.

"As in other procedures, I strive for as natural an appearance as possible and try to maintain the normal rolling curves and shapes of the tummy," explains Dr. Poole. "Most women have too much skin for a mini, and I most often do a full tummy tuck. I always do some muscle repair, or plication; pulling the rectus muscles together tends to bring the waist in, flatten the tummy, and give a better contour to the abdomen. I always try to contour the belly button area, so there is a normal little indentation where the belly button is situated."

"It's important with abdominoplasty to make the belly button look natural," agrees **Brian J. Lee, MD**, of Fort Wayne, Indiana. "I've seen procedures in which the native umbilicus was left too large, so you see a different color skin in the middle. I like to remove some of the fatty abdominal tissue in the area where I'm going to bring the belly button out. This creates nice, gentle curves where the tissue slopes down into the belly button. Otherwise the navel can look like a button on a flat board."

"There have been many descriptions on how to re-create the umbilicus, and there are many ways to achieve a nice looking belly button," says Dr. Mariotti. "However, I believe any round scar is rarely aesthetically pleasing or natural looking. A surgeon should always try to avoid a flat, round belly button. A slight depression leading toward the belly button as well as a subtle hood and vertical elongation in conjunction with an abdominoplasty all help transform the stretched out skin into a more feminine abdomen."

The surgeon separates most of the skin and fat from the abdominal wall, all the way up to the ribs and sternum, lifting a large flap to expose the fascia overlying the abdominal muscles.

"Traditionally, an abdominoplasty involved wide undermining of the skin, which prohibited any simultaneous liposuction of the upper abdomen. Newer techniques allow us to safely add liposuction to the procedure when indicated, which has expanded our ability to provide a comprehensive treatment of the abdomen," says **Mario Loomis, MD**, of Middletown, New York.

"I nearly always use liposuction in conjunction with an abdominoplasty, and I find I can get better results with ultrasonic liposuction. It's easy to thin out the lower abdomen, but patients can be left with fullness in the upper abdomen. I find that using ultrasonic liposuction in this area provides much better results," says **John Burnett, MD**, of Fresno, California.

"The goal is to contour the most aesthetically pleasing form possible, and I will frequently combine, in a safe fashion, liposuction and abdominoplasty to achieve the most favorable results," agrees **Christopher Morea, MD**, of Raleigh, North Carolina.

The fascia is tightened with permanent sutures. The skin flap is then pulled back down, excess is removed, and a hole is cut in the newly tightened skin through which to position the navel. The incisions are stitched closed. Most often, small drainage tubes will be placed within the abdominal tissues to help prevent fluid accumulation.

In performing a limited abdominoplasty, the surgeon's initial incision is shorter, and an incision around the navel is not necessary. In addition, with the limited procedure, the skin flap is only separated between the incision line and the navel. It is then stretched down and stitched back into place, with the excess skin being removed.

In addition to a traditional full abdominoplasty or a limited abdominoplasty, there are other variations designed to treat specific problems. "If a patient has a great deal of laxity in the hips and waist area, I'll do what's called the high lateral tension abdominoplasty," says Dr. Poole. "This gives me the ability to not only tighten the tummy but to pull up on the outer waist and also a little on the outer thigh area."

"The procedure must always be tailored to the patient. Some only need a very limited or 'mini' abdominoplasty, while others require a more extensive procedure — for example, massive weight loss patients may need a circumferential procedure requiring a longer scar," says **Michael R. Schwartz, MD**, of Camarillo, California. "For me, the goal is to remove as much of the loose skin as possible along with aggressive tightening of the abdominal wall muscles to correct the stretching, which usually is a result of pregnancy though sometimes it can be due to aging alone."

"In some instances, an endoscopic procedure can be done," says **Joseph P. Hunstad, MD**, of Charlotte, North Carolina. "The endoscopic approach has rather limited applications, but it's an excellent procedure for women who have excess fat but no skin laxity and just slight muscle laxity. Using an endoscope and working through small incisions, we thoroughly liposuction the abdomen and tighten the muscle. The scars, around the belly button and within the pubic hair, are virtually undetectable."

POST OP

Depending on the extent of the work to be done, a full abdominoplasty usually takes two to five hours to perform; a partial abdominoplasty generally takes an hour or two. A full abdominoplasty is usually performed under general anesthesia, although sedation (twilight) anesthesia is sometimes used.

"General anesthesia is very safe today, but I perform all my procedures using local anesthesia combined with sedation," says **Alfonso Barrera, MD**, of Houston, Texas. "I feel it is even safer, there's less blood loss during surgery, and the patient achieves a quicker recovery, with less nausea and vomiting."

Many surgeons will recommend an overnight stay for pain management, since moderate to severe discomfort is often best controlled with intravenous pain medication for the first 24 hours. Some surgeons have had very good results in minimizing patient discomfort by utilizing pain pumps, catheters that release small amounts of anesthetic, and other post-surgical anesthetic application.

"I've witnessed a tremendous increase in the number of abdominoplasty patients over the past five years," says **Richard D. Anderson, MD**, of Scottsdale, Arizona. "I'd have to say that it's probably because the results of the procedure have improved so greatly, but I also think one of the main reasons is the advent of a device called the pain pump. In the past, patients would be in recovery for days; it was uncomfortable and painful. Now, with the pain pump, which involves a catheter inserted beneath the skin that releases non-narcotic pain medication, patients have a much more pleasant recovery. The device is usually left in for about three to five days. Removal is simple and just requires taking off some tape and removing the tube; about 90 percent of my patients do it themselves."

"In the past, patients had to remain in the hospital for several days because of severe pain. I now use the pain pump (.25 percent Marcaine infusion) in my abdominoplasty patients, and they are able to go home the same day, with minimal or no pain," says Dr. Barrera.

"I also use a pain pump in all my patients, which often eliminates the need for prescription pain medication and helps keep patients much more comfortable," agrees Dr. Alizadeh.

Dr. Morello is among those surgeons who do not advocate the use of pain pumps for abdominoplasty patients. "I apply the same concept to abdominoplasty that I do with breast augmentation: Less surgical trauma is associated with less pain. I practice precise and delicate surgery, avoiding blunt dissection. I perform abdomino-plasty as an outpatient procedure. I don't use pain pumps, and my patients are not calling me and complaining of pain."

Following surgery you will be closely monitored in a recovery area. Dressings, such as gauze, will usually be applied to your abdomen and covered with tape or an elastic bandage. As mentioned earlier, with a full abdominoplasty, you may spend the night in the hospital or surgical facility, although some patients are allowed to go home a few hours after the procedure.

Your abdomen will probably be swollen for the first few days. Whether a pain pump is used or your surgeon prescribes other medication, any pain should be largely controlled. Although straining, bending, and lifting must be avoided and you will be instructed not to stand up completely straight for some time, you will be advised to get out of bed for short walks on your first day following surgery. This will help promote blood circulation, and it is important that you not sit for prolonged periods of time during the first several days.

Your surgeon may advise you to sleep on your back with a pillow placed under your knees. He or she will also instruct you on showering and maintaining your dressings, which may be changed or removed within a week following surgery. At that time, any surgical drains will also probably be removed.

In addition, you may need to wear a support garment for several weeks once the dressings and bandage have been removed. Stitches will generally be removed in stages, with surface stitches usually coming out in five to seven days and deeper sutures, which have ends protruding from the skin, will be removed in two to three weeks.

"I perform all of my abdominoplasties as outpatient procedures. Patients can go home the same day, but they must follow a recovery regimen, which includes not lifting anything weighing 10 pounds or more for six weeks after surgery and wearing a compression garment for two weeks following surgery," says **Michael Horn, MD**, of Chicago, Illinois. "I always put in drains and leave them in for at least a week after surgery, if not more. Although patients' activity will be limited during recovery, it is important that they ambulate almost immediately to prevent the formation of blood clots."

"Seroma, the most common complication of abdominoplasty, can be reduced to a minimum by certain techniques both during and after surgery," says Dr. Mahjouri. "We remove the upper and lower drains in sequential fashion after the fifth and seventh post-operative day. We have found that this contributes to a very low incidence of this nuisance complication."

Following surgery, swelling and bruising will sub-side over several weeks, yet it may take months for all swelling to disappear. Some numbness over portions of your abdominal area may persist for some months. It is normal for scars to appear to worsen before they begin to look better. This may continue for three to six months as scars heal; they may not begin to flatten and fade to a lighter color for nine months to a year.

"I use Arnica with all my surgeries, which I find helps minimize and shorten the duration of any bruising and swelling," adds Dr. Horn.

How well you feel and how soon you can return to work may depend on your physical condition and the strength of your abdominal muscles before surgery. Recovery time can vary greatly between individuals. Some people are able to resume nonstrenuous work within one to three weeks following surgery and most normal activities, including mild exercise, after a few weeks. Others need to rest and recuperate for at least three to four weeks before returning to work.

Although vigorous exercise should be avoided, a

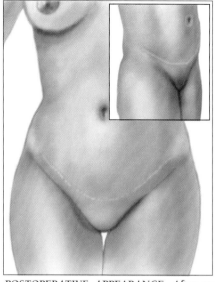

POSTOPERATIVE APPEARANCE. After an abdominoplasty, or tummy tuck, the abdomen is firmer with a flatter contour. Scars from the procedure are permanent but ideally fade and become less noticeable. Scar placement in the lower abdomen is generally below the bikini line.

gentle exercise program, as advised by your surgeon, will help you heal better, reduce swelling, lower the chance of developing blood clots, and improve muscle tone. It is normal to experience some mild, periodic discomfort, but any severe pain should always be reported to your doctor. You should avoid sexual activity for a minimum of two weeks; your plastic surgeon will advise you on this and all matters related to your healing process.

LOOKING AHEAD

Most patients who have realistic expectations are highly satisfied with their abdominoplasty. In most cases, if you follow a balanced diet and exercise regularly, don't gain a substantial amount of weight or become pregnant, the results of your abdominoplasty should last for many years. Of course, the force of gravity and effects of aging do not stop, and you may at some time in the future decide to undergo a secondary procedure.

Editor's Viewpoint

The first documented abdominoplasty performed for aesthetic purposes dates back to 1890. As would be expected, it was a far less sophisticated procedure than is performed by plastic surgeons today. Over time, this early procedure was further expanded and refined, evolving into what we know as the "traditional" abdominoplasty, illustrated on page 188. The traditional abdominoplasty, which has been practiced for decades now, may still be the most frequently performed abdominoplasty technique.

With the introduction of body contouring with liposuction (lipoplasty) in the early 1980s, surgeons began combining this newer technique with abdominoplasty. This stimulated the development of variations on traditional surgical contouring of the abdomen. It was recognized that a good percentage of patients who might have undergone a traditional abdominoplasty in the past could, in fact, be treated with liposuction alone. For many other patients, a mini-abdominoplasty, or a procedure less extensive than the traditional approach, could be offered with selective and judicious use of liposuction. As surgeons gained further experience, it was noted that for some patients it was best and safest to perform abdominal contouring in stages, performing abdominoplasty and liposuction in separate surgical sessions. In addition, surgeons learned that through suctioning of the flanks and waist, the torso could be more effectively contoured and the final results of abdominoplasty significantly improved. All of these considerations require careful planning and a high degree of customization for each patient.

Today, plastic surgeons continue to refine their techniques of combining abdominoplasty with liposuction. Current studies have focused on methods of preserving the delicate lymphatic vessels; this can allow more extensive liposuction to be safely carried out simultaneously with abdominoplasty, eliminate the need for postsurgical drains, and reduce the occurrence of seroma (clear fluid that can be trapped in a pocket under the pulled-down skin and soft tissues, which may require syringe aspiration or surgical intervention). These potential refinements in abdominoplasty should continue to improve the already excellent results obtained from this procedure.

— *Peter B. Fodor, MD*

BODY LIFTS AND MASSIVE WEIGHT LOSS

People who have been obese for much of their lives often perceive bariatric surgery as the doorway to a new life, yet they are frequently unprepared for the next challenge facing them. They may feel exhilarated by the feat of having lost massive amounts of weight, but at the same time their hopes of looking as good as they feel are marred by the vast quantities of hanging skin that remain.

Massive weight loss patients, often having rid themselves of 100 pounds or more, still can't feel comfortable wearing form-fitting clothes or a bathing suit; even their ability to exercise is compromised because of excess skin — loose, sagging tissue cascading over the abdomen, groin, arms, legs and back — that inhibits physical activity.

"A bariatric procedure is sort of a 'miracle' — it dramatically changes a person's life," says **Adam L. Basner, MD**, of Lutherville, Maryland. "Patients who have undergone successful bariatric surgery are happy and grateful, and they feel so much better about themselves both medically and physically. Unfortunately, though, after the weight is lost they are still burdened by tremendous amounts of loose skin. Taking care of that problem is the final step in the transformation of their lives."

"Patients often present with a very challenging group of physical concerns following significant weight loss," adds **Scott Holley, MD**, of Portage, Michigan, "but the typical weight-loss patient already possesses the critical ingredients for success: the determination and resolve to transform his or her appearance and

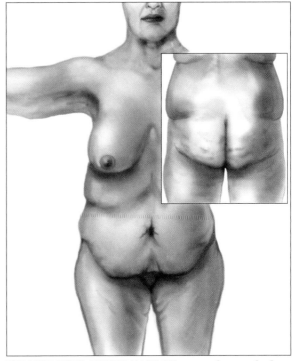

PREOPERATIVE APPEARANCE. Women and men who have undergone massive weight loss frequently are left with large amounts of loose, hanging skin that does not conform to their reduced body contour. In both women and men, there may be folds of skin around the waist, and buttocks, breasts, and upper arms may appear saggy.

well-being. I particularly enjoy the opportunity to apply traditional techniques in new ways to help patients achieve dramatic change."

"Gastric bypass patients who come to plastic surgeons after losing 100 pounds or more have really challenged our abilities to recontour the body," says **Michael Rose, MD,** of Shrewsbury, New Jersey. **Andrew Elkwood, MD,** also of Shrewsbury, observes, "This difficult work has forced us to re-evaluate our body contouring techniques. The result is that current techniques are safer, faster and produce superior results."

Besides requiring the surgeon's technical skill and aesthetic judgment, surgery following massive weight loss is among the most challenging from the standpoint of patient safety. Patients may be nutritionally compromised for an extended period following bariatric surgery, and this can impact both the safety and success of their subsequent plastic surgery. That's why there may be a significant waiting period between the time a patient achieves his or her desired weight loss and the start of body contouring.

Once the transformation with plastic surgery has begun, it often takes a year or more until all areas needing correction can be addressed. Although it is possible to undergo multiple procedures within the same surgical session, your plastic surgeon may recommend that contouring be done in stages rather than all at once. While this approach requires more patience on your part and more time before you see your final result, for some patients it is the safest and most effective surgical plan.

"It's important to really look at each person as a whole," says Dr. Basner. "Patients may initially complain about one area — their belly or their arms — but in reality they have many areas of concern. It is important to get a sense of what they'd like to accomplish, all their short- and long-term goals, so we can formulate a surgical plan that addresses everything in a safe yet timely manner. It may sometimes, but not always, be possible to achieve everything in one session."

Body contouring following massive weight loss is generally very extensive surgery performed under general anesthesia and often will require a brief hospital stay. If more than one surgical session is needed, your plastic surgeon will discuss with you the projected timetable for the various stages of your surgery. You will need to allow adequate time for preparation and recovery from each stage of your transformation.

"In preparing for body contouring procedures including lower body lifts, patients are best served by attaining the lowest weight they think possible for them and sustaining that weight for at least three months," explains **Joseph M. Perlman, MD,** of Spring, Texas. "In planning the surgery for these patients, it is important to sit with them, discuss all the areas they want treated, and plan the proper staging of the procedures. For example, if I am planning an extended medial thigh lift with a long

LENGTH OF SURGERY
Generally three to eight hours.

ANESTHESIA
Usually general anesthesia.

LENGTH OF STAY
Depending on extent of surgery, hospitalization of two to five days may be necessary.

RECOVERY
Initial moderate to severe discomfort; walking may be difficult for a week or two; assistance with ambulation immediately after surgery is essential for safety; return to light activities within two weeks and more strenuous activities in four to six weeks.

SCARS
Extensive; will appear red at first, then fade and usually become much less noticeable over time.

RISKS/POSSIBLE COMPLICATIONS
Risks are greater when multiple procedures are performed at the same time. Some potential complications can be avoided by carefully following your surgeon's instructions.

In addition to the usual risks associated with anesthesia, other risks include:
- Excessive bleeding.
- Infection.
- Separation of incision lines: Though this usually heals with wound hygiene, surgical revision may sometimes be necessary.
- Nerve damage: Can result in partial numbness of the legs; usually temporary.
- Hematoma: Collection of blood beneath the skin; can be treated without compromising result.
- Seroma: Collection of fluid under skin, usually not severe and does not alter cosmetic result.
- Pulmonary emboli: Extremely rare; a blood clot that travels to the blood vessels in the lung.
- Tissue loss.
- Poor healing: Can result in raised or widened scars; in the long term, scar revision surgery may be indicated.
- Contour irregularities: Additional treatments can improve results.

The above-listed risks may be only some of those that your surgeon will discuss with you in greater detail during your consultation.

vertical incision as well as the inguinal (groin region) incision, then I will limit my surgery to the medial thigh lift and abdominoplasty. The remainder of the lower body lift (hips and buttocks) is planned as a second stage procedure, together with a breast lift, which may or may not include augmentation, and brachioplasty (upper arm lift)."

"Because several areas typically need to be addressed, it's best to develop a broad surgical plan so that a harmonious appearance is maintained throughout the body, as much as possible, during the various stages," says **Alexander Majidian, MD**, of Calabasas, California. "I find that it's usually best to start with the trunk, since that unifies the upper and lower body. I think it makes sense to first correct the midsection, abdomen, sides, and back, and do a lateral thigh and buttock lift. After the midsection has been firmed and contoured, we can evaluate what needs to be done to restore the breast and inner thighs. We generally stage procedures two or three months apart for those areas, the upper arms, and sometimes the face and neck."

Whether plastic surgery following major weight reduction is done in one operative session or in stages, the transformation is likely to be quite dramatic. "Certainly within a year, we will have created a 'new you,'" adds Dr. Majidian.

THE CONSULTATION

"Plastic surgery following massive weight loss can be quite challenging," says **Eric Mariotti, MD**, of Concord, California, "but I particularly enjoy this area of practice. I love to hear the patients' stories about their transformation. What finally made them decide to undergo bariatric surgery? How has their life changed? What do their friends and family think? How much weight have they lost and how good do they feel now? It's important to hear each of their unique stories before helping them with their final makeovers. It helps me to better understand their motivation and goals."

Your appearance should be greatly enhanced by body lift surgery, but you should not expect perfection. Additionally, you will need to accept the permanent scarring that these procedures produce. "I warn my patients, particularly those who have achieved massive weight loss, that skin stretched from previous weight gain and loss has a higher likelihood of needing minor revisions or tightening procedures because of

the poor elasticity," says Dr. Mariotti. "No matter how tight I make the skin with the original procedure, after six months or so there will often be some degree of relapse."

When consulting with a surgeon for body contouring following massive weight loss, it is important that you are completely honest and forthright with regard to your medical history, as well as your goals and expectations. Tell your surgeon if you plan to lose any additional weight; he or she may not want operate until your weight has stabilized. Your plastic surgeon will need to review your entire medical history, including any medications you may currently be taking, whether you suffer from any allergies or medical conditions, and what prior surgeries you have had, including the details of any bariatric procedures. Your overall health and nutritional status must be assessed. Your surgeon may require additional studies and consultations with other physicians who have treated you to determine whether you are an acceptable candidate.

During the consultation, your surgeon will examine you to determine the extent of excess fat and hanging skin and to evaluate the supporting tissues. If multiple areas of your body need correction, you and your surgeon will discuss which areas you consider the highest priorities and whether operations must be staged over a period of time. Your surgeon will give you his or her recommendation as to the most reasonable surgical plan.

Dr. Holley stresses the importance of considering the various details of surgery, from the timing of staged procedures to risk factors and cost. "During the consultation, I carefully detail for each patient the technical steps necessary to achieve his or her goal. Considerable thought must be given to the inherent risks and financial implications for each patient before a comprehensive plan can be determined. My goal is to guide my patient through a staged surgical plan that safely delivers maximal enhancement in the least number of surgeries."

Do not hesitate to ask any questions or discuss all concerns you may have. The information provided by your plastic surgeon should include both the benefits and risks of specific procedures being considered. He or she should be able to give you a very good idea of the type of results you can expect, as well as problems that could be encountered in the course of your treatment.

PREPARATION

Your surgeon will give you instructions about how to prepare for surgery. For this type of surgery, smoking can have a profoundly negative effect on healing and can seriously compromise your chances for a successful and safe surgery. If you smoke, your surgeon may ask you to quit for a period of time before and after your operation. He or she will also give you guidelines on eating, drinking and medications, such as avoiding aspirin, anti-inflammatory medications, and certain vitamins and supplements that promote bleeding.

As with all surgery in general, whether performed in an outpatient facility or in the hospital, you should arrange to have someone drive you to the surgical facility and determine who will be your primary caregiver during the early recovery phase. Following lower body lift surgery, you will not be able to stand upright at first or walk normally for up to a week. At the same time, however, it will also be important for you to get out of bed and walk very soon after surgery to reduce the chance of blood clots that could pose a serious threat to your health. Contouring procedures of the upper body also impose certain temporary restrictions on your normal activities. Following your hospital stay, it is essential for you to have someone who is capable of assisting you around the house until you are able to manage on your own.

THE SURGERY

Unlike the relatively short-term weight gain of pregnancy, after which the body can usually regain its shape, years of obesity break down the skin's elastic fibers; the tissues are permanently damaged and cannot return to their previous state. Also unlike pregnancy, or more marginal weight gain, the tissue expansion from obesity is generalized, spread out over the entire body.

Patients who have lost a great deal of weight often have contour problems that include the abdomen, hips, back, buttocks, and outer thighs. In addition, they may require contouring of the upper body. Breasts or chest, upper arms, and even the neck and face may exhibit the same kind of loose, hanging tissue as the lower body.

Lower body lifts including belt lipectomy address multiple problems of the lower body. Other procedures that may be recommended, either individually or in combination, include abdominoplasty, outer thigh and buttock lift, inner thigh lift, breast lift, upper arm lift,

neck lift, and face lift. (You should refer to other chapters in this book for more detailed information about these individual procedures.)

In some cases, traditional contouring techniques may be modified to address the particular problems created by obesity and subsequent weight loss. "In performing abdominoplasty for the massive weight loss patient, it is necessary to take into consideration that these patients not only have skin excess in a vertical direction but also in the horizontal direction," says **Archibald S. Miller, MD**, of Tulsa, Oklahoma. "That's why it is often necessary to use both a horizontal incision and a vertical incision for reforming the patient's lateral abdominal wall. The surgeon can make a V excision, remove redundant skin and close the abdomen, pulling it toward the center and thus making the patient's waist smaller."

Albert Cram, MD, of Coralville, Iowa, explains why massive weight loss patients have unique circumferential

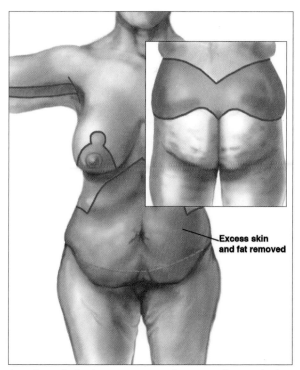

Excess skin and fat removed

A variety of plastic surgery procedures may be required to address different problem areas of the body following massive weight loss. When multiple procedures are needed to restore a more normal appearance, they usually will be performed in stages over a period of time.

problems of their upper body as well as their lower body. "In the upper body, the skin over the breastbone and over the spine doesn't expand with weight gain. So, after weight loss all the excess tissue that remains is literally hanging onto those two points. For example, the crease underneath a woman's breast — called the inframammary crease — is normally shaped like a semi-circle or half moon, but in massive weight loss patients its normal shape and position are severely distorted."

Al Aly, MD, also of Coralville, continues, "What we basically do in our upper body lift technique is to address several areas of the body simultaneously. By eliminating excess tissue of the upper arm that extends onto the chest wall, we are able to restore the infra-mammary crease to its correct position. This, in turn, helps us to eliminate the upper back rolls. Once we have re-established a normal base for the breast, we may perform a breast reduction, a lift or sometimes a combined augmentation and lift. In a male, we usually will need to perform a breast reduction to restore a more masculine contour of the chest."

LOWER BODY LIFT

Lower body lifts include a variety of procedures that can be performed alone or in combination and that target specific areas of the lower body including the abdomen, lower back, hips, buttocks, and thighs. People who have lost a substantial amount of weight, whether through diet and exercise or bariatric surgery, are often candidates for one or more lower body lifting procedures.

There are other individuals who may be excellent candidates for these procedures targeting the lower body. Many people experience sagging lower body contours due to the effects of aging or multiple pregnancies. Some people simply have inherited the lower body characteristics — localized excess fat and poor skin tone — that would make them appropriate candidates for lifting procedures. However, keep in mind that these procedures are not designed for overall weight reduction, and people who are obese or whose weight fluctuates widely may not be suitable candidates. Likewise, if you are considering pregnancy in the future, your plastic surgeon may advise you to wait until your childbearing is completed before undergoing procedures to enhance your lower body contours. While having undergone the surgery will not impact your pregnancy, the weight that you gain could cause

you to lose the aesthetic benefits of your prior body lifting procedures.

Procedures may take from three to eight hours. Lower body lift surgery is usually performed under general anesthesia, in which case you would be asleep and unaware throughout the procedure. Depending on the extent of surgery, you may need to be hospitalized. In the case of massive weight loss patients requiring lengthy and complex operations, hospitalization may be two to five days.

The incisions for a full lower body lift can be designed in a number of different patterns, depending on your anatomy, the extent of correction required and, often, your clothing preferences. Whatever pattern is used, however, incisions will necessarily be long and may extend around the entire trunk of the body. Liposuction may be done in conjunction with body lifting procedures.

Lower body lifting procedures necessarily result in significant scarring. Your plastic surgeon will make every effort to design the incisions so they can be hidden by your preferred style of swimsuit and undergarments. In this way, scars usually can be designed to be inconspicuous, though they will always be visible without clothing. Most patients find that the resultant scars, which fade and usually become much less noticeable over time, are a small price to pay for getting rid of the excess fat and hanging or loose, poorly toned skin that was so bothersome to them in the past. To be able to wear a swimsuit or shorts without embarrassment can be a liberating experience.

Belt Lipectomy

One technique for lifting the lower body is commonly called a belt lipectomy, because — with a long incision similar to a belt in the back and a more abdominoplasty-like incision in the front — it addresses the excess around the complete circumference of the lower trunk. A belt lipectomy is designed specifically to correct multiple problems of the lower body: hanging skin and fat in the abdominal area, outer thigh and hip excess, back rolls, an ill-defined buttocks, and lack of a waist. For this reason, it is frequently the procedure of choice in treating patients who have lost large amounts of weight.

"A traditional lower body lift treats the thighs and lower trunk together but does not create a waist and an aesthetically improved buttock and lower back; the belt lipectomy does all of this," explains Dr. Aly. "The lower body lift often places the scars about a third of the way down the buttocks, where they can be hidden by undergarments. For patients, including many men, who don't care as much about defining the buttocks and would rather limit scars, this is a very appropriate procedure. But, again, it does nothing to cinch the waist."

Dr. Cram adds, "We treat many massive weight loss patients. Oftentimes these patients have had their waist definition obliterated by an enormous amount of excess skin. The technique for performing a belt lipectomy essentially cinches the tissues right at the level where we want to create a waist. And when a waist contour has been achieved, it naturally helps to better define the shape of the buttocks."

"When you add the circumferential component and do the belt lipectomy, you really get correction all the way down to the knees," says **Malcolm Z. Roth, MD**, of New York, New York. "This is a much more difficult procedure than a standard abdominoplasty. It takes more time and involves excision of much more skin. There's more potential for blood loss, and some patients may even need blood transfusion. Drains often need to stay in longer. But the results are worth it. Instead of being an operation that lets someone look a little better in a bikini, there is the potential to change a person's life. In the case of massive weight loss patients, the weight loss is the biggest achievement; but now that the hanging skin is gone, they can go to the beach again. It really turns the page. They say, 'Wow look at me; I'm a new person!'"

Precise marking of the patient before surgery is crucial. **Gary D. Hall, MD**, of Leawood, Kansas, stresses, "I find that even more so than in other surgeries, pre-op marking and planning is vital to assure the location of scars and that the surgery will go smoothly. I mark all patients in a standing position; that way we can approximate the stretch of the skin, and the patient can see where we plan for the scars to end up."

The procedure can take many hours and involves turning the patient several times to work on the tissue around the entire middle section of the body — front, sides, and back. The skill and experience necessary to perform this difficult procedure cannot be overstated, and the patient must be carefully monitored throughout surgery to help ensure safety.

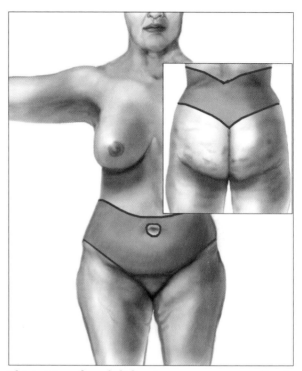

The incisions for a belt lipectomy may vary according to individual anatomy. Generally, incisions in the front are positioned low, similar to an abdominoplasty, and in the back are placed high, in a location similar to a that of a belt around the waist.

Usually, the surgeon will begin by treating the abdomen first. Although incision length depends in large part on the amount of skin to be removed, the most common pattern uses a long incision from hipbone to hipbone, just above the pubic area. As mentioned earlier, your surgeon will place this within the bikini line whenever possible. In most cases, a second incision is also made around the navel.

The surgeon then separates most of the skin and fat all the way up to the ribs from the abdominal wall, lifting a large flap to expose the fascia, which overlies the abdominal muscles. The fascia is tightened with permanent sutures. The skin flap is then pulled back down, excess is removed, and a hole is cut in the newly tightened skin through which to position the navel. The incisions are then sutured.

To address the back, the patient is turned to the side, or directly onto the stomach, and excess skin and fat from the side to the mid back is removed. Most patients

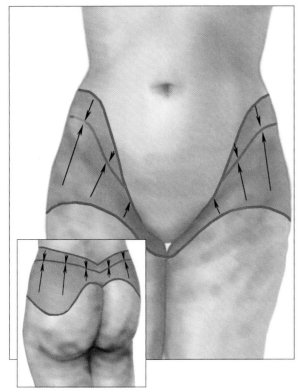

The incisions for a thigh and buttock lift target these specific areas for lifting and shaping. The thighs and buttocks may be lifted as part of a belt lipectomy or as an isolated procedure, as shown.

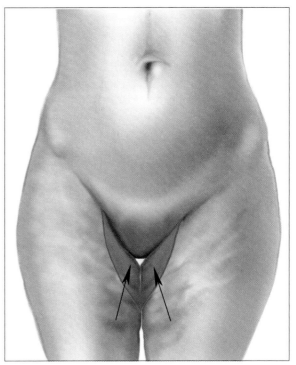

The incisions for a medial (inner) thigh lift, which may be performed as an isolated procedure, are extensive but usually can be relatively well concealed. Another technique (not shown here), which may be necessary when tissue excess is more significant, results in a vertical scar along the entire length of the inner thigh.

require liposuction to reduce the outer thighs. Back rolls are reduced, and the outer thighs and buttocks are lifted.

Each of these maneuvers is done to a different degree depending on the needs of the patient. The same sequence is performed on both sides of the body. A number of drains, small plastic tubes, are usually left under the skin to collect excess fluid and blood.

"Patients will need to have drains," says Dr. Miller, "Removing the drains too soon can cause complications, such as seroma (a collection of fluid underneath the skin). Adequate drainage for an adequate time is important."

Your surgeon should describe in detail each procedure that is recommended and give you an idea of the operating time involved. Keep in mind that multiple procedures performed together increase the risks of surgery. You will want to discuss the risks of individual procedures and combination procedures with your

plastic surgeon. As mentioned earlier, some surgeons prefer to stage lower body surgery, often treating the abdomen first and the back at a later time. Additionally, the thighs and buttocks can be lifted in a separate procedure, if desired.

THIGH AND BUTTOCK LIFT
Lifting of the thighs and buttocks can be performed as isolated procedures to remove excess skin that causes wrinkles and folds. Liposuction may be performed during these procedures to remove excess fat deposits. The tightening and lifting effect of this surgery can allow you to feel more confident wearing clothing that accentuates or reveals thigh and buttock contours.

For patients with only a moderate degree of skin and fat excess resulting from aging or weight loss, significant improvement can be obtained with an inner thighplasty technique requiring incisions limited to the groin fold.

When tissue excess is more significant, usually due to massive weight loss, a different thighplasty technique, requiring an incision along the entire length of the inner thigh, may be the best approach. While this scar is more readily visible, the resulting improvement is also significant. In patients with the most severe degree of tissue looseness, the two techniques may be combined for optimal results.

While these procedures do not change the texture of your skin, because of their tightening effect, they may offer some improvement in the appearance of irregularities of the skin surface, such as the "orange peel" or dimpled appearance of cellulite.

POST OP

Following surgery you will be closely monitored in a recovery area. Dressings, such as gauze, will usually be applied to the incisions and covered with tape or an elastic bandage. You will be fitted with a compression garment or elastic pressure bandage to protect the incisions and help promote natural shrinking as well as tightening of the skin.

A belt lipectomy will usually require a hospital stay of various lengths. In addition to early ambulation, depending upon your surgeon's preference, measures including intermittent calf compression and anticoagulation therapy (sometimes for as long as two weeks following surgery) will be used to reduce the risk of thrombophlebitis and more serious associated complications. The early postoperative period can be one of severe discomfort for the patient. There are a number of effective techniques that your plastic surgeon may implement to considerably reduce postoperative pain.

There will be significant bruising, swelling and soreness. You may need assistance in walking, but you will be instructed to do so frequently throughout the early stages of your recovery. Your bed may have to be adjusted to position your body at the right angle for comfort and safety, and you may need cushioning support as well. Stitches that are not absorbed by your body will be removed within 10-14 days after surgery. For the most extensive surgeries, it could take up to two weeks before you are able to completely resume normal, nonstrenuous activities. Vigorous exercise must be avoided for a longer period of time. Although you will probably see improvement in your appearance after the first week, it may be four to six months

until the final result of your surgery becomes fully apparent. Remember that recovery time can vary greatly between individuals. Your surgeon will give you personal instructions on how to care for yourself during your recovery.

Contour depressions are the most common aesthetic problem occurring after many lower body lifting procedures. This can often be improved by injections of fat taken from your own body. Although one of the goals of the surgery is to create a symmetrical body contour, some asymmetry is often present. Our bodies are naturally asymmetrical to a degree, and unless asymmetry following your procedure is pronounced, you should not find this particularly bothersome.

LOOKING AHEAD

Undergoing plastic surgery after massive weight loss is sometimes a long road, but it's a road most patients would choose to follow again. Finally the benefits of having lost so much weight can be more fully realized. Patients

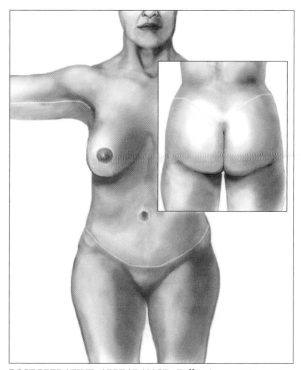

POSTOPERATIVE APPEARANCE. Following surgery, areas of the body that previously were obscured by hanging skin and residual excess fat look tighter and firmer, giving the entire body an improved contour.

typically experience a freedom of physical movement and a psychological boost that is almost beyond words.

"My experience is that patients are usually thrilled with their results," says Dr. Basner, "although improvements from this type of surgery are not perfect and scars are significant."

The results of body contouring after major weight loss can restore a more aesthetic appearance. Surgery cannot, however, completely restore the contour and quality of tissues that existed before major weight gain. The tremendous stress that obesity places on all the body's tissues takes its toll, and loss of skin elasticity may result in some relapse of looseness over time.

"Patients who start with a tremendous amount of lax skin will always end up with a little laxity," says Dr. Basner. "Most people come in with that understanding and are realistic about what we are trying to achieve. Many have gone to support groups through the bariatric centers, and this also helps give them a realistic idea of what can and cannot be done."

The scars resulting from surgery will be permanent and visible, although they can be effectively concealed by most styles of clothing. Finally, these procedures will not prevent future weight gain. If, through lack of attention to diet or exercise, you put on a significant amount of weight following body contouring, you can expect to lose many of the benefits gained.

Realistic expectations, patience in achieving final results, and commitment to maintaining a healthy lifestyle are three factors that contribute to patient satisfaction following plastic surgery to restore the body after massive weight loss. The fourth factor is selecting a surgeon who has the training, skill, experience and interest in this unique area of plastic surgery. By choosing your surgeon wisely, you can help protect your safety and also turn your dreams of a "new you" into your new reality.

It is estimated that, nationally, approximately 150,000 bariatric procedures are performed each year. Today's less invasive approaches have made bariatric surgery appealing to many more patients, and it is anticipated that this will continue to be a rapidly expanding area of medical practice.

The need for body contouring surgery following massive weight loss has also increased dramatically. According to the American Society for Aesthetic Plastic Surgery's annual statistics, more than 213,000 body contouring operations requiring skin resection were performed by plastic surgeons in 2005. This type of surgery is challenging in more than one respect. Attention to additional safety considerations, familiarity with rapidly evolving technical innovations, and a profound understanding of the emotional needs of these patients are all of paramount importance. It is important for patients who need body contouring after massive weight loss to select a plastic surgeon with significant experience in this highly specialized area of plastic surgery.

As we learn more about the special needs of massive weight loss patients, plastic surgeons are developing ways to achieve better and more predictable results from body contouring. For example, we now can not only remove excess skin, but also shift, reposition, and sculpt the remaining tissues to provide volume for deflated body areas such as the breasts and buttocks. This means that the final aesthetic outcome is greatly enhanced. Facial surgery, with modified face lift techniques, may also be performed to complete the "new look." For these patients, who often are both physically and emotionally exhausted from the ordeal of losing 100 or more pounds, plastic surgery truly offers a "new lease on life."

As you heard from our experts, plastic surgery after massive weight loss is indeed a difficult undertaking, for both patients and surgeons. However, the life-changing rewards for patients, both functional and aesthetic, make it among the most satisfying of all the procedures performed by plastic surgeons.

— Peter B. Fodor, MD

UPPER ARM LIFT
Brachioplasty

Droopy upper arms are most commonly caused by loose skin, often resulting from weight loss, and localized excess fat. As people gain weight, the skin on their upper arms stretches to accommodate the increased volume and then may fail to contract following weight loss. This loose hanging skin, which resembles a swinging hammock, can be an embarrassment, especially when wearing sleeveless clothing or a swimsuit. Brachioplasty (upper arm reshaping surgery) can

remove excess tissue and reduce the circumference of the upper arm.

Brachioplasty usually requires an incision that begins in the underarm area, called the axilla, and typically extends down the inside of the upper arm. The length and exact placement of the incision varies and depends on the amount of tissue to be removed, but in some cases, it may extend down the entire upper arm. Your surgeon will do his or her best to position the resulting scars so that they are not visible when the arm is lowered in a resting position along the torso.

"There is no perfect operation to correct severe contour deformities of the upper arms," says **Fereydoon S. Mahjouri, MD**, of Fridley, Minnesota, "Many patients seeking this surgery are those who have undergone massive weight loss. I find that normally these patients are extremely grateful to improve their upper arm contours and do not object to scars, if they are placed in locations that are less visible during daily activities and when patients view themselves undressed."

Although liposuction is sometimes performed to suction out fat deposits in conjunction with arm reduction surgery, liposuction alone is not an option for patients with loose, poorly toned upper arm skin. When hanging upper arms are caused primarily by excess skin, or by a combination of excess fat and loose skin, arm reduction surgery is usually the best remedy. On the other hand, liposuction, which requires only tiny incisions, may be effective by itself if the amount of excess fat is moderate and if skin is tight and elastic enough to contract sufficiently following fat removal.

PREOPERATIVE APPEARANCE. Excess fat and loose, hanging skin can cause embarrassment and reluctance to wear styles of clothing that expose the upper arm.

Brachioplasty is generally not recommended for patients who have had a mastectomy or operations involving the axilla lymph nodes. The procedure may also be unsuitable for those who have had multiple infections in the underarm area, since drainage may already be impaired and further surgery could lead to permanent arm swelling. Patients suffering from a condition known as axillary hyperhidrosis, or excess sweating under the arms, may also be unsuitable candidates for a traditional brachioplasty.

While brachioplasty can remove excess tissue, reduce flabbiness, and give your arms a more contoured appearance, it will not improve muscle tone.

THE CONSULTATION

You should tell your surgeon if you plan to lose a significant amount of weight, since he or she may not want to operate until your weight has stabilized. Your plastic surgeon will need to review your entire medical history, including any medications you are currently taking, whether you suffer from any allergies or medical conditions, and if you have had any prior surgeries. He or she will examine you to determine the extent of the excess fat and loose skin in your upper arm, and how loose the supporting tissues have become.

Your surgeon should describe the procedure in detail, including the surgical technique, type of anesthesia he or she plans to use, and where the surgery will be performed.

Your surgeon will also discuss the scars that will result from brachioplasty. The visibility and appearance of scars can vary greatly from person to person, depending on how the procedure is performed and upon an individual's healing characteristics. However, any patient choosing to undergo brachioplasty should be aware that a scar may be visible with the arms raised and possibly in other arm positions as well.

Although the vast majority of patients are very satisfied with their brachioplasty, it is impossible to guarantee perfect results. Any type of surgery may require minor revisions to achieve an optimal final outcome.

Visible scarring is the biggest drawback to this procedure. Your surgeon will try his or her best to make the scars as inconspicuous as possible, but brachioplasty scars may be difficult to hide. Most patients who choose brachioplasty are so anxious to improve their upper arm contour that they are willing to accept the scars. If you are unwilling to accept the resultant scars, you should not have this surgery.

As in other aesthetic procedures, the best approach to brachioplasty is one that is customized to the individual patient's needs. With this goal, plastic surgeons have developed variations to traditional brachioplasty techniques that can, for some patients, reduce visible scarring.

"For hanging skin of the upper arms, I use an approach that usually confines the scar to the axillary (armpit) area," says Lawrence S. Reed, MD,

LENGTH OF SURGERY
Generally one to three hours.

ANESTHESIA
Usually local anesthesic with intra-venous sedation, or general anesthesia.

LENGTH OF STAY
Outpatient, home the same day.

RECOVERY
Intial mild to moderate discomfort; prescription pain medication for two to five days; back to work in one to two weeks; swelling peaks in two to three days and improves over two weeks; usually minimal or no bruising; avoid strenuous exercise for about one month, heavy lifting for at least six weeks.

SCARS
Visible on underside of arm; scars may appear raised or widened.

RISKS/POSSIBLE COMPLICATIONS
Serious complications, while possible, are unlikely. Some potential complications can be avoided by carefully following your surgeon's instructions.

In addition to the usual risks associated with anesthesia, other risks include:
• Tissue loss.
• Infection; Usually treated only with wound hygiene.
• Hematoma: Collection of blood beneath the skin; can be treated without compromising result.
• Changes in nerve sensation.

The above-listed risks may be only some of those that your surgeon will discuss with you in greater detail during your consultation.

of New York, New York. "This avoids the need for the traditional scar that runs from the armpit to the elbow. I have worked on perfecting this technique for over 20 years. I find that it can be used for over 90 percent of the arm lift patients I examine. In most cases, the incision is hidden in the armpit, and full use of the arms is normally achieved in nine to 12 weeks."

Al Aly, MD, and Albert Cram, MD, of Coralville, Iowa, often deal with severe deformities such as those resulting from massive weight loss and, consequently, believe that "less" is not always "best" when it comes to brachioplasty. "The massive weight loss patient's upper arm excess doesn't stop at the upper arm; it actually flows into the chest wall," says Dr. Aly. "So, if the surgeon attempts to limit scars to just the armpit and upper arm, as with a traditional arm lift, not enough tissue can be removed and results will be disappointing."

"We developed a technique in which the incision crosses from the arm, or across the axilla, onto the chest wall," says Dr. Cram. "This allows us to remove enough tissue so that we achieve a very nicely contoured upper arm. The resultant scars have not been a problem for our patients, who are extremely pleased."

PREPARATION

Your surgeon will give you instructions about how to prepare for surgery and guidelines on eating, drinking and medications, such as avoiding aspirin or anti-inflammatory medications that promote bleeding.

As with all surgery in general, whether performed in an outpatient facility or in the hospital, you should arrange to have someone drive you to and from surgery and to assist you for a day or two after you return home.

THE SURGERY

Brachioplasty is an outpatient procedure, and patients can usually return home the same day. Arm reshaping surgery generally takes between one to three hours and is performed under either general or sedation (twilight) anesthesia.

Before anesthesia is administered, your surgeon will have you either sit or stand while he or she marks the area of excess fat and skin to be removed. After anesthesia has been administered, the surgeon will make incisions in the underarm and usually along the inner surface of the arm. To help minimize scar contraction, the incision may be made in a zigzag or curved pattern.

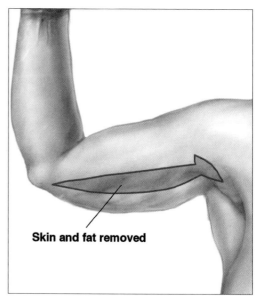

Skin and fat removed

A common brachioplasty technique uses an incision along the inside of the upper arm. Liposuction may be used to reduce or contour the fat layer. Excess tissue is cut away, and the remaining tissues are tightened and sutured into place. (Liposuction alone, which requires only tiny incisions, may be an option for patients with moderate excess fat and elastic skin that will conform to the new, reduced arm contour.)

As discussed earlier, incision patterns may vary according to individual patient needs and surgeon preference.

Liposuction may be employed to suction off some fat or to contour the fat layer. Excess tissue is cut away, and the remaining tissues are tightened and sutured into place. A small drain may be placed beneath the skin to reduce fluid levels at the incision site, which can help the skin to better adhere to the underlying tissue.

POST OP

Following surgery you will be closely monitored in a recovery area. Dressings, such as gauze, will usually be applied to the incisions and covered with tape or an elastic bandage. You will most likely still feel quite groggy while in the recovery area. You may have several layers of stitches in your upper arm. To help protect the surgery and better allow the newly contoured skin to adhere to the underlying tissues, a special compression garment will be placed around your arm.

Pain following the procedure should be mild to moderate, and your surgeon will prescribe pain medication to help you feel comfortable over the next two to five days.

Recovery time can vary greatly among individuals; however, the recovery period following brachioplasty is usually one to two weeks. Swelling will be mild to moderate and should peak two to three days following surgery, although it may take up to 14 days to subside. Elevating your arm with pillows may help reduce swelling and increase comfort. Any stitches that are not self-absorbing will be removed about one week following surgery. You will be able to shower on the third day after surgery and will probably be able to return to work within one to two weeks.

It is important to avoid any lifting or other vigorous movement of the arms until advised otherwise by your surgeon. Typically, patients can resume mild exercise in about two weeks, though strenuous workouts should be avoided for about four weeks, and heavy lifting for at least six weeks. You should usually avoid sexual activity for a minimum of two weeks; however, as each case is individual, your plastic surgeon will advise you as to the best recovery schedule for you.

LOOKING AHEAD

Most patients with realistic expectations are highly satisfied with their brachioplasty surgery. Your upper arms will appear firmer and better toned. Patients often gain a more positive self-image and feel more comfortable in clothing that exposes their upper arm contours. You will probably notice improvement in your appearance during the first week; results will further improve over the next three to six months as scars heal and begin to

fade. It can take six months or more before the final appearance of scars can be seen.

The aging process affects virtually all areas of the body and contributes to fat accumulation and sagging skin. However, the contouring effects of arm reshaping surgery are usually long-lasting, provided you do not gain or lose a significant amount of weight.

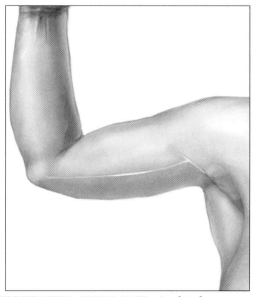

POSTOPERATIVE APPEARANCE. Brachioplasty removes excess skin and fat, giving your arms a firmer, more toned appearance. Incision patterns vary according to individual patient needs and surgeon preference, but effort is always made to position scars so they will be as inconspicuous as possible and hidden with arms in the resting position.

Editor's Viewpoint

Aesthetic surgical reshaping techniques for the upper arms, depending on individual patient needs, range from liposuction (lipoplasty) alone to extensive tissue resection. The resulting scars also vary from inconspicuous to significant.

Liposuction alone is sufficient for many patients. For others, a relatively conservative approach is to limit the incision to the hollow of the armpit, producing a scar that is visible only when the arms are raised above the head with the armpit in full view. When skin excess is more extensive, such as in older patients and following massive weight loss, a longer incision is necessary. In such cases, the resulting scar travels down the entire length of the inner aspect of the arm.

Recent advances in brachioplasty have resulted in significant technical improvements — not necessarily in the length of scars, but certainly in the quality of scars associated with the more extensive, traditional operation. As a result, brachioplasty has become acceptable to a larger number of patients, many of whom in the past would have declined the procedure due to the visibility of the scar.

— Peter B. Fodor, MD

BUTTOCK, CALF, AND PECTORAL AUGMENTATION

Some of the more common body contouring procedures discussed in this book — such as liposuction, breast augmentation and abdominoplasty — are performed hundreds of thousands of times annually in the United States. For example, in 2005, according to the American Society for Aesthetic Plastic Surgery, there were over 455,000 liposuction procedures and nearly 365,000 breast augmentations. In contrast, despite the significant media hoopla concerning procedures such as buttock, calf and pectoral augmentation, the actual numbers of these procedures are quite low. In fact, the 2005 numbers for all three procedures combined totaled less than 3,000, with buttock augmentation accounting for most of this figure.

Nevertheless, there is a small group of individuals for whom these less commonly performed contouring procedures fill an important need. Some people, regardless of engaging in appropriate exercise, are unable to achieve an appearance of enhanced, or sometimes even normal, muscular development of the chest and legs. In most cases, this is a matter of heredity. Conditions such as pectus excavatum, or funnel chest, are actual deformities that may be corrected or improved with specially designed implants. Likewise, certain individuals may have congenitally flat buttocks and seek correction of this perceived defect. Others may have normal buttocks but desire a fuller and more rounded buttock contour.

Buttock, calf, and pectoral (male chest) augmentation offer otherwise fit and healthy individuals the option to achieve an enhanced muscular appearance. This is often accomplished with insertion of solid silicone implants that recontour the body by augmenting muscles or skeletal structures. Alternatively, buttock augmentation may be achieved with fat injections.

THE CONSULTATION

The consultation is a time for the surgeon and patient to get to know and feel comfortable with each other. The patient should feel completely confident that the surgeon is fully qualified. If you haven't read our earlier chapter about choosing a doctor who is certified by the American Board of Plastic Surgery, you may want to do so now.

In aesthetic plastic surgery, good communication between surgeon and patient is a vital component of achieving a successful outcome. Everybody's sense of aesthetics differs. It is extremely important that you tell your surgeon exactly how you perceive your appearance problem and how you would like to look.

Your surgeon will need to determine if you are a suitable candidate for surgery and to review your entire medical history, including any medications you are taking, information about previous surgeries or medical treatments, and any medical conditions you may have such as diabetes, high blood pressure, blood clots, or heart disease.

Your current weight and whether you plan to lose or gain weight in the future are also important factors you should discuss with your surgeon. In the case of calf or pectoral augmentation, your surgeon may want to know what efforts you have made to enhance specific muscles through exercise.

Body implants have a variety of risks that you need to consider very carefully. These include the possibility of infection, displacement, contracture of scar tissue around the implant that can cause "hardening" at the implant site, nerve and muscle damage, and the need for corrective surgery if the implants ever need to be removed.

If you are considering buttock, calf, or pectoral augmentation surgery, it is important that your surgeon is well experienced with body implants. Most plastic surgeons do not receive a lot of requests for this type of surgery, and many are reluctant to perform these operations due to the potential for complications. In some instances, however, the benefits to patients may outweigh the risks. This can only be determined, in each individual case, after a frank and thorough consultation with a trained and qualified plastic surgeon.

PREPARATION

Before undergoing any of these procedures, you will be given instructions about how to prepare for surgery. Your surgeon will also give you guidelines on eating, drinking and medications, such as avoiding aspirin or anti-inflammatory medications that promote bleeding.

As with all surgery in general, whether performed in an outpatient facility or in the hospital, you should arrange to have someone drive you to and from surgery and to assist you for a day or two after you return home.

BUTTOCK AUGMENTATION

Men and women who are unhappy with the appearance of their "flat" buttocks may benefit from buttock augmentation. There are two methods to achieve a fuller buttock contour — implants and fat injections.

If implants are used for augmentation, they may be placed underneath the gluteal muscles through a small incision in the upper gluteal crease. Buttock implants are not at all like the implants used for breast augmentation. Instead of a silicone shell filled with sterile saline or gel, buttock implants are made of soft but solid silicone molded into appropriate shapes and available in a number of sizes. Your plastic surgeon will choose the proper fit based on your desired results and the limitations of your anatomy.

If you and your surgeon decide on fat injections instead of implants for buttock augmentation, your procedure will begin with removal of your own fat, using a suction device or syringe, from a selected donor site. Usually a combination of several donor sites is needed to provide sufficient fat; common sites include the abdomen, waist, hips, flanks and thighs. After being processed, the fat is injected into the buttocks. Because a

LENGTH OF SURGERY
Usually two to two and a half hours.

ANESTHESIA
Local anesthetic and intravenous sedation, or general anesthesia.

LENGTH OF STAY
Usually outpatient procedure, home the same day.

RECOVERY
Initial mild to moderate discomfort, can be controlled with pain medication; minimal activity for several days; swelling, bruising improve in three to 10 days; back to work time line depends upon procedure; avoid strenuous exercise for about three to six weeks.

SCARS
Usually visible but undetectable when wearing clothing or most swimwear.

RISKS/POSSIBLE COMPLICATIONS
Serious complications, while possible, are unlikely. Some potential complications can be avoided by carefully following your surgeon's instructions.

In addition to the usual risks associated with anesthesia, other risks include:
- Implant displacement or extrusion: Surgery would be needed to restore proper position; extrusion may produce unsightly scars.
- Infection: Rare, may require removal of the implant and possible hospitalization with antibiotics.
- Seroma: Collection of fluid under skin; usually not severe and does not alter ultimate cosmetic result.
- Hematoma: Collection of blood beneath the skin; can be treated without compromising result.
- Contracture of scar tissue around the implant: Causes unnatural firmness.
- Numbness: Rare; often temporary when it occurs, but can be permanent.

The above-listed risks may be only some of those that your surgeon will discuss with you in greater detail during your consultation.

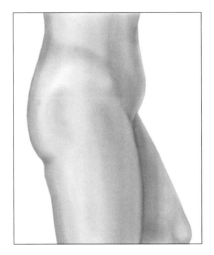

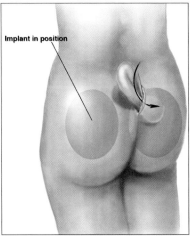

Implant in position

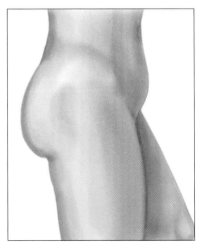

PREOPERATIVE APPEARANCE. Some individuals, especially women, are bothered by the appearance of flat or poorly contoured buttocks.

Solid silicone implants are inserted through a small incision at the crease between the buttocks. Alternatively, injections of fat harvested from other body sites such as the abdomen, hips, flanks, and thighs may be used for buttock augmentation (not shown).

POSTOPERATIVE APPEARANCE. Following augmentation, the buttocks have greater projection and a more aesthetic shape.

certain amount of the injected fat will be resorbed, your surgeon will overcorrect the treatment areas. This means that your initial result will likely produce greater augmentation than you desire, but with the aim of achieving a final result that meets your expectations.

THE SURGERY

Buttock augmentation with implants generally takes about two hours to perform, usually with the patient under general anesthesia. Your surgeon will make a two- to three-inch incision along the midline between the buttocks. Working through this incision, your plastic surgeon will lift the gluteus maximus, or buttock muscle, and form a pocket into which he or she will place the implant. This method is then repeated for the other buttock. Before closing the incisions, your surgeon will ensure that the implants are placed in a way that they are symmetrical and appear natural, making any necessary adjustments.

He or she will then close the incision and wrap the area with compression bandages, which will protect the wound and help to reduce swelling and discomfort.

POST OP

There is generally less pain and faster recovery with fat injections than with buttock implants. After fat injections,

you will experience mild discomfort, but most normal activities can be resumed within the first week. Pain medication will help you feel more comfortable. You will be instructed to wear a compression garment, to help reduce swelling and provide support, for a few weeks.

Because the muscles in the buttock area are involved in so many body movements, you will experience moderate discomfort for the first five to seven days following placement of buttock implants. You should expect to feel tender, and it will be uncomfortable for you to sit or lie in positions that put pressure on your buttocks. Walking may also create discomfort for the first few days. Your plastic surgeon will prescribe pain medication to help keep you as comfortable as possible. It is recommended that you have someone stay with you for the first night, as you may be quite immobile.

Bandages will be removed two to three days after the surgery, and you should be able to resume some normal activities, such as showering, at this time. Usually, you should be walking and sitting much more comfortably about seven days following the surgery. During the recovery process, some swelling and bruising are to be expected. You should be able to resume full activities including vigorous exercise within four to six weeks. Immediate results of augmentation will be apparent soon after surgery but final results may take longer. The implants may not feel fully a part of your body for as long as six to eight months following the procedure.

CALF AUGMENTATION

Calf implants first became popular with body builders whose calf muscles had failed to develop adequately with exercise. Since then, others who are bothered by thin or shapeless calves have chosen surgical calf augmentation. The procedure involves the placement of an implant deep under the thick tissue beneath the skin and fat of the leg. Virtually undetectable, implants can increase the bulk and add to the contour of the calf area.

THE SURGERY

Calf implants are made of soft silicone molded into solid shapes. The variety of available shapes and sizes allows your plastic surgeon to choose implants that will complement the shape of your legs according to your goals for the procedure. Calf augmentation with implants generally takes up to two and a half hours to perform, either with local anesthetic and intravenous sedation (twilight anesthesia) or under general anesthesia. Whether you sleep through the procedure or are sedated and unaware of what is going on, you will not feel any pain. Your surgeon will make a small incision in the back of the knee and, working through this incision, usually will place two implants in each leg, inserting them into pockets formed over the calf muscle.

POST OP

You can expect moderate postoperative pain and swelling as well as soreness and stiffness following calf augmentation. Walking will be difficult and uncomfortable at first. Your surgeon will prescribe medication to alleviate your pain for five to seven days. During this time, you should try to keep your activity level to a minimum. You should be able to return to sedentary work in one week; however, if your work requires strenuous activity or being on your feet, you will probably want to wait about three weeks or until the pain decreases significantly. Your surgeon will remove the sutures within seven to 10 days.

Using a footstool or some other method of keeping your legs elevated as much as possible will help minimize swelling and discomfort over the first three to four weeks. Wearing shoes with higher heels will help minimize pain during the initial recovery period. Your surgeon will advise you to wear compression stockings or ace bandages for the first several weeks. This will also help to minimize swelling and discomfort. You should be able to resume normal activities about six to eight weeks following surgery.

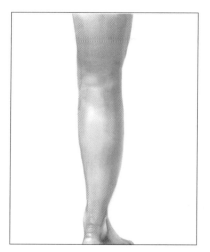

PREOPERATIVE APPEARANCE. Calf muscles and contour may remain underdeveloped despite an appropriate exercise program.

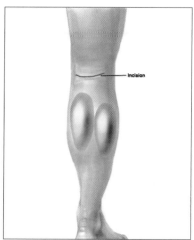

Through an incision at the back of the knee, silicone implants are inserted into pockets formed over the calf muscle.

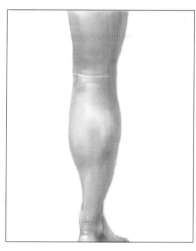

POSTOPERATIVE APPEARANCE. For individuals desiring a more muscular-appearing calf, augmentation with implants can provide the desired results.

PECTORAL AUGMENTATION
(MALE)

Men whose chests do not respond to exercise and remain underdeveloped can achieve greater chest volume and aesthetic contour with pectoral implants. In addition, patients with chest wall deformities — when the muscle has not developed or the skeleton is asymmetrical — can often obtain better chest wall proportions through the use of implants. Pectoral implants are pliable yet much firmer than those used for breast augmentation. They approximate the feel of a well-developed pectoral muscle. These implants are available in a variety of shapes and sizes so your surgeon can choose the proper fit to accomplish your goals for the procedure. A single implant can often be used to achieve the desired results.

THE SURGERY

Pectoral augmentation with implants usually takes approximately two hours and is generally performed with either local anesthetic with intravenous sedation (twilight anesthesia) or under general anesthesia.

Working through an incision in the armpit, at the areola (the pigmented skin surrounding the nipple), or inconspicuously placed in the lower breast, your surgeon will create a pocket under the major pectoral (chest) muscle or just under the fascia covering this muscle. He or she will then insert an implant sculpted to the exact size and shape necessary to achieve your desired result. The implant is secured in place using a few small self-dissolving sutures, after which the incision is closed and the wound is covered with a small dressing.

POST OP

You should avoid lifting your arms for the first few days following surgery. If your work is sedentary, you should be able to return to the office in about five to seven days. If your job is more strenuous, it may take as long as three weeks before you can return to work. Your surgeon will also instruct you to elevate your chest with pillows when you are in a reclining position, either awake or sleeping. You should be able to resume your normal activities, including exercise, about six weeks following your surgery.

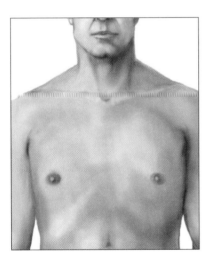 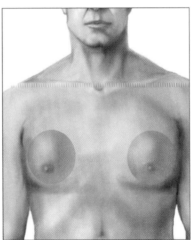 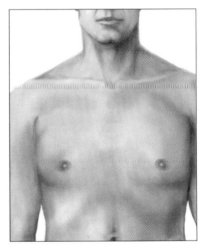

PREOPERATIVE APPEARANCE. Physical fitness does not always produce a muscular, well-contoured chest. In addition, some men may have muscle or skeletal abnormalities that cause a sunken chest or noticeable asymmetry (not shown).

Working through an incision in the armpit, at the areola (the pigmented skin surrounding the nipple), or inconspicuously placed in the lower breast, the surgeon creates a pocket into which a silicone implant is inserted. The size and shape of the implant is selected to precisely fit each patient's anatomy and best achieve his aesthetic goals.

POSTOPERATIVE APPEARANCE. Following pectoral augmentation, the chest appears fuller with well-developed muscles.

LOOKING AHEAD

Many patients find great satisfaction from undergoing augmentation of their buttocks, calves, or pectoral muscles. They find that with time the implants seem to become part of their body and they are no longer aware of them.

As mentioned earlier, there are significant risks involved in this type of surgery. If patients do not follow instructions to severely limit their activities immediately following surgery, implants may shift or other complications such as bleeding and fluid accumulation may occur. Any of these events could require additional surgery. If an implant needs to be removed for any reason in the future, it can result in disfigurement and the necessity for surgical intervention to help restore a more normal appearance.

These potential complications are things that patients selecting this type of surgery must be willing to accept as possibilities, but also do their part to avoid. For certain individuals, however, the benefits of attaining a more muscular appearance or an aesthetically pleasing buttock contour are worth the risks.

Editor's Viewpoint

Body implants may be used for strictly aesthetic purposes to enhance the volume and contour of the buttocks, pectoral area, biceps, and calves. They may also be used to treat deformities caused by disease or to improve congenital anomalies. For example, polio may result in significant calf deformity. Poland's Syndrome, though rare, often leads to underdevelopment of one side of the chest. In instances such as these, surgical augmentation of the specific body part can produce a more normal appearance. As described and illustrated in this chapter, custom made or prefabricated solid silicone implants with various degrees of softness/firmness are inserted through well-hidden incisions placed within natural body folds.

An alternative, which I prefer for some patients even though it is less readily available in the United States, is a silicone gel-filled implant specifically manufactured for buttock augmentation.

When available in sufficient quantities, fat taken from the patient's own body can be an excellent alternative to implants. Generally, the buttocks are more likely to be augmented in this way than the calf or chest areas. Long-term survival of the transferred fat is highly technique-dependent. In many of my patients, I have found fat survival to be far superior to what I initially expected. Like many surgeons, I generally prefer fat injection rather than insertion of a foreign body (implant), when possible. Current clinical research is investigating whether stem cells harvested from a patient's own fat can be used to enrich fat before it is injected for augmentation purposes, thereby improving its survival and achieving longer-lasting aesthetic results.

— Peter B. Fodor, MD

Laser Hair Removal • 238

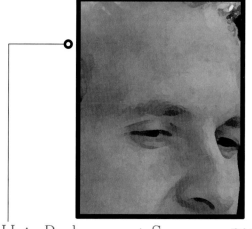

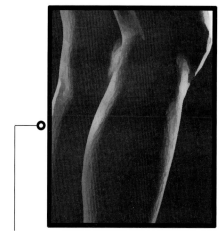

NONSURGICAL AND
ANCILLARY COSMETIC PROCEDURES

NONSURGICAL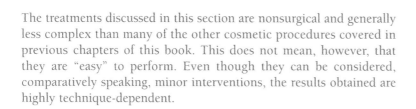
AND ANCILLARY COSMETIC PROCEDURES

The treatments discussed in this section are nonsurgical and generally less complex than many of the other cosmetic procedures covered in previous chapters of this book. This does not mean, however, that they are "easy" to perform. Even though they can be considered, comparatively speaking, minor interventions, the results obtained are highly technique-dependent.

In most states, nurse practitioners, aesthetic technicians, and other licensed personnel can legally perform some nonsurgical cosmetic procedures. When properly trained, these nonphysicians are often very capable of carrying out treatments such as laser hair removal, microdermabrasion, and light chemical peels. However, close supervision by the aesthetic surgeon or physician who is ultimately responsible is an important assurance of competence and patient safety.

There are many nonsurgical procedures that are particularly dependent on the advanced training, skills, and experience of an appropriate physician specialist. Among these are certain injectable treatments, ablative lasers, and deeper skin peels. These procedures have significant risks, and your safety depends on the qualifications of whomever you select to administer them.

During the last few years, the Medi-Spa concept, in association with aesthetic plastic surgery practices, has become quite popular. This trend, affording a wide array of aesthetic services under one roof, is a logical progression toward total patient care and appears to be the wave of the future.

When performed in a safe environment — by a trained and qualified physician or, in some cases, by a nurse or licensed technician under physician supervision — nonsurgical procedures can provide significant benefits. They can be very effective when performed alone or can serve as "frosting on the cake" when offered as ancillary procedures in combination with aesthetic surgery, often enhancing the quality and longevity of surgical results.

INJECTABLE TREATMENTS FOR AESTHETIC FACIAL ENHANCEMENT

Injectable treatments for aesthetic facial enhancement described in this chapter include botulinum toxin (Botox, or BTX) and soft tissue fillers. These nonsurgical techniques are an effective bridge for younger patients who may have begun to show some early signs of aging but don't yet need full surgical procedures.

They may be appropriate for patients of almost any age who can benefit from additional facial volume (soft tissue fillers), or for patients undergoing facial surgery whose results can be further enhanced by adjunctive treatments. Surgeons frequently recommend some of these procedures as maintenance or touch-up for patients who have already undergone facial surgery or as an alternative for individuals who cannot undergo surgical procedures because of medical conditions or other reasons.

"There has been a paradigm shift in cosmetic surgery over the last 10 years," maintains **Fanny dela Cruz, MD**, of West Bloomfield, Michigan. "More and more, we are focusing on maintenance therapy rather than major cosmetic procedures. There is a whole new clientele for cosmetic enhancements: fit, healthy, young men and women who are starting to see early signs of aging and unwelcome changes in their appearance. At this point, they want only minimal procedures. A good example is correcting wrinkles in the lip area or enlarging the lips using fillers such as Restylane and Radiesse."

Unlike surgery, most injectable treatments provide only temporary results and must be repeated periodically.

"Increasing the volume of the external tissues of the face by the injection of fat or another type of filling material is not a permanent solution for long-lasting rejuvenation," says **Jack A. Friedland, MD**, of Phoenix, Arizona. "Initial improvement is temporary at best, and the procedure has to be repeated for maintenance of results. Therefore, I feel this type of procedure should be considered ancillary rather than primary — meaning that it can complement surgical procedures but certainly cannot replace them."

This fact has not detracted from the popularity of injectable procedures. However, some patients do approach them with the expectation that they are a substitute for surgical procedures such as a face lift, brow lift or eyelid surgery. While some nonsurgical procedures can soften facial wrinkles and even alter brow shape, it is important to understand that the results of nonsurgical procedures are not the same as the results of surgery. Yet there are unique benefits to many nonsurgical procedures. One of the primary benefits is that treatments such as Botox and various injectable fillers require virtually no downtime or very little recovery. In addition, the risks associated with these procedures are generally less than those associated with surgery. Cost may be initially less than a surgical procedure, but patients must keep in mind that repeat treatments will add more expense over time.

"A single 10-minute Botox procedure can, for a fraction of the cost and none of the surgical risks, rebalance facial expression by weakening specific muscles, if used correctly," says **Dean Kane, MD**, of

Baltimore, Maryland. "I am able to raise brows, reduce scowl lines, and reduce forehead furrows, crow's-feet, and most lipstick lines with Botox. I can lift the corners of the mouth, get a gentle lift of the jowl, and reduce the neck lines and bands. Previously, most of these procedures needed surgery or could not be performed. There are limits though. When the skin sags beyond the ability of the underlying muscle to lift it, a surgical procedure will be necessary."

Gary R. Culbertson, MD, of Sumter, South Carolina, adds that the temporary nature of injectable treatments can sometimes be a benefit. "To get rid of frown lines, consider Botox injections first and possibly to see what you might look like after a brow lift. The results of Botox can last up to six months. If you like the results, then you may wish to consider a more permanent surgical solution such as a brow lift."

Whatever type of injectable treatment you are interested in, keep in mind that "nonsurgical" does not mean "nonmedical." This area of aesthetic medicine has attracted many unlicensed and unqualified practitioners, and there have been well-publicized instances in which patients were seriously harmed by injections of tainted or nonmedical grade substances used by these individuals. Just as it is recommended to select an experienced board-certified plastic surgeon for your aesthetic surgery, it is also vital to select a trained and qualified physician to administer or supervise your nonsurgical treatments.

You also need to know that some injectable treatments you may have read about are either not approved by the Food and Drug Administration (FDA) for use in the United States, or they may have FDA approval for certain uses and not others. When a product is FDA-approved for a specific purpose and physicians use the product for additional types of treatments beyond those that are officially approved, this is called an "off-label" use. Off-label use of injectable products is not uncommon — in fact, many of the popular cosmetic uses of Botox are technically "off-label." Nevertheless, you should be made aware of any off-label use as part of your informed consent to undergo a procedure.

THE CONSULTATION

The consultation is a time for you and the surgeon to get to know and feel comfortable with each other. You should feel completely confident that the surgeon is fully qualified. If you haven't read sections in the beginning of this book about choosing a surgeon who is certified by the American Board of Plastic Surgery, you should do so now.

Your surgeon may evaluate several factors, including your skin quality, facial structure and volume, the type and location of facial wrinkling, contraction of your facial muscles, position of your brows, and any other aspects of your facial appearance that may bother you. All these factors

LENGTH OF INJECTABLE PROCEDURES
Generally 10 to 45 minutes.

ANESTHESIA
Usually local anesthetic or topical numbing agent; seldom any for Botox.

LENGTH OF STAY
Usually performed as a routine appointment in doctor's office.

RECOVERY
Although there may be temporary bruising, swelling or redness, patient can generally return to normal activities immediately or within a few hours following treatment.

RISKS/POSSIBLE COMPLICATIONS
When performed by a qualified and experienced physician, the risks associated with injectable treatments are relatively minor. However, as with any medical procedure, there can be unanticipated outcomes.

Some of the risks and complications associated with injectables include:
• Infection or abscess.
• Scarring, lumps, or nodules.
• Asymmetry.
• Peeling and open sores.
• Allergic reaction.

The above-listed risks may be only some of those that your surgeon will discuss with you in greater detail during your consultation.

will help your surgeon determine if you are a suitable candidate for one or more injectable therapies. He or she will also review your entire medical history, including any medications you may currently be taking and conditions that could cause problems. These might include (depending on the type of injectable treatment being considered) active infections or sores that have not healed; allergies to beef, bird, or bovine products; autoimmune diseases; or the rare allergy to lidocaine.

You and your surgeon will work together to determine the best treatment plan for you. Depending on the type and depth of your wrinkles, the condition of your skin and the extent of overall facial aging, your surgeon may discuss other procedures that might better achieve your goals, such as face lift, brow lift, eyelid surgery, or skin resurfacing. These procedures, in appropriately selected patients, are often performed in conjunction with the use of Botox and soft tissue fillers.

"I've been using soft tissue fillers for the past few years and have found that they provide a tremendous enhancement to some of the aesthetic surgical procedures we do," says **Larry A. Sargent, MD**, of Chattanooga, Tennessee. "A good example is lip augmentation. In the past, there were few good options for significant lip enhancement with a natural appearance. Today, soft tissue fillers such as hyaluronic acid can make a big difference in shaping and enlarging the lips with relatively little risk and overall good results."

BOTOX

Botox is a product name for botulinum toxin (BTX) Type A. Botox injection is a popular nonsurgical method to temporarily reduce or eliminate frown lines, forehead creases, crow's-feet around the eyes, and in some instances, bands or cords in the neck. It can also be used to decrease nostril flaring and improve downturned corners of the mouth.

Wrinkles such as crow's-feet, frown lines, and horizontal forehead creases are usually caused by repeated muscle contraction associated with facial expressions. The cosmetic form of botulinum toxin, used as a therapeutic agent, blocks certain nerve impulses and temporarily inactivates the muscles that cause these wrinkles. The action of Botox is well targeted to the specific muscles that control facial expressions, and surrounding muscles are not impacted. Your surgeon's understanding of facial anatomy is paramount in achieving a natural-looking result.

"I think Botox is best used in the upper third of the face for frown lines, forehead furrows, and crow's-feet," says **Gustavo Galante, MD**, of Munster, Indiana, who adds, "It can be used for lines around the mouth, but there is more room for error in those areas. The muscles in the upper face are used largely for expression, whereas those around the mouth are more functional — for eating, talking, and kissing. It's critical that the surgeon knows the anatomy of the area being injected."

Botox injections will not only smooth certain types of facial wrinkles, but the treatment will also slow the process of further wrinkle formation.

"In addition to its temporary qualities in reducing furrows, Botox helps to prevent fine lines from becoming deeper, because it weakens the muscles that cause deep wrinkle formation," says **Alexander G. Digenis, MD**, of Louisville, Kentucky.

That's why people as young as their 30s and even 20s, who want to prevent wrinkles before they happen, as well as older women and men can be appropriate candidates for Botox injections.

But wrinkle reduction and prevention are not the only uses of Botox. Today, plastic surgeons frequently use BTX, often in combination with soft tissue fillers such as collagen or hyaluronic acid (Restylane, Hylaform or Captique), for facial shaping.

"Botox is best used in the upper part of the face for brow shaping rather than wrinkle reduction, and in the lower part of the face to dramatically reduce the gravitational effects that pull down the corners of the mouth and create a marionette line," says **Laurie Casas, MD**, of Glenview, Illinois.

First used in the late 1960s to treat neurological disorders and since 1997 to treat facial wrinkles, BTX has proven to be safe; there have been no documented systemic complications associated with BTX injections to date. Side effects can include a burning sensation during injection, local numbness, slight swelling and bruising, but most are not long lasting. Some patients report minor headache pain or mild flu-like symptoms for several days. Allergic reaction is very rare.

The procedure

Your plastic surgeon can inject Botox in his or her office, exam room, or other ambulatory setting. While you contract the muscles that correspond to the area to be treated, the surgeon locates the best injection site and administers the Botox into the muscle using a very small needle.

It would seem that Botox injections are easy to administer, but the success of your Botox therapy is extremely technique-dependent. Injections must be placed precisely to provide effective treatment, minimize the side effects mentioned above, and avoid complications.

"Although Botox has been around for years, there is still no standard 'formula' for its proper administration," says **Eric Mariotti, MD**, of Concord, California. "I still believe there is just as much art as there is science for the best aesthetic results. No two patients are alike and each must be evaluated critically to determine the dosage and placement of injections. In inexperienced hands, a little too much here or not enough there can lead to an unnatural appearance."

For example, if Botox is injected improperly, the eyelids can droop, brows may be asymmetrical, or facial expressions may look unnatural. Although temporary, these problems can take a few months to resolve. Difficulty in swallowing associated with treatment of neck bands is a serious, although rare, complication. A qualified and experienced plastic surgeon has the skill and knowledge of facial anatomy to lessen the risk of unexpected side effects and complications. He or she understands how the various facial muscles interact and can administer the toxin in strategically placed locations to achieve exactly the desired effect, whether it is smoothing frown lines and neck cords or modifying brow shape.

"When patients come in who just want Botox to reduce their horizontal forehead lines, I always tell them it is also a good idea to inject some into the vertical frown line area and crow's-feet." says **J. Vicente Poblete, MD**, of Avon Lake, Ohio. "In the course of trying to alter facial aesthetics, if we only treat the elevator muscles to remove the forehead lines and do nothing to the other muscles, the eyebrows may droop. That's because another set of muscles, called the depressors, will overpower the weakened elevator muscles."

Post-treatment

Following treatment, your surgeon will advise you to avoid lying down or massaging the injection areas for a few hours so that the toxin does not spread to nearby muscles. You should begin to see the effects within a

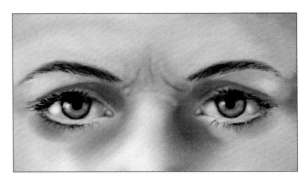

PREOPERATIVE APPEARANCE. Frowning causes muscle contraction, which in turn creates skin wrinkles and furrows.

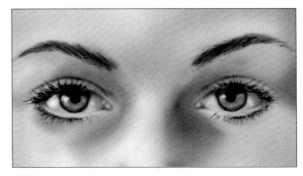

POSTOPERATIVE APPEARANCE. Following Botox injection, the muscles that cause frown lines are temporarily inactivated so that even when the patient tries to frown (as shown here), the area between the eyebrows in the lower forehead remains smooth. Results can last from two to 12 months, but four to six months is average.

few days, and improvement may continue for about 10 to 12 days. Results can last anywhere from two to 12 months, though the average seems to be about four to six months. Patients who continue with long-term Botox therapy may find that the effects of injections seem to last longer than in earlier stages of treatment. Occasionally, patients may experience no effects from Botox injection; in such cases, touch-up injections typically produce the desired results.

INJECTABLE SOFT TISSUE FILLERS

A vibrant sound is full and rich. Likewise, a youthful, vibrant face is characterized by fullness and smooth contours rather than a gaunt or hollowed-out appearance. But over time, the wear and tear on muscles and tissues from normal, everyday facial expressions and movements combine with the effects of gravity and exposure to the elements to break down the underlying tissues that support your skin. Laugh lines, crow's-feet, and other facial wrinkles, as well as soft tissue depletion, can cause you to look older and less vibrant than you feel.

"The addition of volume enhancement, instead of only skin excision and tightening, creates a more natural and rejuvenated result, which is most likely longer-lasting as well," says **Michael Parker, MD,** of Akron, Ohio. "The 'new-age' cosmetic plastic surgeon does not rely on just one or two procedures to correct problem areas; we are now using multiple modalities, such as skin tightening, laser resurfacing, Botox, and various fillers, in an effort to achieve the maximum enhancement. Of course, this has largely been brought about by technological advancements in the field, and I think that's the wave of the future for cosmetic surgery."

Today, natural or biocompatible substances such as injectable collagen (Zyderm, Zyplast, Cosmoderm, Cosmoplast, Isolagen), hyaluronic acid (Restylane, Hylaform, Captique), calcium hydroxylapatite (Radiesse), poly-L-lactic acid (Sculptra), and fat are helping to restore a more youthful appearance for millions of women and men. Research is ongoing, and new products are constantly being developed that further expand the choices available to physicians and patients.

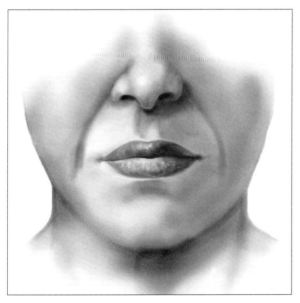

PREOPERATIVE APPEARANCE. Aging causes descent of soft tissues, resulting in volume loss in the cheek areas and deep facial lines and folds.

The specific applications and techniques for injectable soft tissue fillers are also expanding as physicians learn how to use these products, alone and in combination, to achieve better and more refined results. In addition to treating facial lines and wrinkles, soft tissue fillers can reduce the appearance of scarring caused by acne, chicken pox or injury; augment lips and cheeks; and even shape noses and chins.

"I would estimate that 99 percent of the fillers used in this country are used to fill lines, wrinkles, and lips. That's probably how I use about 50 percent of my fillers," says **Michael Kane, MD,** of New York, New York. "The other half I use for facial shaping, which is often essential to creating a youthful appearance. An old advertisement for collagen showed a 'before' picture of a woman with a lot of fine lines in her face, and an 'after' picture without lines. The strange thing was, she didn't look any younger in the 'after' picture. When we age, the fat descends from the cheekbones and accumulates at the jowls. By building up the cheekbones and then using Restylane to fill the indent in front of the jowls, disguising it, I can truly give the face a younger shape."

Fillers can be used in conjunction with skin resurfacing procedures or surgical procedures such as a face lift or brow lift to enhance the facial rejuvenation process and achieve a harmonious effect. Your plastic surgeon can advise you which fillers will work best for your specific needs. Considerations will include the areas for correction, the extent of volume needed, your skin pigmentation (some fillers may not be appropriate for darker-skinned individuals), any allergies that you may have to specific products, and whether a surgical procedure might offer a better or more permanent solution.

There are two main categories of injectable fillers: resorbable (temporary, since they are resorbed by the body over time — effects typically last three to nine months), and nonresorbable (permanent or at least generally longer-lasting than resorbable fillers). It has long been thought that the "ideal" filler would be one that is both biocompatible and permanent. However, many physicians and patients have come to recognize the relative benefits of temporary fillers. As we mature, our faces change in subtle ways; temporary fillers provide us with the opportunity to modify our facial contours in sync with the natural changes that occur with the aging process or in combination with aesthetic surgical modifications.

COLLAGEN

Approved by the FDA in 1981, collagen is a popular soft tissue filler used primarily for nonsurgical lip augmentation and treatment of nasolabial folds. Although allergy to bovine-based (derived from cows) collagen occurs in less than five percent of the population, it is the primary risk associated with the product, and you will need to undergo allergy testing before your first treatment with bovine-based Zyderm or Zyplast. The test involves the injection of a small amount of collagen beneath the skin of your forearm, which you will be instructed to watch carefully for about a month. If you do not develop a reaction, such as redness or swelling in the area of the injection during this time, it is safe to proceed with treatment.

There are other formulations of collagen, Cosmoderm and Cosmoplast, that are made from human-derived sources and do not require you to be allergy-tested prior to injection. Yet another option is Isolagen, a process in which your own collagen-producing cells are cultured from a small skin sample, often easily removed from behind your ear, and then injected in the treatment site. However, this can be a somewhat more expensive alternative. Because today there are other soft tissue fillers with significantly longer-lasting results, collagen is no longer the most widely used soft tissue filler.

The procedure

Collagen contains an anesthetic, lidocaine, which helps diminish any discomfort. Patients may still feel a slight stinging or burning sensation at the beginning of the injections. In patients with a lower pain threshold, an additional topical or local anesthetic can be used.

As with all injectables, selection of the injection points is critical. Your plastic surgeon will mark the sites, often choosing several injection points for each area to be treated. He or she will then inject the collagen with a fine needle at several points along the treatment area. Depending on the length and depth of the wrinkle, several injections may be needed. Your surgeon will slightly overfill each area, since part of the injected solution is saline and local anesthetic that will be absorbed by the body within a few days. Your surgeon may ask you to hold a hand mirror to select and help monitor the sites as well as decide when they are sufficiently corrected. The procedure generally takes between 15 to 45 minutes, depending on the areas to be treated.

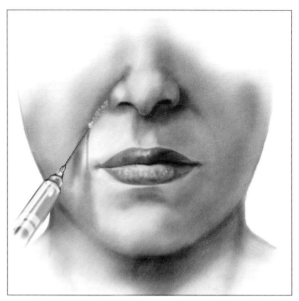

"Fillers" such as hyaluronic acid, collagen, and fat can be injected with a tiny needle beneath the skin wrinkle or indentation, filling or 'volumizing' the area treated.

Post-treatment

Following your collagen treatment, you may experience some stinging or throbbing at the points of injection. This will subside rather quickly; in addition, any redness or swelling that may appear should disappear within 24 to 48 hours. In some cases, notably with fair-skinned patients, redness may last for a week or more. If tiny scabs should form over injection sites, they will heal quickly and without visible marks.

Bandages are not needed, and you can resume normal activities immediately. Your surgeon will advise you to avoid direct exposure of the treated areas to sunlight. You will be able to wear makeup with sunscreen protection the following day. If any of your symptoms or aftereffects persist beyond the periods specified, you should contact your surgeon.

Your results should be fully apparent within one week. Collagen treatments are temporary. Duration varies among individuals and can also be affected by the patient's lifestyle, physical characteristics, and the area of the face that is treated, with areas most affected by muscle movement having a shorter duration. Typically, the length of time between retreatments is about three to six months.

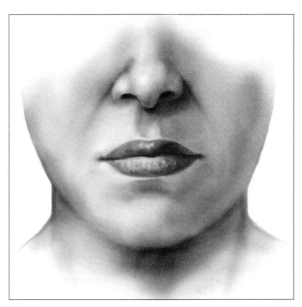

POSTOPERATIVE APPEARANCE. Following injection with a soft tissue filler, the nasolabial fold is less pronounced, creating a smoother facial contour.

HYALURONIC ACID

Today, the most popular pharmaceutical fillers are those with hyaluronic acid. Among the best-known hyaluronic acid products available in the U.S. are Restylane, Hylaform and Captique, all of which are FDA approved. Hylaform uses a form of hyaluronic acid obtained from rooster combs. Restylane and Captique are within the category of fillers known as non-animal, stabilized hyaluronic acid (NASHA) products. Manufacturers state that no pre-treatment allergy testing is required for any of these products, but there is some debate about this among physicians. In the case of Hylaform, individuals with known allergies to bird products could be at risk of allergic reaction. Even for NASHA products, some physicians have reported incidents of apparent allergic response, though this appears to be extremely rare.

Dr. Kane says, "If you look at a photo of a 60-year-old patient when she was 20, you will usually see that her brows haven't fallen appreciably. They've deflated a little bit. So, if you build the brow back up with a little Restylane and then use Botox to weaken some of the muscles around the brow that pull it down as well as around the upper bone of the eye socket, the brows look terrific — like they looked at 20 years old, and very natural."

Hyaluronic acid (HA) occurs naturally in all living organisms and is a natural component of connective tissues, including the skin. HA's function in the body is to cushion and lubricate, and it has been used to treat joint pain. HA products come in a variety of formulations that differ in the size of their injectable microspheres (tiny crystals), making some products better suited for treating deeper wrinkles and creases while others are better for thin, superficial lines. In addition, the largest microsphere formulations are more suitable for large-volume augmentations in areas such as the cheeks and chin.

"In facial contouring, my favorite combination of fillers is fat and Restylane," says **Diane Duncan, MD**, of Fort Collins, Colorado. "Many people believe that both do similar things. This is not true. I use fat in the superficial subcutaneous plane to achieve a soft, broad fill, while Restylane is used intradermally to fill lines, localized hollows, add definition, and correct asymmetry."

The procedure

Your surgeon may give you a local anesthetic to help alleviate discomfort, but you might still feel some stinging or burning from the needle. Injection techniques for hyaluronic acid products can vary according to the area being treated. Material may be injected in a series of "threads" or in serial punctures. Plastic surgeons who have received training in the use of injectable HA products are able to use their knowledge of facial anatomy and technical skill to place filler materials in the manner and location that will create the most natural-looking augmentation. Because the injected material is not absorbed into the body as readily as fat, overfilling is not necessary. Depending upon the areas to be treated, the procedure may take from just a few minutes to as much as half an hour.

Post-treatment

Although you can resume normal activities immediately following your HA treatment, you may experience some mild redness and swelling for a few days. More pronounced swelling is possible but unusual. Some patients have experienced side effects including mild headache, nausea, flu-like symptoms or even muscle weakness, which is rare. Most symptoms, if they occur, are not long-lasting.

Your surgeon will advise you to stay out of the sun and to avoid outdoor activities in the cold until any redness and swelling disappear. Of course, any abnormal or progressive pain or symptoms should be reported to your surgeon immediately.

Results of HA injections generally can be expected to last from six months to, in some cases, a year.

CALCIUM HYDROXYLAPATITE (RADIESSE)

Radiesse (formerly called Radiance) is a soft tissue filler made from a form of hydroxylapatite, which is a natural material found in bones and teeth, suspended in gel. It typically is used for the treatment of deeper facial wrinkles or to increase volume in the lips. As a normal constituent of bones and teeth, calcium hydroxylapatite should not elicit a chronic inflammatory or immune response.

"There is a plethora of fillers available, and even more are awaiting approval by the FDA. That attests to the fact that the ideal one has not been found. What works best for me is Radiesse," says **Edward J. Domanskis, MD**, of Newport Beach, California, "which does not need pre-testing and is by far the longest lasting of all fillers presently available."

The procedure

Radiesse does not include lidocaine, and your surgeon will use a local anesthetic to help reduce any pain or discomfort. As with the other injectables, you may experience some stinging or burning during the injections. Calcium hydroxylapatite is injected in a fashion similar to other injectable fillers, using a fine needle. The procedure usually takes between 15 to 30 minutes to accomplish.

Post-treatment

Although you can return to most normal activities within a few hours following treatment with calcium hydroxylapatite, you should avoid activities that may strain facial muscles and features, such as singing, shouting, strenuous laughing, chewing gum or tough food, and using a straw for 48 hours. Any minor inflammation or swelling will usually disappear within 24 to 48 hours. In addition, the application of ice should help reduce any swelling.

At this time, Radiesse has achieved the longest results of any of the fillers — up to three years. It can, however, cause firm areas (granulomas) to form under the skin, and there have been reports of permanent hardness, especially when this material is used in the lips. As with all aesthetic procedures, your surgeon will explain the balance between risks and benefits and advise what would best meet your needs.

POLY-L-LACTIC ACID

Poly-L-lactic acid, marketed under the name Sculptra, is one of the newest of the pharmaceutical soft tissue fillers and is used for large-volume augmentations. It is a biocompatible material that can be broken down by the body. That is why it has been used for a long time in absorbable sutures and certain types of implants. According to the manufacturer, no skin testing for allergic reaction is required.

Sculptra is formulated with a suspension of microspheres that, when injected into tissue, stimulate collagen formation and increase the thickness of the dermis (the lower layer of the skin). Over time, this process increases volume in the injected facial areas. Sculptra has been approved by the FDA for use in treating facial wasting, a common side effect of HIV infection. Because of its unique ability to volumize and enhance facial contours, it is being used "off-label" for cosmetic purposes such as cheek augmentation and treatment of mild laxity of the midface and jowls. It may be used as a pretreatment for patients undergoing a face lift. When used in this manner, it helps to provide a fuller soft tissue foundation for skin redraping during the surgical procedure.

The procedure

Sculptra is implanted deeply through multiple injection sites, either in a crisscross pattern or through small tunnels created with a thin needle. Injections may be painful, but resuspension of the material in sterile water and lidocaine prior to injection helps to minimize discomfort. A topical or local anesthetic or a nerve block may also be used to further numb the areas to be treated. A common technique for augmenting the cheek area is to inject the material from inside the mouth.

Patients usually will have from three to five treatments, administered a few weeks apart.

Post-treatment

An icepack may be used to help reduce swelling and bruising. These side effects, as well as redness and some discomfort, should diminish or disappear in a few hours or a few days; however, symptoms sometimes may persist more than two weeks. Still, most patients find that they can return to their home or work immediately following treatment, and can re-apply makeup within a few hours. You will be instructed to massage the treated areas periodically over the next several days.

The patient's own collagen formation occurs over a period of four to six months. During that time, the implant is slowly resorbed, but the soft tissue augmentation increases as this new collagen is formed. Repeat treatments may be necessary to achieve or maintain desired results. Initial results have been reported to last as long as two years.

It is possible that small nodules may form at the injection sites within the first six to 12 months following treatment, but these can generally be dispersed through firm massage or, if necessary, by your surgeon inserting a needle directly into the nodule to break it up.

FAT

Fat has long been used as a soft tissue filler to add volume to the face and lips. Many patients like the idea of using their own fat, rather than a pharmaceutical filler, to restore volume that has been lost through the aging process or to "plump up" areas that lack dramatic contours. One of the benefits of fat injection is that, because the fat is removed from your own body, there is no possibility of an allergic reaction.

Fat can be safely injected into the face by a skilled plastic surgeon. It can also be injected in other areas of the body to fill in dents or depressions. However, to date, fat injection into the breasts has been condemned because of the concern that it could impair future mammographic diagnosis of breast cancer.

The procedure

If your own fat is used, it must be harvested from another part of your body. Usual donor sites include the buttocks, abdomen, or thighs. Fat may be extracted during a liposuction procedure or harvested only for the purpose of reinjection. In the latter case, once the site is selected and cleansed, a local anesthetic, sometimes in combination with oral sedation, is applied. The surgeon makes a tiny incision and uses a syringe or cannula, which is the same instrument used in liposuction, to withdraw a small amount of fat. The fat is then processed and re-injected into the area to be enhanced. The body will absorb some of the injected fat. For this reason, the surgeon will often overfill the area to be enhanced. In addition, the procedure may need to be repeated in the future to compensate for volume loss.

"Fat is an excellent filler, but you have to be very careful, extracting it with low suction to not break up the cells and preparing it very gently, removing the serum so that you inject fat rather than fluid," says **George Marosan, MD**, of Bellevue, Washington. "You then have to inject it under low pressure, in small amounts into multiple layers of the tissues under the skin and muscles, so it can get thoroughly vascularized. The transplanted fat only has about 48 hours for blood vessels to find it before it dies. If you put in a large clump, or overfill, the edge will get vascularized, but the blood supply won't penetrate the mass of fat and it will die. By treating it properly, fat can be very long-lasting. I have patients whose results are still excellent after three years."

Archibald S. Miller, MD, of Tulsa, Oklahoma, adds, "It is very important to inject enough fat. The surgeon must overfill the areas being treated. Thirty to 50 percent of the fat cells will be lost, so overfilling is the only way to get the final result that the patient wants. Initially, this overfilling causes a somewhat distorted appearance but once this resolves, patients will find that they are very happy with the results, which can be virtually permanent."

In some instances, fat may be transplanted rather than injected. Fat, dermis or fascia (a layer of tissue that covers muscles) can be grafted from one area of the body to another to improve contour and create more fullness. Usually grafting is done in conjunction with facial surgery rather than as an isolated procedure.

"There has been an evolution in facial rejuvenation over the past 25 years," says **Michael Epstein, MD**, of Chicago, Illinois. "For a long time, face lifts were the only option until about 15 years ago, when skin resurfacing came to the fore and techniques such as chemical peels and laser resurfacing became more popular. Although these adjuncts improved facial rejuvenation, it was still incomplete. But in the last several years, aided by the use of digital photography and comparisons of old photos with the patient's present appearance, the key role that volume loss plays in facial aging became more apparent. Fat grafting, an excellent method of restoring volume, has also undergone an evolution. Originally it was just harvested and re-injected; however with today's more modern transferring techniques, which better preserve the cells, we can achieve essentially permanent results."

Post-treatment

Recovery from fat injection is much longer than recovery following injection of most pharmaceutical soft tissue fillers. Following fat injection, there will be significant bruising and swelling that may last several days to several weeks. The size and location of treated areas will determine the severity of post-treatment symptoms and the time needed for complete recovery.

Your surgeon will advise you to stay out of the sun until all redness has cleared. Until then, you can wear makeup with sunscreen protection to help conceal any redness or bruising.

There are differing reports concerning how long injected or implanted fat can be expected to last. Most surgeons agree that a significant percentage of the fat will be long-lasting or even permanent, especially if the treated area is one that has limited muscle movement. However, because of fat's resorbable nature, results of fat injections can be somewhat unpredictable in terms of symmetry and longevity. As mentioned earlier, overfilling helps compensate for expected resorption but also may make your initial results significantly "fuller" than desired.

Editor's Viewpoint

Over the last few years, there has been a meteoric rise in the use of injections of Botox for reduction of facial muscle activity and soft tissue fillers for facial rejuvenation and cosmetic enhancement of facial shape. A commonly used approach today is the combination of Botox injections for the upper face and fillers for the lower. These injectable treatments are also popular as adjuncts to facial aesthetic surgery, complementing and sometimes prolonging surgical results. Careful analysis of each patient's physiognomy and aesthetic goals guides the surgeon in designing the best treatment strategy.

Botox injections also have been used very successfully to control migraine headaches and diminish excessive sweating of the forehead, armpits, and palms, an embarrassing problem for some patients.

Injectable treatments are a wonderful tool in treating cosmetic patients, but, like any tool, they can be misused. The physician must practice meticulous technique with careful control of the location and depth of injections based on an intimate knowledge of the anatomy coupled with full understanding of the unique characteristics of the injected material. Inadequately trained practitioners from varied backgrounds are often responsible for the substandard results that all of us have seen, many times on well-known celebrities who appear virtually expressionless from Botox, sporting "over-plumped" lips and "mask-like" faces from overzealous use of fillers. These kinds of results are entirely avoidable.

For all the reasons mentioned by our contributing experts, absorbable and semi-permanent injectables are "the way to go" and will probably remain so for the foreseeable future. Meanwhile, the search for the ideal filler material continues with several promising ones, yet to be FDA-approved, on the horizon.

My personal preference for facial volume restoration has almost completely shifted away from injections of autologous fat (harvested from the patient's own body) to hyaluronic acid and other filler materials. Not so for the body, however, where fat remains the best filling material for post-liposuction defects and buttock augmentation.

There are, however, some exciting developments with regard to autologous fat. At the University of California, Los Angeles (UCLA), we are in the process of research that could greatly enhance the performance of fat as a soft tissue filler. Our research already showed that stem cells are abundantly present in the fat removed by liposuction. These stem cells can be isolated and preserved (like blood in a blood bank) for later use. Enriching fat with stem cells prior to injection should significantly improve its survival in the face and body and eliminate the need for unsightly over-correction to compensate for fat resorption. These findings have led us to reconsider the use of fat for breast augmentation, a practice that has until now been widely condemned on the grounds that it causes calcifications within the breast tissue, resulting in false positive mammograms. More research needs to be done, but it is entirely possible that our own fat may yet become the ideal universal filler.

— Peter B. Fodor, MD

SKIN RESURFACING

Facial rejuvenation surgery is designed to reduce excess tissue and fat, redrape skin and improve facial contours, but it is not effective in treating fine wrinkling of the skin or improving skin texture. That is why plastic surgeons often may recommend one or more skin resurfacing procedures to complete a patient's facial rejuvenation. These procedures also may be performed in conjunction with other nonsurgical therapies such as injections of Botox or soft tissue fillers, or skin resurfacing may be done as a stand-alone procedure for patients of almost any age who seek improvement of their skin's appearance.

Today there are many options for skin resurfacing treatments, from deep to superficial. First, though, it is important to understand that skin resurfacing cannot achieve the same results as, for example, a face lift. Some types of resurfacing treatments may offer skin tightening effects, but these are generally minimal compared with the results obtained through surgical interventions.

The type of treatment recommended for you will depend primarily on the condition of your skin. This, in turn, may be determined by your heredity and by lifestyle factors including sun exposure, nutrition, smoking, alcohol consumption and your daily skin care regimen.

"The earlier we begin to add nutrients, anti-oxidize, internally "moisturize" our tissues and stall the degenerative effects of aging, the longer we can delay surgical procedures and the more effective these less invasive nonsurgical procedures will be," says **Dean Kane, MD**, of Baltimore, Maryland. "In my practice, we promote three fundamental and interactive spheres of 'anti-aging'

management: One is skin protection with sunblock and with internal and external anti-oxidants. Two is nutrition for building and repair of tissues using a low-carb, low-fat, high-protein, well-hydrated diet with low calories and plenty of nutrients, essential fatty acids, minerals, and vitamins. Three is reversal, which involves many components: Retin-A and hydroquinone, and the use of Botox, Restylane and chemical peels."

Samuel Shatkin, MD, of Amherst, New York, agrees and adds, "The best way to keep your skin looking young is a good, healthy diet rich in vitamins, nutrients and especially water. Daily skin management with proper moisturizing and exfoliation using natural fruit acids — glycolic and lactic acids — can further help maintain youthfulness, and even reverse some of the changes that occur from years of sun exposure and daily stresses. Getting into a habit of daily care, just like brushing your teeth on a daily basis, will assure you are keeping your skin fit."

When visible signs of skin damage appear, resurfacing treatments offer a range of solutions. Some types of skin resurfacing procedures have little or no downtime, while others may require a lengthy recovery and you may experience persistent skin redness for an extended period of time. Skin resurfacing treatments may be superficial or deep. They may target only the upper layers of the skin, removing dead cells (exfoliation) and allowing skin cell regeneration, or they may penetrate to deeper layers of the skin to stimulate changes beneath the skin's surface. Lighter treatments are usually most appropriate for younger skin or skin that has minimal sun damage, called photoaging. Deeper treatments may be necessary to achieve dramatic results in more mature skin or skin with moderate to severe sun damage. Treatments that target the collagen deep within the dermis while bypassing the outer skin layers involve less recovery than other deep treatments, but visible results are not as significant. Most resurfacing treatments are performed on the face, but some treatments can be used on the neck, chest, hands, and other areas of the body.

Like some other nonsurgical procedures, skin resurfacing treatments often may be available from non-physician practitioners. While certain treatments, generally those that are most superficial, can be safely administered by a licensed aesthetician or trained medical staff under the supervision of a physician, other skin resurfacing treatments — those that are most invasive or carry significant risks — should be administered only by a qualified physician such as a board-certified plastic surgeon.

"In the wrong hands, lasers are dangerous and can cause permanent damage," cautions **Carl Williams Jr., MD**, of Henderson, Nevada, "Some states do not have regulations governing who can administer laser treatments. Make sure you seek a physician who has laser qualifications and training. Make sure the laser is used in a medical setting, not a salon, spa, or storefront operation. And don't become caught up in the media hype about laser resurfacing or the 'quick lunch-hour face lift.' You can spend a lot of money and have dissatisfying results or complications if you do not do your homework."

Skin resurfacing methods can be classified into several main categories: chemical peels, mechanical abrasion treatments, lasers, and light-based treatments.

"When you're looking at skin, you need to first determine what the specific problems are," offers **Guy Stofman**, MD, of Pittsburgh, Pennsylvania. "There is a variety of issues that may need to be dealt with such as uneven pigment, poor skin texture, wrinkling, and enlarged pores. Every one of these components often must be treated separately with the best modality for each."

CHEMICAL PEELS

Chemical peels date back to the days of ancient Egypt when people would use lactic acid, an active ingredient of sour milk, as an agent to exfoliate and rejuvenate the skin. Aged wine, which contains tartaric acid, served the same purpose during the

---

FAST FACTS
Chemical Peels & Dermabrasion

LENGTH OF PROCEDURE
CHEMICAL PEELS
From 10 minutes to two hours.
DERMABRASION
Generally from 15 to 45 minutes.

ANESTHESIA
CHEMICAL PEELS
Depending on the strength, from none, to local anesthetic with or without intravenous sedation, or to general anesthesia.
DERMABRASION
Depending on the severity of the problem and the extent of the treatment, dermabrasion can be performed under local anesthesia, numbing spray, sedation (twilight) anesthesia, or general anesthesia.

LENGTH OF STAY
CHEMICAL PEELS & DERMABRASION
Outpatient, home the same day.

RECOVERY
CHEMICAL PEELS
Skin color from mild pinkness to severe redness, scabbing, peeling and swelling, depending on the strength of the peel; from 24 hours for light peels to several weeks or longer for deep peels.
DERMABRASION
Slight stinging or tingling subsiding almost immediately following microdermabrasion; moderate discomfort with redness and swelling for up to 14 days following dermabrasion.

RISKS/POSSIBLE COMPLICATIONS
Serious complications, while possible, are unlikely when performed by a qualified physician or, in some cases, by trained and licensed staff under medical supervision.

Risks include:
CHEMICAL PEELS
• Infection. • Unanticipated pigment changes. • Scarring.
DERMABRASION
• Temporary burning, itching, tingling, lightening of treated skin; loss of the ability to make pigment or to tan in treated areas.
• Infection.
• Scarring.
• Flare-ups of skin allergies, fever blisters, or cold sores.

The above-listed risks may be only some of those that your surgeon will discuss with you in greater detail during your consultation.

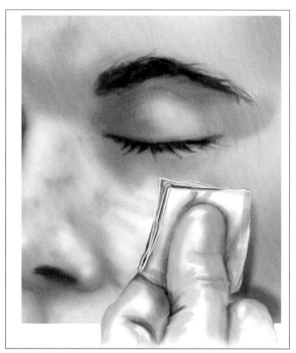

A variety of chemical peels ranging from superficial to deep can be applied to freshen the skin and, in the case of deeper peels, significantly reverse sun damage and improve fine or coarse wrinkles. While a chemical peel can enhance skin tone and texture, it will not tighten sagging skin.

Middle Ages. Today, with scientific advances greatly improving the chemical agents, chemical peels are still a popular nonsurgical technique used to revitalize finely wrinkled, blemished, unevenly pigmented or sun-damaged facial skin.

Chemical peels can also be used to remove pre-cancerous skin growths, treat acne scars and even control acne. The procedure involves using a chemical solution to peel away the skin's damaged outer layers, allowing new cells to grow and produce a smoother, younger-looking skin surface. Chemical peels may sometimes be performed in conjunction with a face lift to improve and smooth the skin's texture, but they are in no way a substitute for a surgical procedure. The results of chemical peels can be long-lasting, but the skin will continue to age and may be more easily damaged by sun exposure unless adequate sun protection (UVA/UVB sunscreen, dark glasses and a wide-brimmed hat) is used regularly.

While there is a wide variety of peeling agents, those used most commonly are alpha hydroxy acids (AHAs), trichloroacetic acid, (TCA) and phenol. Other peeling agents include beta hydroxy acid, vitamin-A based tretinoin and Jessner's solution (a mixture of lactic acid, salicylic acid, alcohol and resorcinol).

The strength of any chemical peel can be adjusted to specifically address each patient's individual needs. This means, however, that even alpha hydroxy acid peels, which are generally considered the lightest peels, can be mixed at a higher percentage to increase the effects — and also the risks of complications if administered by an untrained and unqualified practitioner.

"Glycolic acid is a great superficial peel for the acne patient, or to get rid of some of the superficial dirt and pigmentation that can cause mottling and splotching," offers Dr. Kane. "Phenol peels provide much deeper penetration, but many physicians feel it is too difficult to control. TCA's concentration can be varied, usually from 5 to 30 percent, giving it great versatility in treating many different problems from acne to pigmentation, and, when it is allowed to penetrate even deeper in the dermis, in tightening the skin similar to the effects of a laser but with more control and no thermal injury."

"When performed in conjunction with a home skin care program that incorporates the use of Retin-A," advises **Laurie Casas, MD**, of Glenview, Illinois, "a peel can provide patients with a very measurable change in the quality, texture and color of their skin. Improvements may include a more even pigment and a natural glow. Peels help to exfoliate the upper layers of the skin so that the new skin underneath has a healthier, more radiant appearance."

THE CONSULTATION

The consultation is a time for you and the physician who will administer or oversee your skin resurfacing treatments to get to know and feel comfortable with each other. You should feel completely confident that the physician is fully qualified. Your skin resurfacing procedure may be performed by, or under the supervision of, a board-certified plastic surgeon. Other types of physicians, such as dermatologists or ENT/facial plastic surgeons, also perform many of these procedures. One of the benefits of selecting a board-certified plastic surgeon is that he or she has a wide range of procedures, both nonsurgical and surgical, to offer you in meeting your specific goals.

Your surgeon will help you to determine if you are a suitable candidate for skin resurfacing. Patients with darker skin types may not be good candidates for deeper peels. Depending on the procedure recommended for you, a full medical history may be requested. It may be important for your surgeon to know if you have ever had an outbreak of herpes or shingles, and if you have a personal or family history of heart disease. Patients with a history of herpes or shingles can experience cold-sore breakouts following a chemical peel, and a family history of heart disease can have negative implications for patients undergoing certain types of chemical peels. Some medications you may be taking can also negatively affect your outcome. There are measures your surgeon can take to minimize all of these risks, but only if he or she knows your medical history in advance of the procedure.

Your surgeon will discuss the overall appearance of your face and the condition of your skin. Depending upon your goals, he or she may recommend different or additional procedures. When you and your physician have agreed on the appropriate procedure, or procedures, for you, he or she will explain the details, including risks and recovery time.

AHA

Alpha hydroxy acid (called AHA), often in the form of glycolic acid, is generally the gentlest of the peel solutions. This type of peel can provide an alternative for people with mild skin problems, such as areas of dryness, minor sun damage, or uneven pigmentation, who want little or no downtime but seek a fresher, brighter-looking complexion. Glycolic acid, like other peels, can be applied at various concentrations usually beginning at 30 percent and up to 70 percent.

The Procedure

Since the AHA peel will cause only a slight stinging sensation during the application, no anesthetic is needed. Unless being performed in conjunction with other surgical procedures, the peel will most likely be performed in the doctor's office or treatment room. A light peel may be applied by your surgeon or by a specially trained member of your surgeon's staff, such as a licensed aesthetician or nurse.

Depending upon the solution's concentration, treatment usually consists of a series of six to eight peels over a period of two to four months. Each peel usually takes no more than 10 minutes. First the patient's face is thoroughly cleansed, then the AHA solution is applied to the face. No dressing, covering, or ointment is necessary following the application. Although some stinging, redness, irritation, and flaking may occur, they will usually subside as the skin adjusts to the treatments. After a light AHA peel, patients are usually able to return to normal activities the same day or the day following treatment. Results range from a more "glowing" complexion to, with repeated use, modest reduction in fine lines and improvement in skin texture.

Some patients may be good candidates for a home skin care regimen to improve skin texture utilizing a topical glycolic acid liquid, lotion or cream at a concentration of 10 to 14 percent. Depending upon the patient's needs, the mixture may also include Retin-A or a bleaching agent. It is important for the patient to return to the physician's office after several weeks to determine if any adjustments need to be made. Even mild peels and glycolic acid products can leave your skin more vulnerable to future sun damage. Your surgeon may recommend daily use of a sunscreen with adequate UVA and UVB protection.

TRICHLOROACETIC ACID (TCA)

Trichloroacetic acid (TCA) can be used at low strength for a mild peel but is generally used to produce a medium-depth peel that treats fine surface wrinkles and, for some patients, may be effective in treating superficial blemishes, age spots or other pigment problems. TCA peels also may be used to treat precancerous conditions of the skin.

Your surgeon may advise a specific regimen to prepare you for your TCA peel. Various solutions are often used to pre-treat the skin. These include Retin-A, a prescription medication derived from Vitamin A, which allows the TCA solution to penetrate the skin more deeply and evenly, or an AHA cream may be used if your skin will not tolerate the Retin-A. Hydroquinone, a bleaching agent, is often used in conjunction with either of these pre-treatment regimens. The pre-treatment period may last for more than a month.

The Procedure

The TCA chemical solution, which has a slight numbing effect on the skin, acts as an anesthetic; an additional oral or topical anesthetic is usually unnecessary but may be used if the concentration of TCA is high. You may receive a sedative both prior to and following the procedure to keep you more comfortable.

Your face will be thoroughly cleansed and the TCA solution applied. A full-face TCA peel should take from 15 to 60 minutes. You will probably feel a burning or stinging sensation followed by some numbness for about 10 to 15 minutes during the application. Once the desired depth of penetration has been reached, your physician will neutralize the TCA's effects by applying iced saline. Following the application, your face may be covered with an oil-based ointment, steroid ointment, or vegetable shortening. This will help keep your skin moist and help promote healing. Two or more treatments are often required to achieve your goals. These subsequent treatments can be spaced out over several months. Treatments utilizing a milder solution, however, can be repeated monthly.

Post-treatment

You may experience moderate itchiness and mild to significant swelling, depending on the strength of the solution. This should subside in approximately one week. You will be instructed how to care for your face, which will include twice-daily washings followed by the application of an ointment. Within a few days, the superficial layers of facial skin will turn crusty, subsequently cracking and flaking or peeling off. This process can last from a few days to a couple of weeks, after which your new skin will become apparent, although appearing quite flushed. Your skin should appear smoother and fresher and be healed well enough to allow you to return to normal activities a week to 10 days following the procedure. Your doctor will tell you when you can resume normal skin care. As with all skin resurfacing procedures, it is important to protect your skin from the sun.

PHENOL

Phenol is the strongest of the chemical peel solutions; it achieves the most dramatic results, and the effects of just one treatment can last for many years. It does, however, have its drawbacks, not the least of which is a permanent and noticeable lightening of the treated area. That's why phenol is not recommended for darker-skinned people and is usually only suitable for patients with very fair skin.

Phenol may be recommended for treatment of blotches on the skin caused by pregnancy, sun exposure, birth-control pills or illness. It is also used to treat coarse facial wrinkles, severe sun damage or precancerous growths. Phenol is usually not used on areas other than the face, since scarring may result if it is applied to the neck or other areas of the body.

In patients with fair, unfreckled skin, where the contrast with the untreated areas won't be obvious, phenol can be used on specific facial regions, such as around the mouth to reduce the vertical lines that cause lipstick bleed, or on the entire face. Because today's patients generally prefer skin-resurfacing methods requiring less downtime, phenol has fallen out of favor in recent years. However, newer phenol formulas that reduce the depth of the peel are allowing phenol to experience a revival of sorts.

The Procedure

Although like TCA, the phenol solution has some anesthetic qualities, your surgeon may give you some additional pain medication and a sedative to aid in your comfort. Full-face phenol peels take about one to two hours. The procedure can be performed under sedation (twilight) anesthesia, although general anesthesia may be used. Whether you are awake and unaware of what is going on or you are unconscious, you will not feel any pain during the surgical procedure. Phenol peels used to treat smaller areas, such as above the upper lip, may only take 10 to 15 minutes to perform. Phenol peels are generally outpatient procedures, and the patient can return home the same day. You should, however, arrange for someone to drive you to and from the procedure.

Phenol is applied in a similar fashion to the other peels, with the physician applying the solution to the thoroughly cleansed facial area. After the procedure has been completed, you may have an ointment such as petroleum jelly or a waterproof dressing applied to the treated area.

Post-treatment

You will normally feel moderate discomfort for several days following the procedure, which can be treated with a mild prescription pain medication. If you have undergone a full face peel, your entire face, including the area around your eyes, may be quite swollen. This is temporary and will improve over the next seven to 10 days. If the treated area was covered with a waterproof adhesive, your physician will remove it in one or two days and may instruct you to cover the area with antiseptic powder several times a day. The treated area will scab over and flake off within seven to 10 days revealing healthy, smooth skin, which at first will be bright red, as though sunburned. Although you may be presentable with makeup after two weeks, it will take two to three months or longer for the redness to fade. Loss of skin pigmentation in the treated areas is permanent, and you most likely will need makeup to blend these areas in with the rest of your face or your neck.

Treated areas will never be able to tan and must be protected from the sun. Your physician may recommend a high SPF sunscreen for everyday use.

DERMABRASION

Dermabrasion is a form of mechanical resurfacing that is similar to "sanding" the skin. The procedure uses a hand-held instrument that abrades or scrapes the skin, removing its upper layers. Dermaplaning is a similar procedure that uses a different type of instrument, either a mechanical blade or surgical scalpel.

"In our practice, we emphasize hands-on skin care," says **James A. Matas, MD**, of Orlando, Florida. "Rather than using a machine, we do dermaplaning, which is actually scraping the top layer of the skin. Dermaplaning prior to performing a chemical peel allows the peel to penetrate more efficiently and be more effective." Dr. Matas adds that proper skin care can enhance the results of other aesthetic procedures. "I've found skin care to be a vital component of the rejuvenation process. In cases where patients have severe sun damage, I will often insist that they begin skin care before I'll perform any facial surgery."

The removal of the skin's upper layers with dermabrasion allows them to be replaced with healthier skin cells, resulting in a smoother skin surface. The procedure is most frequently used for the treatment of facial scars, such as those caused by acne. Since each treatment typically improves acne scars by 20 to 40 percent, multiple treatments may be necessary to achieve a patient's desired result.

Similar to the deeper chemical peels, dermabrasion is also effective in reducing the appearance of vertical wrinkles around the mouth. It can be used on small areas of skin and on patients with somewhat darker complexions. The treated area usually will blend with the surrounding skin so there is little noticeable difference in the pigmentation, although there is a risk of permanently lighter pigmentation.

Although dermabrasion can be quite effective, it is important that patients have realistic expectations. As mentioned above, repeat procedures may be required, especially for deeper wrinkles and scars, which often may be significantly improved but not erased.

THE CONSULTATION

Your surgeon needs to first determine if you are a suitable candidate for dermabrasion. For example, patients with a history of oral herpes need to take medication, under the care of a physician, to lessen their chances of an outbreak. Should they have an outbreak during the healing period, it can spread to the entire treatment area and result in permanent scarring. Patients who are prone to keloids, hyper- or hypo-pigmentation, are dark-skinned, darkly tanned, or do not heal well from burns may not be good candidates for dermabrasion.

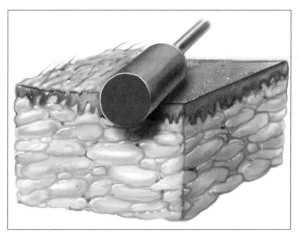

Dermabrasion, which uses a small "sanding" instrument to abrade the upper layers of skin, is sometimes recommended to treat small areas of skin, or the full face, affected by deep wrinkles or acne scars.

In addition, patients should generally not have a dermabrasion treatment on any area where they have undiagnosed lesions, warts, recent herpes outbreak, stages three-four acne, active Rosacea, pigmentation problems, or if they have auto-immune system disorders or unstable diabetes. Your physician will advise you about whether or not you should proceed with treatment. Regardless of whether you fall into any of the aforementioned categories, he or she will want to review your entire medical history.

Your surgeon will examine the overall appearance and condition of your skin and check for prior scars. Depending upon your goals, he or she may recommend different or additional procedures. Your consultation will include an explanation of the details of the procedure, including risks and recovery time.

The Procedure

Dermabrasion is an outpatient procedure that takes 15 to 60 minutes and can be performed in a physician's office or in a medical facility or hospital. Your doctor will use a high-speed rotary wheel to scrape off the top layers of skin. Depending on the severity of the problem and the extent of the treatment, the procedure can be performed under local anesthesia, numbing spray, sedation (twilight) anesthesia, or general anesthesia. You should be able to return home the same day.

Post-treatment

You can anticipate moderate discomfort, which will be relieved with prescription pain medication, for the first three to seven days. Your surgeon will also prescribe an ointment to apply daily after face washing to help reduce scabbing and promote healing. Your face will be red and swollen for a week or two, after which your new skin will emerge. You should be presentable in public, with makeup, about 10 days following the procedure, but even after healing the treated areas will appear sunburned for about four to six weeks. After that, your natural color should return and the final result will be apparent. Skin will remain sensitive to the sun for some time, and it is important to wear an effective sunscreen, both immediately and long term.

The results of dermabrasion are permanent or long-lasting; however, your skin will continue to age and may form new wrinkles.

MICRODERMABRASION

Microdermabrasion is a much gentler treatment than dermabrasion and can be used to freshen facial skin that has light sun damage, spotty pigmentation, and fine wrinkling. It is an effective method of clearing clogged or enlarged pores, or refreshing a dull or oily skin texture.

"Microdermabrasion can diminish the appearance of scars and facial spots that have increased pigment," says Dr. Casas. "It can often be combined with peels and a home care skin program to achieve great improvement in skin texture and pigment."

A hand-held device continually sprays tiny crystals on the skin and then sucks them up along with the dirt and dead skin that has been dislodged. This combination of gentle abrasion and suction exfoliates the skin. As with light chemical peels, a series of treatments over a period of weeks or months is recommended to achieve maximum benefits such as reduction of fine lines. Treatments must continue to maintain results.

The process usually takes between 15 and 45 minutes for the face, and treatment of additional areas of the body, such as the neck, upper chest and hands will lengthen the procedure time.

Discomfort is limited to a slight tingling or stinging immediately following the procedure, but an anesthetic is unnecessary. Microdermabrasion is performed on an outpatient basis, usually in the doctor's office and often by a trained and licensed aesthetician or nurse. Under this type of care, patients undergoing microdermabrasion have little risk of complications. However, those with sensitive skin may experience greater irritation following the procedure. Most patients can go back to their normal activities immediately after treatment.

LASERS

An acronym for Light Amplification by Stimulated Emission of Radiation, lasers generate a concentrated stream of bright, pulsed light that can be used to help correct a variety of skin conditions. While some laser treatments result in complete skin resurfacing, others only help diminish fine wrinkles and discoloration. Lasers can penetrate deeply into the skin and promote reorganization of collagen, which helps diminish wrinkles and improve skin tone. They also have somewhat of a tightening effect, which can aid skin tone and appearance.

Although an effective method of facial rejuvenation, laser treatment is not a substitute for surgical procedures such as a face lift. Laser resurfacing may sometimes be performed in conjunction with another facial aesthetic procedure, such as a face lift or eyelid surgery.

"Laser peels can provide significant and long-lasting improvement of sun-damaged, unevenly pigmented, or coarsely wrinkled facial skin," says **Mark Sofonio, MD**, of Palm Springs, California, "Peels can be performed with superficial or deep lasers and may be used on your entire face (avoiding your brows and lips) or on a limited area, such as the vertical wrinkles around your mouth. Carbon dioxide lasers are generally the strongest and may be recommended if you have fair skin, severe sun damage, and deep wrinkles. Variants in the laser energy can create a milder treatment for broader use."

"There are different types of lasers that can be used for a variety of purposes — to help diminish pigmented areas, fine lines, scars, and to reduce unwanted hair," says Dr. Casas, who adds, "The future may bring lasers that can tighten the deeper layers of the skin and actually reduce skin laxity on any area of the body."

ABLATIVE LASERS

The carbon dioxide (CO_2) laser and Erbium laser (Er:Yag) are both ablative lasers, which means that they resurface the skin by vaporizing damaged skin layers and allowing healthier cells from deeper layers to surface and form a new, smoother outer layer of skin. This process achieves, by a different mechanism of action, effects similar to those of chemical peels and dermabrasion.

"We usually address fine lines with a carbon dioxide-based resurfacing laser," says **Alexander G. Digenis, MD**, of Louisville, Kentucky. "Although there were some problems with the laser in the past — such as over-lightening of the skin and sharp lines of demarcation between treated and non-treated areas, particularly at the jawline — plastic surgeons have developed techniques to eliminate such problems and provide excellent results. For example, most hypopigmentation problems were caused by treating the skin too deeply. We now treat at a much shallower depth, in each application and overall. We also treat areas such as the jawline by feathering the border onto the neck, which reduces any demarcation."

The laser can be used on the entire face or on specific areas to effectively treat wrinkles, blotchiness, age spots, and scars from acne or other causes. The CO_2 laser penetrates more deeply than the Erbium laser and produces more dramatic results. It can even produce a mild tightening effect; this effect generally is not sufficient to produce dramatic improvement in overall skin laxity, but it may be beneficial in certain areas such as the lower eyelid.

FAST FACTS
Ablative, Nonablative Lasers & Intense Pulsed Light

LENGTH OF PROCEDURE
ABLATIVE & NONABLATIVE
Generally from 15 to 60 minutes.
INTENSE PULSED LIGHT
About 20 minutes.

ANESTHESIA
ABLATIVE
Depending on the severity of the problem and the extent of the treatment, the procedure can be performed under sedation (twilight) anesthesia or general anesthesia.
NONABLATIVE
None required.
INTENSE PULSED LIGHT
Topical anesthetic may be used.

LENGTH OF STAY
ABLATIVE, NONABLATIVE & INTENSE PULSED LIGHT
Outpatient, home the same day.

RECOVERY
ABLATIVE
Back to work, two weeks; more strenuous activities, four to six weeks; complete fading of redness, up to six months.
NONABLATIVE
Virtually immediate.
INTENSE PULSED LIGHT
Typically pain-free; some redness may follow treatment and last for one or two hours.

RISKS/POSSIBLE COMPLICATIONS
Serious complications, while possible, are unlikely when performed by a qualified physician or, in some cases, by trained and licensed staff under medical supervision.

Risks include:
ABLATIVE
• Burns or injuries caused by laser heat.
• Scarring.
• Abnormal changes in skin color.
• Flare-ups of cold sores and, rarely, other infections.
NONABLATIVE
• Purpura (rupture of small blood vessels) may occur.
• Activation of herpes virus causing cold sores; rare.
INTENSE PULSED LIGHT
• Blistering or slight bleeding.
• Long-lasting pigmentation problems: Lightened or darkened areas of skin (hypo- or hyperpigmentation) can occur and last anywhere from three to 12 months.
• Permanent pigmentation changes.

The above-listed risks may be only some of those that your surgeon will discuss with you in greater detail during your consultation.

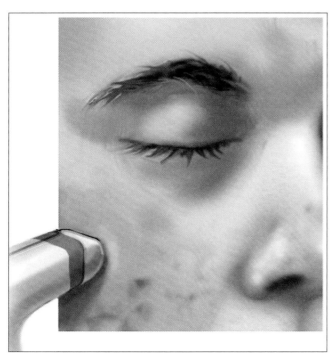

A variety of laser- and light-based treatments are available to effectively treat fine wrinkles, uneven pigmentation, age spots, and other skin problems. Ablative lasers achieve the most dramatic results and can require significant healing time. Nonablative lasers and light-based treatments generally result in more subtle improvements with little or no downtime.

"The carbon dioxide, or CO_2, laser, has been the gold standard ablative laser since the 1980s," says **Richard O. Gregory, MD**, of Celebration, Florida. "When we make the first pass with the laser, we are largely just disrupting the surface skin cells, which we can wipe away, removing a lot of the dull look of the skin. Treating the surface you also get some heating of the deeper cells, but the second, third, and subsequent passes are what really heat the deeper levels of the dermis. It is this deeper heating that shortens the collagen fibers and induces new collagen formation. The shortening gives you an almost immediate tightening effect. This effect is always greater in areas of thinner skin, such as the lower eyelids. Over a period of time, the healing process includes the growth of new vascular tissue and, ultimately, collagen remodeling."

The Erbium laser can vaporize very thin layers of skin and produces less thermal effect than the CO_2 laser,

which means that recovery is quicker but, again, results are more limited. Particular skin characteristics, such as thickness and texture, may influence whether a patient is a good candidate for either type of ablative laser resurfacing.

"As they age, my patients come in more often to correct a 'negative' facial expression, or to fill in lines and hollows, than for facial 'tightening,'" offers **Diane Duncan, MD**, of Fort Collins, Colorado. "Therefore, I tend to do a lot of noninvasive facial procedures. Fat grafting combined with Erbium laser resurfacing is a favorite treatment; it can truly help to restore a more youthful look and add elements of beauty."

THE CONSULTATION

Patients who are prone to keloids, hyper- or hypopigmentation, are dark-skinned, darkly tanned, or do not heal well from burns may not be good candidates for ablative laser skin resurfacing. People with ethnic ancestry where darker complexions are predominant may be prone to hyper- or hypopigmentation. In addition, patients with an impaired immune system, those who have used isotretinoin, a powerful drug for the treatment of acne, in the past 12 to 18 months, or had extensive radiation therapy, burns, or poor healing in the treatment area, may be advised not to undergo laser therapies. Your surgeon will determine if you are good candidate for treatment. Regardless of whether you fall into any of the aforementioned categories, he or she will want to review your complete medical history.

Your surgeon will examine the overall appearance and condition of your skin and check for prior scars. Depending upon your goals, he or she may recommend different or additional procedures. Your consultation will include a discussion of the details of the laser procedure, including risks and recovery time.

Preparation

Your surgeon may advise a pre-treatment plan to prepare the skin for laser resurfacing. This may include the use of alpha hydroxy and Retin-A to help stimulate collagen and aid in rapid healing. Skin bleaching agents are also often used to help avoid pigmentation irregularities that sometimes can occur after treatment. Your doctor or a member of the medical staff will also tell you how to care for your skin immediately following treatment and may suggest a maintenance regimen for long-term skin care. As with all medical procedures involving the use of sedatives and anesthesia, you should arrange for someone to drive you to and from the facility and to assist you when you first arrive home.

The Procedure

Laser resurfacing is usually an outpatient procedure that takes anywhere from 15 to 90 minutes and can be performed in the physician's office-based facility or an outpatient surgical center. You may be admitted to a hospital for more extensive resurfacing procedures or if laser therapy is performed in conjunction with other surgical procedures. The procedure can be performed under sedation (twilight) anesthesia, although general anesthesia may be used if resurfacing will be extensive or performed with other surgery. Whether you are awake and unaware of what is going on or you are unconscious, you will not feel any pain during the surgical procedure.

After covering your eyes and teeth with protective guards, your surgeon will perform laser resurfacing by passing the activated laser back and forth over the treatment area until reaching the appropriate depth in the dermis to achieve the desired correction. He or she will then cover the newly resurfaced skin with protective creams or ointments. Some doctors also cover the treated area with dressings, which will remain in place for the first five to 10 days of healing.

"The problem with the laser when it first became popular in the 1990s, was that physicians tended to over-treat the skin, and consequently there were complications," offers Rick J. Smith, MD, of East Lansing, Michigan. " I think it's important to ablate the skin slowly. I always expect to do a secondary procedure in six to nine months. By the second time around, the skin is much healthier, and it heals in four or five days instead of seven to eight days. It's a matter of giving the skin an opportunity to heal."

Post-treatment

You will most likely experience mild to moderate swelling, itching, and discomfort after the procedure. Your surgeon will prescribe medication and the use of ice packs to help you feel more comfortable. If a dressing was used, your surgeon may replace it with a fresh one within two days following the procedure. He or she will completely remove the dressing after about a week and apply a thin layer of ointment.

Your skin, which may be bright pink or red for weeks or months following the procedure, will probably take a couple of weeks to heal, during which time it will ooze, crust and peel. The newly exposed skin will be raw and sensitive, and your surgeon will instruct you how to care for it. It is very important to follow these instructions precisely. Inconsistent or incomplete care can delay healing, increase irritation, and cause infection. You will be presentable in public with makeup after about two weeks. Your doctor will instruct you about the importance of protecting the treated area from the sun, both immediately and long term.

"With our protocol, we apply a fibrin glue dressing immediately following the procedure, cover the skin with something like Vaseline to keep it very moist, and then four days later we'll start using Collagenase to break down any crusting that may develop," says Dr. Smith. "That way we keep the skin really clean. I tell patients to expect to be healed in seven to eight days and to be able to wear makeup in 10 days. Redness will last for months, but it can be well camouflaged with makeup."

It may take up to several months for you to see your final result, with significant improvement in skin quality and a fresher, smoother appearance. The results of laser skin rejuvenation are long-lasting; however, the aging process will continue. Over the ensuing years, the natural elements will take their toll, and your normal facial movements will eventually cause a recurrence of dynamic wrinkles. Protecting your face from the sun will help increase the longevity of improvements in your skin's texture. Laser treatments can be repeated as needed.

NONABLATIVE LASERS

Nonablative lasers use longer wavelengths to penetrate the skin's deeper layers while leaving the surface intact. These "gentler" lasers provide a new method to help improve the skin's overall tone and texture by promoting reorganization of collagen and elastin beneath the skin's surface. Nonablative lasers can also correct or improve pigmentation problems including some types of birthmarks. The results of nonablative laser treatments are not immediate, occurring over time as the gradual changes beneath the skin's surface take place. Multiple treatments are required to achieve results. Recovery following each treatment is nearly immediate with no appreciable downtime.

A variety of nonablative lasers is currently being used in aesthetic practices. Some of the laser product names include NLite, CoolTouch, and ThermaCool (or Thermage). The Fraxel laser is yet another form of nonablative laser therapy designed to improve skin texture and pigmentation, including fine lines and wrinkles, surgical, and acne scars, and sun damage. Fraxel delivers a series of microscopic pixel-like laser spots to a small fraction of the skin in the treatment area, preserving areas of unaffected, healthy skin. This allows the healthy cells to promote more rapid healing of the entire area. The technique has been compared to the way in which digital images can be altered pixel by pixel to produce a precisely touched-up photograph.

THE CONSULTATION

Your surgeon will help you to determine if you are a suitable candidate for nonablative laser therapy. Patients who are pregnant or who have a personal or family history of skin cancer, lupus, or Kaposi's sarcoma are advised against having this treatment. The use of certain medications, such as aspirin, anti-inflammatory or photosensitizing medications can affect the results of nonablative laser treatments. Your physician will want to review your entire medical history, including a list of all medications you have taken or are taking.

He or she will examine the overall appearance and condition of your skin and, depending upon your goals, may recommend different or additional procedures. Your surgeon will explain the details of nonablative laser treatments, including risks and recovery time.

The Procedure

With most types of nonablative lasers, the patient will feel a warming sensation during treatment but usually no other discomfort. Topical or injected anesthetic generally is not required. Your surgeon may apply a preparatory gel or ointment and then use the handheld device to pass the laser's pulsing light waves over the treatment area. Depending upon the size of the area and the severity of the problem, treatments can take from five to 60 minutes.

Post-treatment

With no apparent pain or damage following treatment, recovery is virtually immediate. You will be able to wear makeup and return to normal activities without delay. Sensitivity to sunlight is not increased, but the prudent use of sunscreen is always recommended to maintain healthy skin. Full results usually appear within 30 to 90 days. Multiple treatments are usually required to achieve optimal results.

INTENSE PULSED LIGHT

Intense Pulsed Light (IPL) therapy is another type of nonablative skin resurfacing treatment that uses emissions of high intensity pulses of light to penetrate the skin. The improvements resulting from IPL treatment are only in the upper skin layers and may include elimination or reduction of age/liver spots, fine wrinkles, facial flushing, redness, broken capillaries, spider veins, freckles, minor sun damage, port wine stains, and flat birth marks. The procedure causes little or no discomfort as cooling gels or devices are used to regulate skin temperature.

"We're reaching the point where light therapy can help tremendously," says Dr. Stofman. "In an ideal situation, light in combination with tissue fillers, chemical peels, mechanical dermabrasion, or microdermabrasion can keep the aging face younger-looking for a very long time."

"Most of my patients would like to be able to go without makeup so they don't want resurfacing treatments that could create noticeable areas of demarcation," says Dr. Duncan. "I find that microlaser resurfacing and broadband light treatments can correct a lot of the sun damage we see in this part of the country."

"Intense pulsed light can be applied to your neck, upper chest, and other areas of skin damaged by sun exposure," adds Dr. Sofonio.

THE CONSULTATION

Patients who are prone to keloids, hyper- or hypopigmentation, are dark-skinned, darkly tanned or do not react well to burns may not be good candidates for IPL. People with ethnic ancestry where darker complexions are predominant may be prone to hyper- or hypopigmentation. Because insulin-dependent diabetics are at risk for wound-healing and infection problems, they generally are not appropriate candidates, although there are exceptions. If you are diabetic, your plastic surgeon will most likely consult with your primary care physician before proceeding with treatment. Regardless of whether you fall into any of the aforementioned categories, your surgeon will want to review your entire medical history. Your surgeon will examine the overall appearance and condition of your skin. Depending upon your goals, he or she may recommend different or additional procedures. Your surgeon will explain the details of the procedure, including risks and recovery time.

The Procedure

IPL is an outpatient procedure usually performed in a physician's office-based facility or an outpatient surgery center. It may be performed in a hospital if scheduled in conjunction with other surgical procedures. Although this procedure is typically pain-free, your surgeon may apply a topical anesthetic to help ensure your comfort. Then he or she will apply a cold gel to the area to be treated. Your surgeon will then pass computer-controlled, precise bursts of light through the glass surface of the IPL applicator to the skin in the treatment area. Sessions usually take about 20 minutes. You may experience some redness. If this occurs, it generally lasts no longer than one or two hours. Mild blistering can occur for up to a week.

Post-treatment

Although you can resume your normal activities immediately following IPL treatment, you should protect treated areas from UV light by wearing adequate sunscreen. A series of treatments is usually necessary, and depending on the conditions being treated and skin type, your surgeon will formulate the best plan to meet your needs. The average treatment plan usually includes four to six treatments, with each lasting about 20 minutes. Although often subtle, the results of IPL can be long-lasting, with results from a full series of treatments.

Editor's Viewpoint

The cosmetic benefits of skin resurfacing are the result of a process of injury and wound repair that occurs at various tissue depths, depending on the selected treatment modality. The body responds to the action of the chemical peel, dermabrader, laser, or other light-based device in the same way that it repairs any wound. These steps include the growth of new, small blood vessels in the treated areas, creation and reorganization of collagen, thickening of the dermis, and other natural processes that all contribute to skin rejuvenation.

Whatever the modality of treatment, the induced mechanism of repair is similar. The depth of injury defines the severity of the response and, in turn, determines the side effects, length of recovery, and final result. Selecting the proper depth of the injury for any particular patient requires consideration of many factors. Among the most important are the thickness and pigmentation of their skin as well as their expectations for results and acceptance of extended "downtime."

Pre-treatment regimens, used at home for a period of time prior to skin resurfacing, can condition the skin and improve the results of resurfacing treatments. However, the most important factor is the knowledge, skill, and judgment of the individual administering the selected resurfacing method. Even the more superficial resurfacing techniques, used too aggressively, have the potential for complications. Too deep an intervention with any treatment modality can bring about unwanted pigmentary changes and even permanent scarring.

As described in this chapter, there are many different modalities to choose from, allowing for a highly customized approach to each patient's particular needs. As we have pointed out with regard to other cosmetic procedures, a very pleasing result may be obtained by various methods.

Laser technology continues to advance, offering new options. Nonablative lasers, which produce changes beneath the surface of the skin while causing minimal superficial injury, can be a good choice for patients with modest expectations of results. While the search for the "perfect" laser — one that can achieve dramatic improvements with little or no downtime for the patient — goes on, and while plastic surgeons continue to gain a better understanding of the effects of skin resurfacing in general, there has been somewhat of a revival of interest in methods more commonly used in the past. Dermabrasion and chemical peels, including deeper peeling agents with phenol — while perhaps not as "glamorous" as laser technology — are good options for certain patients. In general, these traditional methods are less involved, less expensive, and seemingly just as, if not more, effective in the long run.

Skin resurfacing, by itself or in combination with aesthetic surgical procedures, offers patients the opportunity to significantly reduce the cumulative damage caused by years of sun exposure and other environmental or lifestyle factors. Equally important are preventative and maintenance skin care programs that can, when used on a permanent basis, greatly assist in the quest to "be your best."

— *Peter B. Fodor, MD*

LASER HAIR REMOVAL

$\mathcal{A}n$ evolving technology that has shown significant advancement in recent years, laser hair removal has been proven as an effective means to gently remove unwanted hair from the face, upper lip, and underarms, as well as larger areas such as the neck, chest, breasts, back, abdomen, bikini line, and legs. The laser works by pulsing a penetrating light to the hair follicle and temporarily generating enough heat to cause injury to the follicle and inhibit hair growth.

Although the first hair removal lasers, which were ruby lasers, were best at removing dark hair from light skin and sometimes caused darker skin to blister or discolor, newer lasers may be more effective on all skin complexions. However, in patients with primarily lighter colored hair, intense pulsed light treatment may be another option. Your plastic surgeon will advise you of the best treatment for your individual situation.

Laser hair removal has been called permanent, but most patients will need to undergo repeat treatments. Hair grows in cycles and because the laser targets only actively growing, visible hair, follicles not affected by the treatment will still produce hair. Most patients require multiple treatments over weeks and months. Arrested hair growth has been reported in some patients after a series of treatments, but this is not the norm and should not be expected. Some patients experience periods as long as two years without hair growth, while others require treatment at three- to four-month intervals.

THE CONSULTATION

The consultation is a time for you and the surgeon to get to know and feel comfortable with each other. You should feel completely confident that the surgeon is fully qualified. If you haven't read sections in the beginning of this book about choosing a surgeon who is certified by the American Board of Plastic Surgery, perhaps you should do so now.

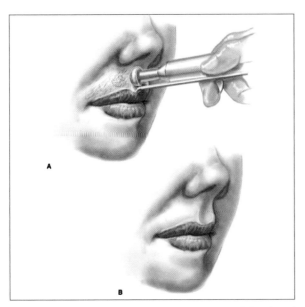

A. PRE-TREATMENT APPEARANCE. Unwanted facial and body hair can be removed by treating the follicle (base of each hair) with a small, handheld laser.
B. POST-TREATMENT APPEARANCE. Following treatment, the skin appears free of hair. Multiple treatments are usually required to target other hair follicles and maintain results.

Your surgeon will determine if you are a suitable candidate for laser hair removal and will want to review your entire medical history, including any medications you may currently be taking. He or she may ask you to avoid taking certain medications, such as aspirin and other nonsteroidal anti-inflammatory drugs, and some dietary supplements such as niacin and vitamin E, which can increase the risk of complications. Other factors that can negatively affect results include a history of abnormal scarring, excessive sun exposure, allergies, and herpes infection. If you have a suntan, your surgeon will most likely tell you to wait until it fades completely before proceeding with treatment, since a tan increases the risk of side effects such as blistering and discoloration.

PREPARATION

Because laser hair removal affects only short, visible hair, your surgeon will have you shave the area to be treated a few days before the procedure so it will present as short stubble at the time of treatment. Although laser hair removal usually creates only mild discomfort and can be performed without an anesthetic, your surgeon may advise you to apply a cream containing the anesthetic lidocaine 45 minutes prior to your treatment.

THE PROCEDURE

Laser hair removal treatments are usually performed in your plastic surgeon's office or outpatient facility. The procedure generally takes from 15 to 90 minutes, depending on the size of the treatment area. Your surgeon, or a specially trained technician under medical supervision, will perform the treatment by pressing a handheld laser to the skin and activating it for short bursts lasting only a second or so.

You will wear goggles during the procedure to protect your eyes from accidental exposure to laser light. Although discomfort is generally mild, you should not be alarmed if you smell a rather strong odor of singed hair during the procedure.

POST TREATMENT

Although you will be able to return to work immediately following treatment, you may experience some redness and slight swelling. It is not uncommon for skin to turn a pale purple color. This will usually subside within several days. Although less common, temporary scabbing and blistering is possible. You should avoid unprotected exposure to the sun for three to six months following treatment.

LENGTH OF SURGERY
Generally 15 to 90 minutes.

ANESTHESIA
Usually unnecessary or topical cream.

LENGTH OF STAY
Outpatient, home the same day.

RECOVERY
Can usually return to normal activities immediately following treatment. Any swelling, redness, or inflammation will usually resolve within several days.

RISKS/POSSIBLE COMPLICATIONS
When performed by a qualified and experienced physician or specially trained technician under medical supervision, the risks associated with laser hair removal are few. As with any medical procedure, however, the outcome can never be fully predicted.

Some risks and possible complications include:
• Temporary pain, swelling, redness, or blistering.
• Permanent scarring or skin discoloration; very rare.

The above-listed risks may be only some of those that your surgeon will discuss with you in greater detail during your consultation.

HAIR REPLACEMENT SURGERY

$\mathcal{A}$ full head of hair is associated with vitality and sexuality. No wonder that across cultures and throughout history great attention has been paid to the condition, care, and grooming of the hair. Hair loss is a common condition and one that can be deeply troubling. Men are not the only ones to suffer from hair loss. Some researchers estimate that 20 percent of all women will

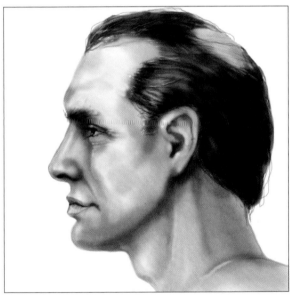

PREOPERATIVE APPEARANCE. Hair loss, a common occurrence for men and not uncommon among women, can occur in a variety of areas and patterns. A receding hairline, large bald areas, or patchy areas of hair loss can cause loss of self-confidence and can make a person look older than he or she feels.

experience some degree of hair loss, usually caused by aging, illness, or menopausal hormone changes.

Whether male or female, those wishing to correct hair loss have found little hope in an endless array of over-the-counter or special-order creams and lotions, most of which have proven to be of dubious value if not downright worthless. Topical prescription drugs can vary greatly in effectiveness from patient to patient, and while some may be helpful in preventing future hair loss, they generally do nothing to stimulate new hair growth.

Until recently, even surgical solutions such as hair transplantation left much to be desired, often leaving telltale signs such as relatively large punch grafts, or plugs, each of which contained many hairs and were quite noticeable. To many patients, the resultant clumps of hair, planted in the scalp like cornrows in a field, were more embarrassing than their original baldness.

Fortunately, the science and art of hair transplantation has evolved considerably. Today's methods, such as the so-called "megasessions," deliver vastly improved results. Rather than treating just a small section of the scalp at a time, or inserting large plugs containing many hairs, the megasession technique accomplishes a transplant that, for some patients, can deliver a natural-looking, permanent result in a single session.

Most patients are very happy with their hair transplants, yet it is important to understand that no matter how successful the surgery, you may never have the coverage you had before any hair loss occurred. Other than being in good health, the only prerequisite for hair transplantation is that you must have sufficient hair density at the back and sides of the head to serve as the donor sites.

THE CONSULTATION

The consultation is a time for the surgeon and patient to get to know and feel comfortable with each other. The patient should feel completely confident that the surgeon is fully qualified. If you haven't read sections in the beginning of this book about choosing a surgeon who is certified by the American Board of Plastic Surgery, you may want to do so now. Although not all plastic surgeons choose to perform hair transplantation, they usually can refer you to someone with whose qualifications and results they are familiar.

Your surgeon will evaluate the condition of your scalp, your hair growth and loss. He or she will review your hereditary factors and ask if you've had any previous hair replacement surgery. Your surgeon will also need to review your entire medical history, including any medications you may currently be taking, whether you suffer from any allergies or medical conditions, and if you have had any prior surgeries.

PREPARATION

Your surgeon will give you instructions about how to prepare for surgery. He or she will also give you guidelines on eating, drinking and medications, such as avoiding aspirin or anti-inflammatory medications that promote bleeding. You should arrange to have someone drive you to and from your hair transplantation procedure.

THE SURGERY

All hair transplant surgery involves moving hair-bearing scalp from a donor site on the head and to bald or thinning areas. Surgeons use varied techniques to accomplish this and, as in other forms of aesthetic surgery, the patient's individual characteristics often dictate the best method. Grafts — whether mini, micro, punch or strip grafts — are usually most appropriate for achieving moderate corrections of bald or thinning hair. Transplantation may be conducted in one session or over multiple surgical sessions.

Round-shaped punch grafts usually contain about 10 to 15 hairs each; mini-grafts contain about two to four hairs, and the micro-graft contains one to two hairs. Another alternative is the slit graft, for which slits are created in the scalp and the grafts containing about four to 10 hairs are inserted into them. Similarly, strip grafts are long and thin and contain 30 to 40 hairs each.

During a hair transplantation megasession, between 1,000 and 2,500 micro- or mini-grafts of the patient's own hair can be inserted. Using these

LENGTH OF SURGERY
Usually two to six hours, depending upon technique.

ANESTHESIA
Usually local anesthetic and intravenous sedation, although general anesthesia may be used.

LENGTH OF STAY
Outpatient procedure, home same day.

RECOVERY
Initial mild to moderate discomfort; resume most normal activities, including return to work, in one to two weeks; scabbing for two weeks; transplanted hair falls out and grows back over a two or three month period; final result in eight months to one year.

SCARS
Usually undetectable with micro- or mini-grafts, sometimes can be seen with other techniques.

RISKS/POSSIBLE COMPLICATIONS
When procedure is performed by a qualified surgeon, complications are infrequent and usually minor.

- Patchy hair growth: Less common when using mini- or micro-grafts.
- Wide scars: With scalp reduction technique, can result from tension on scalp.
- Grafts not "taking."
- Bleeding: rare and easily controlled.
- Infection.

The above-listed risks may be only some of those that your surgeon will discuss with you in greater detail during your consultation.

numerous tiny grafts, the surgeon can eliminate the plug-like look and scarring associated with earlier techniques and can artfully craft a natural-looking hairline.

Flap surgery is a considerably different method. With flap surgery, the surgeon cuts out a section of bald scalp and then lifts a flap of hair-bearing skin, leaving one end still attached to preserve the original blood supply. This flap is then moved over the area from which the bald scalp was removed and is sewn into place. Although this technique has been in use for decades, its popularity has been limited because of its downsides, which can include an unnaturally abrupt and dense hairline and scarring at both donor and recipient sites.

Tissue expansion is another method of hair replacement surgery. The surgeon inserts a device called a tissue expander beneath hair-bearing scalp that is adjacent to a bald area. Over a period of weeks, the balloon-like device is inflated with saltwater, which causes the skin to expand and even grow some new cells. It also, however, creates a huge bulge over a several-week

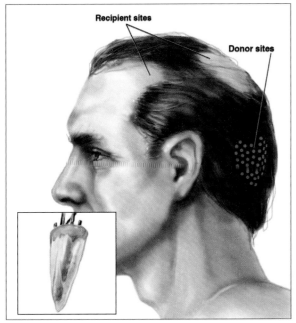

Recipient sites

Donor sites

Among the more common hair transplantation methods, the use of micro- and mini-grafts involves removal of tiny ellipses of hair-bearing scalp (inset) from a donor site and insertion of these grafts into hair loss, or recipient, sites. Other techniques such as flaps, tissue expansion, or scalp reduction may be more efficient albeit less natural-looking alternatives for correction of extensive bald areas.

period. After about two months, the skin beneath the hair has usually stretched enough, and in another procedure resembling flap surgery the expanded skin is brought over to cover the bald area.

Scalp reduction presents another method of hair replacement surgery dealing with hair loss. This technique, sometimes called advanced flap surgery, is not suited for the frontal hairline and only works for coverage of bald areas at the top and back of the head. With scalp reduction, the surgeon injects the scalp with a local anesthetic and removes a section of bald scalp. Depending on the patient's individual characteristics, sections can be removed in varied patterns such as an inverted Y-shape when a large amount of coverage is needed. Other shapes include a U-shape and a pointed oval. The surgeon then loosens and pulls hair-bearing skin surrounding the cut-out area, bringing the sections together and securing them with stitches. The patient often feels this tension as a tugging sensation, and there may be temporary discomfort.

Scalp reduction may require multiple surgeries over many months, with each session involving a healing cycle. Multiple surgeries are necessary because most patients' skin is not elastic enough to allow for removal of more than just a few square inches at a time. Scars may be very noticeable between procedures, and it is not uncommon for the head to feel extremely tight for quite a long time.

There are instances in which these somewhat more inconvenient methods are an appropriate choice — particularly when coverage is needed over a large area, which would take a long period of time and many surgical sessions to accomplish using individual grafts. For properly selected candidates, though, the megasession using mini- and micro-grafts is an attractive option with minimal downtime.

"Performing hair transplantation by the method of conducting a megasession, and using mini- or micro-grafts, eliminates many of the problems, such as the large punch grafts or plugs, or the temporary deforming bulge on the scalp associated with the tissue expansion technique," says **Alfonso Barrera, MD**, of Houston, Texas, "but the method alone is no guarantee of success. To obtain a truly natural-appearing result, the surgeon needs to be skilled and experienced and have the patience and temperament to pay strict attention to a multitude of details, such as the natural inclination and orientation of the hair. Although most people's hair is angled forward at 45 degrees, some have hair that grows at different angles and in different directions, such as upward or to the side. It is important to transplant hair that imitates the hair native to that area. We have to use very tiny grafts and place them with extreme accuracy to prevent problems, such as pitting and cobblestoning."

This technique is usually performed as an outpatient procedure under sedation (twilight) anesthesia, where a sedative is administered followed by a long-acting anesthetic that will render the treatment area completely numb for the entire day. If the patient wishes, sedation can generally be reduced after the first hour of surgery, allowing the patient to be awake and alert although feeling no pain or discomfort. Depending on the number of grafts, the procedure usually takes four to six hours to perform.

To perform a megasession hair transplant, your surgeon will remove an ellipse of hair-bearing scalp from the back of the head, the donor site. This site is stitched closed and the resulting scar is well hidden within the hair. Unlike the punch grafts, where a tube-like instrument made of sharp carbon steel is used to punch out a round graft from the donor site and insert it in the treatment area, mini- or micro-grafts are inserted in very small slits about 1.5 millimeters apart in the bald area. The surgeon must place the grafts with great skill and precision. To achieve the most natural appearance, he or she must select grafts that contain hair that is growing in the proper direction for the area into which they are being placed. Furthermore, being able to feather the individual hairs contained in the tiny grafts at the hairline greatly enhances the natural look. The grafts and slits are so small and heal so well that they usually leave no visible scars.

POST OP

Following hair transplantation, a turban-like bandage will be applied to the treatment area. This can usually be removed after 48 hours, at which time you will be able to wash your hair. Depending on how you feel and your individual situation, you will be able to resume normal activities, such as returning to work, within a few days. Your surgeon may, however, instruct you to avoid vigorous exercise for at least three weeks so as not to greatly increase blood flow to the scalp and cause possible bleeding. He or she may

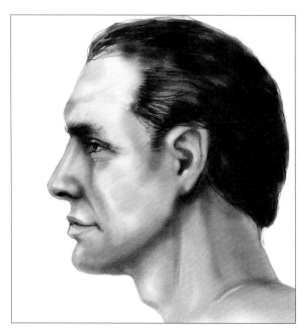

POSTOPERATIVE APPEARANCE. The results of most hair transplantation methods are natural-looking and permanent. Grafts taken from donor sites will continue to grow in the transplanted area, creating a fuller, more youthful-looking head of hair.

also advise you to avoid sexual activity for at least 10 days following surgery.

Sutures will be removed in seven to 10 days. Many small scab-like crusts will form in the treatment area over the next two weeks and as these dry, they will fall off. Between two to four weeks following the procedure, some of the transplanted hair will fall out. This will start growing back within two to three months. The final result is usually evident within eight to 12 months. Although many patients achieve their desired result in one session, some repeat the procedure after one year to achieve even greater density.

LOOKING AHEAD

The results of most hair transplantations are permanent. That's because hair growth is controlled by genetic information that is stored in the hair root, and most people are not "programmed" to lose hair at the back of their head, from where the grafts are removed. Hair taken from this area usually will continue to grow in the transplanted area for a lifetime.

HAND REJUVENATION

Although patients seeking to rejuvenate their appearance most often are concerned first about their face, the hands are another highly visible area of the body that can reveal aging. Exposure to the elements and the passing of years both take their toll on the appearance of your hands. Youthful hands are full with smooth and relatively blemish-free skin, but as hands age, skin loses its elasticity, pigmented spots begin to develop, and the loss of fatty tissue accentuates the appearance of unsightly veins.

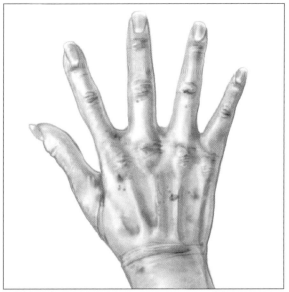

PREOPERATIVE APPEARANCE. The aging hand appears bony, wrinkled, and displays unattractive pigmentary changes.

After someone has undergone facial procedures to achieve a more youthful appearance, hands that looked bony and blotchy appear incongruous. That's why, in recent years, there has been growing interest in procedures to rejuvenate the hands. These cosmetic procedures are increasingly seen as desirable adjuncts to other types of rejuvenating surgery.

Hand rejuvenation may involve staged procedures that treat both the skin and the tissues.

These include topical application of products such as Retin-A and glycolic acid derivatives, laser or intense pulsed light treatments, chemical peels, microdermabrasion, and sclerotherapy for treatment of veins. Natural or synthetic soft tissue fillers can be injected to plump the tissues of the hands and help restore the fullness of youth.

Many of the products, materials, and devices used in hand rejuvenation are also used to treat other parts of the body, such as the face and the legs, and are covered in further detail in other sections of this book.

Many people are not aware that, in addition to the benefits, hand rejuvenation has risks. The hands have a slower rate of healing than the face, which can increase the possibility of infection, scarring, and pigmentation problems. Hand rejuvenation should always be performed or supervised by a qualified physician.

THE CONSULTATION

The consultation is a time for the surgeon and patient to get to know and feel comfortable with each other. The patient should feel completely confident that the surgeon is fully qualified. If you haven't read sections in the beginning of this book about choosing a surgeon who is certified by the American Board of Plastic Surgery, you may want to do so now.

Good communication between you and your surgeon is vital to a satisfying outcome. It is essential that you know exactly what bothers you about the changing appearance of your hands and that you can specifically describe the problem to your surgeon. When you express these openly and precisely, your surgeon can better give you an accurate idea of what you can realistically expect.

In determining if you are a suitable candidate for hand rejuvenation, your surgeon will review your entire medical history. He or she will examine your hands to evaluate the aging changes that have occurred. It is important to make sure that the condition of your hands is not due to dermatologic conditions, such as eczema or even skin cancer, which may require a different type of treatment.

Your surgeon will discuss with you the treatment that he or she recommends. Included in this discussion should be a reasonable estimate of how many treatments may be required and over what period of time before results are achieved. Many of the treatments for hand rejuvenation require maintenance, and your surgeon will indicate as much as possible how often repeat treatments may be needed in order to maintain the benefits.

In general, rejuvenation of the hands may involve both treatment of damaged skin and restoration of tissue volume.

SKIN RESURFACING TREATMENTS

Methods for treating the skin include chemical peels, microdermabrasion, intense pulsed light, and lasers. Prior to some of these treatments, patients often are placed on a regimen of at-home care that may include topical application of Retin-A, alpha-hydroxy acids (such as glycolic acid), and hydroquinone bleaching cream applied directly to age spots. In some cases, these treatments alone may provide sufficient improvement and side effects are limited. If bleaching creams are used to treat spots, they should be carefully applied to avoid surrounding skin. If used as a pre-treatment, topical products may be continued for a number of weeks prior to the patient undergoing more extensive rejuvenative procedures.

Chemical Peels

Chemical peels can be used to revitalize finely wrinkled, blemished, unevenly pigmented, or sun-damaged skin on the hands. Chemical peels are also effective in treating pre-cancerous skin growths. The procedure involves using a chemical solution to peel away the skin's damaged outer layers, allowing for new cells to grow and produce a smoother, more evenly pigmented skin surface. The results of chemical peels are not permanent, and they do not stop or slow down the aging process. In addition, following

For fast facts about the various methods of hand rejuvenation, please refer to the chapters in this book that pertain to each:

SOFT TISSUE FILLERS
can be found in Injectable Treatments for Aesthetic Facial Enhancement.

CHEMICAL PEEL,
MICRODERMABRASION,
INTENSE PULSED LIGHT,
AND LASERS
can be found in Skin Resurfacing.

SCLEROTHERAPY
can be found in the chapter on Spider Vein Treatment.

RISKS/POSSIBLE
COMPLICATIONS
Please refer to the chapters listed above for possible complications for each method of hand rejuvenation.

Your surgeon will discuss possible risks and complications of these procedures with you in detail during your consultation.

a chemical peel the skin will be even more vulnerable to sun damage so careful sun protection is mandatory.

Chemical peels most commonly used in hand rejuvenation include glycolic acid, Jessner's solution, and trichloroacetic acid (TCA). For deeper pigmentation problems, stronger solutions may be used, but with protracted healing time and greater risk of complications. Adverse effects may include post-treatment hypopigmentation or hyperpigmentation, noticeable demarcation between treated and untreated areas, and scarring.

Glycolic acid, the most superficial of the peel formulas, is sometimes called an alpha-hydroxy acid (AHA) peel or "fruity" acid peel. This type of peel can provide an alternative for people with mild skin problems, such as areas of dryness, minor sun damage, or uneven pigmentation. Glycolic acid, like other peels, can be applied at various concentrations. For example, a 70-percent glycolic acid peel provides deep penetration and may be used to treat particularly stubborn age spots.

Trichloroacetic acid (TCA) is generally used to produce a medium-depth peel that treats fine surface wrinkles, superficial blemishes or pigment problems. Once healed, TCA peel will not diminish your skin's ability to produce pigment. However, the newly formed layers of skin will be quite sensitive. Because of the hand's constant mobility and reduced blood supply, healing may be protracted. Sun exposure must be avoided for as long as several months, and sun protection should be maintained for life.

Microdermabrasion

Microdermabrasion can be used to gently freshen skin that has been damaged by the sun and the effects of aging. A hand-held device continually sprays tiny crystals on the skin, and then sucks them up along with the dirt and dead skin that have been dislodged. This combination of gentle abrasion and suction exfoliates the skin. As with light chemical peels, a series of treatments over a period of weeks or months is recommended to achieve maximum benefits. Treatments must continue to maintain results. Microdermabrasion is often performed by a trained and licensed aesthetician under medical supervision.

Intense Pulsed Light

A relatively new therapy for skin care, Intense Pulsed Light (IPL) therapy uses emissions of high intensity pulses of light to penetrate the skin. IPL reduces or eliminates many visible skin problems on the hands, including age/liver spots, freckles, and minor sun damage; the goal is overall improvement in skin pigmentation and texture. The procedure causes little or no discomfort since the skin is protected with a cooling gel. Light pulses are emitted through a hand piece that is applied to the skin, covering a relatively large area rather quickly.

Lasers

While some laser treatments result in complete skin resurfacing, others are designed to diminish localized discolorations such as age spots. When used on the hands, such spot treatment is usually the primary aim. Multiple treatments may be required.

Some physicians feel that overall resurfacing of the hands using either the carbon dioxide (CO_2) laser and Erbium laser (ER: Yag) has too many side effects to be useful. Both these devices are ablative lasers, which means that they resurface the skin by vaporizing damaged skin layers and allowing healthier cells from deeper layers to surface and form a new, smoother outer layer of skin. If a large area of the hand is treated with one of these types of lasers, patients may require sedation or regional anesthesia. Following treatment with ablative lasers, healing time can be extensive. However, for some patients, the more dramatic results achieved by these resurfacing treatments may be worth the extended recovery time and higher risk of complications.

Nonablative lasers use longer wavelengths to penetrate the skin's deeper layers while leaving the surface intact. These gentler lasers are a new method used to help remove certain skin discolorations, improve texture, and with repeated treatments, help promote reorganization of collagen and elastin. Following treatment with nonablative lasers, there is no appreciable downtime. However, results are not as dramatic as with ablative lasers.

In addition to using resurfacing techniques to treat surface irregularities of the skin, various methods are also used to add volume to the hands.

SOFT TISSUE FILLERS

Today, materials such as injectable collagen, hyaluronic acid (Restylane, Hylaform, Captique), and fat can be used to help restore a fuller, more youthful appearance to the hands. Because so much material must be injected, at significant expense to the patient, fat is often the substance of choice for hand rejuvenation. Newer materials such as injectable poly-L-lactic acid (Sculptra) may prove to be useful as well.

Injections to the hands are usually performed with the patient under local anesthesia. Material typically is injected through the web spaces between the fingers and into the dorsum (top portion) of the hand. Additional injections may be made along the tops of the fingers. Because of the large volume of material needed for effective treatment of the hands as well as the thinness of the skin, proper injection technique into deeper tissue layers is extremely important. For some materials, immediate light massaging by the surgeon will help smooth the contour. Following the procedure, patients may be instructed to restrict hand movements for several days or longer. Repeat treatments are necessary to maintain results.

Additional information on these filler materials appears in the Injectable Treatments for Aesthetic Facial Enhancement chapter.

SCLEROTHERAPY

Another procedure used in hand rejuvenation, sclerotherapy, is also used to treat spider veins in the legs and face. Patients who may not be good candidates for hand sclerotherapy include women who have undergone radical mastectomy, individuals with a dialysis shunt, or those with injury to the deep veins. The veins of the hands are normal veins of large caliber, requiring higher doses of sclerosant than are used in, for example, facial areas. Although there are a number of alternative sclerosants, one of the most frequently used is hypertonic (high concentration) saline.

After injection, the area may be massaged and then wrapped; bandages may stay in place for anywhere from two to 24 hours, depending on the surgeon's instructions. Typically, two or more sessions are required to treat the hands. Results of sclerotherapy of the hands are often permanent.

LOOKING AHEAD

Although the hands are often overlooked when assessing one's appearance, clearly they are an area of the body that shows significant signs of aging. Patients who desire a totally rejuvenated appearance may wish to take advantage of advances in cosmetic procedures and technology that have made hand rejuvenation an achievable goal. The results of these procedures are generally not permanent, and maintaining youthful looking hands requires a commitment to continue therapies indefinitely. It is also important to shield your hands from further damage from the elements, particularly sunlight. With proper attention and protection, your hands can be as attractive and youthful as the rest of you.

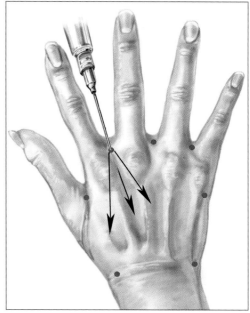

Injections of soft tissue filler often are placed through the web spaces between the fingers and into the dorsum (top) of the hand. Additional injections may be made along the tops of the fingers.

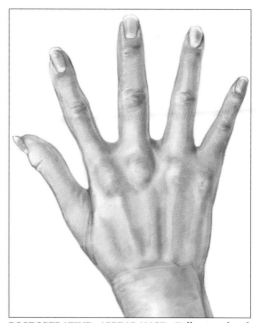

POSTOPERATIVE APPEARANCE. Following hand rejuvenation procedures, the dorsum (top of hand) and fingers appear fuller, and skin texture and pigmentation are improved.

SPIDER VEIN TREATMENT

There are several effective ways to treat spider veins (telangiectasias) — those stringy, unsightly clusters of red, blue, or purple veins, and small superficial varicose veins, which most commonly appear on the thighs, calves, and ankles. Treatment modalities include laser treatment, sclerotherapy, and simple coagulation with a fine electro-cautery needle.

LASER TREATMENT

Lasers can be used to effectively treat small and medium size spider veins. They are an excellent option for patients who are fearful of needles as well as for those who do not tolerate sclerotherapy or whose vessels do not respond to sclerotherapy.

A properly skilled and experienced physician using the correct type of laser can accurately direct strong bursts of light energy through the skin, causing the targeted vein to slowly fade and disappear. The treatment is noninvasive, and the administration of pain medications or local anesthetic usually is not necessary. Cooling the area helps alleviate any discomfort. Laser treatments typically last 15 to 20 minutes, and a treatment regimen to remove spider veins in the legs, depending on the severity of the condition, usually consists of two to five sessions, with the average being three treatments administered at three-month intervals.

Spider veins will appear darker and more visible imme-diately following laser treatment but will fade over two to six weeks. Patients will usually see a 30 to 40 percent improvement in leg spider veins following each treatment session. Some possible side effects associated with laser

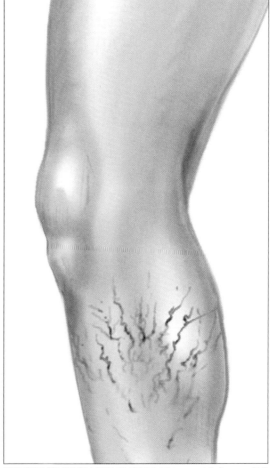

PRE-TREATMENT APPEARANCE. Thin, unsightly, purplish veins (spider veins) appear in clusters on the legs.

treatment of leg veins include redness or swelling of the skin immediately following treatment, which usually disappears within a few days, and skin discoloration, usually disappearing within one to two months.

SCLEROTHERAPY

Sclerotherapy is the most commonly used treatment for spider veins. Treatment involves the injection of a sclerosing solution, such as concentrated saline, which causes the veins to collapse and seal shut by scarring. The scarring is not visible and the spider veins literally disappear. Sclerotherapy may also remedy the bothersome symptoms associated with spider veins, including aching, burning, swelling, and night cramps. Sclerotherapy is predictable and relatively painless. Patients often require two to six sclerotherapy sessions to achieve their desired results. Repeat sessions can sometimes be performed as soon as one month apart.

THE CONSULTATION

The consultation is a time for the surgeon and patient to get to know and feel comfortable with each other. The patient should feel completely confident that the surgeon is fully qualified. If you haven't read sections in the beginning of this book about choosing a surgeon who is certified by the American Board of Plastic Surgery, you may want to do so now. In aesthetic plastic surgery, good communication between surgeon and patient is a vital component of achieving a successful outcome. It is extremely important that you tell your surgeon everything that bothers you about the appearance of your veins. Treatment modalities affect only veins that are visible; they will not prevent new veins from surfacing in the future. Your surgeon will discuss your goals and help you arrive at realistic expectations for the procedure.

He or she will need to review your entire medical history, including any medications you may currently be taking, whether you suffer from any allergies or medical conditions, and if you have had any prior surgeries. Some conditions that may preclude sclerotherapy include hepatitis, AIDS, or other blood-borne diseases. Your surgeon will examine your legs, checking for any signs of deep vein problems, and may even use a handheld ultrasound device to detect any backflow within the venous system. Neither laser treatment nor sclerotherapy will affect deep vein problems, and these problems must be treated before treatment of the surface veins can be successful in the long term. Your surgeon will also ask about other leg problems, such as tenderness, aching, pain, or itching. Prior to sclerotherapy, you may be given guidelines on eating, drinking, smoking, and medications, such as avoiding aspirin or anti-inflammatory medications that promote bleeding.

LENGTH OF PROCEDURE
Generally 15 to 45 minutes.

ANESTHESIA
Usually unnecessary.

LENGTH OF STAY
Outpatient, home the same day.

RECOVERY
Can usually return to normal activities within three to 10 days following treatment. Any redness or bruising will likely resolve within one month.

RISKS/POSSIBLE COMPLICATIONS
When performed by a qualified and experienced physician, the risks associated with sclerotherapy are few. As with any medical procedure, the outcome is not fully predictable.

Some possible risks and complications include:
• Blood clot formation.
• Severe inflammation.
• Adverse allergic reaction to sclerosing solution.
• Pigmentation irregularity (usually temporary) and telangiectatic matting (when fine reddish blood vessels appear around the treated area).
• Skin necrosis: Can occur if solution injection misses vein and is injected into skin or fat; would result in a small wound that should heal in five to 10 days but could leave a scar.

The above-listed risks may be only some of those that your surgeon will discuss with you in greater detail during your consultation.

PREPARATION

You should not wear any type of moisturizer, sunscreen, or oil on your legs on the day of the procedure. For convenience, you may want to bring some shorts to wear during the treatment process and slacks to wear home afterward.

THE PROCEDURE

Each sclerotherapy session generally lasts from 15 to 45 minutes, depending on the area being treated. While you lie on the examination table, the surgeon will cleanse the area with antiseptic solution and inject the sclerosing agent into the veins to be treated. Injections are usually placed about one inch apart along the length of the spider veins.

A normal session may comprise anywhere from five to 40 injections, however, often one injection placed at the base of a "tree" of spider veins, may cause all the interconnected branches to collapse. You will probably feel a slight burning sensation with each injection; but because the needles are extremely small, any discomfort will usually be mild. Anesthesia is unnecessary. After injecting the solution, your surgeon will probably cover the injection sites with cotton balls and tape.

POST-TREATMENT

The cotton balls and tape can usually be removed within 48 hours of your sclerotherapy treatment. Your surgeon will probably instruct you to wear medical-grade compression hose or ace bandages around the clock for anywhere from three to 10 days, removing them only to bathe. He or she will also ask that during this initial recovery period you refrain from taking hot baths, squatting, prolonged standing or sitting, particularly with crossed legs, heavy lifting, running, or any strenuous activity that could, at this early stage, lead to re-dilation of the blood vessels and compromise your results. Your surgeon will probably instruct you to walk for short periods to help prevent blood clots from forming in deep veins of the legs.

You may experience some cramping in your legs during the first few days following sclerotherapy. This will soon diminish and medication is usually unnecessary. You should not be surprised to see some bruising and redness at the injection sites. Your treated veins will probably look worse before they get better. Although bruising usually diminishes within one month, some discoloration may not completely fade for up to a year.

After the initial recovery period, usually about five days, you should be able to resume normal activities, although you probably won't want to wear clothing that reveals your legs for about two weeks.

LOOKING AHEAD

Most patients are extremely pleased with the results of spider vein treatments. They find the skin on their legs appears younger, healthier and clearer. Many patients who used to shun shorts and short skirts, or felt uncomfortable baring their legs in a bathing suit, feel a wonderful sense of freedom in being able to once again wear these garments without embarrassment.

Although the improvement in treated veins is generally permanent, new spider veins may emerge in the future. Of course, you can always have additional therapies if new veins surface, but your legs will look better as a result of your initial treatments.

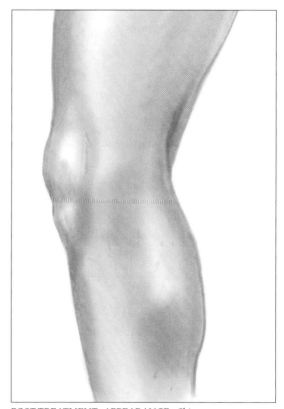

POST-TREATMENT APPEARANCE. Skin appears younger, healthier and clearer following laser treatments or multiple injections of a sclerosing agent that collapse and seal vein clusters.

■ SPECIAL TOPICS

AESTHETIC PLASTIC SURGERY
for men

Throughout this book, our experts have emphasized that cosmetic surgery must be "customized" to suit the individual needs of each patient. And while we have not talked extensively about the differences between men and women, it is certainly true that different considerations may apply to plastic surgical treatment of the male patient. Some of these factors involve modified surgical approaches due to common male physical characteristics and others have more to do with differences between male and female aesthetics. But first, let's examine the growing phenomenon of men undergoing appearance-enhancing surgery.

CHANGING TECHNIQUES AND ATTITUDES

It's a fact that attitudes about cosmetic surgery have changed. Men are more interested in their appearance, and society exhibits a growing obsession with youth, which many people feel translates to competitiveness in the workforce as well as greater satisfaction in one's personal life. And while more women than men actually undergo cosmetic surgery, almost as many men as women say they approve of it. In fact, a 2006 consumer survey sponsored by the American Society for Aesthetic Plastic Surgery (ASAPS) showed that 52 percent of American men generally approve of cosmetic surgery, and 79 percent say they would not be embarrassed about having surgery themselves.

Statistics show that the number of men seeking an enhanced appearance through cosmetic procedures is significant — approaching 1 million per year. In 2005, it is estimated that men comprised between nine and 12 percent of those undergoing cosmetic surgery and nonsurgical cosmetic treatments. According to ASAPS,

the most popular surgical procedures for men in 2005 were liposuction, rhinoplasty, eyelid surgery, male breast reduction, and face lift. Nonsurgical procedures finding the greatest acceptance among men included Botox, laser hair removal, microdermabrasion, Restylane, and laser skin resurfacing.

Yet, the impression that more men are opting for aesthetic plastic surgery mainly because of attitudinal changes misses an important point: In the past, results of cosmetic surgery were not nearly as good as those achieved today, and the special challenges of male aesthetic surgery were yet to be resolved. With facial rejuvenation surgery, for example, scars that could not be well hidden and a noticeable shift in hairline were simply not acceptable to most men — and, indeed, barely acceptable to many women.

Today, options such as endoscopic surgery, using very small incisions that can be well concealed, or other incisional approaches designed specifically to avoid hairline shift have made the benefits of aesthetic surgery more accessible to men.

"It can be reasonably argued that the main reason for the increasing numbers of women and men undergoing cosmetic procedures is the same for both," says **Robert W. Bernard, MD**, of White Plains, New York. "And that is that the results of aesthetic plastic surgery have gotten so much better. Patients undergoing rejuvenative treatments can expect to look refreshed rather than 'operated.' And those wanting to augment, reduce or enhance specific features of their face and body can do so more quickly, safely and subtly than in the past."

Men generally have thicker skin than women and a richer blood supply. The downside: With facial surgery, they tend to bleed more and are at greater risk for the formation of a hematoma, pooling of blood under the skin that sometimes requires surgical removal. On the other hand, men usually heal very well, with good quality scars that are difficult to detect.

FACIAL CONSIDERATIONS

A significant difference between men and women is the presence of facial hair, and this must always be considered when planning a face lift in a male patient. A surgeon treating a male patient has to note how high the beard-growing skin extends up the cheeks or how far down the neck in order to plan the correct surgical approach for each patient.

"For men, you have to consider the beard pattern and beard color," says **Bruce F. Connell, MD**, of Santa Ana, California. "If a man has brown hair but a reddish beard, you don't want to elevate the beard up into the temple area."

Following a face lift, due to the pull and subsequent redraping of the facial skin, a portion of the beard may end up in the tragus, which is the curved skin in front of the ear, or behind the ear. This is not considered a "mistake" of surgery but, rather, an expected outcome. The solution is either to shave these areas regularly or to undergo laser hair removal as a more permanent remedy.

Baldness, a receding hairline, thinning hair, and the potential for hairline or sideburn shift are other challenges in male aesthetic surgery. Incisions may be custom-designed to deal with these problems. It is important to discuss with your plastic surgeon how he or she plans to address these issues — where incisions will be placed and how discreet they will likely be when healed.

When rejuvenating the eyelids and elevating the brows, plastic surgeons must consider the important differences between male and female facial aesthetics. A dramatically elevated and arched brow is distinctly feminine and should be avoided in the male patient. Likewise, excessive removal of upper eyelid skin on a male patient may result in an over-feminized look.

"One big difference in eyelid surgery with men and women is that in a man there is rarely need for any upper eyelid skin to be removed," says Dr. Connell. "If a man looks sad and you simply raise the eyebrow, it makes him look energetic and wide awake."

Men frequently seek lower eyelid surgery to reduce under-the-eye bags and puffiness, which can make them appear tired and even unhealthy. Nonsurgical treatments such as Botox and soft tissue fillers can further refresh the eye and forehead areas, reducing frown lines and creating a more relaxed look.

Many men are concerned about their neck, which is often one of the areas to show significant signs of aging. If the problem is simply excess fat, liposuction may be the answer. But often, there is significant skin sagging as well, which is best corrected in conjunction with a face lift. Although men are increasingly willing to undergo face lift surgery, there are instances in which male patients may prefer an isolated procedure to address problems with the neck. These alternatives are described in our chapter, Neck Contouring and Rejuvenation. Men generally are satisfied with modest improvement that can sometimes be achieved by more limited procedures.

About a quarter of all rhinoplasties, chin augmentations, and cheek implant procedures are performed on male patients. With these surgeries, as well, the plastic surgeon must keep in mind the facial characteristics that comprise a masculine appearance.

In general, a masculine nose is longer and straighter than a female nose. A masculine chin is often termed a "strong" chin and can be more prominent than what might be considered aesthetically appealing for a female. Cheek implants for a male are usually for the purpose of correcting excessive facial flatness rather than creating high, dramatic cheekbones, which are considered feminine.

Naturally, the patient's own personal sense of aesthetics is as important, or more important, than accepted ideals of "masculine" and "feminine" traits. As in all aesthetic surgery, it is important for the plastic surgeon and patient to thoroughly discuss the goals for surgery and agree on what is realistic. For whatever reason, men often have been found to be less accepting of significant changes in their appearance, especially in conjunction with rhinoplasty surgery. That's another reason why doctor and patient must get to know each other and feel comfortable prior to undertaking any type of cosmetic surgery.

THE MALE BODY

In addition to facial cosmetic surgery, male body contouring is a rapidly expanding area of plastic surgery practice. Liposuction — which, in men, is most often used to reduce double chins, "love handles" around the waist, abdominal fat, and enlarged male breasts — is usually performed as an outpatient procedure. Involving only small incisions that are virtually undetectable when healed, liposuction is appealing because of its effectiveness and fairly short recovery time; most patients undergoing the type of liposuction procedures mentioned above can return to normal, nonstrenuous activities in about one week.

Body sculpting with liposuction, sometimes called "etching," can be used to enhance an already well-toned physique.

"I published my first article on liposuction etching, a liposuction technique used to improve the athletic contour of the muscles of the male chest and abdomen, in 1991," says **Henry A. Mentz, MD**, of Houston, Texas. "Although originally designed for the abdominal or 'six-pack' muscles, since 2004 it has also been used to etch and define the pectoral muscles. We can create muscular enhancement by leaving fat over muscle, or etch muscular definition by removing fat at the perimeter of the muscles. Good candidates for the procedure have good skin elasticity, well-developed abdominal and chest muscles, a desire to enhance their muscular contour, and will follow an exercise maintenance program."

More extensive excisional surgeries, such as abdominoplasty (tummy tuck) and post-bariatric body contouring, are also performed on men with great success. These procedures require a longer recovery and leave significant scars, but for properly selected candidates they offer body contour improvements that can enhance both the way a man looks and feels about himself.

LOOKING AHEAD

In addition to facial rejuvenation, facial contouring, and body contouring surgery, procedures such as hair restoration, skin resurfacing, and injectable treatments (Botox and soft tissue fillers) are increasingly sought by men. There are a variety of techniques and materials used for these procedures, and the selection is based upon a thorough evaluation by your surgeon and an assessment of your personal goals. These common aesthetic procedures are covered in detail in other sections of this book.

What is most important to note here is that the continuing boom in minimally invasive or nonsurgical procedures definitely is not limited to women. And why should it be? These procedures are perfectly adapted to busy lifestyles, provide subtle and natural-looking results, and generally carry minimal risks. As men become better informed regarding the benefits of such procedures, we can expect the numbers of men taking advantage of these new and constantly developing treatments to climb even higher.

Many factors have led to the increased numbers of men opting for aesthetic plastic surgery. People are living longer and retiring later. It has been said that "50 is the new 30," and people generally want to continue to look as good as they feel. Vast improvement in results, increased public acceptance, and an ever-increasing number of satisfied patients have all contributed to aesthetic plastic surgery's gain in popularity.

For men, as for women, the decision to undergo aesthetic surgery is an intensely personal choice. Many men continue to have misconceptions about what plastic surgery can or cannot achieve for them. Perhaps they believe that because they are bald or have thinning hair, facial rejuvenation is not an option. Or maybe they still believe that "real men" don't have cosmetic surgery. The latter idea, fortunately, is no longer prevalent in our society, which recognizes that both men and women have the capacity and desire to improve their appearance through plastic surgery. Thanks to today's advances in techniques and technology, plastic surgeons have solutions for most of the common problems that men face as they age or as they develop a mature concept of who they are and how they want to look.

Because men generally don't wear makeup or style their hair in a way that makes it easy to conceal incision sites, they are particularly leery of visible scars or any indication that they have undergone cosmetic surgery. And the truth is that making incisions undetectable takes time, surgical skill, and artistry. The potential advantages of choosing a board-certified plastic surgeon as discussed elsewhere in this book cannot be overemphasized, from the perspectives of results, patient safety, and patient satisfaction. The key to a successful outcome is to find the right plastic surgeon — one with whom you feel comfortable, who has experience in male aesthetic surgery, and who understands male aesthetics as well as your unique personal aesthetics. A qualified plastic surgeon will carefully evaluate you for surgery and advise you on which procedure, or combination of procedures, can best meet your individual needs. ᵞ

Editor's Viewpoint

Both men and women have very similar reasons for wanting to look their best. Thanks to advances in aesthetic surgery, men can now enjoy the superior results that are routinely achieved for women — provided that they select a surgeon who understands the uniqueness of male aesthetics and the technical nuances that are often necessary for truly natural-looking enhancement of the male face and body.

This chapter highlights the change in attitudes of men toward aesthetic surgery and the factors that fueled this change. Today, it is not only entertainers and other individuals in the public eye who opt for plastic surgery. Men from all walks of life have discovered the benefits of aesthetic surgery in both their personal and professional lives. Although I practice in proximity to Hollywood, the men coming to see me are increasingly from businesses and professions such as finance, teaching, law enforcement, and sales.

While national statistics on cosmetic surgery show that between nine and 12 percent of all aesthetic surgical and nonsurgical interventions are performed on men, it seems that the percentage may be significantly higher in major urban settings. For example, in my Los Angeles practice, between 18 and 20 percent of procedures are performed on male patients.

In addition to Botox injection — an extremely popular treatment among men, who often want to reduce the appearance of frown lines that make them look perpetually angry or irritable — minimally invasive endoscopic facial rejuvenation and refinements in body sculpting, such as abdominal and pectoral etching, have played a significant role in the greater acceptance of aesthetic surgery by men. As plastic surgeons continue to develop additional noninvasive, minimally invasive, and limited scar treatments, most certainly the number of aesthetic procedures performed on men should rise exponentially in the future.

— Peter B. Fodor, MD

AESTHETIC PLASTIC SURGERY
for teens

Based on media attention, it may seem as though teen plastic surgery is a new and explosive phenomenon. The fact is that less than two percent of all cosmetic surgical and nonsurgical procedures are performed on people aged 18 and under, according to 2005 statistics from the American Society for Aesthetic Plastic Surgery (ASAPS). Nevertheless, teens are an important group for whom plastic surgery can have a significant impact.

BODY IMAGE, ACCEPTANCE, AND SELF-ESTEEM

For some teens, societal and peer pressure to conform to generally accepted standards of appearance can be devastating. When a young child has protruding ears that lead to ridicule and taunts from classmates, or when a teenage girl is impaired both physically and psychologically by excessive breast development that is out of proportion with the rest of her body, surgical intervention may often be the right solution.

Critics may say that young people must simply "learn to live with" those aspects of their appearance that are troubling to them, even implying that this is the proper way to "build character." Yet science would suggest that demanding they do so may be putting them at a disadvantage, not only now but throughout their lives. Well-documented studies have shown that as early as nursery school and through the formative years of elementary school, social attitudes are forged in favor of children who are more attractive. And attitudes in favor of attractive individuals persist throughout adulthood. It is easy to see that, in certain circumstances, plastic surgery can contribute to a better quality of life for young people, both during their formative years and for their entire adult lives.

This is not to say that every teen who feels somewhat awkward or dissatisfied with his or her appearance is a good candidate for plastic surgery. On the contrary, responsible board-certified plastic surgeons spend significant time when evaluating teens for plastic surgery to be certain that surgery is the best option for a particular young person. Surgeons are well aware that the decisions about surgery made today will be the decisions young people live with for the rest of their lives.

"Plastic surgery in itself does not create happiness," points out **Frederick N. Lukash, MD**, of Manhasset, New York, "but it can be a tool to help young patients achieve their personal best and build self-esteem that will impact them positively for their entire lives."

Most people are totally supportive of children with birth defects, who in the past would have been societal outcasts, undergoing reconstructive plastic surgery to create a more normal appearance so they can take their place in society's mainstream. In many cases, children with prominent ears and adolescents with physical challenges such as oversized or asymmetrical breasts, gynecomastia (male breast enlargement), a nose that is significantly out of balance with their other facial features, or a receding chin can also benefit from plastic surgery.

"I have seen remarkable changes in attitude among the teens on whom I have performed procedures such as breast reduction and rhinoplasty," says **Robert W. Bernard, MD**, of White Plains, New York. "Some have gone from being shy and introverted to being very upbeat and outgoing. It's wonderful to see that kind of transformation."

Most plastic surgeons have many stories about their adolescent patients for whom plastic surgery has been a positive experience. Yet more common than surgical procedures among teens are nonsurgical treatments. Among 18 and under individuals, the most commonly performed procedures are laser hair removal, chemical peel, and microdermabrasion — the latter two for their ability to improve acne and skin texture. Commonly performed surgical procedures are rhinoplasty, otoplasty, and breast reduction, all of which are performed in both females and males.

There are many considerations when evaluating if plastic surgery is the right choice for a particular individual. However, significant research suggests that plastic surgery in young people can, for properly selected patients, be the right choice.

PATIENT SELECTION

Plastic surgery for adolescents has an appropriate place, and that is when it is done for the right individual at the right time and for the right reasons. The decision to operate must be based on the patient's physical and emotional condition, needs, and ability to understand the outcome. In the case of rhinoplasty (reshaping of the nose) for example, the patient must understand that he or she initially must restrict activities to protect the operated nose from injury and, also, that a touch-up to achieve optimal results is not unusual. With a breast reduction, the teen must fully appreciate that the operation will leave permanent and visible scarring on the breasts. More important, teens must have the maturity to understand that while undergoing plastic surgery may significantly improve a feature of their face or body, it will not necessarily improve their relationships with people or make their lives "perfect." They will still have to deal with the problems, insecurities, and normal challenges of growing up.

In order to make the right decision about whether surgery is appropriate, the patient's physical condition and emotional readiness must be fully considered. The patient should be in generally good health and maintain healthy lifestyle habits, particularly in terms of nutrition and exercise. Some young people visit a plastic surgeon seeking liposuction as a weight loss solution; in most cases, they are sent them home with the advice to change their eating habits and start exercising. Liposuction may be a reasonable option, however, for a teen of normal weight who has hereditary fat bulges in localized areas of the body (such as thigh "saddlebags" or back rolls) that simply will not respond to dieting and exercise.

The family must be actively involved in the consultation process, and child psychiatrists and other professionals can be involved to help make decisions. It is important, however, to be certain that the motivation for undergoing plastic surgery actually comes from the adolescent and not from a well-meaning parent, relative or friend.

"When evaluating a teen for rhinoplasty surgery, I always take some time to speak alone with him or her, without parents or anyone else in the room," says Dr. Bernard. "I want to find out what this young person is thinking and whether, when we are alone, he or she might reveal, 'It's really my parents who want me to do this.'"

Another factor that should be considered is how long the teen has expressed the desire to make a change in his or her appearance, and whether these feelings are generally consistent over time. During the teen years, it is not uncommon for young people to experiment with different "looks" — a new hairstyle, hair color, style of clothing, and so on. Plastic surgery is, of course, a permanent change, which is why it is critical that young people considering surgery have a clear idea of exactly what bothers them about their appearance and how they would like to change it. A teen who tends to be inconsistent with likes and dislikes about personal style may not be ready to commit to a surgical alteration.

Some procedures must be age-appropriate — for instance, typically, girls starting at age 13 and boys at age 15 can be candidates for rhinoplasty because their noses are sufficiently developed. While unusual, rhinoplasty can be performed at an earlier age in exceptional cases, as long as both the young person and parents understand that revisions may be necessary in the future.

Determining the physical and emotional readiness of the patient is just one part of the decision-making process. Milestone timing is crucial for successful procedures, and young people can benefit from entering new chapters in their lives feeling good about themselves. Prominent ears ideally can be repaired prior to the start of school. If the procedure is justified and patients are well adjusted, it is most beneficial to have the experience behind them prior to socialization.

Between high school and college and between middle school and high school are often optimal times for certain procedures in order to minimize the social and psychological impact on the patient and allow for a smooth emotional transition. It is important for parents to be aware of the importance of timing and plan their consultation well in advance of when they ideally would like their child to undergo surgery.

CHOOSING THE RIGHT PROFESSIONALS

It is extremely critical to choose professionals who are especially sensitive to the needs of young people and preferable to find those who have worked extensively with this age group. If you haven't already read the chapter, Choosing a Qualified Surgeon, in the front part of this book, you may wish to do so now.

"Responsible board-certified plastic surgeons will look at the individual patient and make an informed decision based on the risks, benefits, and expected outcomes of surgery," states Dr. Lukash. "The surgery must be appropriate and necessary. The surgeon must be able to determine what is beneficial and what is nonsense — like the teenager who thinks surgery is a 'quick fix' for other problems or whose goal is to look like a favorite celebrity — and if necessary, to say 'no' to performing surgery."

Cosmetic plastic surgery is not only about external beauty. It is about helping people feel better about themselves, which in turn builds self-confidence. In essence, plastic surgeons can help individuals to achieve their personal best. Helping a young person feel normal and accepted can provide a foundation upon which he or she can build success — both now and for an entire lifetime. ⅄

Young people with aesthetic deformities are often subjected to ridicule by their peers. Their self-consciousness and, often, feelings of social unacceptability can lead to reclusiveness and other behavioral problems.

For children and teens who have the necessary internal motivation, physical maturity, and emotional stability, achieving a more normal appearance through plastic surgery can have far-reaching benefits. Not only do these patients often become more outgoing, assertive and confident, but also it is not uncommon for school grades to improve and even for previously unrecognized leadership qualities to emerge.

I have had an ongoing personal interest in the subject of plastic surgery for teens. In the early 1980s, I initiated a long-term study on the effects of rhinoplasty performed in adolescents. Follow-up after surgery in the study group was a minimum of 10 years. The findings were extremely supportive of the long-term benefits of rhinoplasty in teenagers with bona fide deformities. I cherish the many personal letters of gratitude received from this group of patients over the years.

On the other hand, plastic surgeons sometimes see teens in consultation who, in response to peer or parental pressure or media influence, are highly determined to undergo plastic surgery for correction of very minimal aesthetic defects. In such cases, it is important for teens and their families to understand why plastic surgery, undertaken prematurely and for the wrong reasons, may not be in their best interests.

The competent aesthetic plastic surgeon, in addition to possessing the necessary technical skills, will also be of assistance to the patient and his or her family in sorting out the intricate and highly individual physical and emotional factors surrounding aesthetic surgery for teens.

— Peter B. Fodor, MD